A Belief in Humanity: The Untold Story of Conciliar Humanism

A Belief in Humanity: The Untold Story of Conciliar Humanism

The Twentieth-Century Retrieval of Sapiential Consciousness

Thomas D. Carroll

⌒PICKWICK *Publications* · Eugene, Oregon

A BELIEF IN HUMANITY: THE UNTOLD STORY OF
CONCILIAR HUMANISM
The Twentieth-Century Retrieval of Sapiential Consciousness

Copyright © 2024 Thomas D. Carroll. All rights reserved. Except for brief quotations in critical publications or reviews, no part of this book may be reproduced in any manner without prior written permission from the publisher. Write: Permissions, Wipf and Stock Publishers, 199 W. 8th Ave., Suite 3, Eugene, OR 97401.

Pickwick Publications
An Imprint of Wipf and Stock Publishers
199 W. 8th Ave., Suite 3
Eugene, OR 97401

www.wipfandstock.com

PAPERBACK ISBN: 979-8-3852-0736-7
HARDCOVER ISBN: 979-8-3852-0737-4
EBOOK ISBN: 979-8-3852-0738-1

Cataloguing-in-Publication data:

Names: Carroll, Thomas D. [author].

Title: A belief in humanity: the untold story of conciliar humanism : the twentieth-century retrieval of sapiential consciousness / by Thomas D. Carroll.

Description: Eugene, OR: Pickwick Publications, 2024 | Includes bibliographical references.

Identifiers: ISBN 979-8-3852-0736-7 (paperback) | ISBN 979-8-3852-0737-4 (hardcover) | ISBN 979-8-3852-0738-1 (ebook)

Subjects: LCSH: Theological anthropology—Catholic Church. | Catholic Church—Doctrines. | Catholic Church—Doctrines—History—20th century. | Vatican Council (2nd : 1962–1965 : Basilica di San Pietro in Vaticano). | Catholic Church and philosophy.

Classification: BX830 C37 2024 (paperback) | BX830 (ebook)

VERSION NUMBER 09/10/24

Scripture quotations are from New Revised Standard Version Bible: Catholic Edition, copyright © 1989, 1993 National Council of the Churches of Christ in the United States of America. Used by permission. All rights reserved worldwide.

This book is dedicated to the memory of His Eminence George Cardinal Pell AC (1941–2023), a man of faith, a beloved priest, a remarkable scholar, a proud Australian, and a good friend. His untimely death prevented his writing a foreword to this book as he promised.

Requiescat in pace

Contents

Introduction | ix

1. A Meeting of Minds | 1
2. Back to the Future | 10
3. Being Conscious | 19
4. Thinking about Humanity | 29
5. A Human Agenda | 37
6. Empires of the Mind | 46
7. Signs of the Times | 52
8. Friends of Wisdom | 67
9. Christian Wisdom | 80
10. Practical Wisdom | 85
11. Awake to God | 95
12. Living in the World of Today | 105
13. The Denial of God | 118
14. Human Crisis? | 131
15. Thinking without Foundations | 138
16. World of a Person | 147
17. Learning from Others | 152
18. Thoughtful Foundations | 161
19. A Tapestry of Thought | 171
20. A Search for Learning | 180
21. An Outsider? | 190
22. A Definite Insider | 209
23. In Need of Recovery | 219

24. A Return to Metaphysics | 228
25. A Person Who Thinks | 233
26. The First Truth | 239
27. What If? | 254
28. A Generous Service | 268
29. A Work in Progress | 281
30. Being without God? | 291
31. Living in Uncertain Times | 302
32. Beyond Categories | 312
33. Definitely Something More? | 322
34. Together in Christ | 332
35. Loving in God | 344
36. A Thoughtful Legacy | 353
37. A Vision of Humanity | 362

Conclusion | 371

Bibliography | 375

Introduction

"Faced with today's evolving world, an increasing number are asking really basic questions or feeling them with a new urgency: What is man and woman? What is the meaning of suffering, evil and death, which persist even in the midst of such progress?" As I once wrote, "while curiosity might have killed the cat, human beings have thrived on their capacity to ask questions,"[1] but in an ordered and disciplined manner—a way of thinking originally used by Saint[2] Augustine (354–430), Bishop of Hippo Regius. Reflecting on his turbulent personal life, the foremost thinker of the first millennium of the Christian era continues to inspire, who sought to better understand our shared humanity. Approached from the perspective of newly acquired Christian faith writing his seminal autobiography *Confessions*, he laid foundations for Christian anthropology, from the Greek *anthrōos* 'human being.' Described as "a single work in thirteen books written in AD 397," Augustine documented the truth he found in a 'restless' human person; "behind this fundamental act of the self, lay powerful and evident anxieties—evident on every page"[3] in the opinion of James J. O'Donnell, author of *Augustine, Sinner & Saint: A New Biography* (2005). Wherein the young convert finds God through understanding his humanity as being loved by God, as he concludes this seminal book, reflecting on words from the Gospel of Matthew 7:7–8: "From you let it be asked. In you let it be sought. At your door let us knock for it."[4] A propitiatory

---

1. Carroll, "Human Activity," 37.
2. Once a person's canonized status as a saint is recognized, or someone in the process of moving toward canonization, either as blessed, venerable or servant of God, this is presumed in the book.
3. O'Donnell, *Augustine's Confessions*, 1:xvii–xx.
4. Augustine, *Confessions*, 370.

way of thinking which characterized his thought as he sought to grapple with life's big questions; one which speaks to our time.

These introductory words could easily have been written by someone today. Living in the digital world of the twenty first century, wherein our life as a human being seems to be "changing, rapidly, and, for the worse!"[5] A claim addressed by Leslie Williams, a Congregationalist Christian and visiting scholar from Yale Divinity School (1822) in her remarkable book *When Anything Goes: Being Christian in a Post-Christian World* (2016). Building on her earlier book *Night Wrestling: Struggling for Answers and Find God* (1997), she draws attention to the mixed emotions aroused when human beings ask questions of profound consequence about themselves, "the kind of deep, unsettling questions that can threaten faith and rob us of peace." Thinking in this postmodern world wherein *anything goes* she situated this perennial quest for self-understanding within the enigmatic experience of love. Namely, as human beings she claims, "we are beggars for love, our hands outstretched, clasping a cup, hoping for contributions from passers-by"; words worth requoting. Approaching our human vulnerability found in the capacity to love, understood as mutually reciprocal wherein we give each other what we can and have received from each other, we come to the recognition that we are opaque to ourselves no less than to others. Encountering these circumstances, she claims "only when God walks by is the cup filled to overflowing." Namely, as we recognize the Incarnate face of the Person of Christ who walks with us as the source of God's grace and mercy given through his redemptive act of self-sacrificing love.

Thinking in an atmosphere of unbridled uncertainty, how can we make sense of our humanity, our being human in such a world immersed with Artificial Intelligence, inhabited by beings suspiciously human. How can we tell the difference? Does it matter? Perhaps science has all the answers as we have been repeatedly assured but wait, there seems to be something more being human, something special behind these questions, someone who asks them. An awareness which takes us beyond the boundaries of science which speak to a shared concern as we try to understand what we are being human, our humanity. Furthermore, given the paradoxical character which seems to characterize our existence, how can we account for ourselves as a biological and material being who is naturally oriented towards other human beings,

---

5. Williams, *When Anything Goes*, xiv, 53.

INTRODUCTION

similarly enigmatic and capricious. That is, how can we understand our evident capacity to choose to live together as social and political beings through the exercise of personal freedom. A sphere of human activity rarely discussed by those who continue to use a scientific way of thinking despite their ethical claims; let alone their rejection of God. Such as the proponents of twenty first century 'transhumanism' and the 'World Transformation Movement' (1983), suitable partners for a philosophical conversation undertaken in this book.

These 'unprecedented' words, first quoted to introduce this book, were written by men living last century. Namely, over two thousand and three hundred Catholic bishops and religious leaders from around the world, known as 'Council Fathers,' who were summoned by Saint Pope John XXIII (1958–63) to answer these basic questions. As they assembled in a reconstructed Saint Peter's Basilica in the Vatican City 'fit for the purpose,' for what came to be known as the Second Ecumenical Vatican Council (1962–65) or Vatican II, referred to as the Council. Not for the first time will this adjective be used, which implies never done or known before. Writing as a collective person, typical for ecumenical councils, they offered their response in an unprecedented document simply addressed to 'humanity,' of a distinctive integrative philosophical and pastoral orientation which came to characterize a form of conciliar thought known as 'conciliar humanism,' the consequence of an extended moment of *sapiential* consciousness, from the Latin *sapere* 'be wise.' Wherein we find the Council's unprecedented 'belief in humanity,' the subject of this book.

This is original thought which speaks about joy and hope, pain, and sorrow—human emotions we experience and share together. These are incredible words, from the beginning of this Constitution, an official document which represents the highest teaching authority, compared to decrees or declarations, from an ecumenical council of the universal Church. This original thought is documented in *Gaudium et Spes: Pastoral Constitution on the Church in the World Today*.[6] Understood as the consequence of the Council's unprecedented human agenda, it was the last of four Constitutions, the final, longest, and most anticipated document produced over three years. Literally the Council's last words, this Constitution drew immediate and international media attention and acclaim as indicative of the Church's acquired sense of openness

---

6. Tanner, *Decrees of the Ecumenical Councils*, 2:1069. The source of conciliar thought quoted in this book.

to the contemporary world, to 'the world of today.' A way of thinking based on a network of three interrelated ideas, introduced in *Gaudium et Spes*: namely, "human person" (para. 3), "community of persons" (para. 12), and "human solidarity" (para. 32). Ingeniously appropriated from contemporary European philosophy, this original network represents a thoughtful synthesis based on a creative juxtaposition between philosophical and sociopolitical thought and pastoral concerns, which came to characterize the originality of conciliar thought, a partnership between thought and action. A way of thinking inspired by, among others, the practical philosophy of Athenian philosopher Aristotle. (384–322 BC) Approached through its unprecedented recognition of our shared humanity and our shared concerns; expressed in the original idea of 'human solidarity.'

Unprecedented thought coming from an unexpected Council, conciliar humanism represents an original, remarkable, and equally unprecedented way of thinking about our shared humanity, one which emerged during the twenty first and last ecumenical council to be held of the universal Church. An adjective which also speaks to the originality of the subject and content found in this book as never previously discussed. In a nutshell, conciliar humanism represents an original Christ centred integral philosophical understanding of our shared humanity. One especially found in the content of two Council documents when read together; namely *Gaudium et Spes* and *Dignitatis Humanae: Declaration on Religious Freedom*, officially promulgated by Saint Pope Paul VI (1963–78) on the final day of Council proceedings 7 December 1965. The subject of my philosophical and historical reading and related background commentary, characterized as 'back to the future.' Approached as literally the last words of the Council, its final testament whereby conciliar humanism remains the Council's final testament bequeathed to the 'world of today.'

Moving into this book, while contemporary thinkers might cautiously disassociate themselves from gender specific translated language used in the question 'what is man,' being mindful of current issues regarding gender neutrality, to think twice before using 'man' for human or 'mankind' for humanity. Previous scholars and especially philosophers were not so inclined in their efforts to discuss humanity and to identify human nature as being essentially different from other forms of animate life, categorized as *homo sapiens*, and will be quoted as such. Typical for thinking in the West, philosophers use reason and ordered thought to explore life's big questions; characterized as 'doing philosophy.' A human activity generated by three w's: 'what am I,' 'who am I', and the question which initiates this ordered process, generated by a sense of wonder, 'why?'

A studied awareness well recognized by the practical metaphysical realism found in the Aristotle's thought. Traditionally expressed as 'why is there something rather than nothing,' namely, the awareness that there is something real in the first place. Prompted by this thought, the sense of being human, of my human 'existence,' a further question may be asked, 'why am I here,' and if I am here, 'what is the purpose and meaning of my life.' Approached from the perspective of history, this sequence of interrogative thought generated the study of being human, the study of being itself and the study of what is right and wrong, ways of thinking categorized as anthropological, metaphysical, and ethical, in response to life's big questions we ask. Traditionally approached from a broader religious, philosophical, or scientific perspective, or a mixture thereof as found in conciliar humanism.

Inspired by the popular expression 'back to the future' used for the 1985 American science fiction film and its equally popular theme song, "The Power of Love" by Huey Lewis and The News, this book probes the genesis and legacy of this original way of thinking about humanity during the Council. A project initiated by the further reading of *Gaudium et Spes* and *Dignitatis Humanae*, set against their philosophical and historical, cultural background, wherein we find an integrative way of thinking about ourselves as human beings, one which is accessible to everyone. As such, conciliar humanism represents a 'good news story,' approached as a thoughtful consequence of an "act of love," to quote an expression used by Archbishop Karol Wojtyła (1920–2005), one of the leading lights during the Council, and someone who was particularly influential in drafting these documents wherein we find his philosophical thought.

As a way of understanding our shared humanity, conciliar humanism is best approached as a 'symphony of ideas,' an original network of three interrelated ideas, human person, community of persons, and human solidarity. This represents an instance of broad new thinking which occurred during the Council, original thought understood as a synthesis of 'fidelity and dynamism' to employ the original words of Pope Benedict XVI (2005–13) out of context, which best describe the intent of this symphonic work. An appropriate metaphor for understanding the genesis of conciliar humanism, drawn from the structure of Western classical music as an extended composition of music consisting of multiple distinct sections or movements, usually four, which when brought together constitute a 'symphony.'

Reflecting the legacy of conciliar humanism, Pope Francis offered this characterisation: "Human life is like an orchestra that performs well if the various instruments are in harmony and follow a score shared by all." Aspirational words he spoke on April 4, 2017 to participants during a conference to celebrate the fiftieth anniversary of Pope Paul VI's seminal encyclical *Populorum progressio* (1967). Written soon after the Council, this document represents the first attempt to consolidate conciliar humanism as a way of thinking about humanity, especially its network of three basic ideas, human person, community of persons and human solidarity, which constitute the Council's belief in humanity. Original thought discussed in my book by means of three related ideas used during the Council to understand our shared humanity: namely, the act of an individual human person's moral 'conscience,' the sense of 'participation' shared within a community of persons, and the shared awareness of our humanity through the idea of 'solidarity'; one being directed to God. From the Latin words, *scire* 'to know,' *participare* 'share in,' and *solidus*, 'unity.' Equally expressive of our shared awareness as human beings found in "feelings of oneness, concern and love towards the whole human family" (*Gaudium et Spes*, para. 3).

When looking for the composer of this thoughtful music we find it is the consequence of a collaborative effort on the part of several leading figures; two popes who convened the Council, namely John XXIII and Paul VI and several bishops who, while comfortable using Catholic philosophical thought, looked beyond these traditional parameters for new ideas, which they found in twentieth century European philosophy. Interestingly, two 'Council Fathers,' those entitled to speak during the Council and to vote on Council documents, namely the Belgian Cardinal Leo Jozef Suenens (1904–96), Archbishop of Mechelen-Brussels (1961–79) and the Polish philosopher bishop Karol Wojtyła (1920–2005), Archbishop of Kraków (1964–78), who knew each other while post graduate students living in the Belgian Pontifical College in Rome (1844), held canonical doctorates in both Catholic theology and in contemporary philosophy, quite unusual for the time among the well-educated Council Fathers. These two men would become 'leading lights' during the Council.

INTRODUCTION

Furthermore, these personal connections play a significant role in the genesis of conciliar humanism as a remarkable instance and consequence of a retrieval of *sapiential* consciousness; from the Latin *sapere* 'be wise.' Namely, a premodern form of Christian philosophical awareness, characterized by the capacity to synthesise, to bring together and to unify various strands of diverse thought within a whole. A way of thinking later characterized as 'integral' from the Latin *integrare* 'to make whole,' to employ the original idea of the French philosopher Jacques Maritain (1882–1973) used for the title of his seminal *Integral Humanism* (1936); who shared this consciousness as a 'friend of wisdom.' An awareness which inspired this popular book read by Catholics, whose content was well known to the assembled Council Fathers. Perhaps due to what occurred during the Council, this *sapiential* awareness re-emerged during the twentieth century through the auspices of Archbishop Wojtyła who later became Saint John Paul II (1978–2005). As the great philosopher pope of the twentieth century, he reintroduced this word within contemporary Catholic discourse writing his seminal papal encyclical *Fides et Ratio* (1998). Embedded within *sapiential* consciousness, the intent of this way of thinking is captured in the inspirational words of Julene Siddique, the English composer and social commentator: [we need] "critical thinking coupled with constructive creativity" by people with "personal strength and integrity based on values and belief in a higher purpose." A remarkable alignment between thought and action found in the genesis of conciliar humanism.

Written in a conversational style, I have used the 'question and answer' approach initiated by Socrates (circa. 470–399 BC), the enigmatic thinker from Athens, for providing information from my reading and related commentary on the sources wherein we find the tenets of conciliar humanism. Furthermore, this approach provides the means to better understand the collective thought processes and influences which directed this original way of thinking. Commonly used as a means of ordering our thought when doing philosophy, the content of this book is directed by three interrelated questions, why, what and who. While ideas such as human person and community, considered synonymous with Conciliar thought are now ubiquitous in contemporary Catholic discourse, one might ask sixty years on, where did they come from? Which leads into why write another book about the Council? What was talked about during the Council, and who does it speak to, who benefits from this conversation? Approached from this broader context, why

INTRODUCTION

was another ecumenical council held at this time? What was the subject matter discussed which had not been talked about previously? And finally, who benefits from this discussion, where is the legacy? Questions taken up in this book.

Understood as a "symphony of ideas," this original thought is encapsulated by the expression "communion of salvation"; originally used by Jacques Maritain to characterize the German philosopher Max Scheler's (1874–1928) understanding of the universal Church.[7] Wherein we find the ongoing significance of conciliar humanism as a means to address three related issues in twentieth first century thought of an anthropological, sociological, and theological orientation, through the ideas of human person, community of persons and human solidarity.

In posing these questions I recall the observation made by John O'Malley, the American Jesuit church historian when he introduced *What Happened at Vatican II* (2008). While "library shelves are filled to overflowing with books about Vatican II,"[8] he asked whether anything had been omitted "from the crowd of volumes on these shelves?" Though many record the "drama of the Council" and the hermeneutic challenge posed in understanding its documented thought which opened the Church's windows onto the world of today, is anything missed? My response is an emphatic yes, which has generated this book; namely, the existence of a major lacuna within the study of the Council and its original thought. One which is addressed by a wide-ranging discussion about the genesis and legacy of conciliar humanism, hitherto unrecognized. Now approached from my philosophical reading and historical commentary on the background of *Gaudium et Spes* and *Dignitatis Humanae* as containing this original thought. Conducted by means of a conversation, about the circumstances of its evolution arising from the Council's human agenda, the unprecedented use of ideas taken from contemporary European philosophy by Council Fathers in writing their documents, and finally, the ongoing influence or legacy of such thought; subject matter, rarely researched, nor discussed in an organized manner.

Accessing this original thought wherein we find a remarkable consonance of related ideas, an element of detective work is required. In so far as Council documents only reference scriptural, papal, and doctrinal sources rather than identify individual names. By means of this investigative

---

7. Maritain, Foreword to *Walls Are Crumbling*, xiv.
8. O'Malley, *What Happened at Vatican II?*, 2.

INTRODUCTION

approach we can better understand how these ideas were drawn together from diverse sources, taken from Catholic tradition and doctrine, papal thought, especially regarding twentieth century teaching on social justice, along with ideas from twentieth century European philosophy, which are drawn together within a remarkable tapestry of original thought; from which there is much to learn sixty years on.

The subject of this book, written by a diocesan Catholic priest, teacher, and pastor, for a general readership. Namely, for anyone interested in learning about the philosophical thought of those living in the tradition of Catholic Christianity, past and present; as 'taking hints from the past.' Notably as this operated during the Council whereby we catch a glimpse into how conciliar thought functions, and to better understand the human, philosophical, and personal connections. Necessary background against which we can understand the genesis of conciliar humanism and its philosophical significance as a remarkable study of our shared humanity accessible to everyone. Namely, as the theoretical means of 'dialogue' with the 'world of today.' Whereby the ideas of others are respectfully engaged with and shared in the mutual pursuit of truth, wherein human life is affirmed as being inviolable and invaluable. As such, "humanity remains the substance of our Catholic tradition" in the words of James Hanvey, the English Jesuit and social theorist.[9]

Recognized from Antiquity on, the written word found in books has been characterized as "carriers of civilization"; "books are humanity in print," in the words of Barbara W. Tuchman (1912–89), the self-trained historian and popular American author.[10] Written by human beings with a story to be told, even a cookbook says something about the author. Whether God's or a human being's, each book reflects a personal story. As observed by the Polish Catholic philosopher Stefan Swieżawski (1907–2004), "every book has a history of its own," introducing his *St. Thomas Revisited* (1995).[11] My own story began during the 2009–10 European winter semester while participating in a graduate seminar "on the history and content of *Gaudium et Spes*" in the Faculty of Theology led by Professor Mathijis Lamberigts; a former teacher and friend. When I returned on sabbatical leave from teaching at the Catholic Institute of Sydney (1954) to my *alma mater*, the Katholieke Universiteit Leuven (1425). Already familiar with this seminal document, my rereading

9. Hanvey, "Dignity," 211.
10. Tuchman, *Bulletin*, 16–32.
11. Swieżawski, *St. Thomas Revisited*, xv.

awakened further interest as to how ideas which seemed familiar, such as 'human person' and 'community of persons' were incorporated in this document and more to the point why? I had a suspicion the source was found in the thought of the enigmatic German philosopher Max Scheler (1874–1928), the subject of my graduate study at Leuven's *Hoger Instituut voor Wijsbegeerte* (1889) 'Higher Institute of Philosophy.' My curiosity aroused, I began looking for connections which might confirm my impression, whereby I came to appreciate the influence of the Polish bishop Karol Wojtyla. As a young priest he had made a critical study of Scheler for postdoctoral *Habilitation*; whereby he appropriated the idea of the 'human person.' In making these connections, human and philosophical, I recalled my previous meeting with Saint Pope John Paul II (1978–2005) in January 1985 while on winter holiday in Rome with a group of American seminarians, through the generous assistance of the Belgian Cardinal Leo Jozef Suenens (1904–96). The former Archbishop of Mechelen-Brussels (1961–79), he was one of the leading lights during the Council. Having identified myself, "an Australian priest studying philosophy," we spoke of our mutual interest in the thought of Scheler. Ever the teaching pastor, holding my hand with his finger extended in mindful instruction, the Holy Father encouraged me to pursue my study of philosophy, as he had done, through our mutual search for Truth in the service of the Church; one which continues to this day.

Negotiating the complex interconnections found between historical, philosophical and sociocultural thought and pastoral concerns, along with their associated personal and thoughtful connections which informs the genesis of conciliar humanism, I recall the words of Pope Benedict (2005–13) as he opens his inaugural papal encyclical *Deus Caritas Est* (2005): "Being Christian is not the result of an ethical choice or a lofty idea, but the encounter with an *event, a person*, which give life *a new horizon* and *a decisive direction*" (para. 1; emphasis added). Expressive of Conciliar thought, these words which his successor Pope Francis "never tires of repeating" as he writes in his Apostolic Exhortation, *Evangelii Gaudium on the Proclamation of the Gospel in Today* (2014), offer a helpful means to move through the content in this book.

Obviously, the Council represents the unprecedented event which occurred during the twentieth century, consequential, seminal, and especially *sapiential*, whereby the universal Church addressed the fundamental issue "what is human" envisaged as providing the theoretical means of 'dialogue' with the contemporary world about our shared humanity. As an emergent leading light, the person is Archbishop Karol Wojtyła. One of the youngest Council Fathers, and an accomplished philosopher, he was a pivotal figure whose thought underpins the network of ideas which make up conciliar humanism, understood as a 'service to humanity.' Catholic and open to dialogue with the world of today, conciliar humanism offers the thoughtful means whereby we discover the integrity in being human together found in the face of Christ as we look into the faces around us, known and unknown, our sisters, and brothers, broken yet saved—a Christ centred understanding, approached as an instance of Incarnational soteriology. As such, conciliar humanism signifies a visionary network of ideas of far-reaching consequence, observed by Cardinal Karol Wojtyla in *Sign of Contradiction* (1978): "the Church of our day has become particularly conscious of this truth [namely, the transcendence of the human person]; and it was in light of this truth that the Council succeeded, during the second Vatican Council, in re-defining her own nature."[12]

Narrating the story of conciliar humanism, I have been inspired by the expression *probing the riches of Vatican II* used by David G. Schultenover. Namely, it's time to explore, to dig deeper into the documented thought before us, found in *Gaudium et Spes* and *Dignitatis*; in other words, to probe as a doctor examines a patient. While for many these documents may be very familiar, and their content presumed, having read them for over sixty years, perhaps this familiarity may conceal something? Namely, an original way of thinking, hitherto unrecognized, brought together within an original network of three related ideas, whereby we discover the Council's 'belief in humanity,' a source of hidden riches to be scrutinized further.

Approaching this process of probing and discovery, my thought was directed by the familiar words "back to the future," namely to understand where this original thought came from, and where it leads, to appreciate the connection between persons, popes, clergy, and laity, especially philosophers and their ideas, which directed my attention to a shared awareness, an extended moment of *sapiential* consciousness. Another story yet untold about an assembly of "friends of wisdom" thinking in the tradition of lived Catholic Christianity during one of the consequential moments of Catholic thought of the twentieth century, a moment of *sapiential* consciousness. In so doing, I was inspired

---

12. Wojtyla, *Sign of Contradiction*, 177.

INTRODUCTION

by reading *The Genesis of Heidegger's Being and Time* (1993), written by Theodore Kisiel, Professor emeritus of philosophy at Northern Illinois University (1894). Ten years in writing, like my own undertaking, *Genesis* represents the first factual and conceptual commentary on *Being and Time* (1927), one of the formative philosophical books of the twentieth century, wherein he explores the mindset which informs Heidegger's original project; an approach similarly undertaken in writing this book. Furthermore, I have adopted the idiosyncratic approach of a self-characterized "ruthless synthesiser" Yuval Noah Harari, an Israeli "public intellectual and historian," which he applies to understanding "what is human," found in his three popular books *Sapiens" Brief History of Humankind* (2011), *Homo Deus: A Brief History of Tomorrow* (2015) and *21 Lessons for the 21st Century* (2019).

Written in a deliberate conversational style, I invite you to undertake a thoughtful excursion, "to wander in mind" in the sense of Ancient Greek *alucinor*, to consider the broad circumstances, personal connections and thoughtful ideas which inform the genesis and legacy of conciliar humanism. Namely, to participate in a discussion something like the weekly conversations held between interested persons and Richard Heffner (1925–2013), the Dowling Professor of Communications and Public Policy at Rutgers, the State University of New Jersey (1766) and animated host of the popular television series *Open Your Mind*.

Furthermore, I have identified three twentieth century European Catholic philosophers who made a study of humanity their priority, whom I naturally consider the 'right people' whose original thought was creatively used in conciliar humanism. Namely, the phenomenological ethical personalism and philosophical sociology of the German philosopher Max Scheler (1874–1928), the existential Thomism and social personalism of the French Catholic philosopher Jacques Maritain (1882–1973) and the phenomenological Thomism of the Polish philosopher and bishop Karol Wojtyła (1920–2005).

Perhaps for many negotiating this philosophical terrain of twentieth century European Catholic thought might represent an intellectual *terra incognita*, to recall the words of Adolf von Harnack (1851–1930), the German Lutheran historian quoted in *Catholicism: The Story of Catholic Christianity* (2013). However, suitable guidance for the traveller doing philosophy as a Catholic is found in the particular use of history; namely, our ideas are embedded within a narrative of thoughtful ideas and personal connections in their historical and cultural setting.

INTRODUCTION

Axiomatic for this journey are two basic premises: "ideas change the world," a thought which captures the twentieth century use of ideology, the science of ideas, but equally important is the corollary, "no idea occurs in a vacuum"; namely, the meaning of our ideas captured in words is always drawn from within a context; a thinking within a text. Oriented towards the pursuit of truth as thinking Catholics, our ideas are generated and operate within a network of thoughtful meaningful connections as we engage a written text, wherein we find originality; herein "context is necessary." A rewording of the pithy expression "context is everything" attributed to A. D. Garrett in *Everyone Lies* (2014), a pseudonym used by the internationally acclaimed British crime writer Margaret Murphy. This contextual methodology, "with the text," informs my philosophical reading and historical commentary as it informs original thought found in *Gaudium et Spes* and *Dignitatis Humanae*.

Furthermore, engaging these 'voices of the past' I am reminded of the metaphor of a 'landscape' used by the French Catholic philosopher Blaisé Pascal (1632–62), a contemporary of another formative figure in Western philosophy, René Descartes (1596–1650). Writing in his *Pensées* (1657–58), a posthumous publication of fragments of his ideas, later referred to as the "Apology for the Christian Religion," Pascal observes "a landscape from afar is a landscape, but, as one approaches it becomes houses, trees, grass, ants, and so on, *ad infinitum*. All that is comprehended in the word 'landscape'" (para. 65), namely, accessing these 'voices' found in conciliar humanism is a matter of perspective, from which we can understand the whole; thereby the acquisition of meaning in understanding the emergence of conciliar humanism is afforded by a 'layered approach' towards the philosophers discussed in this book. By employing my layered methodology, I offer a philosophical "landscape with figures" to adapt an expression used by G. K. Chesterton (1874–1936), the prolific British Catholic journalist and philosopher, in his classic biographical sketch *Saint Thomas Aquinas: The Dumb Ox* (1933). Alternatively, the expression "beneath every history, another history" is equally applicable, taking inspiration from Dame Hilary Mantel's (1952–2022) acclaimed historical novel *Wolf Hall* (2009).[13]

Finally, to appreciate the legacy of conciliar humanism, my conversation has been guided by anthropological, sociological and theological issues used by the Italian bishop Giovanni D'Ercole in his 2013 lecture

---

13. Mantel, *Wolf Hall*, 55.

"The Church, an Instrument of Peace in the Contemporary World: 50 Years after Encyclical *Pacem in terris*."[14] Wherein he approached the significance of conciliar thought, especially in *Gaudium et Spes* through a discussion of the influence of Pope John XXIII's encyclical *Pacem in Terris* (1963). The opening words of *Dignitatis Humanae* are a direct quote from this encyclical: "The dignity of the human person is a concern of which people of our time are becomingly increasingly more aware" (para. 5). Issues which provide a thoughtful means to engage current trends in thinking about humanity, namely, 'transhumanism,' and 'World Transformation Movement' whereby we can appreciate the ongoing relevance of conciliar humanism discussed in this book.

---

14. D'Ercole, "Church."

1

A Meeting of Minds

To BETTER UNDERSTAND THE creative and interpretative mechanism which underpins the acquisitive process of thought during the Council which informed conciliar humanism, the twenty-first-century phenomenon known as 'ThoughtWorld' might be helpful. As it operates like the concept of a 'lifeworld' popularized during the twentieth century by the German philosopher Edmund Husserl (1859–1938) for the ground of what we know within lived experience. According to its promotional material, ThoughtWorld is "not just another social media platform," but rather, it is envisaged as a "bridge" built to encourage people "to think, find compromises, collaborate with others, and to be unafraid to pose new ideas, even bad ones," quoted thought which captures the activity of Council Fathers in thinking about our shared humanity. Furthermore, approached as a phenomenon of human interaction the *Acta synodalia Concilii Oecumenici Vatican II* (1970–2000) is an invaluable resource. Written in Latin the official language of the Council and the Church, this offers an invaluable resource as it documents in thirty-two volumes the interactive thought world of Council proceedings, characterized as 'who said what.' For instance, concerning the transmission of thought documented in Schema XIII, which came to be known as *Gaudium et Spes*, Archbishop Wojtyła offered fifty-six interventions, compared to four interventions offered by Cardinal Suenens, another leading light who was especially involved in drafting these documents, and four by Father Joseph Ratzinger (1927–2022), a *peritus* speaking on behalf of the German bishops. Helpful information wherein numbers count.

A BELIEF IN HUMANITY: THE UNTOLD STORY OF CONCILIAR HUMANISM

"Ideas change the world," claimed Jeffrey Sachs, the American economist during the inaugural Montreal Millennium Promise Conference on the prevention of global poverty on November 9, 2006. In so doing, he was recalling the thought behind Sir Winston Churchill's (1872–1965) understanding of "empires of the mind." Namely, his recognition of the power of a new idea which offers the means of transforming the way we live and think.[1] This book concerns another empire of the mind generated during the Council, the idea of a 'human person,' used by the Council to express the 'something more' about being human. Namely, the recognition that there is something special about being human, the 'Factor X' which reveals the "essential human quality underneath" in the opinion of Francis Fukuyama, the American political scientist, as he writes in *Our Posthuman Future: Consequences of the Biotechnology Revolution* (2002).[2] However, and herein lies the extraordinary originality found in Conciliar thought about being human, namely, this idea is embedded within an incredible network of three interrelated ideas, 'human person,' 'community of persons,' and 'human solidarity' which together constitute a remarkable way of thinking about our shared humanity, a network which encompasses conciliar humanism, wherein we find the Council's belief in humanity.

Sixty years ago, this conversation would not have been possible nor intelligible: "Why has Christ not yet returned, why so long a wait for the end of times?" In response to these rhetorical questions the French Benedictine theologian Ghislain Lafont (1020–2021) employs an enigmatic thought, "to give us time to believe in the human person." Continuing this conversation, he claims "Christ died because he believed in the human person." An extraordinary conversation used by the American Jesuit Ladislas Orsy, a specialist in canon law, to introduce his article "The Divine Dignity of Human Persons in *Dignitatis Humanae*" in *50 Years On: Probing the Riches of Vatican II* (2015). Wherein the American Jesuit literally 'probes' the significance of the idea of 'human person' as the key to understanding the seminal thought documented in *Dignitatis Humanae* generated during the Council. Reading this article was both an inspiration and a challenge when writing my book, namely, the awareness that someone else drew similar conclusions as I had done concerning the pivotal status of the idea of 'human person,'

---

1. Stengel, "Power of Ideas."
2. Fukuyama, *Our Posthuman Future*, 149–50.

approached as a hermeneutic key, but more significantly, its role within a philosophical network of original and interrelated ideas which together constitute conciliar humanism. A remarkable realization which emerged from my rereading of *Gaudium et Spes*. The challenge arose as I began to understand the significance of this idea not in isolation but how it was embedded within this network of original ideas.

A way of thinking generated during an extraordinary 'meeting of minds' comprising over two thousand and three hundred Catholic bishops and religious leaders from around the world. Truly multinational, multilingual, multicultural, this was an enormous gathering of people, a meeting of minds thinking in the tradition of lived Catholic Christianity. One which generated an equally enormous amount of speculative and critical thought and accompanying paperwork, which was eventually reduced to sixteen official documents, wherein we find the ingredients of conciliar humanism, especially found in two of them.

Access to conciliar thought was made available through the *Acta synodalia Concilii Oecumenici Vatican II* wherein we can appreciate the collective mindset of the Council. This invaluable resource documents the process whereby conciliar thought was drafted, approached as a complex process which incorporated ideas taken from thousands of individual submissions offered by individual Council fathers, from groups of Council fathers according to nationality, and from Roman officials. These ideas were discussed in the numerous sub-committees appointed by the Council, and finally brought before the Council during a public session, when individual Council Fathers were entitled to offer a spoken 'intervention' of twenty minutes on a prepared topic or issue arising from drafts of proposed texts; original thought which finally found its way onto the Council floor. Whereupon this was further discussed and eventually voted on by Council Fathers during a full session of the Council. Following their approval, these documents were submitted to the pope for his official promulgation. From this rather labyrinthine process taken over three years sixteen documents were received, some of their content codified as Church teaching. Original thought currently found in the two volume English translation *Decrees of the Ecumenical Councils* (1990) edited by Norman P. Tanner, the British Jesuit church historian.

Asked to explain this process in simple words Maureen A. Kelly, an American Catholic theologian and Leuven alumna, recalled the imaginative thought of her teacher when writing her 'Prologue' to *Vatican II in*

Plain English: The Council (1997).³ Namely, that of the Flemish Jesuit Piet F. Fransen (1913–83) who personally witnessed the Council as a *peritus*, a theological expert appointed to advise the Belgian bishops during Council proceedings. When asked in class to recall what he had seen, this elderly theologian spoke of the significance of a 'synchronicity' between "events and people." An original idea of Carl G. Jung (1875–1961), the renowned Swiss psychiatrist and 'depth' psychologist, which Fransen used to understand the thoughtful transmission of "ideas" taken without any direct causal connection during the Council from "the right people." Ideas taken from diverse sources, drawn from traditional Church teaching, from papal encyclicals, and from contemporary European philosophers, which were then ingeniously used by the Council Fathers, wherein we find the genesis of conciliar humanism. Understood as a thoughtful interaction within a network of "meaningful coincidences between events, persons and ideas." Approached as a remarkable confluence of ideas, this came together during the Council without any direct causal relationship as an extended moment of *sapiential* consciousness. One which occasioned a Christ centred original, synthetic, and integrative pattern of philosophical thought about our shared humanity.

"For by his Incarnation the Son of God united himself in some sense with every human being. He laboured with human hands, thought with a human mind, acted with a human will, and loved with a human heart" (*Gaudium et Spes*, para. 22). Eloquent thought, taken from *Gaudium et Spes*, which reflects the Christological orientation of the Council's understanding of our shared humanity, captured in the words of Pope Benedict XVI: "God's love can become concrete and can almost be experienced in history with all its painful and glorious vicissitudes." Words which his successor Pope Francis quoted during his closing World Youth Day homily on January 27, 2019, which address the orientation of conciliar humanism as portrayed in the religious art *Descent from the Cross* (1435) by the renowned Flemish artist Rogier van der Weyden (1400–1464).

One might ask how does religious art of the fifteenth century, speak to those living in the twenty-first century? An answer is found within the content of this book, wherein we appreciate the significance of conciliar humanism portrayed in *Descent from the Cross*, summarily expressed in the opening words of *Gaudium et Spes*: "the joys and hope and the sorrows and anxieties of people today," human vicissitudes of

---

3. Huebsch, *Vatican II in Plain English*, 11.

those receptive "to the message of salvation communicated to everyone" (para. 1). Approached through the narrative of my philosophical reading, and related historical and cultural commentary on a remarkable, though hitherto unnoticed way of thinking about our shared humanity which emerged during the Second Vatican Council, namely, conciliar humanism.

Original thought which represents an innovative Christ centred, integral philosophical understanding of our shared humanity, offered as a reasonable way of thinking accessible to believers and unbelievers alike. Based in part on Max Scheler's understanding of personal love as a distinctive human activity, wherein we find the meaning of our shared human existence. Original thought captured in the words of Pope Benedict: "Jesus' entire earthly existence, from conception to death on the cross was a single act of love," spoken to introduce the subject of his Angelus address on September 25, 2005 on *Jesus Caritas* 'Jesus Love.' Ever the consummate theologian, the recently elected pope explores this thought through the lens of these expressive words, already quoted but worth repeating: "God's love can become concrete and can almost be experience in history with all its painful and glorious vicissitudes." Circumstances which characterize the enigma of being human, well expressed in the opening words of *Gaudium et Spes*: "The joys and hopes and the sorrows and anxieties of people today."

In so doing, the pope draws attention to a fundamental connection between humanity and the Triune God in the Person of Christ, portrayed by "the tears and sorrows" van der Weyden ingeniously placed on those who observed the "countenance of Christ," understood as "a symphony of sadness." Expressed in the collapsed figure of Jesus' mother at his side, with tears from her eyes which draw attention to our own sense of human vulnerability in the experience of grief, suffering and pain occasioned by the death of a loved one. Approached from this perspective of human experience shared by all, Van der Weyden's religious art captures the originality of conciliar humanism, informed by its incisive and unique understanding of our shared humanity found 'in' the Person of Christ, a "knowledge of man" moving towards an awareness of the nature of the Triune God. As Pope Paul recalls the words of Christ recorded in the Gospel of John (14:9), "He who sees me also sees the Father" in his final address to the Council.

Approached through the narrative in this book, van der Weyden's religious art *Descent from the Cross* (1435) remains a powerful portrayal of the spirit of conciliar humanism and its original network of ideas, 'human person,' 'community of persons,' and 'human solidarity,' expressed in these opening words of *Gaudium et Spes* which capture the human vicissitudes of those receptive "to the message of salvation communicated to everyone." Whereby this famous art speaks to those living in the twenty-first century as an instance of 'incarnational soteriology.' Summarily expressed in the defining paragraph of this landmark Pastoral Constitution: "For by the incarnation the Son of God united himself in some sense with every human being, freely shedding his blood as the innocent lamb, suffering for us, he not only sets us an example to follow in his footsteps, but opens a way in which life and death are sanctified" (para. 22).

Arguably the most famous human being who ever lived, the Sacred Scriptures do not record any physical description as to what Jesus actually looked like, the opening premise used by a self-identified Quaker, Joan E. Taylor, the King's College London art historian, for her highly original *What Did Jesus Look Like* (2018). Over the course of Western cultural history, recognized as a 'visible religion' Christians have used art to graphically express their spiritual beliefs and to communicate their faith in Jesus Christ, the Incarnate Son of God. Based on the hypothesis concerning the reciprocity between image and meaning, this is found in the correspondence between humanity and divinity portrayed in the religious art evocatively captured in *Descent from the Cross*. Originally designed to be a 'masterpiece' by a budding artist, the Flemish painter Rogier van der Weyden, following his successful apprenticeship under Robert Campin (1378–1444), the so-called 'Master of Flemalle,' in the old city of Tournai in the Walloon province of Hainaut. This religious art was undertaken when he relocated to Brussels, the administrative capital city in what was then Spanish Netherlands, part of the Hapsburg Empire under the Holy Roman Emperor Charles V (1500–58).

Commissioned in 1435 by the St. George Guild of Crossbowmen in the Flemish city of Leuven, some ten years after its famous *Katholieke Universiteit Leuven* (1425) was established as a *studia generalia* by Pope Martin V (1369–1431), this religious art on Baltic oak was to be placed on the main altar in their chapel in the local church *Onze-Lieve-Vrouw van Ginderbuiten*, 'Our Lady Without the Walls,' and when required, carried in their regular religious processions through the city on major feast days. Under circumstances not unusual for the time, having been acquired through rights of inheritance by King Phillip II of Spain (1527–98) as an 'item of significance,' van der Weyden's altar piece was subsequently removed from the chapel in Leuven, and transported by sea to Spain, eventually to be placed in Madrid's world-famous *Museo del Prado*. Opened in 1819 as the national art museum of Spain, this contains one of the finest collections of European art dating from the twelfth century, where *Descent from the Cross* remains on permanent display.

Standing in front of Madrid's famous religious art, rather than looking at the *Prado's* less well-known 'Mona Lisa' painted by the workshop of Leonardo da Vinci (1452–1519), I was able to recall my thoughtful connections originally made during my sabbatical leave which afforded me with a very productive opportunity to reread the content of *Gaudium et Spes*, living in the city where this religious art was originally located, whereby I found inspiration for this book. Now in the presence of van der Weyden's religious art, I found myself as intended similarly disposed for meditative contemplation on the sufferings of Christ, hemmed in, and jostled amid an enthusiastic group of curious observers. Though anyone who tried to view da Vinci's extremely popular 'Mona Lisa' (c. 1503–16) in the Louvre (1793) would dismiss any impression that such boisterous behavior in front of a famous work of art is unusual.

As a remarkable piece of religious art *Descent from the Cross* represents a unique symbiosis between contemporary artistic and religious trends. Namely, as an instance of 'Northern Renaissance humanism,' whereby van der Weyden moves away from the traditional Gothic style in art which dealt with symbols towards a more vivid form of 'flesh and blood' human naturalism, found in the artistic representation of Christ's lifeless humanity captured in sorrowful pain. In so doing, this religious art represents an example of *devotio moderna*, namely, a sociopolitical movement of religious reform within Catholic spirituality found in the Low Countries including Flanders during the late fourteenth century. Where it was employed as a means for apostolic and pastoral renewal within the local community, a means of promoting the individual person's spiritual recovery through genuine pious and devotional practices, such as humble mediation.

Whereby the Flemish artist draws the viewer into the salvific scene of Christ's redemptive sacrifice, to experience the shared sense of shock, suffering and pain by those who observed the face of Christ, "the Word made flesh." A powerful testimony to the vicissitudes of human emotions, captured by the portrayal of 'tears and sorrows' on all nine figures van der Weyden has ingeniously assembled, closed in around Christ's lifeless body, as someone "born to save" was lowered from the cross, in the presence of St. John the Beloved Disciple and St. Mary Magdala, both witnesses to His Crucifixion, while being held by Joseph of Arimathea and supported by Nicodemus, a high ranking pharisee, positioned to the right. Together with His pale faced mother, collapsed aside swooning in grief, the viewer is offered a "symphony of sadness." Alternatively, approached as a "sculptured altarpiece," a chiselled frieze or *tableau vivant* in the style of his teacher Campin, found in van der Weyden's particular use of live models uncommon for the time.

By means of which *Descent from the Cross* offers a structured and emotionally charged work of great originality, characterized as a "synthesis of gesture and emotive power." One expressed in the introductory words of *Gaudium et Spes*, "the world has been liberated by Christ, who was crucified and has risen so that it would be transformed according to God's purpose" (para. 2). This human gathering of consequence portrayed by van der Weyden replicates the religious community assembled around the Eucharistic table of sacrifice. Furthermore, this art is especially evocative of the Council's original use of the expression *communio personarum* applied to the faith filled 'community of persons' gathered around the altar during the celebration of mass, characterized as a "communion of salvation." An instance of incarnational soteriology, this original thought found in conciliar humanism was generated during a twentieth-century extended meeting of minds, characterized by *sapiential* consciousness.

Namely, as a celebration of God's unconditional incarnate love, offered in sacrifice for our salvation through the person of Jesus Christ, "the New Adam." Thought well expressed by the "teacher of humanity," the foremost medieval scholastic theologian and another millennial figure infused with this distinctive form of consciousness, Thomas Aquinas as he writes about Christ in his famous *Summa Theologica* (1265–74): "who as man is the way for us to tend towards God" (1.2).[4] A tendency expressed more colloquially in the contemporary words of Ghislain Lafont who characterized Christ as "a man for others," exemplified in his salvific love towards those in need of salvation, namely, someone for everyone. Expressed in van der Weyden's portrayal of the human face of the suffering Incarnate truth, considered by the American art historian Elmer A. Carmean Jr. (1945–2019) as "an altar piece loaded with symbols that

---

4. Cited in Lafont, *Imagining the Catholic Church*, 93.

point all the way back to Adam and look forward to the Resurrection," as he begins his 2019 article "Decoding Sacrifice and Salvation," written for *The Wall Street Journal* (1889), published several months before his death from cancer on October 12, 2019.

By means of his radical portrayal of humanity, enacted through the redemptive activity of Christ's suffering, death, and resurrection, the Flemish artist literally draws the viewer into the salvific scene of Christ's sacrifice, to experience the sense of shock, suffering and pain occasioned by the death of "the Word made flesh." A powerful artistic testimony to our shared human emotions which characterize what we share as human beings, especially our human vulnerability experienced with others through our shared grief and loss, as we come to better understand ourselves.

2

Back to the Future

ALWAYS MEMORABLE, OPENING WORDS matter. They draw attention to something which follows, they set the tone and offer a preview of what you can expect, as found in these well-known words "all human beings are born free and equal in dignity and rights. They are endowed with reason and conscience and should act towards one another in a spirit of brotherhood." Because we are human, and only because of our humanity, we possess certain inalienable rights. Aspirational thought about being human offered in Article One of the Universal Declaration of Human Rights proclaimed by the United Nations General Assembly in Paris on December 10, 1948. Drafted by representatives with different legal and cultural backgrounds from all regions of the world, this was truly a global statement about humanity of universal significance. Wherein, we find set forth for the first time the fundamental rights to be universally protected for 'simply' being human; henceforth, December 10 is celebrated as Human Rights Day. However, as will become clear, there's nothing simple about being human.

To celebrate in 2018, the seventieth anniversary of this foundational moment, the popular expression "back to the future" was chosen by the editors of the *UNESCO Courier: Many Voices, One World* (1948) for its October-December volume, the official magazine published by the United Nations Educational, Scientific and Cultural Organization. Undoubtedly one of the greatest documents in human history, two decades later another unprecedented document was published on December 7, 1965, this time from the Catholic Church, which received similar publicity and international media acclaim for its promotion of our shared humanity, namely *Gaudium et Spes: Pastoral Constitution on the Church in the World of Today* (1965). As well as their shared human orientation, these foundational documents of the twentieth century addressed the inherent dignity and value of being human as a human being.

On closer scrutiny, the evolution of these documents had much in common, especially as a thoughtful consequence of a collective mindset, what I characterize as a "meeting of minds." Whether an assembly of the members of the recently established United Nations meeting in Paris or an assembly of Catholic bishops and religious leaders gathered in St. Peter's Basilica in the Vatican City, both sought the theoretical means to better understand our shared humanity.

A remarkable love story, the American science fiction film *Back to the Future* (1985) follows the time travels of a young teenager Marty McFly as he attempts to reenkindle the relationship between his parents initially falling in love, the reason for his own existence and to somehow get back to the future, suitably accompanied by the theme song "The Power of Love" by Huey Lewis and the News. While taken as the *leitmotif* for the celebration of the Declaration's seventieth anniversary, this well-known expression best reflects the orientation of my book as a "behind the scenes" philosophical, historical, and cultural detour into the past to discuss the genesis of a remarkable 'love story.' Namely, that of conciliar humanism, a way of thinking generated during the Council wherein, we find the theoretical means to engage the 'world of today' based on the recognition of our shared humanity, driven by the healing power of Christian love towards others, revealed in the suffering humanity of the Incarnate Word, Jesus Christ.

Known as "the man who loved wisdom," I would add of "practical wisdom" in Aristotle's sense, the French philosopher Jacques Maritain was someone who ingeniously combined philosophical thought with a profound awareness of socio-ethical concerns, wherein we find the inspiration for conciliar humanism in Maritain's seminal and well-known *Integral Humanism* (1936). Following the liberation of Paris which began on August 19, 1944, as a prominent Catholic figure, Maritain was appointed French ambassador to the Holy See by General Charles de Gaulle (1890–1970) later that year until 1947. When he was chosen to lead the French delegation to the UNESCO symposium on 'human rights' held in Mexico on November 6, during which he represented the Holy See, after which he accepted a resident professorship at Princeton University (1746) until 1952. Elected its President, Maritain opened the symposium in 1947 with an inspiring speech *La Voie de la paix*. That year was of particular significance for Maritain with the publication of his two philosophical books, *The Person and the Common Good* (1947) and *Existence and the Existent* (1947). Following the Council, he spoke on "the spiritual conditions of progress and peace" to UNESCO assembly on April 21, 1966 during his last visit to the United States. Later recalling the fundamental differences of approach about being human raised during the Mexico symposium, Maritain observed: "Yes, they said, we agree about the rights but *on condition that no one asks us why?* That 'why' is where the argument begins."[1]

Later used as the basis of the UN's "International Covenant on Civil and Political Rights" (1966), "these [human] rights derive from the inherent dignity of the human person." When read together these foundational documents, the Declaration and Covenant, like *Dignitatis Humanae* and *Gaudium et Spes*, remain consequential for their ongoing promotion of humanity. Moving into the twenty-first century, they provide a theoretical and especially philosophical framework to address sociopolitical issues within contemporary discourse. Such as the inexcusable and persistent blight of systemic racism, which can assume many forms and can occur in many places. A phenomenon of the twentieth century, racial prejudice is something like "Dark Matter," an ingredient of little value though critically present within human society seemingly incapable of studied resolution.

Other possible issues effecting contemporary humanity might be "climate change" and the ongoing ecological repercussions of "global warming" brought on by human activity on the natural environment, the expansive use of scientifically engineered artificial intelligence or the human issue of gender identify and associated rights of LGBTQI+ persons. Contemporary scientific and ethical issues within twenty-first-century discourse which find a resonance in Huxley's fictional futuristic literature, in his dystopian vision of humanity living in a *Brave New World*, an opportunity to explore the legacy of conciliar humanism.

This was certainly the mindset of the editorial staff of *Many Voices, One World* when they choose "to take a detour into the past to enable us to better orient ourselves in the future" hence their choice of this popular expression 'back to the future.' One which also informs my choice to write this book on the "untold story of conciliar humanism." Namely, by

---

1. McCrudden, *Understanding Human Dignity*, 2–3n4.

traveling back to the philosophical, intellectual, and cultural world of the mid twentieth century, we find "lessons for the future" in the opinion of Mark Goodale, Professor of Cultural and Social Anthropology at the University of Lausanne (1537). Whereby he sought to uncover "a hitherto little-known part of the history of the Declaration" through an analysis of the origins and philosophical foundations of human rights, a subject he later developed in *Reinventing Human Rights* (2022).

Characterized as "one of the most important and least-publicized UNESCO projects," this worldwide symposium on "what is human" addressed the philosophical foundations of human rights held in Mexico in 1948, chaired by Jacques Maritain. Convened in preparation for the subsequent drafting and adoption of the Universal Declaration, this symposium discussed material prepared from around sixty responses to an extensive survey sent between 1947 and 1948, "dispatched to an impressive list of social institutions, state organizations, and individuals," and collated under the supervision of another French philosopher Jacques Havet (1919–2002), chair of the UNESCO Sub-commission on Philosophy and Humanistic Studies, a diplomat and graduate from the *Ecole normale supérieure* (1794). Circumstances replicated years later in preparation for the Council under the direction of Domenico Tardini (1888–1961), Cardinal Secretary of State for the Vatican City, having been tasked with this responsibility by Pope John.

An approach similarly undertaken in writing my book concerning the genesis and legacy of a remarkable, though relatively 'unknown' way of thinking generated during the Council, conciliar humanism, found in the content of two remarkable documents *Gaudium et Spes* and *Dignitatis Humanae* when read together; there is much to be learnt from the opening words of the former. Characterized as "the Council's most mature document,"[2] the unprecedented opening words of *Gaudium et Spes* drew considerable attention to the human orientation of its content. Whoever thought a Catholic document bearing such doctrinal authority would begin with a celebration of human emotion: "the joys and hopes and the sorrows and anxieties of people today." Yet it goes further, these human emotions are shared by everyone, they speak about what we share in common, "there is nothing truly human which we do not share together." As intended, these words introduce the Council's "message of salvation to be communicated to everyone" (para. 1).

---

2. Gaillardetz, "Ecclesiological Functions," 83.

Not for the first time, thinking within a religious context were words spoken of such enormity as found in the opening words of Genesis, "In the beginning God . . . ," words of ultimate cosmic and human significance, which were taken up by the author of the prologue in John's Gospel, "in the beginning was the Word." Unique to this Gospel, none of the other Gospels has a beginning like this; these words were probably taken from a contemporary hymn that was in use within the Johannine community. Words which reflect thought of a philosophical orientation, perhaps that of Philo Judaeus from Alexandria who lived sometime during the first half of the first century. Characterized as a 'Hellenistic' thinker, he was proficient in Jewish, Islamic and Christian thought, and believed the early books of the Old Testament were embedded with philosophical meaning, as found in the opening words of Genesis.

Ultimately derived from acts of faith, the biblical books speak the language of humanity, found in the human experience of concrete relationships between God and human beings. However, as well recognized by the great Catholic convert, Augustine, bishop of Hippo Regius (354–430) in the north African Roman province of Numidia, an extraordinary thinker of the first millennium equally familiar with contemporary forms of philosophical thought, no matter how true it is that human beings seek God, God always takes the initiative, as Augustine narrates his personal story in his well-known autobiography, originally entitled *Confessions in thirteen books*. Furthermore, this encounter with God is always personal and as such requires an active response which forms community, an original thought which would direct conciliar humanism through the influence of Scheler. A remarkable and unprecedented way of thinking found in *Gaudium et Spes*, but not in isolation, as there is a much smaller companion piece of writing, *Dignitatis Humanae*. Here again we can learn much from the opening words of the Declaration "on religious freedom": "The dignity of the human person is a concern of which people of our time are becoming increasingly more aware," a direct quote from Pope John's papal encyclical *Pacem in Terris* (1963)

Perhaps a digression might be useful. While the expression 'human person' is commonly associated with the Council for obvious reasons due to its frequent employment in *Gaudium et Spes* and *Dignitatis Humanae*, I return to my original question asked years ago, "where did it come from?" Namely, where is the source of this thought? It is certainly used by Pope John in paragraph fourteen of his *Pacem in Terris*, 'on establishing universal peace in truth, justice, charity, and liberty' published on April 11, 1963 months before his death on June 3. However, approaching this source there seems a discrepancy. It appears Pope John adds something in his re-reading of the thought of his predecessor Pope Leo XIII: "true freedom, freedom worthy of the sons of God, is that freedom which most truly safeguards *the dignity of the human person*" (emphasis added). However, when reading the original source from Leo's encyclical *Libertas praestantissimum* "on the nature of human liberty" (1888), wherein he criticized prevalent forms of liberalism in politics and economics, this expression is not used, perhaps a liberty taken by Pope John? Referring to the context of Leo's translated thought wherein he distinguishes various forms of liberty, such as liberty of worship, liberty of speech and of the press, liberty of teaching, he finally arrives at 'liberty of conscience' in paragraph thirty, the source where Pope John finds this quoted thought. However, Leo speaks of "the dignity of man and is stronger than all violence or wrong." There is no mention of 'human person' by Leo, he only writes of 'man,' the choice of words is rather telling. This points to the originality of Pope John's thoughtful attempt to broaden an understanding of being human in the direction of a 'human person,' an orientation employed in *Gaudium et Spes*, based on its original use in *Dignitatis Humanae*.

Literally 'returning yearly,' anniversaries are an important aspect of our life as human beings, a claim commonly recognized. Whether recalling the date when an event took place, such as the opening of the Council on October 22, 1962, or when a document was published, such as December 7, 1965, when *Gaudium et Spes* and *Dignitatis Humanae* were promulgated, or March 26, 1967 when the papal encyclical *Populorum Progressio* "on the development of peoples" was published, or the foundation of an institution, a saint's feast day or a person's birthday. These human celebrations, whether communal or individual constitute an important component in our daily lives, whereby we discover 'we are not alone.'

Thinking philosophically within the tradition of shared thought of those living Catholic Christianity anniversaries can be understood as 'multidirectional.' Wherein we find an opportunity for thoughtful reflection, to re-read an important document, and in so doing, to revisit the ideas of the past with a view of thinking into the future while living in the present; this method of re-reading was practiced by the popes of the twentieth century, characterized as "champions of humanity," who sought to address practical issues of social justice. Generally the term *Catholic social teaching* refers to papal encyclicals and other documents issued since 1891 when Pope Leo XIII (1878–1903) published his landmark encyclical *Rerum Novarum* "on the Condition of Labor" (1891), which set the benchmark for this Catholic way of thinking with issues concerning social justice, such as "the fair and equitable distribution of resources, opportunities and privileges, wherein individual's rights are recognized and protected." A pattern of thought taken up by Pope Pius XI (1922–39) to celebrate the fortieth anniversary of Leo's groundbreaking document with his own encyclical *Quadragesimo Anno: Forty Years After: On Reconstructing the Social Order and Perfecting It Conformably to the Precepts of the Gospel* (1931), wherein he outlined the ethical implications arising from our social and economic life. Writing in 1991 Pope John Paul II continued this tradition of re-reading with his social encyclical with the rather predictable title *Centesimus Annus* (1991) to recall the thought of *Rerum Novarum*.

However, another seminal document appeared on the twentieth-century landscape of papal social teaching, when Pope Paul VI wrote his sixth encyclical, two years after the Council, namely, *Populorum Progressio: On the Development of Peoples* (1967), wherein we find a consolidation of a particular philosophical way of thinking which emerged found in conciliar humanism. As the pope concludes his encyclical with this aspirational thought: "Genuine progress does not consist in wealth sought for personal comfort or for its own sake; rather it consists in an economic order designed for the welfare of the human person, where the daily bread that each man receives reflects the glow of brotherly love and the helping hand of God" (para. 86). Original thought which Pope John Paul II engaged writing his encyclical *Sollicitudo Rei Socialis: On Social Concern* (1987) on the twentieth anniversary of *Populorum Progressio*.

As an original form of thought, conciliar humanism represents the Council's creative juxtaposition between philosophical thought and pastoral concerns, an instance of Aristotle's "practical philosophy," which generated a contemporary form of Christian humanism announced in *Gaudium et Spes*, "we are witnesses that a new humanism is being born" (para. 55). A way of thinking which emerged within an intellectual atmosphere, in response to "the accumulating problems and dangers of the twentieth century," which in the opinion of the French historian Jean-Luc Barré, the first biographer of Jacques Maritain, influenced the re-direction of Maritain's original thought, moving from "speculative philosophy to the philosophical defence of democracy, social justice, and the freedom of the human person,"[3] a sociopolitical philosophical way of thinking which generated his seminal *Integral Humanism* (1936).

A novel way of thinking which set the scene for conciliar humanism which brings together philosophical ideas and pastoral concerns, especially through the influence of two leading figures during the Council familiar with this approach. Namely, Maritain's close friend and philosophical interlocutor Giovanni Battista Montini (1897–1978), the well-read Cardinal Archbishop of Milan (1954–63), who would become Pope Paul VI, and Karol Wojtyła (1920–2005), the recently appointed Archbishop of Kraków. The latter well respected for his input during the Council by the former, a confidant of Maritain, who as pope exercised considerable influence in directing the philosophical and pastoral orientation found in conciliar humanism, which received his papal endorsement. Furthermore, intended as a means of 'dialogue' with the contemporary "world of today," the network of ideas found in conciliar humanism were then used by the pope in his next papal encyclical *Populorum Progressio* (1967). A word originally used by Athenian philosophers in Antiquity, it was rehabilitated by Martin Buber (1878–1965), the twentieth-century Jewish religious thinker from Austria, as the basis of his "philosophy of dialogue." And subsequently employed by the pope as a means of moving the Catholic Church from its former "ghetto mindset" towards a thoughtful interaction engaging the "world of today."

Equally familiar with Maritain's thought though approached from a different perspective, Wojtyła represents another influential figure in the genesis of conciliar humanism. As a young Catholic philosopher teaching Christian social ethics in Lublin, Wotyła had been introduced to *Integral Humanism* (1936) by his colleague, the Polish philosopher Stefan Szieżawski. Having worked with Maritain while on sabbatical leave in Paris during the early 1930s when this book was being prepared, the accomplished senior Polish philosopher returned to Lublin's "School of Thomist Philosophy" an enthusiastic proponent of Maritain's original thought which he enthusiastically shared with his young colleague. A thoughtful engagement Wojtyła took up during a series of lectures in 1949 entitled "what is Christian humanism?" Later, Wojtyła identified this subject as a possible topic for discussion during the Council in his 1959 letter in response to Cardinal Domenico Tardini, the Vatican's Secretary of State, who was tasked by Pope John XXIII to seek out suitable

---

3. Barré, *Jacques and Raïssa Maritain*, xii–xiii.

topics for discussion during the Council. While later recognized as "the Pope who rescued Western humanism" by his biographer George Weigel during an interview he gave on November 10, 2011 for the ABC, Australia's national broadcaster, Weigel might well have been referring to Pope Paul VI rather than speaking of his successor Pope John Paul II.

3

Being Conscious

MOVING INTO THIS BOOK, I invite you to consider the thought of Belgian Cardinal Désiré-Joseph Mercier (1851–1926), a well-known twentieth-century proponent of Thomism, found in *The Origins of Contemporary Psychology* (1897): "For whom are we philosophizing, unless it be for the men of our times? And what is our object, unless it be to attempt a solution of the doubts which are an obsession in our contemporaries?"[1]

As a "synthesis of fidelity and dynamism," conciliar humanism offers the theoretical, especially philosophical means to engage contemporary concerns shared by all, first and foremost the ongoing quest to understand our shared humanity. Introducing his seminal commentary on what came to be known as *Gaudium et Spes* (1965), then Professor Ratzinger recalls the assessment of the French cleric Gabriel-Marie Garrone (1901–94), Archbishop of Toulouse (1956–66), that the "real soul of schema XIII was in man and the human condition,"[2] namely, understanding our humanity in what Ratzinger calls the "age of Positivism." A way of scientific thinking without God generated by the thought of its so-called "founder," Auguste Comte (1798–1857), the French philosopher and social theorist, who coined the expression "sociology." Having repudiated formal religious belief at an early age, Comte became the figure head of a generation of thinkers who repudiated Cartesian rationalism in favour of the historical and empirical study of human existence using the methodology of science. Famous for inspiring the "religion of

---

1. Mercier, *Origins of Contemporary Psychology*, 344.
2. Ratzinger, "Dignity of the Human Person," 118.

humanity," Comte's thought captured the Godless spirit which generated the modern scientific worldview as it came to dominate early twentieth-century European thought, which initiated the 'crisis of humanity,' a worldview which persists to this day as it informs twenty-first-century 'transhumanism' and the World Transformation Movement.

Employing the rhetoric of "crisis," the German Lutheran philosopher Karl Jaspers (1883–1969), an existential thinker who was optimistic about the possibilities of human existence, sought to counter the contemporary malaise he found in contemporary European thought by promoting a new mode of global historical 'consciousness' using an existential methodology which generated his seminal book *The Origin and Goal of History* (1949), wherein he introduced the concept of an 'axial age.' A descriptive expression currently used by philosophers and sociologists to designate a pivotal and unprecedented moment in human history during the first millennium BC between 800–300, which generated what came to be known as 'consciousness.' Namely, the initial awareness among human beings to understand themselves embedded within the process of their search for meaning and an explanation of their origins. A dramatic shift towards human consciousness first expressed in Socratic thought.

During this unprecedented moment, characterized as the 'age of thinkers,' the spiritual and religious foundations of humanity were simultaneously and independently laid by Eurasian thinkers such as Confucius and Lao-Tse in China, Buddha and the Upanishads in India, Zarathustra in Persia, Elijah, Isaiah, and Jeremiah in the Judeo prophetic tradition in Palestine and the poet Homer and philosophers Parmenides of Elea, Heraclitus of Ephesus and Socrates of Athens and his student Plato, philosophers whose thought initiated the so-called 'era of consciousness.' Engaging Jasper's original idea, this became the subject of widespread debate among academics, vigorous, and often acrimonious, an idea creatively used by Karen Armstrong, the British author on comparative religion, in her popular book *The Great Transformation: The Beginning of Our Religious Traditions* (2006). Recently the Canadian philosopher Charles Taylor has characterized this Age as initiating "the era of transcendence," discussed in his seminal book *Sources of the Self: The Making of the Modern Identity* (1989). Recognized as a distinctive human capacity to move beyond our self-awareness, at no other time in human history was this understanding of ourselves so seriously challenged as during the late nineteenth and early twentieth centuries, a period which marks "the demise of transcendence," circumstances which the Council Fathers sought to address as men of the twentieth century.

Recognized in *The Blackwell Companion to Consciousness* (2007) as "anything that we are aware of at a given moment forms part of our consciousness, making conscious experience at once the most familiar and most mysterious part of our lives." A recognizable human phenomenon which remains "puzzling and controversial," symptomatic of an "era of apparent contradiction," human consciousness re-emerged as the subject of philosophical interest during the twentieth century. Notably by the German philosopher Edmund Husserl (1859–1938) through his promotion of "phenomenology," the study of what appears or is experienced in consciousness. Reliant on the thought of another German philosopher Franz Brentano's (1838–1917) recovery of the scholastic notion of 'intentionality,' Husserl identified this notion as the distinctive feature of consciousness, found in the experience of being directed "towards" something or someone. Based on Husserl's restorative thought, the study of consciousness approached as a human phenomenon set the philosophical agenda during the twentieth century, especially in European thought, discussed by the Alsatian born American philosopher Herbert Spiegelberg (1904–90) in his landmark two volume *The Phenomenological Movement: A Historical Introduction* (1960).

Understood as the science of phenomena, as distinct from the study of the nature of 'being' found in ontology, phenomenology represents "the unprejudiced, descriptive study of whatever appears to consciousness, precisely in the way it so appears" as described by Dermot Ryan in his introduction to *The Phenomenology Reader* (2002). An approach first outlined by Husserl in his two volume *Logical Investigations* (1900–1901), written from the perspective of Aristotelian realism wherein he criticizes the prevalent subjectivism found in contemporary 'psychologism,' the view that logic is based on psychology. Namely, Husserl's scientific study of how the human mind operates through the use of perception, feelings, emotions, across a broad spectrum of mental phenomena used as a means of resolving philosophical problems. However, his next book represents a reversal of thinking which might be characterized in the mode of Cartesian rationalism, found in *Ideas on a Pure Phenomenology and Phenomenological Philosophy* (1913), written while teaching at Freiburg where one of his students was Martin Heidegger (1889–1976), who was to succeed Husserl as professor of philosophy following his retirement.

Traditionally approached as a human activity, doing philosophy begins with a commonly asked question, 'what am I?' A way of thinking initially examined by Socrates (around 470–399 BC), an equally 'engaging and infuriating' little person who walked around annoying Athenian society. While this ultimately led to his untimely death, his critical method of inquiry has been used as an effective means of acquiring knowledge and further information by means of an ordered series of questions, whereby we learn more. An interrogative process which lies at the foundations of Western thought, as observed by Sir Isaiah Berlin (1909–97), the Latvian born British social philosopher and historian of ideas in his essay "The Purpose of Philosophy" (1962): "the questions themselves are only intelligible if, and only it, we know where to look for the answers," which are found in the use of philosophy.[3] However, philosophy was not always philosophy, a realization which emerged during the twentieth century.

While over the course of Western history the meaning of philosophy, from Greek *philosophia* 'love of wisdom,' might have changed it has always retained its distinctive human orientation, found in the use of rational thought to 'think things through.' While commonly used its meaning is difficult to pin down, one which perhaps reflects its subject matter, like other difficult words such as 'human,' 'love' or 'person,' each readily understood but equally resistant to precise definition.[4] Approached as a human activity, it was originally recognized in the fragmented thought of Heraclitus of Ephesus in one of his aphorisms: "Philosophical men, namely, shall have knowledge of a great many things.[5] As Felix M. Cleve (1890–1985), the Jewish born Austrian émigré to the US continues, the thought of this Ionian philosopher marks a strange coincidence with modern usage of this expression as "a man searching for ultimate truth."

Whereby contemporary philosophers generally 'shy away' from explaining 'what philosophy is' in favour of an explanation 'how philosophy' is undertaken in the Socratic tradition, giving examples of the sorts of things philosophers think about, wherein we find the activity of 'doing philosophy' in thinking about humanity which generated conciliar humanism. Well expressed by Pope John Paul II as he introduces *Fides et Ratio* (1998) wherein he defines this human interrogative process of rational thought: "the study of *philosophy* is directly concerned

3. Berlin, *Concepts and Categories*, 1.
4. Swieżawski, *St. Thomas Revisited*, 8.
5. Creve, *Giants*, 1:xxii.

with asking the questions of life's meaning and sketching an answer to it" (para. 3). An approach ultimately used as a means towards understanding our human capacity to think about the nature of God and about ourselves, a twofold capacity denied during the twentieth century in some forms of European philosophical thought.

So called 'classical philosophy,'[6] which emerged within Greek Antiquity during the first millennium BC in the city state of Athens, was built on the universal recognition that humans are naturally embodied animate beings who are rational and naturally social, directed towards other human beings, creatures who live with others in a *polis* or 'state,' outlined in Aristotle's *The Nicomachean Ethics* (340 BC). While over the course of recorded history one dimension of being human, approached as either rational, social, or spiritual has been prioritized. During the twentieth century European Catholic philosophers sought to bring these diverse understandings together, thereby achieving a recovery of an 'integral' or whole understanding of being human, one which seeks to bring together everything that makes us a 'human being.' In the words of *Gaudium et Spes*: "Being a unity of body and soul, humanity concentrates in its physical dimension the elements of the material world, which reach their peak in the human and raise their voice in free praise of the creator" (para. 14). An understanding which embraces the diversity which makes us human, as a physical, material, emotional, social, and spiritual being brought together in the 'human person.' Characterized as a *living synthesis*, this original way of thinking was inspired by Maritain's "Christian manifesto' entitled *Integral Humanism* (1936) and Scheler's original understanding of 'philosophical anthropology.'

Access to the thought of this enigmatic quintessential philosopher from Athens, from which others have learnt, is found in the *Dialogues of Socrates* written by his student Plato (c. 429–347 BC), and the *treatises* written by Plato's student Aristotle (384–322 BC), thereby establishing what might be described as a form of 'philosophical awareness.' Furthermore, this method of critical questioning functioned within what we might call a 'conversation' between several people holding different points of view concerning a particular subject, in response to a specific question, such as what is 'piety' or 'justice' asked by human beings. Later characterized as 'dialectic' by Plato, this interrogative method facilitated the pursuit of truth through the form of reasoned

---

6. Adamson, *Classical Philosophy*, 7.

argumentation practiced to this day. Namely, that in the search for truth "ideas do not occur in a vacuum" but rather represent the consequence of a profound and thoughtful engagement with the ideas taken from other thinkers about what is real and true, and how to act ethically, to do good and to avoid evil, who have directed their critical attention toward understanding the world around us.

Based on Socrates' ingenious use of an ancient Greek aphorism *know thyself* inscribed above the portal of the Temple of Apollo at Delphi, wherein he employed reason as a means to speak about ourselves as being conscious, through his model of 'an examined life' prompted by our natural human curiosity, thereby initiating the so-called "Socratic turn to consciousness," later used by the German philosopher Max Scheler through his innovative study of our value oriented emotional life. Furthermore, as a human activity, philosophy represents an integrative communal activity. Found in the ethos of the traditional "school of philosophy," established by Plato's Academy and Aristotle's Lyceum, which set the pattern for the later philosophical societies established at the Universities of Munich (1472) and Göttingen (1734) and the University of Lublin's (1918) "School of Thomist Philosophy," wherein ideas were critically engaged, discussed, and shared, an interrogative practice which remains axiomatic for participating in the conversation undertaken within this book. Currently, philosophy is designated by the English academic philosopher Simon Blackburn as "human thought become self-conscious."[7]

As a distinctive human activity, doing philosophy is initiated by asking a question which generates an inquisitive and purposeful search for meaning in the pursuit of truth in understanding the world around us through the disciplined use of reason, prompted by a sense of wonder that "there something rather than nothing." Based on the premise "all men desire to know" what is real, the Athenian philosopher Aristotle wrote his famous study of 'being *qua* being' originally designated as 'first philosophy,' later renamed *Metaphysics*. This activity of rational thought was commonly associated with "wise men" who were considered skilled and clever thinkers; however, the expression "Sophist" was also used by Plato, Aristotle's teacher to disparage the activity of so-called 'professional' thinkers 'for hire.' Namely, itinerant teachers who taught 'rhetoric,' the art of using language to persuade or influence others, to anyone willing

---

7. Blackburn, *Oxford Dictionary of Philosophy*, v.

to pay for this service, such as the Greek thinker Protagoras of Abdera (c. 490–c. 420 BC) or the Sicilian Gorgias of Leontini (c. 483–376 BC), rather than to think in search for the truth.

While many recognize a disjunction between theory and action, Aristotle's original philosophical realism was essentially an integrative way of thinking about what possesses 'being' or what is, whereby he recognized their interdependence which informs his discussion concerning the nature of 'being,' the study of ontology, through an interrogative process of "distinguishing without separating" the various forms of knowing, as discussed in his *Nicomachean Ethics* 1139–41, his best-known study of ethics. Set against the pursuit of human happiness, Aristotle explores the meaning of 'practical philosophy' by differentiating various ways of knowing, hierarchically ordered from the lowest form of *episteme* or scientific knowledge based on observation and induction. Whereby he moves onto *techne* or a technical knowledge of how to do things, then onto *phronesis* understood as 'practical wisdom,' the awareness of what is conducive to producing the good, *nous* or 'intelligence' found in the direct intuition of the first principles of 'being,' and finally, the attainment of *sophia* or 'wisdom,' understood as "scientific and intuitive knowledge of the highest goods."

Familiar with this pattern of hierarchically structured thinking, which came of characterize traditional philosophical thought, Augustine was the first Christian thinker, who was infused with *sapiential* consciousness, to integrate this way of thinking within a theological context. Found in book nine of *The Trinity*, published around 417, wherein he employs the distinction between *scientia*, a knowledge of historical facts, and that of *sapientia* or wisdom, one which subsequently informs the difference between natural or scientific knowledge and theoretical knowledge acquired through the infusion of wisdom, a way of thinking wherein we find the genesis of conciliar humanism thought which continues to this day. As discussed by Jonathan Attard in "Rediscovering *Sapientia* in an Age Riddled by *Scientia*: Prophetic Knowledge in Thomas Merton" (2017), a master's thesis submitted to the Faculty of Theology at the University of Malta (1592).

Like all sentient animals, human beings make observations throughout life; we notice the warmth of the sun, hear the clap of thunder, and see the flash of lightning. And yet, precisely because we are human, we can participate in more complex patterns of thoughtful activity, such as calculation and speculative thinking, expressed in our use of language as a means of communicating our thought and ideas. However, probing these levels of human activity which are accessible to scientific scrutiny, there is the awareness that there is much more to what we are as human beings, traditionally approached as *Homo sapiens*.

An issue taken up during the 2009 Melbourne International Film Festival which featured *Examined Life: Excursions with Contemporary Thinkers* (2008). A Canadian film screened to great acclaim, produced by the American born writer and cultural activist Astra Taylor whereby she sought to "take philosophy to the streets." Attempting to learn how to live as human beings through a conversational and entertaining journey of ideas with eight iconoclastic philosophers as they strolled through particular locations chosen for their personal significance: literally moving philosophy "out of the dark corners of the academy and into the streets." A reminder as the promotional blurb states, I would add if ever one was needed, that "great ideas are born through profound engagement with the hustle and bustle of everyday life, not in isolation from it," as claimed by the engaged spirit of twentieth-century European existentialism. However, not all shared this favorable assessment, as observed by one of the participants, the American moral philosopher Martha Nussbaum who spoke on the topic of 'justice' as reported in *The Point* magazine. Wherein she claims this form of "pop philosophy" was "a betrayal of the tradition of philosophizing that began, in Europe, with the life of Socrates."[8]

While he remains one of the ancient Greeks that everyone has heard of, unlike philosophers after him, Socrates left no written account of his own thought, as it appears he was unable to write. Thereby we are reliant on contemporary, secondary sources to access his original thought, found in the *Early Socratic Dialogues* written by his student Plato, another formative figure in Western philosophy. Original circumstances which seem to contradict his medieval depiction by Matthew Paris (c. 1200–1259), the Anglo-Norman Benedictine monk from St. Albans Abbey in Hertfordshire, in a fortune telling tract entitled *Prognostica Socratis Basilei*, 'The Prognostications of Socrates the King [and a magician],'[9] part of a collection of manuscripts held in the Bodleian Library (1602) at the University of Oxford (1096), named after its founder Sir Thomas Bodley (1545–1613), the English diplomat and scholar. Wherein the portrayal of these classical figures in Western thought, the

---

8. Nussbaum, "Inheriting Socrates," para. 2.
9. Lewis, *Art of Matthew Paris*, 387.

relationship between a teacher and student, was "reinvented and reinscribed," a typical practice during the Middle Ages.[10] Later reproduced as a picture postcard for sale in its bookshop, which was purchased by the postmodern Algerian born French philosopher Jacques Derrida (1930–2004) on June 4, 1977 during his visit to the Bodleian, and subsequently used as the front cover for his book, *The Post Card: From Socrates to Freud and Beyond* (1980). Considered a national treasure, I was privileged to read this tract with the assistance of the head librarian, a specialist in medieval Latin abbreviations, while on sabbatical leave in Campion Hall (1898) in Oxford during November 2015.

The famous dictum, the unexamined life is not worth living, was made by Socrates as part of his defence during the criminal proceedings against him, as recorded by Plato, a saying which underscores Socrates' lifelong commitment to the pursuit of self-awareness. Whereby he employed an interrogative approach, doing philosophy as a characteristic human undertaking, generated by our natural curiosity and the systematic use of abstract and reasoned thought. A cyclic process initiated by a question, such as "what is human?" and following a thoughtful conversation wherein various opinions are appraised and much is learnt within this educative process, whereby we return to the same question more well informed, a process undertaken reading this book.

Citing the opinion of the popular English historian Paul Johnson in *Socrates: A Man for Our Times* (2011), this argumentative figure whom he characterized as the "Great Question Master" was more interested in "*how* to think" rather than "*what* to think,"[11] initiating a thoughtful process of "question and answer" between several people holding different points of view about a particular subject. Later called 'dialectic' by Plato, this form of reasoned argumentation has served as the philosophical touchstone for the human pursuit of truth used to this day. Found in the ongoing employment of a philosophical orientation of human thought, which in the words of Pope John Paul II "defends the capacity of reason to know the truth." Emblematic thought expressed during his address to the American bishops on October 24, 1998, which both generated and informs the legacy of conciliar humanism. Prompted by a resurgence of interest during the twentieth century in understanding our shared humanity, based on the recognition of our human capacity

---

10. Camille, "Dissenting Image," 131.
11. Johnson, *Socrates*, 91.

'to choose' to think about God, generated by our related 'capacity for transcendence' which directs the choices we make as human beings, an awareness which inspired conciliar humanism.

Approached from the perspective of religious belief and the use of philosophy we might ask, is there something we share as living beings, something which specifies us as being human? In so doing, we need to address what are the qualities or characteristics which define our 'nature,' more traditionally understood, or as a 'condition,' more scientifically approached. Moreover, to explain whether humans are different from other forms of animate life, and if so, what is the meaning and purpose of human existence? What has been referred to as "the something more" or "X factor" which the Council ingeniously called a 'human person,' whereby two strands of twentieth-century European philosophical thought, humanism and personalism, are brought together.

4

Thinking about Humanity

As a pattern of philosophical thought with a human orientation, 'humanism' remains an ambiguous though persistent expression used to this day; it is defined in *The Oxford Dictionary of Philosophy* (1994) as "any philosophy concerned to emphasize human welfare and dignity."[1] Over the course of Western history this orientation has assumed many variants; however, whether approached from its original pagan, then Christian, atheistic or secular perspectives, these draw attention to the inherent dignity of being human as something important and valuable, in response to this perennial philosophical question, what is human? A common enough question to which everyone seems to have an answer, presumably shared by all; however, there is nothing more prone to misunderstanding than a response to this question. And herein we find the enigma of being human.

Over the course of history this resilient way of thinking about humanity has informed Western civilization and culture, wherein human discourse was approached from a mixture of religious and philosophical perspectives until the nineteenth century, when these were replaced with the emergence of the human sciences. Nevertheless, whether approached from religious, philosophical, or scientific perspectives, until the nineteenth century these drew attention to the inherent value and dignity of humanity and a legitimate subject for studied discussion. Namely, to understand that human beings are essentially different from other forms of animal life, based on the recognition of our human capacity for ordered

---

1. Blackburn, *Oxford Dictionary of Philosophy*, 178.

thought, the ability to think rationally, and in our capacity to choose, to exercise of free will. Whereby humans were categorized as *Homo sapiens* by Carl Linnaeus (1707–61), the Swedish biologist, as the most common and widespread species of primate.

However, circumstances changed following the demise of religious belief generated during the eighteenth-century Enlightenment, whereby the nineteenth century marks a consolidation of this rational way of thinking living in a world where science gained ascendency, as a reactionary and reductive way of thinking about humanity. Namely, one which denied the spiritual integrity of the human being in possession of an immortal soul, in favour of a purely biological and material being without a soul, as one physical organism among many, a way of thinking marked by the arrival of the French philosopher Paul Ricoeur's (1913–2005) so-called 'masters of suspicion.' Namely, the German philosophers Friedrich Nietzsche (1844–1900) and Karl Marx (1818–83) and the Austrian founder of 'psychoanalysis' Sigmund Freud (1856–1939) whose critical thought generated further variants of humanism, now approached from 'atheistic' and 'secular' perspectives, moving into the twentieth century.

Currently understood as a socio-ethical, non-religious way of thinking, contemporary humanism employs the use of reason and a scientific methodology to claim "human beings have the right and responsibility to give meaning and shape to their own lives," a topic discussed during the International Humanist Conference held in Glasgow, sponsored by the Scottish Humanist Society, between June 3–5, 2022. Recognized as one of the most pervasive ideologies of the twentieth century, humanism was recently presented as "a progressive philosophy of life" by the American Humanist Association with the innocuous motto "good without God." However, the true character of this harmful atheistic and secular ideology is discussed in a compilation of essays published as *Philosophers and God* (2009), written at "the frontiers of faith and reason" by a group of philosophers and theologians in response to what they call "the continued popular polemic against theism" living in a postmodern world wherein "aggressive secularism" and "secular humanism" remain our critical opponents.

Thinking in a postmodern digital world, little seems to have changed from the intellectual and cultural milieu "which in a sense defied the Council" in the opinion of Pope Paul VI, expressed during his address to close the final plenary session of Council proceedings on December 7, 1965. Provocative thought well documented in *The Drama of Atheist*

Humanism (1944) by Henri de Lubac, another key figure operating "behind the scenes" in shaping the human agenda and subsequent direction of thought during the Council. These various forms of contemporary humanism, atheistic and secular, mirror the two-fold denial which characterized twentieth-century European thought, namely, the denial of our human capacity to think about the nature and existence of God, found in prevalent forms of atheistic rationalism, materialism, and naturalism, which were addressed during the First Vatican Council (1869–70) in its Dogmatic Constitution "on the catholic faith," promulgated on April 24, 1870. And the inevitable denial of our human capacity for transcendence, once God is taken out of the picture and everything is permitted, found in the reduction of humanity to a biological species and a material physical being among many, a way of thinking which was challenged during the Second Vatican Council. Recently, the American Catholic political commentator George Weigel has characterized these denials as the "common rejection of the God of the Bible" which inevitably led to the "annihilation of the human person."[2]

During his final address to the Council, Pope Paul VI used this occasion to outline what he thought the Council had achieved; in so doing, he drew attention to a new form of humanism. One based on a Christ centred integral philosophical understanding of our shared humanity which was generated over the life of the Council in response to a question we all ask. Succinctly expressed in *Gaudium et Spes*: "Believers and unbelievers are almost at one on considering that everything on earth is to be referred to humanity as its centre and culmination. But what is humanity itself?" (para. 12). This fundamental question was emphatically answered in the affirmative, which set the Council's unprecedented 'human' agenda and its subsequent celebration of the integrity of human life through its innovative use of the idea 'human person,' a way of thinking which initiated the "era of the human person" within Catholic discourse.

Nowhere more so than in these evocative words from *Gaudium et Spes*: "Thus, we are witnesses that a new humanism is being born in which the human is defined above all in terms of our responsibility to our sisters and brothers and to history" (para. 55). Unprecedented thought which marks the generation of a new Catholic way of thinking about our shared humanity found in the 'human person.' Highly original thought which hours later Pope Paul VI would endorse with these iconic words as he

---

2. Weigel, *To Sanctify the World*, 22.

formally closed the Council on December 7, 1965. Recalling the words of Christ in the Gospel of John, "He who sees me, sees also the Father" (14:9), the pope takes ownership of this original thought with his claim: "our humanism becomes Christianity, our Christianity becomes centred on God, in such sort that we may say, to put it differently: a knowledge of man is a prerequisite for a knowledge of God."

Herein we find the nexus of conciliar humanism, namely, as a Christ centred integral philosophical understanding of our shared humanity, expressed in *Gaudium et Spes*: "Whoever follows Christ, the perfect human being, become more of a human being. By this faith the church is able to preserve the dignity of human nature" (para. 41). A radical, from the Latin *radax* 'root,' or foundational way of thinking about our shared humanity in Christ which was generated in response to the question 'what am I.' Unlike the first ecumenical councils which used ideas found in colloquial Greek language, such as *prosopon* 'person' and *hypostasis* 'of one substance' to affirm the tenets of Christian faith, namely, to better understand the theological issue of the divinity of Christ. Now, the twenty first and last to date such council adapted this God centred way of thinking to thinking about our shared humanity, using ideas taken from twentieth-century European Catholic philosophy, from the phenomenological ethical personalism of Max Scheler, from the Thomistic humanism of Jacques Maritain and from the Thomistic personalism Karol Wojtyla, brought together with ideas from Catholic tradition, wherein we find inspiration for conciliar humanism.

An awareness set against the background of contemporary philosophical interest in the study of humanity, about being human and the human being, by contemporary Europeans such as Gabriel Marcel's (1889–1973) *The Philosophy of Existence* (1948) and two volume *The Mystery of Being* (1951), Henri de Lubac's (1896–1991) *The Drama of Atheist Humanism* (1944) and Maurice Blondel's (1861–1949) *Action* (1893) along with Jewish philosophers, the Austrian Martin Buber's (1878–1965) seminal *I and Thou* (1937) and Lithuanian Frenchman Emmanuel Levinas's (1906–95) *Existence and Existents* (1947) and *Totality and Infinity: An Essay on Exteriority* (1961). Understood as a remarkable confluence of thought, set against the landscape of twentieth-century European Catholic philosophy, wherein we find the broad background to understand the genesis of conciliar humanism.

Namely, as the Council sought to better understand what we share in common as human beings with the Incarnate Word in response to the perennial question 'what is human.' By means of this interrogative process, the Council Fathers sought to regain our thoughtful access to understanding the Triune God which had been denied, living in a world characterized by the popular "polemic against theism." Understood as the consequence of the twentieth-century reductive understanding of humanity and its twofold denial, namely, the denial of our human capacity to think about the idea of God's existence and the related denial of our human capacity for transcendence, which generated various forms of 'aggressive secularism' and 'secular humanism,' a twofold denial which conciliar humanism sought to address. Moving into the twenty-first century, little seems to have changed from the time of the Second Vatican Council when gauging the intellectual and cultural climate of our day, living in a postmodern digital world *where anything goes*, as observed in *Philosophers and God: At the Frontiers of Faith and Reason* (2009).[3] Written by a group of philosophers and theologians in response to *Philosophers without God: Meditations on Atheism and the Secular Life* (2007). Sixty years on it is opportune to begin this conversation, whereby we recognize this highly original synthesis of philosophical thought generated during the Council. Understood as the consequence of the twentieth-century retrieval of a pre-modern Christian form of consciousness, known as *sapiential*. A way of thinking well expressed in *Gaudium et Spes*: "The intellectual nature of the human person reaches its final perfection, and needs to do so, through the wisdom which gently draws the mind to seek and love what is true and good, and which leads it through visible realities to those which are invisible" (para. 15).

Perhaps the Canadian Christian philosopher Jens Zimmermann represents a notable exception to the apparent neglect concerning the circumstances which inform conciliar humanism by Catholic thinkers let alone anyone else, when he claimed: "From the Catholic side, Vatican II has provided an important push for the idea of Christian humanism by recovering the incarnation as the theological centre of theology,"[4] a claim which opens his *Re-Envisioning Christian Humanism* (2017). A specialist in this subject whereby he asserted in an earlier publication that Christianity represents the "first proper humanism" introducing his *Incarnational Humanism* (2012),[5] a project he pursued later writing *Humanism & Religion: A Call for the Renewal of Western Culture* (2012).

3. Cornwell, *Philosophers and God*, xviii.
4. Zimmermann, *Re-Envisioning Christian Humanism*, 10.
5. Zimmermann, *Incarnational Humanism*, 15.

Nevertheless, notwithstanding his erudite scholarship, he joins the ranks of contemporary Catholic theologians, like the German Cardinal Walter Kasper, who appreciate the emergence of theological anthropology as a field of study initiated by the Council's original human agenda, an approach expressed in the words of the American theologian Richard McBrien (1936–2015) writing in *Catholicism* (1994), "no theology can begin without immediate attention to the question of human existence."[6] Furthermore, little attention has been given to the philosophical orientation of thought which directs the Council's understanding of the human being who actually thinks about God, Christ, the Church, redemption and our moral and spiritual life, an understanding found in conciliar humanism, let alone from whence it came?

Namely, as the Council's original way of thinking about our shared humanity, accessible to all regardless of religious affiliation, which it understood as a "service to humanity." This original expression encapsulates the Council's "belief in humanity," to borrow the words of Ghislain Lafont (1928–2021), the French Benedictine theologian, through its unprecedented use of philosophical thought, nuanced by anthropological, metaphysical, and sociological concerns, brought together and unified within a network of three original ideas, human person, community of persons, and human solidarity. By means of which conciliar humanism represents the consequence of the twentieth-century retrieval of *sapiential* consciousness.

Sixty years on, it's time to probe a little deeper into this original form of twentieth-century Catholic thought found in conciliar humanism. To understand the originality of the network of its three interrelated ideas, innovative thought studied through the lens of a philosophical rereading of two foundational Council documents accompanied by a guided historical and cultural commentary in the form of a discussion. Wherein we find background information to better understand the genesis of conciliar humanism and its abiding legacy. Namely, how this thought originated and to access the unexplored philosophical, historical, and personal connections which direct this original thought. Approached from within a format which brings together, for the first time, the philosophical thought of three twentieth-century European Catholic philosophers, who 'on the face of it' seemingly share very little in common, other than a general interest in philosophy, though approached from different

---

6. McBrien, *Catholicism*, 75.

vantage points. Furthermore, while the French layman and Polish bishop are recognizably Catholic, some might challenge this attribution to the German layman. However, on closer scrutiny this was not the case, as recognized by Karol Wojtyła while writing on Max Scheler for his *Habilitation* (1954), a post-doctoral piece of written research required for promotion as a 'professor' in the European university system.

While Scheler unexpectedly died in 1928 well before the Council, we not only need to understand his original thought which brought together various strands of twentieth-century European thought, namely, phenomenological ethical personalism and philosophical sociology between 1900 until 1921 when this Jewish convert was well-known throughout Germany as a Catholic philosopher, but more significantly, to understand how this thought was ingeniously used by the Council Fathers, especially through the influence of Karol Wojtyla, and brought together in a remarkable 'synthesis of fidelity and dynamism,' to quote the words of Pope Benedict out of context, namely, found in the 'untold story of conciliar humanism.' Understood as a 'symphony of ideas,' originally used by the Council, namely, human person, community of persons, and human solidarity, which together constitute conciliar humanism as a thoughtful response to the twentieth-century 'crisis of humanity.'

As such, the tenets of conciliar humanism represent a "communion of salvation."[7] An expression originally used by Jacques Maritain, a Catholic convert to characterize the thought of another Catholic convert, Max Scheler's understanding of the universal Church. Now applied to this network of three philosophical ideas, drawn from the latter's original phenomenology of religious activity embedded within a triadic structure.

An expression taken from the Preface to *Walls Are Crumbling: Seven Jewish Philosophers Discover Christ* (1953) by Monsignor John M. Oesterreicher (1904–93), of Moravian Jewish origin, who was a Catholic convert like Scheler and Maritain. A prominent anti-Nazis activist during the 1930s, following the German annexation of Austria in 1938, known as the *Anschluss*, when he fled to Paris where he met Maritain; however, the German invasion of France in 1940 forced him to flee again, this time to American. Working at the Institute of Judaeo-Christian Studies which he established in 1953 at Seton Hall University (1856), a private Catholic research university, Oesterreicher became a leading advocate of Jewish-Catholic reconciliation and one of the principal architects of

---

7. Maritain, Foreword to *Walls Are Crumbling*, xiv.

the Council's seminal *Nostra Aetate* Declaration "on the church's relation to non-Christian religions." The shortest Conciliar document of six paragraphs, promulgated on October 28, 1965 by Pope Paul VI. This unprecedented document was addressed to "the human race in our age," wherein we find the "promotion of unity and charity among people" based on the recognition of what "human beings have in common," namely, "what brings them together" (para. 1), a remarkable thought which foreshadows conciliar humanism.

5

A Human Agenda

"TODAY THE CHURCH IS witnessing a crisis underway within society. While humanity is at the threshold of a new age, immensely serious and broad tasks await the Church, as in the most tragic periods of her history," understood as a "human crisis." Descriptive thought used to characterize the twentieth century; these words are equally applicable to the twenty-first century as it confronts the "crisis of truth." These words introduce the 'painful' diagnosis made by an elderly Pope John XXIII who was certainly attuned to the "signs of the times," writing in his Apostolic Constitution *Humanae Salutis* whereby he formally convened the Council on December 25, 1961, whereby the universal Church would address the issue of 'human salvation.'

This remarkable though neglected document informs the remote background to understand the genesis of conciliar humanism, as an instance of Incarnational soteriology. Found in the pope's innovative and purposeful use of this date, familiar to Christians and embedded with theological and especially human significance. Namely, the annual celebration of the birth of Jesus Christ, the Word Incarnate, wherein we think about the arrival of the human presence of God, brought into the world through the birth of a child who would atone for the sins of humanity.

Given what we celebrate at Christmas, the pope envisaged the forthcoming ecumenical council as an opportunity to think again on the significance of the humanity we share with the One born for our human salvation, a thought expressed in the words of Augustine "for our sake God became man" (*quia pro te Deus factus est homo*; Sermon 85). Later, these words were purposefully used by Pope Benedict XVI, an eminent Augustinian scholar, as he begins his seminal Christmas Address to the Roman Curia on December 22, following his papal election on April 19, 2005, wherein he offers an invitation to understand "the true meaning of Christ's birth," namely, to live eternally "in communion with the Most Holy Trinity."

While his predecessor was the pope who espoused the Conciliar idea of 'human person,' now his successor would be the pope who espoused the Conciliar idea of *communio*, 'a community of persons,' an instance of the new way of thinking he had referred to during his Address. As our hearts are filled with joy and hope at Christmas, to echo the introductory words of *Gaudium et Spes*, this celebration is tinged with the recognition that the Saviour "born for us" will also "die for us," as the Constitution's introduction continues, found in "the sorrows and anxieties of people today." Approached as a "communion of salvation," the celebration of the human birth of the God-given source of our shared human salvation enacted on the Cross, is well captured in the religious art of van der Weyden.

Herein we find the significance of Pope John's unprecedented manifesto to address the concerns of "people today," which was taken up ten days later, after the Council had begun. Amid growing dissatisfaction with the preparatory material organized for discussion by the Roman Curia, the Council Fathers, namely, those entitled to speak during Council proceedings, known as 'interventions,' and to vote on proposed documents, delivered their own 'message to the world': "We urgently turn our thoughts to the problems by which human beings are afflicted today. As we undertake our work, therefore, we would emphasize whatever concerns the dignity of the human person, whatever contributes to a genuine community of peoples."[1] Whereby it is understood they took ownership of Council's proceedings and set in motion its distinctive human agenda and its subsequent original philosophical pastoral orientation of thought. Given the collective nature of ecumenical councils, much can be read into the intent of this message from the Council Fathers, expressive of their shared concern for the 'human person' directed towards those living 'out there.'

While this 'message' received minimum coverage in the media, the American Jesuit church historian John O'Malley considers these words "an adumbration of the council's future direction," namely, its human

---

1. O'Malley, *What Happened at Vatican II*, 99.

agenda and the distinctive philosophical pastoral orientation of thinking which generated the characteristic expressions, 'human person,' 'community of persons,' and 'human solidarity,' a network of three interrelated ideas which form the basis of conciliar humanism. An original way of thinking which informs the Council's unprecedented outreach towards the whole of humanity, living in a broken world 'out there.' An awareness of this philosophical orientation and pastoral concern which was shared by many Council Fathers who contributed to this message, especially those familiar with twentieth-century European philosophy, men of the twentieth century like Cardinal Giovanni Battista Montini (1897–1978) from Milan, Cardinal Leo Jozef Suenens and Archbishop Karol Wojtyla, who likewise shared the lovable pope's gospel inspired philosophical acumen and pastoral openness to humanity or that of Cardinal Josef Frings (1897–1978) from Cologne, who certainly lived up to his episcopal motto *Pro Hominibus constitutus*, 'disposed towards humanity.' Who along with Blessed Bishop Clemens August von Galen (1878–1946), the so-called "lion of Münster" who denounced the "worship of race," was created a cardinal by Pope Pius XII (1939–58) in recognition of their very public and passionate denunciation of Hitler and National Socialism, especially their outspoken condemnation of the regime's policy of systemic racism against European Jews, "an injustice crying out to heaven," one which required a philosophical and pastoral response.

One found in the thoughtful collaboration during the Council between Frings and the recently appointed professor of dogmatic theology, Joseph Ratzinger, his unprecedented choice for a theological advisor: one of the youngest experts *periti* appointed to a Council. Sharing the same human agenda Ratzinger had previously delivered a lecture "What Is Man?" at the University of Tübingen (1966–69) during the early 1960s, approached from a theological perspective. Wherein looking for something "one and true," Ratzinger finds this in the person of Jesus Christ, "the crucified and the risen." Approached from this perspective Ratzinger claims, "man is the only authentic image of God," wherein we find looking outwards "the humanization of religion," and looking inwards towards "man's final breakthrough to himself" found in the person of Christ.[2] Ideas which informed the so-called 'Frings-Ratzinger connection,' one of the collaborative "behind the scenes" activities, along with

---

2. Ratzinger, "What Is Man?," para. 18.

the so-called 'Lublin connection,' which inform the personal background to conciliar humanism as a philosophical orientation.

An awareness which informed Pope John's Apostolic Constitution *Humanae Salutis*, published on Christmas Day 1961 as a fitting opportunity to propose the Council's thoughtful response to the perennial question, "what is human," which arose living in the chaotic and turbulent world of the mid twentieth century. One initiated by "painful considerations" which the pope diagnosed as "the danger of nuclear war" and "the ongoing dehumanization of men" which occurred at Auschwitz-Birkenau and found in the prevalent forms of "atheistic materialism, affluent hedonism and abject poverty," all of which occasioned what he called "the crisis of humanity," namely, the climate of uncertainty about the identity of being human. As such, "this much neglected document,"[3] reflects the pope's abiding interest as he directs attention to "the salvation of humanity" as a universal concern, which set the scene for the Council's remarkable 'human agenda' and integral philosophical orientation of thought, especially found in *Gaudium et Spes* and *Dignitatis Humanae*, wherein we find conciliar humanism.

Unlike the previous twenty gatherings of the universal Church, wherein ideas were either denounced as heretical nor specific thought defined, now this surprisingly convened assembly by a recently elected 'caretaker' pope directed attention to an unprecedented issue within Catholic thought, namely, to understand 'humanity' lived as such, one which set the Council's human agenda. Expressed in the concluding words of *Gaudium et Spes*, wherein this "holy synod" sought to identify the "deeper foundations" found in the "universal fellowship" of our shared humanity, through the promotion of "mutual esteem, respect and harmony," expressive of the Council's "belief in humanity" found in conciliar humanism. A good news story summarily expressed in the opening words of this remarkable document, "believers and unbelievers are almost at one in considering that everything on earth is to be referred to humanity as its centre and culmination. But what is humanity itself?" Asked and answered by the assembled Council Fathers in their original and distinctive form of original thought about our shared humanity.

Reading these "signs of the times," Pope John sought to move "toward a new order of human relationships," expressed in the introductory words of *Gaudium et Spes*: "For it is the human person that is to be saved,

---

3. Kobler, *Vatican II*, 19.

and human society to be restored. It is around humankind therefore, one and entire, body and soul, heart and conscience, mind and will, that our whole treatment will revolve" (para. 3). Wherein the Council offers a broad characterisation of its original integral philosophical understanding of humanity brought together in the original idea of a 'human person.' An awareness of our humanity which built on the traditional theological definition of "person" as "an individual substance of a rational nature" by the early sixth-century Roman philosopher Boethius (c. 477–524), towards an integral philosophical and sociopolitical understanding found in the Council's idea of the 'human person.'

A remarkable vision of humanity, conciliar humanism was the consequence of this momentous event held over four years and remains a good news story for everyone, namely, as a distinctive pattern of Catholic thought based on the Council's recognition of our shared humanity, found in the twofold connection between philosophical ideas and pastoral concerns. A way of thinking found within an original network of three interrelated ideas, human person, community of persons, and human solidarity. Literally its last words addressed to 'humanity,' following the unanimous approval of *Gaudium et Spes* and *Dignitatis Humanae* by the Council Fathers on December 7, 1965.

Intimations of which were given by Karol Wojtyla, the recently appointed Archbishop of Kraków on January 13, 1964, on his return to Rome during an interview on October 19, 1964 for Vatican Radio, one loaded with significance: "The human person is an element of the doctrine of the Second Vatican Council. They (Council and Church) regard the call concerning the dignity of the human person as the most important voice of our age. This is eloquently expressed in the encyclicals of John XXIII and Paul VI, as well as in the work of the Council, especially in the Declaration on Religious Freedom and the schema on the relation of the Church to the modern world, which is currently under discussion."[4]

Wherein Archbishop Wojtyla not only identifies the current sociopolitical concerns the Council Fathers addressed through their human agenda but also their integrative philosophical approach prompted by these pastoral concerns infused by their retrieval of a distinctive form of Catholic consciousness characterized as *sapiential*. A shared awareness which drew inspiration from recent papal social teaching and contemporary

---

4. Boniecki, *Making of the Pope*, 241–42.

European philosophical thought, a novel approach first observed by Michael Novak (1933–2017), the American journalist sent by the *National Catholic Reporter* (1964) to observe Council proceedings. Published in *A New Generation: American and Catholic* (1964),[5] an approach which sets the background to understand the genesis of conciliar humanism.

This distinctive pattern of Catholic thinking, employing philosophical thought as a means of addressing social justice concerns, was established by Pope Leo XIII (1878–1903) with his two foundational encyclicals, *Aeterni Patris* "on the restoration of Christian philosophy" (1879) and *Rerum Novarum* (1891) on "Rights and Duties of Capital and Labor," which set in place the Leonine program of reform within contemporary Catholic thought. The former marks the official recognition of the tradition of Catholic thinking known as 'Thomism,' the philosophical and theological thought established by the medieval scholastic thinker Thomas Aquinas. Thought now complemented by the pope's revolutionary discussion of social issues, whereby he employed an integrative way of thinking about humanity, which set the pattern for twentieth-century papal teaching on social justice issues built on solid philosophical foundations, published by popes of the twentieth century who would be known as "champions of humanity."

Wherein we find a philosophical orientation towards understanding humanity, based on a theoretical discussion on 'being human' and the nature of the 'human being,' within a consideration of human activity. Namely, a theoretical discussion of practical concerns shared by humans as social beings, recognized as 'practical philosophy.' A subject first discussed by the Athenian philosopher Aristotle in his exploration about ethics, the study of ideas such as 'good,' 'right,' 'virtue,' and 'freedom' applied to practical reasoning, which he regarded as a branch of the natural history of being human, discussed in his ethical treatises such as *Politics, Nicomachean Ethics,* and *Eudemian Ethics*. A central figure in medieval Arabic, Jewish and Christian philosophy, Aristotle's metaphysical realism which he applied to understanding human behavior was used to great effect within the original scholastic synthesis of Aquinas which brought together metaphysical and ethical ways of thinking. A pattern of thought Pope Leo XIII sought to replicate writing his two foundational encyclicals, *Aeterni Patris* (1879) and *Rerum Novarum* (1891). One later used to great effect in the social philosophy of Jacques Maritain.

---

5. Novak, *New Generation*, 91–104.

This 'unitive' connection between philosophical thought and practical social issues came to characterize twentieth-century European Catholic philosophy and directed the orientation of subsequent papal 'encyclicals.' An expression originally used to identify a circular letter sent by a local diocesan bishop to churches under his jurisdiction in the early Church. However, the unprecedented ninety encyclicals written by Pope Leo XIII between 1878 and 1903 established the practice whereby these letters assumed the status of a specific category of papal document. Namely, as a means for the individual pope to offer a form of authoritative teaching or guidance relating to a specific issue of contemporary significance, a practice which continues to this day with Pope Francis' 2015 encyclical on ecology, *Laudato Si'* "on care for our common home."

This distinctive pattern of Catholic thought, connecting philosophical ideas and social concerns, continued with Pope Pius XI's (1922–39) two encyclicals, *Studiorum Ducem* "on St. Thomas Aquinas" published on June 29, 1923 to celebrate the sixth centenary of Aquinas' canonization on July 18, 1323, together with his *Quadragesimo Anno* "on the reconstruction of the social order" published on May 15, 1931 to celebrate the fortieth anniversary of *Rerum Novarum*. Moreover, as well as establishing the practice of building on or rereading the thought found in previous papal encyclicals, Pope Pius XI's *Ubi Arcano Dei Consilio* (1922) anticipates the Council's original understanding of the 'human person,' through his promotion of "the value, dignity and sanctity of human life," and his subsequent encyclical *Divini Redemptoris* (1937) wherein he consolidated this earlier thought with the claim: "Man is a person, marvellously endowed by his Creator with gifts of body and soul." As such, this distinctive pattern found in papal encyclicals was replicated by the Council Fathers in their twofold connection between philosophical ideas and pastoral concerns which informs conciliar humanism, summarily expressed in the words of Archbishop Wojtyła one of the major proponents of this way of thinking, worth repeating: "The human person is an element of the doctrine of the Second Vatican Council. They (Council and Church) regard the call concerning the dignity of the human person as the most important voice of our age. This is eloquently expressed in the encyclicals of John XXIII and Paul VI, as well as in the work of the Council, especially in the Declaration on Religious Freedom and the schema on the relation of the Church to the modern world, which is currently under discussion." Spoken on October 19, 1964 during an interview on Vatican Radio loaded with significance following his return to Rome as the new Archbishop of Kraków, having been appointed by Pope Paul VI on January 13, 1964.

The emergent pastoral awareness of issues concerning social justice discussed in papal teaching of the late nineteenth and twentieth centuries, which defined the papacy of Pope John XXIII may be traced back to his intellectual formation as then Father Angelo Giuseppe Roncalli (1881–1963). Following his ordination as a diocesan priest in 1904 he began teaching church history in the local seminary, working closely with Bergamo's Bishop Giacomo Radini-Tedeschi (1857–1914), recognized as "one of the most important bishops of pre-World War 1 Italian Catholicism," found in his original awareness of "pastoral modernity"[6] which foreshadowed the pope's original appropriation of 'pastoral.' Opportunities soon arose for the young priest from Bergamo to exercise his natural disposition and sensitivity caring for others following his appointment as a Church diplomat working in Bulgaria, Greece, Turkey and finally in France (1925–53), then as Cardinal Patriarch of Venice (1953–58) where he encountered distressing circumstances of those living in a turbulent world which generated in him "a sense that all was not well."

However, it was while working in France as Papal Nuncio that this recognizable scholar of ecclesiastical history complemented his pastoral sensitivity with the rigors of philosophical thought through his regular contact in Paris with prominent French Catholic laymen, philosophers in the Thomist way of thinking. Namely, Jacques Maritain, the author of the recently published *Integral Humanism* (1936), who taught at the Institut Catholique de Paris (1875), written while Roncalli was in Paris, and Jean Guitton (1901–99), professor of philosophy at the University of Paris (1150), known as the *Sorbonne*, and author of *La Pensée modern at le catholicisme* (1934–50). Reading their published thought which consolidated what he acquired during his many discussions with these philosophers, the pope discovered the philosophical language of French personalism to complement his historical awareness and pastoral concern, and the means to confront contemporary issues of social justice. As pope he personally chose the latter as an *auditor*, the first lay person officially appointed to observe the proceedings of an ecumenical council, which he had convened.

Herein we find the foundations for the Council's distinctive twofold orientation of philosophical thought and pastoral concerns directed

6. Faggioli, *John XXIII*, 29.

towards the recognition of God and the promotion of an integral understanding of the human person, based on the awareness of our shared humanity and the pursuit of our collective well-being, which informs conciliar humanism as the consequence of *sapiential* consciousness. Understood as a unique conflation of philosophical and theoretical ideas mixed with pastoral and sociocultural concerns, arbitrarily designated as 'philosophical' and 'pastoral,' which characterize the essentially *synthetic* interactive process of thought which generated conciliar humanism during an extended moment of *sapiential* consciousness. Namely, during a moment of infused Christian wisdom informed by the work of the Spirit, structured around a complex network of three interrelated ideas, human person, community of persons, and human solidarity, in response to practical issues and pastoral concerns. A unitary way of thinking which brought together ideas drawn from contemporary trends of European philosophy, phenomenology, and variants of French and German personalism, with thought drawn from traditional Catholic philosophy, scholastic and contemporary forms of Thomism, such as 'being,' 'person,' 'act,' 'conscience,' and 'participation,' within an original "synthesis of fidelity and dynamism" to quote the phrase of Pope Benedict. The consequence of *sapiential* consciousness, this integrative way of thinking about our shared humanity, accessible to "believers and unbelievers alike," conciliar humanism unalterably changed contemporary Catholic discourse as the product of this wisdom consciousness.

6

Empires of the Mind

As already recognized, "ideas change the world" in the words of Jeffrey Sachs, whereby he recalled Churchill's iconic thought "empires of the mind." Spoken midway through the Second World War (1939–45), at his most eloquent best, by Britain's great war time prime minister and someone who was well known to "put ideas together," whereby he suggested future global conflict would be generated by ideas and ideology: "the starting point for the conquest of the world would now be the human mind. It would be ideas, not nations, that would be at war in the future." Speaking in the United States to receive an honorary Doctor of Laws from the prestigious Harvard University (1636) on September 6, 1943, repaying the compliment given to President Franklin D. Roosevelt (1882–1945) by the equally prestigious Oxford University (1096) in 1941, he sought to marshal the available allied military resources necessary, not only in the defence of his country, but in anticipation of the military invasion of Europe to liberate it from the Axis powers. Speaking from the steps of its Memorial Church, this Noble laureate for Literature, referred to the "greatness of Anglo-American unity and amity."

In so doing, Churchill outlined a twofold strategy on the interchange between action and thought, based on their shared 'responsibility' to combat a common and multifaceted foe, namely, 'tyranny' found in violent action "on the fields of war or in the air" and "in the realms of thought, which are consecrated to the rights and dignity of man." By the use of this ingenious and anticipatory distinction, Churchill promotes the recognition of what we share as human beings, namely, our humanity as being foundational for the exercise of legitimate authority, political control, and international influence. Thereby constructing what he calls "empires of the mind" rather than "empires of the past," such as Roman or British, which took away "other people's provinces or land or grinding them down in exploitation." In Churchill's opinion, "the conquest of the world" would now begin with the human mind, with ideas outlined in his 1943 commencement address at Harvard.[1]

A former atheist, now one of Christianity's foremost proponents, the Oxford Anglican theologian from Northern Ireland, Alister McGrath finds merit in Churchill's speech, especially his claim "empires of the future will be empires of the mind" as he introduces his *The Twilight of Atheism* (2004).[2] While McGrath refers to contemporary atheism as another 'empire of the mind,' Churchill was probably thinking of the source of this conflict found in the antagonism between two contemporary totalitarian systems of thought, the political ideologies of German National Socialism allied with Spanish and Italian Fascism, organized around the idea of race and those of Communism and Marxist Socialism, around the economic idea of class. Both are radically dehumanizing ideologies which drew inspiration from modern atheism, another 'empire of the modern mind.' As observed by John Gray, the English political philosopher writing "The Atheist Delusion" in the *Guardian* on March 14, 2008: "when atheism becomes a political project, the invariable result is an ersatz religion that can only be maintained by tyrannical means." Taking up this thought, America's evangelical Protestant intellectual Nancy Pearcey adds "by secret police and death camps" as she writes in *Finding Truth: 5 Principles for Unmasking Atheism, Secularism, and Other God Substitutes* (2015).[3]

Understood as a means of transforming the way we live and think, wherein we find the power of a new idea, herein we find the significance of the idea of a 'human person.' Used by the Council to express that there is 'something more' about being human, namely, approached in the thought of Francis Fukuyama, the American political scientist, as the 'X factor' which reveals the "essential human quality underneath" as he writes in *Our Posthuman Future: Consequences of the Biotechnology Revolution* (2002).[4] However, notwithstanding this significance, further is to be gleaned with the realization that this new idea is itself part of an

1. Berlin, *Proper Study*, 605–27.
2. McGrath, *Twilight of Atheism*, x.
3. Pearcey, *Finding Truth*, 135.
4. Fukuyama, *Our Posthuman Future*, 149–50.

original network of three related ideas: human person, community of persons, and human solidarity, which speak about our shared humanity approached from a Christian perspective. Namely, as a Christ centred integral philosophical way of thinking about our shared humanity which emerged during the Council, and which together speaks eloquently to the world of today about our humanity. Herein we find the meaningful significance of conciliar humanism in a nutshell.

Several years later this atheistic and secular way of thinking about humanity set the scene for the re-emergence of Christian humanism during the Council, when the junior auxiliary bishop of Kraków Karol Wojtyła unexpectedly joined the ranks of Council Fathers. This followed his popular election by the Chapter of the diocesan clergy of Kraków as Archdiocesan administrator '*vicar capitular*' on the death of his Archbishop, Eugeniusz Baziak (1890–1962) on June 15, 1962. Whereby, as a thoughtful and engaged participant, though a relatively unknown minor prelate, over the course of Council proceedings, this young Polish bishop would assume the status as one of the Council's leading lights. Especially following his official appointment as Archbishop of Kraków on January 13, 1964, when Wojtyła joined the ranks of other 'likeminded' Council Fathers, working in conjunction with Pope Paul VI, the former Archbishop of Milan, the so-called "pope of the Council," along with Cardinal Suenens, who like Wojtyła held doctorates in both traditional Catholic theology and in contemporary European philosophy, something unique among the Council Fathers, and Cardinal Josef Frings ably advised by the young Professor Joseph Ratzinger, as they returned to this original form of Catholic philosophical thought about humanity, espoused by the French layman Jacques Maritain in his seminal book *Integral Humanism*. From which emerged a remarkable form of Christian humanism, found in conciliar humanism. Subject matter hitherto rarely discussed, this distinctive pattern of Conciliar thought is found in the shared content of *Gaudium et Spes* and *Dignitatis Humanae*, documents primarily drafted by Wojtyła.

An original philosophical way of thinking about humanity, conciliar humanism reflects the distinctive pattern of Catholic philosophy, living and thinking in the tradition of Catholic Christianity, approached as a continuing conversation undertaken over the course of human history, whereby in the words of Alastair Macintyre, the Scottish born American Catholic philosopher, "we turn and return to dialogue with the important voices from the past, in order to carry forward that conversation in our own time,"[5] formulated in the colloquial expression "back to the future." A pattern of thought first expressed by the twelfth-century metaphor "standing on the shoulders of giants," used by John of Salisbury (late 1110s—1180), an English scholastic philosopher and teacher speaking about the influence of his teacher Bernard of Chartres (died c. 1124), the French Neoplatonist scholastic philosopher.

Following this established pattern between thought and action, Pope Paul concludes the theoretical component of his encyclical *Populorum Progressio* in paragraph forty-two with a discussion of what he calls "transcendent humanism" or elsewhere, "a full-bodied humanism, one which points towards God as the ultimate source of human self-improvement and the meaning of human life." In this context the pope could well have been talking about conciliar humanism and the sources which inspired this original thought which he directly quotes. Such as the thought taken from his philosophical mentor, Jacques Maritain's *Integral Humanism*, but also inspiration from other French Catholic philosophers, such as Blaise Pascal's (1623–62) *Pensées* (1670) when he quotes "man infinitely surpasses man" or thinking along a similar vein the pope refers to the Jesuit Henri de Lubac's (1896–1991) well known *The Drama of Atheist Humanism* (1944). Wherein de Lubac critically engages attempts to construct a humanism without the recognition of God, namely, the atheistic thought of the German philosopher Ludwig Feuerbach (1804–72), the atheistic nihilism of the German philosopher Friedrich Nietzsche (1844–1900), and the atheistic scientific positivism of the French social theorist Auguste Comte (1798–1857). Thinkers who set the broader scene to understand the genesis of conciliar humanism.

Finally, from these cursory observations, the author of *The Drama of Atheist Humanism* was another significant behind the scenes figure during the Council, performing a key role in shaping conciliar thought, for which he was subsequently created a cardinal-deacon by Pope John Paul II on February 2, 1983. This well-known French intellectual was also a proponent of the thought of another French philosopher Maurice Blondel (1861–1949), especially his "philosophy of action," which followed his doctoral thesis *Action* (1893). During the Council these philosophical connections came together through the participation of another leading Council father, Archbishop Karol Wojtyła. Not only did he share an esteem for Blondel's philosophy of action, but he worked very

---

5. MacIntyre, *God, Philosophy, Universities*, 1.

effectively with de Lubac during the Council, especially on the famous Schema XIII, which became *Gaudium et Spes*.

Interestingly, de Lubac refers to the fact Wojtyla had told him that during the Council he had been writing a book on "the metaphysic sense and mystery of the PERSON." This was eventually published as *Person and Act* (1969), for which Wojtyla is primarily known, though it was initially mistakenly translated as *The Acting Person*. From de Lubac's eyewitness account of "a person of the very highest qualities," it was evident that, for the young archbishop, the idea of "the fundamental uniqueness of each person" was necessary to combat the prevalent atheistic ideologies of the time.[6] Once again, these personal connections and philosophical ideas inform the genesis of conciliar humanism.

Set against the "fiercely ambitious ideology of secular humanism," the Council offered a Christ centred integral philosophical vision of human nature and the world, a new way of thinking which reflected a contemporary European philosophical orientation. One directed towards understanding "the whole man as a phenomenon—using an expression of the current age," which Pope Paul VI had summarily expressed during his 'final address' to the Council on the last day of the seventh plenary session on December 7, 1965, by his use of the term *hominem integrum*. Namely, to identify human nature as a whole, namely, "the true man, integral man" employing Maritain's language, which is informed by his recognition that "God is; He actually exists; He lives; He is a person." Wherein we find a remarkable synthesis of philosophical and theological thought which facilitates the awareness of the whole human being in their complete integrity as open to God through Christ; addressed theologically, found in "the face of Christ, the Son of Man, is seen in the face of every man, especially when it has become translucent with tears and sorrows." Reflecting on the consequence of the original thought which emerged during the twenty first ecumenical council, Jacques Maritain introducing his final book, *The Peasant of the Garonne* (1968) directs attention to the Council's synthesis of "great germinal ideas of Christian wisdom." Namely, the Council's recognition that the "true idea of freedom" is now embedded within its original understanding of "the true idea of the human person," wherein we find their dignity and rights, as

---

6. Lubac, *At the Service*, 171–72.

the Church honours humanity found in "Christ's gaze on our brothers and sisters, regardless of religious affiliation."[7]

Two mutually connected redemptive events which constitute the Paschal Mystery, found in the Incarnate Person of Christ, in whose life baptized Christians share as human persons, now approached from the philosophical perspective of Scheler's phenomenological ethical personalism. Whereby Scheler draws attention to the 'human person,' either an individual or what he calls a 'communal person,' who reveals their personal identity through their activity within mutual love towards each other; as such, 'being' is understood as a verb rather than a noun. A particular way of thinking which informs conciliar humanism as it emerged from an extraordinary moment of thoughtful reflection, one which set in motion 'a new age' for Catholicism whereby the Church looked at the human face of a broken world in need of healing—portrayed by religious lithograph "In His Image" (1967) by the American artist William Zdinak (1925–93), "the image of God in the face of Jesus formed by the faces of humankind."

Approached as a new way of thinking which emerged during the Council, this understanding was expressed in his claim in *Populorum Progressio*: "we cannot allow economics to be separated from human realities" (para. 14). Namely the pope's use of ideas from conciliar humanism which offer an adequate understanding of the human being, one suitable for his exposition on the development of economic growth. In his discussion of human life and human development he draws attention to "the reality of human solidarity" (para. 17). An idea he develops in understanding our shared responsibility though "promoting human solidarity" (para. 48). Interestingly, he only draws attention to the idea of 'human person' in his concluding remarks, circumstances which I find suggestive concerning the employment of an original network of ideas within conciliar humanism, rather than a predominant idea, namely that of the 'human person.'

---

7. Maritain, *Peasant*, 2.

7

Signs of the Times

EVERY GENERATION STRIVES TO interpret the time it lives in, living in "the world of today." Wherein we try to move towards something better, relying on our best hopes, during the twentieth century this was directed by the critical attention given to understanding our humanity. Thinking which inspired Pope John XXIII, who employed the biblical expression "signs of the times," used in the Gospel of Matthew (16:3), to initiate an extraordinary extended moment of thoughtful reflection in our Catholic history, one which transformed the Church as "the human face of Christ." Like the Lunar landing, the Second Vatican Council emerged from a three-year period of intense preparation which set in motion "a new era," that of the "human person."

Recalling the Lunar landing, many of us may still remember that extraordinary moment, when on July 20, 1969, the American astronauts Commander Neil Armstrong (1930–2012), accompanied by Buzz Aldrin, the lunar module pilot, became the first humans on the moon. "Our eyes glued to the TV screen" as they climbed down from the *Eagle* and set foot on the lunar surface, with these well-rehearsed words "that's one small step for a man, one giant leap for mankind." A step which represented the "best of our humanity" and the culmination of human scientific achievement thus far. While the success of the Apollo mission marked the accomplishment of an advanced technological project undertaken over eight years, initiated by American President John F. Kennedy (1917–63), following his appeal to a special joint session of Congress on May 25, 1961 "to land a man on the moon," it was only the beginning of "a new age" in the words of Armstrong speaking at a post-flight press conference.

Over the next three and a half years, ten astronauts followed in their footsteps, with the commander of Apollo 17, Gene Cernan (1934–2017) on leaving the lunar surface for the last time to date on December 14, 1972, claiming: "We leave as we came and, God willing, as we shall return, with peace, and hope for all mankind." However, these enormous strides made in science and technology to send human beings to the moon sat uncomfortably with the unparalleled global and indiscriminate violence perpetrated against fellow human beings, found in the sociopolitical regimes of Fascism, Nazism, and Communism. Symptomatic of the enigma of humanity, these are expressions of "the power of evil," one of "gigantic proportions" in the estimation of Pope John Paul II writing in his last book, *Memory & Identity: Personal Reflections* (2005).[1] Taken together these atheistic forms of totalitarian governance inform the conflictual background which contributed to the general malaise concerning humanity during the twentieth century. A challenge recognized by the French philosopher Albert Camus (1913–60), which was taken up during the Council, wherein we find a new way of thinking about our shared humanity within Catholic thought. One which initiated a new age focused on "the human person."

While every ecumenical council "occurs at a unique point in history," following the thought of Joseph F. Kelly in *The Ecumenical Councils of the Catholic Church: A History* (2009),[2] the Second Vatican Council took place "in a world unlike any of its predecessors," convened in "a changing world it changed the Church" to paraphrase his thought. In response to the broad philosophical and sociopolitical background of twentieth-century European atheistic humanism and its twofold denial, the Second Vatican Council sought to address the contemporary malaise, occasioned by the denial of our human capacity to think about the idea of God, and of our human "capacity for transcendence."

Like the Lunar landing four years later, the Council which opened on October 22, 1962 marked the end of an extensive and prolonged period of preparation, involving for the first time in the history of the Catholic Church a broad process of world-wide consultation. Based on replies to the June 1959 consultative letter addressed to the world's

---

1. John Paul II, *Memory and Identity*, 189.
2. Kelly, *Ecumenical Councils*, 179.

Catholic bishops and religious leaders. Written by the Cardinal Secretary of State Domenico Tardini (1888–1961) as president of the Ante Preparatory Commission, these eventually produced seventy working plans or *schemata* of proposed topics for discussion: "more than double the quantity of texts produced by all previous councils put together" in the summation of then Professor Joseph Ratzinger writing in *Theological Highlights of Vatican II* (1966).

"With the Second Vatican Council broad new thinking was required, its content was certainly only roughly traced in the conciliar texts but determined its essential direction," as found in the original network of ideas which inform conciliar humanism. Following his papal election on April 19, 2005, Pope Benedict addressed these words to the curial officials gathered to receive his Christmas message on December 22, 2005, wherein he identified the nature of this conciliar thought as being novel, innovative, tentative though directive, perhaps an instance of this authoritative thoughtful work in progress is found in the Council's 'belief in humanity.' While no official teachings were defined nor heretical thought condemned as practiced in previous ecumenical councils, more than sixty years on we are still experiencing the ripple effects of the Council's thoughtful legacy found in conciliar humanism. Wherein we find the Council's belief in humanity, inspired by Pope John's twofold exhortation for an 'openness to the world' and a 'respect for the human person' in his statement *Gaudet Mater Ecclesia* as he opened Council proceedings on October 22, 1962.

Following his unexpected resignation from the papacy, now emeritus Pope Benedict joined his successor Pope Francis in co-writing his unprecedented inaugural encyclical, *Lumen Fidei* "on the light of faith" (2013) wherein they identify their appreciation of this documented legacy which speaks to the meaning and purpose of being human together found in the Incarnate Person of Christ: "The Second Vatican Council enabled the light of faith to illumine our human experience from within, accompanying the men and women of our time on their journey of faith" (para. 6). Several years later Pope Francis found another opportunity to address this new way of thinking, one which has certainly influenced the way he thinks. Addressing the hundreds of thousands of young pilgrims attending the XXXI World Youth Day Final mass on July 31, 2016, held on a site specifically designed for this purpose named *Campus Misericodiae*, 'Field of Mercy' located about fifteen kilometers from the center of the Polish city of Kraków, Pope Francis exhorted those present to share his belief in a "new humanity," "one that rejects hatred between peoples, one that refuses to see borders as barriers and can cherish its own traditions, without being self-centred or small minded." Thought which raises the question, wherein the novelty for this "new humanity" is to be found, and compared to what?

Answers were found in the new way of thinking generated during the Council, found in conciliar humanism. While Francis was too young to be present during this momentous event, his language betrays its thoughtful influence, in what might be characterized 'the spirit' of this new way of thinking. Several years later another opportunity arose to further address this original thought as Pope Francis recalled the legacy of conciliar humanism on the anniversary of *Populorum Progressio* wherein he identified the foundations for an ongoing "Christian philosophy of culture," one inspired by Pope Paul's promotion of an "integral and solidary humanism." A way of thinking guided by his own understanding of a Christian humanism, inspired by what he seen evolve during the Council from its very beginning as then Cardinal Giovanni Battista Montini, and what he had read, namely Jacques Maritain's *Integral Humanism*, the seminal work of his philosophical mentor.

Whereby Pope Francis endorsed the philosophical foundations of conciliar humanism as being suitable for the implementation of pastoral activity with its human socioeconomic and ethical themes, issues of social justice taken up by his predecessors, in Pope John Paul II's *Sollicitudo Rei Socialis* (1987), and especially in Pope Benedict's *Caritas in Veritate* (2009).

Now drawing attention to our inherent social awareness shared with humanity, Pope Francis explored the natural and cosmic connections within the Universe which direct this awareness. Connections originally discussed by the Council in *Gaudium et Spes* which drew inspiration from the Franciscan vision of our shared ecological awareness, eloquently expressed by St. Francis of Assisi (1181–1226) in his religious song *Canticle of the Sun*, wherein God is praised for creating the great breadth and diversity within the natural world. A way of thinking Pope Francis now developed as he appropriated the Umbrian phrase *Laudato si'* for the title of his second encyclical in 2015. Wherein Pope Francis builds on the Council's understanding of 'human solidarity' within this new way of thinking as he speaks of "fraternal" and "ecological humanism," the latter inspired by the Council's unprecedented discussion of our human interaction, our "activity" with the "whole of nature" and within human culture found in chapter 3 of *Gaudium et Spes*. Appropriating this phrase Pope Francis invites the reader "on a journey towards sustainability in the spirit of an integral ecology," language reminiscent of Maritain's thought, which further betrays the new thinking found in conciliar humanism.

An ownership Pope Francis assumed when he approved a working paper produced by the Congregation for Catholic Education published on April 16, 2017 entitled "Educating to Fraternal Humanism: To Build a Civilization of Love 50 Years after the Encyclical *Populorum Progressio*." Inspired by recent conciliar thought, Pope Francis recalls his call for "humanizing education" made during his address to the plenary session of the Congregation on February 9, 2017, and in anticipation of the theme of the forthcoming congress organized by the International Office of Catholic Education for June 2019 in New York on the theme "to educate to solidary humanism: to build a civilization of love." Notwithstanding the ambivalent response to this document, found in the Cardinal Newman Society journal, for the use of the word 'humanism,' and the exercise of caution concerning this word, approached from a Christian perspective found in conciliar humanism; as he reflects during a general audience on September 9, 2021: "There is no place for discrimination or divisive distinction among people who believe in Christ" as he continues," that everyone is made new and equal in Christ who overcomes all ethnic, economic differences, even between the sexes." Words which reflect the new way of thinking found in conciliar humanism.

From the moment Pope John XXIII officially opened the Second Vatican Council on October 22, 1962, its sixteen officially promulgated documents have directed Catholic discourse and liturgical practice; however, it is now opportune to address the failure to discuss the Council's distinctive pattern of philosophical thought about our shared humanity, a consequence of its unprecedented human agenda. Narrated in this book as the untold story of conciliar humanism which offers an unprecedented "behind the scenes" guide to the Council's seminal belief in humanity expressed in its remarkable Christ centred integral philosophical understanding of our shared humanity, our "human solidarity." Later recognized as a "humanism of solidarity" by the American Cardinal Justin Rigali during his address "*Gaudium et Spes* and Its Relevance to Catholic Higher Education" given on September 26, 2005.

As such, conciliar humanism represents a distinctive, though not uncommon philosophical way of thinking about humanity found in humanism. One which Pope Paul VI addressed during his summation of the Council on December 7, 1965, wherein he encouraged ownership of "our new type of humanism." Found in the Council's recognition of the human capacity for transcendence which honours humanity, set against the prevalent "secular humanism" which "in a sense defied the council."

"Why has Christ not yet returned, why so long a wait for the end of times? His response is, 'to give us time to believe in the human person.' Christ died because he 'believed' in the human person."[3] More than sixty years ago such perplexing language would have been unimaginable, let alone intelligible within Catholic discourse. Found in *L'Église en travail de reform* (2011), this highly original thought was posed by the speculative French Benedictine theologian Ghislain Lafont (1928–2021) as he draws attention to the ongoing and critical issue of reform within the contemporary Catholic Church, previously discussed in *Imagining the Catholic Church: Structure Communion in the Spirit* (2000). However, in so doing, the French octogenarian, who well remembered the Council which inspired such original thought, was later quoted in a seminal article "The Divine Dignity of Human Persons in *Dignitatis Humanae.*" An imaginative reflection on the Council's Declaration "on religious freedom" by the Hungarian born American Jesuit theologian Ladislas Orsy, published in the commemorative book *50 Years On: Probing the Riches of Vatican II* (2015). Wherein the American Jesuit engaged the original thought of Lafont who first drew attention to the Council's "belief in humanity" found in its idea of the human person embedded within these final documents: *Gaudium et Spes* and *Dignitatis Humanae.*

Namely, the Council's innovative way of thinking about our shared humanity found in the person of Christ, characterized by Lafont as "a man for others," original thought which informed conciliar humanism as a way of thinking "spoken with the accommodating friendly voice of pastoral charity" in the words of Pope Paul VI during his final address to the Council on December 7, 1965. Now it's time to "look behind the scenes" to examine this remarkable way of thinking which emerged as the consequence of a twentieth-century extended moment of *sapiential* consciousness. As such, conciliar humanism represents a distinctive, though not uncommon Christ centred integral philosophical way of thinking about our shared humanity, which Pope Paul VI summarized during his final address to the Council on December 7, 1965: "our

---

3. Orsy, "Divine Dignity," 347.

humanism becomes Christianity, our Christianity becomes centred on God: in such, that we may say it differently; a knowledge of man is a prerequisite for a knowledge of God."

Whereby Pope Paul VI encouraged those present to take ownership of "our new type of humanism," found in the Council's recognition of the human capacity for transcendence which honours humanity, set against the prevalent atheistic and secular forms of humanism which "defied the Council." In so doing, the pope returned to his original thought expressed on September 29, 1963 as he reconvened the Council, now envisaged as a "journey," following the death of Pope John XXIII on June 3, 1965, as he opened the second plenary session of Council proceedings with the claim: "The journey is made within the framework of human history, bearing all the marks of time, and is conditioned by all the limitations of our present life."[4] This human orientation was later expressed in the evocative words of John Paul II, an ailing pope from Parkinson's disease thirty years into his pontificate: "the Second Vatican Council made room for Christian humanism in its documentation," made by a former Council father who had facilitated this thoughtful process as Archbishop Wojtyła.

Evocative thought he later recalled from the Apostolic palace of Castel Gandolfo on September 20, 2003, when the great philosopher pope opened the International Congress on "Christian Humanism in the Third Millennium: The Perspective of Thomas Aquinas." Held at the Pontifical Academy of Saint Thomas Aquinas (1879), established on October 15, 1879 by the other remarkable philosopher pope of the twentieth century, namely Leo XIII soon after his papal election on February 20, 1878, whereby Pope Leo sought to implement his original program of philosophical reform within Catholic thought, characterized as 'Leonine' and initiated by his papal encyclical *Aeterni Patris: On the Restoration of Christian Philosophy*, published on August 4, 1879. Recalling the timeless wisdom of Aquinas as "doctor of humanity," Pope John Paul II directs attention to the original humanism of this medieval thinker, from someone infused with *sapiential* consciousness, wherein "man comes from God and must return to him." This distinctive God centred understanding of our humanity, found in the thought of Aquinas was understood by Pope John Paul II as a "cultural event that deserves the greatest attention,"

---

4. Kung et al., *Council Speeches*, 19.

namely, as a response to the twentieth-century awareness that "man continues to be a problem" in the words of the pope.

Thought well expressed by Max Scheler, a Catholic convert and philosopher from Munich, when he claimed, "man is more of a problem to himself at the present time than ever before" in his seminal essay "On the Idea of Man" (1915). Inspired by Scheler's original philosophical anthropology, the young professor of Christian social ethics teaching at the Jagiellonian University (1364) Karol Wojtyła first took up the theme of Christian humanism in 1949 during a series of public lectures given to the academic community living in the university city of Kraków, wherein he claimed the "first truth of Christian humanism" was found in "the internal life of God—that in which man by grace receives by filial *participation* (emphasis added) through an analysis of our human spiritual experiences,"[5] later published as *Considerations on the Essence of Man* (2016).

"The human person is one of the elements of the doctrine of the Second Vatican Council," already quoted thought taken from a talk Archbishop Wojtyla delivered on Vatican Radio, entitled "on the dignity of the human person" on October 19, 1964.[6] During this talk the archbishop was keen to point out, while recalling the influence of the papal encyclicals of Popes John XXIII and Paul VI, this thought was embedded within another way of thinking which seems to have come from nowhere, to assume the elevated status as being deeply embedded in the entire teaching of the Council. "Although none of the prepared constitutions or decrees deal with the human person directly," this remains a fundamental idea associated with the Council. Some might say after sixty years, it has become one of the expressions, along with 'people of God,' *communio*, and 'pastoral' which have become synonymous with the Council, ubiquitous in contemporary Catholic discourse. Perhaps it's time for a closer examination, and in so doing, to learn a little more. Namely, while the significance of this idea is incontestable, what has yet to be recognized, that it remains one idea within a network of three original ideas which together make up conciliar humanism: a new way of thinking about our shared humanity. One eloquently expressed in these words from *Gaudium et Spes*: "For by his Incarnation the Son of God united himself in some sense with every human being. He laboured

---

5. Wojtyla, *Considerations*, 197–99.
6. Boniecki, *Making of the Pope*, 240.

with human hands, thought with a human mind, acted with a human will, and loved with a human heart" (para. 36).

Understood as a "synthesis of fidelity and dynamism," conciliar humanism represents a new way of thinking, best approached as a "symphony of ideas." As a distinctive pattern of thinking generated during the Council, conciliar humanism emerged as the consequence of a twofold orientation between philosophical thought and pastoral action; a way of thinking which speaks a language accessible to all about our shared humanity and related concerns, found in the human experience of "joys and hope, the griefs and anxieties" we share, expressed in the words, "the dignity of the human person is a concern of which people are becoming increasingly more aware." These words which introduce *Dignitatis Humanae* are a direct quote taken from Pope John's *Pacem in Terris* (1963), published three months before his death from the effects of stomach cancer on June 3, 1963. This quoted thought identifies the Council's indebtedness to Pope John's original thought and sets the scene for my philosophical rereading of *Gaudium et Spes* and *Dignitatis Humanae*, wherein we find the nexus of conciliar humanism; a way of thinking found in a human connection between philosophical thought and pastoral action under the umbrella idea of "human person."

Perhaps a recapitulation of this connection found in these documents might be helpful. Namely, a theoretical framework is offered in Part One of *Gaudium et Spes*, and an elaboration of pastoral action through a discussion of practical social issues in Part Two of *Gaudium et Spes* and throughout *Dignitatis Humanae*. Within this framework, particular attention is given to issues associated with our personal life, human intimacy, and life affirming activity, especially as they relate to marriage and the exercise of religious freedom. While over the last sixty years much attention has been given to these personal and practical issues, little has been given to understanding the theoretical framework within which these are embedded, especially its integral philosophical orientation as an instance of new thinking which emerged during the Council.

Namely, a God centred way of thinking but with a Christocentric orientation to better understand the universality of our shared humanity. Best expressed in the words of the Apostle Paul to the Galatians: "As many of you who were baptized into Christ have clothed yourselves in Christ. There is no longer Jew or Greek, there is no longer slave or free, there is no longer male and female; for all of you are one in Christ Jesus" (3:28). Furthermore, original thought which takes up the religious idea of *imago Dei* wherein we find the source of our dignity and value now approached from within an 'integral' understanding of being human together. Namely, as a life filled creature comprised of both 'body and soul,' with the inherent capacity to think with a mind, to know the truth and the desire to seek wisdom; herein, we find the originality of Conciliar thought as a positive response to the prevalent reductionistic denial of the human capacity to think and to act. As well as being capable of thought, human beings are also capable of action, though the use of moral conscience, the exercise of freedom and the capacity to embrace the "mystery of death."

Building on the claim that human beings "have been called to communion with God," the Council opens a discussion concerning 'atheism,' understood as the denial of the human capacity "to say anything about God" (para. 19). Interestingly, this framework concludes with paragraph twenty-two, wherein we find a consideration of *Christ, the new human being*. Perhaps one of the most quoted sentences which came from the Council: "It is only in the mystery of the Word incarnate that light is shed on the mystery of humankind" (para. 22), a summation of conciliar humanism. Building on this foundational thought, the Council moves beyond the considerations of the individual human being, towards the recognition of the human disposition towards other human beings, with the claim: "As a God image—human beings have been called to communion with God" (para. 23).

While traditional philosophy recognized the human being as naturally rational and social, now the Council employs the original idea of 'communion' to broaden this understanding, regarding 'the human community' found in chapter 2 of *Gaudium et Spes*, wherein for the first time the idea of a 'communion of persons' (para. 12) was introduced. Approached as an idea with metaphysical significance as well as a corrective to the prevalent world of capitalism and an ethics of individualism, herein the Council seems to expand on Maritain's social personalism. Furthermore, this understanding is broadened by a consideration of the ecological activity of human beings living in the universe. These introductory words from *Gaudium et Spes* express the integral philosophical understanding of our shared humanity, namely a new way of thinking found in conciliar humanism: "For it is the human person that is to be saved, and human society to be restored. It is around humankind therefore, one and entire, body and soul, heart and conscience, mind and will, that our whole treatment will revolve" (para. 3).

While my discussion undertaken in this book involves a rereading of the content found in *Gaudium et Spes* and *Dignitatis Humanae*, it should be noted that the idea of 'human person' appears in three other Council documents. Namely, *Unitatis redintegratio* Decree "on ecumenism" promulgated on November 21, 1964 which speaks of the shared responsibility among all Christians towards a "just appreciation of the dignity of the human person" (para. 12). Within the context of understanding the responsibility given to those entrusted with leadership in the Church, such as local bishops, the document *Christus Dominus* Decree "on the pastoral office of bishops in the church," promulgated on October 28, 1965, exhorts these individuals to give particular attention to the promotion of "the inestimable value of the human person; her or his freedom and bodily vitality" (para. 12).

Finally, the document *Gravissimum educationis* "Declaration on Christian Education" promulgated on October 28, 1965, begins with the fundament claim: "all people of whatever race, condition and age, since they are endowed with the dignity of persons have an inalienable right to an education." Education remains a key to access the philosophical treasures enclosed within the edifice of those thinking in the tradition of Catholic Christianity, especially understanding our human nature, built on the living synthesis between faith and reason. Years later, addressing the fortieth anniversary of *Gaudium et Spes* on September 26, 2005 at the prestigious Villanova University, founded in 1842 and named after the Spanish Augustinian friar St. Thomas of Villanova (1488–1555), the oldest and largest Catholic university in the Commonwealth of Pennsylvania USA, Cardinal Justin Rigali recognized the "new humanism of Vatican II,"[7] namely, what he calls a 'humanism of solidarity.' Wherein we find the means of looking to the future employing this new way of thinking, the necessary resources to meet the enormous challenges of our time understanding the "mystery of man" by drawing attention to the 'human person', the individual, the community, and the entire human family.

Rigali characterized this way of thinking as the employment of all available intellectual resources to find "true and just responses" to meet the enormous challenged of our time. Elsewhere, writing *Reliving Vatican II: It's All about Jesus Christ* (2006) he documented his eyewitness account from his "minor role" during the first two plenary sessions of the Council as a newly ordained priest from the Archdiocese of Los

---

7. Rigali, "*Gaudium et Spes*," 273–81.

Angeles, as another opportunity to endorse the ongoing significance of this original thought from the Council. In a document which builds on twentieth-century papal social teaching, in an effort "to speak to all people in order to shed light on *the mystery of man*," to help find solutions to the "outstanding problems of our time."[8]

Furthermore, while not using this idea directly, two other Council documents share this new way of thinking which gives attention to being human, namely, in a document already mentioned as directed towards those human beings living other religious faith traditions discussed in *Nostra Aetate: Declaration on the Church's Relation to Non-Christian Religions* promulgated on October 28, 1965, and finally, the recognition of our shared humanity 'within' the Church found in the document *Apostolicam Actuositatem* "Decree on the Apostolate of the Laity" on November 18, 1965, which introduced the so-called 'era of the laity' within Catholic life.

Approached by Pope Benedict as a "work in progress," this broad new way of thinking found in conciliar humanism continues to inform Catholic discourse and beyond, wherein we find its legacy. Original thought about what is human generated during the Council which became synonymous with this historic event: namely, human person, community of persons and human solidarity. Thought which Pope Benedict endorsed in his encyclical letter *Caritas in Veritate: Integral Development in Charity and Truth* (2009), wherein he claims: "a humanism which excludes God is an inhuman humanism." Written to mark the fortieth anniversary of Pope Paul's encyclical letter *Populorum Progressio* (1967) wherein this new way of thinking was explored by its foremost proponent. Now, while integrating ideas discussed in paragraph sixteen of the encyclical, drawn from conciliar humanism, Pope Benedict reaffirms in paragraph eighteen the "unconditional value of the human person and the meaning of his growth" and the promotion of self-fulfilment within a "transcendent humanism which gives [to man] his greatest perfection" whereby he absorbs ideas from conciliar humanism within his original form of relational personalism.

Building on the idea of 'community of persons,' Pope Benedict identifies the 'human creature' as a 'dialogical being' defined through a metaphysical understanding of interpersonal relations. In so doing, like Wojtyła before him, the pope moves beyond Boethius' traditional

---

8. Rigali, *Reliving Vatican II*, 24.

understanding of person as a rational substance towards a groundbreaking concept of 'person in relation.' While there is much to be found in Benedict's critical response to contemporary forms of relativism and individualism, in his novel relational ontology based on the traditional interplay between human thought and the data of Christian faith, on a Trinitarian model of partnership between Persons wherein "truth is shared," regrettably this remarkable way of thinking has been given insufficient attention by contemporary Catholic scholars.

Given his claim about truth, it should come as no surprise to find a similar pattern of creative adoption and appropriation of ideas drawn from conciliar humanism by Pope Francis. Found in the claim made by Massimo Borghesi, author of *The Mind of Pope Francis* (2017), that Vatican II gave direction and guidance to the pope's particular way of thinking, understood as "both Catholic and open."[9] Reflecting on its instructive intent, as observed by an earlier biographer, as for many of us "the Council would be Bergoglio's greatest teacher, and the single greatest source, of his pontificate."[10] Addressing members of the National Catechetical Office of the Italian Bishops' Conference on January 30, 2021, Pope Francis claimed "I know that the Lord wants the Council to make headway in the Church." Recalling his earlier claim that "historians tell us that it takes 100 years for a council to be applied. We are halfway there." Whereby the pope takes up thought previously expressed by Massimo Faggioli, a popular Italian layman and church historian writing in *Vatican II: The Battle for Meaning* (2012), when he claimed, historically speaking "the Council is still very young."

It should be noted that a Christ centred theological orientation found within the Council's final documents, *Dignitatis Humanae* and *Gaudium et Spes*, reveals an underlying philosophical way of thinking about our shared humanity which formulates the necessary Christ centred "knowledge of man" disposed towards God. A human orientation aligned with the recent "rediscovery of transcendence" in contemporary theology observed by Ghislain Lafont writing in his Heideggerian inspired *God, Time, and Being* (1998) wherein Christ is presented as "the embodiment of our personal and collective struggles for humanity," characterized as "the man for others."[11] Whereby Lafont counters the criticism of an overly optimistic attitude found in Conciliar thought

9. Borghesi, *Mind of Pope Francis*, 3.
10. Ivereigh, *Great Reformer*, 99.
11. Lafont, *God, Time, and Being*, vii–xi.

towards humanity and "the world of today" by means of a "theology of the cross," portrayed by van der Weyden. Commenting on Pope John's original use of ideas drawn from contemporary European philosophy the American Passionist priest and private research scholar John F. Kobler draws attention to another source of papal authority similarly disposed to this contemporary philosophical connection with humanity as a former Council father, namely as Pope John Paul II when he claims: "the cross is the cradle of the New Man."[12]

A subject taken up in Pope John Paul II's Apostolic Letter *Salvifici Doloris: On the Christian Meaning of Suffering* (1984), wherein the pope locates "the mystery of *Redemption* as being accomplished *through the Cross of suffering Christ*" (para. 3). Understood as an expression of God's love through the person of Christ, as the "human face of Incarnate truth" looking towards our broken humanity, portrayed in van der Weyden's *Descent from the Cross* (c. 1435). Concluding this Apostolic Letter, the pope recalls the inspirational thought found in *Gaudium et Spes*, para. 22, which he frequently quotes, "only in the mystery of the Incarnate Word does the mystery of man take on light" wherein we find the experience of God's love *"fully reveals man to himself."* Words which would have been very familiar as a Council father to Wojtyła in understanding the relationship between suffering and love, an understanding probably facilitated by Scheler's recognition of "the innermost union of suffering and love in Christian doctrine" in his essay "The Meaning of Suffering" (1916)[13] which Wojtyła read preparing for his *Habilitationsschrift* (1954).

Approached as a Christ centred integral philosophical understanding of our shared humanity, conciliar humanism represents the thoughtful consequence of "the 21st Council for the 21st Century," wherein we find the Council's unprecedented "belief in humanity" expressed in *Gaudium et Spes*: "For by his Incarnation the Son of God united himself in some sense with every human being. He laboured with human hands, thought with a human mind, acted with a human will, and loved with a human heart" (para. 36). Language which betrays an "integral" understanding of the whole human being, "body and soul, heart and conscience, mind and will" which reflects the seminal thought found in Maritain's *Integral Humanism* (1936) whereby he introduced this word within contemporary philosophical discourse.

12. Kobler, *Vatican II and Phenomenology*, 172.
13. Scheler, "Meaning of Suffering," 121–63.

Set against the "fiercely ambitious ideology of secular humanism," the Council offered a philosophical response, found in a Christ centred integral philosophical vision of human nature and the world, a way of thinking which reflected contemporary European thought. One directed towards understanding "the whole man as a phenomenon—using an expression of the current age," which Pope Paul VI had summarily expressed during his final address to the Council on the last day of the seventh plenary session on December 7, 1965, by his use of the term *hominem integrum*, namely, to identify human nature as a whole, "the true man, integral man" employing Maritain's language, one which is inspired by his recognition that "God is; He actually exists; He lives; He is a person." Wherein we find a remarkable synthesis of philosophical and theological thought which facilitates the awareness of the whole human being in their full integrity, one open to God through Christ, addressed theologically. This is found in "the face of Christ, the Son of Man, seen in the face of every man, especially when it has become translucent with tears and sorrows."

Reflecting on the consequence of this original thought which emerged during the twenty first ecumenical council, Jacques Maritain introducing his final book, *The Peasant of the Garonne* (1968) directs attention to the Council's synthesis of "great germinal ideas of Christian wisdom." Namely, the result of an extraordinary moment of *sapiential* consciousness, wherein the Council connects the "true idea of freedom" within its original understanding of "the true idea of the human person," the source of our dignity and rights. Unprecedented thought as the Church honours humanity found in "Christ's gaze on our brothers and sisters, regardless of religious affiliation,"[14] a look captured by the lithograph "In His Image," (1967) created by the American artist William Zdinak (1925–93) as "the image of God in the face of Jesus formed by the faces of humankind."

---

14. Maritain, *Peasant*, 2.

8

Friends of Wisdom

"The three decades following the Second World War" are arguably the "most productive in the long history of science" in the opinion of Michael Aeschliman, a Swiss American educator and literary critic, writing his "Foreword" to the revised edition of *The Restoration of Man* (2019). Nevertheless, given this impressive intellectual background, human beings remain "a mystery to ourselves," an ongoing conundrum which requires resolution. Recently approached by James Le Fanu, a retired British General Practitioner and well-known columnist from south London, through a retrieval of the idea of a "human person." An idea with a distinguished lineage within Christian thought dating back to the first Christian philosopher, Augustine of Hippo. As a remarkable friend of wisdom infused with *sapiential* consciousness, he established Christian anthropology as an original way of thinking about being human based on this idea, one which these contemporary thinkers sought to replicate, as during the Council.[1]

Considered "an intellectual giant" of his time, C. S. Lewis (1898–1963), the famous British writer and Anglian lay theologian from Oxford, while primarily known for *The Chronicles of Narnia*, a series of seven fantasy novels published between 1950 and 1956, was also a serious philosopher, author of *The Abolition of Man* (1943), wherein he challenged the contemporary relativism and scientific mindset found in "transhumanism," namely, to re-assert "man's power over nature" which continues to this day. In so doing, Aeschliman surveys the famous twentieth-century

---

1. Fanu, "Between *Sapientia* and *Scientia*."

Christian apologist's argument against this current way of thinking about humanity which reduces being human to a biological organism one among many, espoused by Sir Julian Huxley (1887–1975), the renowned English evolutionary biologist and secular humanist who coined this expression. Taking up Lewis' argument for the "human person" as someone more than a material being, the Swiss cultural commentator employs Augustine's distinction between *scientia* and *sapientia* to disclose the meaning and purpose of human existence through the awareness "that there is more than we can know," found in the idea of a 'human person.' A remarkable claim which encapsulates the central mystery of being human originally envisaged by Augustine, now approached through scientific analysis, accessing what he calls "the splendours of the universe and all that is contained within." Namely, through the recognition of the inherent deficiency Lewis finds in the prevalent materialist scientific understanding of being human, the Swiss commentator argues there is "something more about humanity." More than a material biological entity, the human person remains "a creature with inherent rationality and worth," an invaluable resource for restoring and preserving "the sanity, wisdom and moral order with human culture."

This informed awareness of "something more" also directed the original restorative way of thinking about our shared humanity found in conciliar humanism, especially through the endeavours of the Council Fathers as they assimilated the philosophical thought from three "friends of wisdom," leading twentieth-century European Catholic philosophers: two laymen Max Scheler, Jacques Maritain, and a cleric, Archbishop Karol Wojtyła. Understood as the consequence of a twentieth-century 'retrieval' of *sapiential* consciousness, wherein various and sometimes competing ideas about being human were drawn together from disparate modes of twentieth-century European thought and ingeniously assembled within an all-encompassing whole in their original idea of a 'human person.' A way of thinking understood as the consequence of a rather nebulous concept, the meaning of *sapiential* within the tradition of lived Catholic Christianity is essentially philosophical, contextual, and relational. Namely, as a philosophical awareness of the various relationships which constitute the integrity of being human as a human person, approached as individual or communal, who is directed towards God.

After centuries of neglect, the word *sapiential* re-emerged from the shadows of obscurity, notably through the twentieth-century attention given to 'consciousness.' With a philosophical orientation from Socrates onwards, the study of consciousness became a specific issue during the twentieth century. Recognized by the editors of *The Blackwell Companion to Consciousness* (2007) as "the most familiar and most mysterious aspect of our lives," consciousness became the subject of the interdisciplinary *Journal of Consciousness Studies* (1994). Approached as something distinctively human, and commonly taken for granted "awareness of something at a given moment," consciousness represents a complex phenomenon which received particular attention during the last century, found in the emerging European movement of philosophy established by the German philosopher Edmund Husserl (1859–1938) known as "phenomenology" or the study of phenomenon "that which appears."

Originally used by his friend and fellow phenomenologist Max Scheler for the study of human emotions, approached as a human response to a hierarchy of objective values, detailed in his ground-breaking publications for which he is primarily known, *Formalism in Ethics and Non-Formal Ethics of Values* (1913) and *The Nature of Sympathy and Contemporary German Philosophy* (1913); the subject of this value laden human consciousness was later critically studied by Saint Edith Stein (1891–1942). Another phenomenological realist associated with the University of Göttingen's (1737) "School of Philosophy," having written her doctorate *On the Problem of Empathy* (1917) under the direction of Husserl, she became his first female assistant, an extraordinary achievement within the male dominated German academic life of the day. Following her twofold religious conversion to Christianity and to the enclosed life of a Discalced Carmelite, Sister Theresa Benedicta a Croce was martyred together with a train load of Dutch Jews in the gas chambers of Auschwitz concentration death camp on August 9, 1942. Interestingly, these early practitioners of phenomenological realism drew inspiration from the thought of Augustine, one which continues to this day.

Full of surprises to the end, when tens of thousands of faithful Catholics and visitors alike, witnessed an unprecedented event. Gathered in St. Peter's Square for the concluding ceremony of the Council on December 8, 1965, they saw two laymen among the thousands of mitred bishops, not only invited onto the specially constructed dais in front of St. Peters, but also to be personally greeted by Pope Paul VI, namely, Jacques Maritain and Jean Guillot. Operating 'behind the scenes,' the recognition of these two Catholic philosophers by the pope who was a friend to both speaks to their indirect thoughtful influence during what would become one of the most philosophically oriented ecumenical councils, one infused with *sapiential* consciousness, which spoke to humanity at large. As author of *Integral Humanism*, Maritain then received the pope's message on behalf of the Council Fathers addressed to "men of thought and science," spoken in "a language accessible to all men." Namely through the bond of mutual friendship, this was also an opportunity for an unprecedented gesture of philosophical significance between 'friends of wisdom.'

Furthermore, adding to the significance of this unprecedented papal gesture was the presence of three Polish witnesses, also characterized as "friends of wisdom." Colleagues from the University of Lublin's (1918) "School of Thomist Philosophy," the so-called "Lublin connection," namely, Archbishop Wojtyła, Stefan Swieżawski and George J. Kalinowski. Co-authors of *Philosophy During the Second Vatican Council* (2006), these laymen produced the first commentary on what they had observed during the first two plenary sessions of the Council. Moreover, another witness to this extraordinary closing ceremony and another hitherto unrecognized resource when approaching conciliar humanism was Michael Novak (1933–2017), the American Catholic journalist and philosopher, a former diocesan seminarian trained in theology at the Pontifical Gregorian University (1551) in Rome, author of *A Salute to Jacques Maritain* (2009) and editor of the twenty-three-volume series *The Men Who Made the Council* (1964–65). All of whom were very familiar with the original thought of Jacques Maritain and had observed Council proceedings through the lens of Catholic European philosophy, hitherto unrecognized commentators concerning the genesis of conciliar humanism.

A way of thinking based on Maritain's *Integral Humanism* (1936) and subsequent *The Person and the Common Good* (1946), wherein we find the evolution of his original philosophical approach which combines theoretical and social dimensions. Original thought which was based on Maritain's previous lectures, "The Human Person and Society," given at Oxford on May 9, 1939, and "The Person and the Individual," given at Rome's Pontifical Academy of Saint Thomas (1879) on November 22, 1945, whereby the author of *Integral Humanism* sought to elaborate a "Christian personalism," expressed by one commentator, "[his] personalism might also be termed humanism."[2]

Approached from a different perspective, John F. Kobler, the American Passionist priest and private research scholar writing *Vatican II and*

---

2. Allen, *Christian Humanism*, 36.

Phenomenology (1985) offers a commentary on the philosophical nature of Conciliar though from the perspective of twentieth-century European phenomenology, founded by Edmund Husserl's "study of phenomena," later followed up writing *Vatican II, Theophany, and the Phenomenon of Man* (1991). However, while there is merit in these observations, little attention has been given to the influence of the characteristic expansion of philosophical thought towards understanding the human being found in Wojtyla's original thought inspired by his understanding of Scheler's phenomenological ethical personalism and philosophical anthropology, which informs the genesis of conciliar humanism.

Interestingly, the French philosopher Jean Guillot, the so-called "friend of presidents and popes," as well as being one of the first laypersons officially appointed by Pope John to witness Council proceedings as an *auditor*, was later asked by Pope Paul to address the plenary session of the Council on December 3, 1963 during the Solemn Commemoration of the Council of Trent (1545–53), an unprecedented opportunity given to a Catholic layperson to address the assembled hierarchy of the Catholic Church, along with another Catholic layman Vittorino Veronese (1910–86), the Italian lawyer and former Director-General of UNESCO (1958–61). Operating behind the scenes, the thought of this French philosopher also proved influential in directing what became conciliar humanism.

Given this background of personal connections, the presence of these "friends of wisdom" in front of the doors of St. Peter's Basilica spoke eloquently of their indirect influence on what was one of the most philosophical and pastoral oriented of ecumenical councils, an orientation directed towards understanding humanity previously expressed by the elderly Pope John as he opened the Council on October 22, 1962: "to make use of the medicine of mercy rather than severity,"[3] used as the subtitle of Massimo Faggioli's *John XXIII: The Medicine of Mercy* (2014). Moving into a new millennium, the use of this medical metaphor for our ongoing human spiritual wellbeing became the *leitmotiv* of the papal ministry of Pope Francis, inspired by the words of St. Paul to the Romans (12:13): "those who do works of mercy do them cheerfully." Especially found in his promotion of a "new humanity," "one that rejects hatred between peoples, one that refuses to see borders as barriers and can cherish its own traditions, without being self-centred or small minded."

---

3. O'Malley, *When Bishops Meet*, 27.

An integrative way of thinking which surfaced at critical junctures in world history, such as midway through the last century of the second millennium, during the twenty first and last to date ecumenical council of the Catholic Church. Approached as a seminal and consequential moment within twentieth-century Catholic thought of a definite philosophical pastoral orientation, found in conciliar humanism, which Pope John Paul II characterized in *Fides et Ratio* (1998) as a form of *sapiential* consciousness. One which brought together ideas drawn from traditional Catholic theology, from Aristotelian-Thomist metaphysical realism and from contemporary phenomenology and philosophical anthropology. Taken from the old French *retrover* 'to find again,' another expression of many variants, used in the subtitle of this book, 'retrieval' conveys 'a sense of renewal' wherein we find a thoughtful appropriation of ideas drawn from the past with an eye to the future while accommodating the present: 'back to the future.' A meaning commonly associated with the Italian *aggiornamento* 'bringing up to date' and the French neologism *ressourcement*, 'return to sources.' Expressions connected with the Council, used to convey the original intent of Pope John's innovative methodology based on an awareness of contemporary circumstances which informed the "crisis of being human," found by interpreting "the signs of the times."

Of a philosophical orientation, this sense of retrieval inspired the twentieth-century German philosopher Martin Heidegger's (1889–1976) ground-breaking publication *Being and Time* (1927), wherein he reviews the history of Western philosophy as a means of critically distancing himself from the traditional understanding of Being found in Aristotelian metaphysics, which he characterized as *onto-theology*, and thereby to recover the original sense of 'being' approached in pre-Socratic thought through the study of ontology. In so doing, Heidegger attributes a new meaning to 'being' through a process referred to as "hieroglyphic." Wherein recognizable language was used, such as the German word *dasein* 'being there,' a seemingly unintelligible notion in traditional philosophy, which was given a new meaning within his original existential project of recovery, now translated as 'being human,' thereby reducing ontology to anthropology. A reduction challenged by his friend Max Scheler's understanding of the 'human person' as the basis of his ethical personalism and subsequent philosophical anthropology. This twentieth-century process of thoughtful appropriation and recovery is similarly found within Conciliar thought with its original use of 'human person.' Namely, as the consequence of a thoughtful reengagement between the

Roman philosopher Boethius' (c. 475–524) original concept of 'person' as an "individual substance of a rational nature," and a twentieth-century understanding of the modern notion of 'person' as an ego-centred 'subject,' discussed in variants of French and German Christian personalism, from which emerged the Council's original idea of a 'human person' during an extended moment of *sapiential* consciousness.

"Christian wisdom, which the Church teaches by divine authority, continuously inspires the faithful of Christ to endeavour to relate human affairs and activities with religious values in *a living synthesis*. Under the direction of these values all things are mutually connected to the glory of God and the *integral* development of the human person" (emphasis added). These introductory words were written by Pope John Paul II, by someone certainly infused with *sapiential* consciousness, in his "Foreword" to *Sapientia Christiana* (1979), his Apostolic Constitution "on ecclesiastical universities and faculties." Written soon after his papal election on October 16, 1978, wherein we not only find the appropriation of thought taken from Maritain, who introduced the word 'integral' into contemporary Catholic philosophical discourse but also used by the pope in reference to Council's original understanding of the 'human person.' The consequence of a distinctive pattern of thought characterized as '*a living synthesis*,' a constitutive feature of the philosophical orientation of *sapiential* thought which directs conciliar humanism.

While "wisdom was seen as the embodiment of humanism," as observed by the Italian philosopher Enrico Cantore from the Pontifical University of the Holy Cross (1984), "[contemporary] philosophers seem to have forgotten the sapiential nature of their discipline,"[4] a lapse of memory not found among the Council Fathers, wherein we find an instance of the twentieth-century "retrieval of *sapiential* consciousness." Well known for reintroducing the adjective *sapiential* within contemporary Catholic discourse, the former Archbishop of Kraków, Karol Wojtyła shared a similar consciousness informed by a quest for an appropriate form of Christian humanism with other leading figures during the Council, notably proponents equally familiar with contemporary European philosophy, especially Cardinal Giovanni Battista Montini, Cardinal Suenens, and Cardinal Josef Frings.

Recognized as "friends of wisdom," these prelates were numbered among those persons primarily responsible for the Council's human

---

4. Cantore, "Science and Humanism," 215.

agenda and philosophical orientation which generated conciliar humanism, the consequence of an extended moment of *sapiential* consciousness, inspired by the thought of Jacques Maritain. Known as "the man who loved wisdom," himself infused with *sapiential* consciousness, Maritain was indirectly responsible for the re-emergence of this awareness among the Council Fathers whose collective thought was infused with *sapiential* consciousness having read his seminal *Integral Humanism* (1936). An awareness summarily expressed in the words taken from *Gaudium et Spes* "the need to create a synthesis, or to preserve among men and women capacities for contemplation and wonder which lead to wisdom" (para. 56). From their seminary formation these leading Council Fathers were well qualified and suitably positioned to guide the direction which informed the philosophical thought and pastoral orientation found in *Gaudium et Spes* and *Dignitatis Humanae*, wherein we find the ingredients of conciliar humanism, wherein we find the Council's 'belief in humanity' following its unprecedented human agenda.

The re-publication in 2018 of *The Future of Wisdom: Toward a Rebirth of Sapiential Christianity* (2008) by the American Benedictine monk Bruno Barnhart (1931–2015) from the New Camaldoli Hermitage in the Santa Lucia Mountains of Bir Sur, California, marks a welcome contribution in the retrieval of this original premodern form of human consciousness characterized as *sapiential*, wherein he claims "Wisdom Christianity is rooted in the sapiential writings of the New Testament, particularly the Pauline and Johannine texts."[5] By means of Barnhart's highly original and contemporary discussion of the Christian *sapiential* tradition, he prepares the reader not only to rediscover "the wisdom and power of God in the Christ-event today" but also the realization that "we are on the threshold of a *sapiential gospel*."[6] While interesting and very informative, what struck me as somewhat curious, given the contemporary charter of *The Future of Wisdom*, was the absence of any reference to nor discussion of the contribution made by Pope John Paul II's earlier and highly original recognition of this expression, found in his seminal encyclical *Fides et Ratio* (1998): "philosophy needs first of all to recover its *sapiential dimension*" (para. 81).

Celebrating the fifteenth anniversary of the Pontifical University of the Holy Cross on June 16, 1999, Pope John Paul II claimed: "It is in Christ,

---

5. Barnhart, *Future of Wisdom*, 7.
6. Barnhart, *Future of Wisdom*, 1.

God and Man, that the perfect harmony between nature and grace shines brightly. This marvellous balance has borne countless fruits of knowledge down the ages." A balance found between the various branches of knowledge which still need the light of theology, one "accompanied by *a sapiential philosophy of a genuinely metaphysical range*,"[7] a philosophical orientation he first discussed the previous year in Fides et Ratio (1998), published on September 14, 1998, the Feast of the Holy Cross. Returning to this theme during his address entitled "The Cross illumines all human life," the pope identified the philosophical background against which the issue of humanity was to be understood. Namely, through the tenets of conciliar humanism, an instance of Incarnational soteriology, echoing the thought of Pope Paul VI and that of Cardinal Ratzinger, later Pope Benedict XVI, original thought directed by "a *sapiential* philosophy," generated during the Council in the "words of the wise" which direct the orientation of Gaudium et Spes and Dignitatis Humanae.

However, as Pope John Paul II cautiously observed in Fides et Ratio para. 38, Christianity's initial engagement with philosophy was "neither straightforward nor immediate." Whereby the pagan thinker from Athens, Socrates originally recognized the natural inquisitiveness found among human beings, which generated the desire for learning what is true, a project which lies at the heart of philosophical and scientific enquiry, and the accompanying formal structure of "education," from the Latin *educare* 'to lead out.' First discussed by his student Plato in "the education of the philosopher" in Book 7, Part 8 of The Republic, a Socratic dialogue written around 325 BC, wherein the term 'philosophy' in its true sense as "love of wisdom" was first used. Following the Socratic dialogical approach, instruction in the practice of doing philosophy was through student participation in schools of philosophy, initiated by Plato when he founded the *Academy* (387 BC) in Athens, where another formative Athenian thinker Aristotle studied for twenty years until he established his own peripatetic school of philosophy, the *Lyceum* (334 BC). However, given the pagan ethos of these schools, they were approached by the early Christians as "more of a disturbance than an opportunity" (para. 38), circumstances which soon changed, especially moving into the world of medieval European monotheistic thought, found within Latin and Byzantine Christianity, Jewish, and Islamic faith traditions.

---

7. John Paul II, "Cross Illumines All Human Life," 10, emphasis added.

Operating within our contemporary Catholic philosophical tradition which seeks "a living synthesis," as the pope continues, this was achieved by means of integrating the exercise of our faith within the use of reason, exemplified in the "most elevated synthesis" achieved in the original though of Aquinas who could "defend the radical newness introduced by Revelation without ever demeaning the venture proper to reason." This creative and at times tense interaction between faith and reason remains a perennial issue in the history of Christianity, a characteristic of Catholic thought as being *sapiential*. An expression originally used in biblical studies and applied to the Wisdom literature of the Ancient Near East, the pope ingeniously employs the word *sapiential* within a new philosophical setting. More specifically, whereby "*sapiential* philosophy" is envisaged as a "stimulus," a means of response to the "kind of ambiguous thinking" evident in Heidegger's evocative atheistic existential humanism expressed in the German word *dasein* 'being there,' thought which currently informs the postmodern "crisis of truth." One fuelled by a proliferation of possible answers to the questions we naturally ask ourselves as human beings regardless of religious affiliation: what am I and who am I?

Interestingly, Professor Stefan Swieżawski (1907–2004) from the University of Lublin's "School of Thomist Philosophy" was the first Catholic thinker to highlight the philosophical significance of the *sapiential* thought found in *Gaudium et Spes* in his book *St. Thomas Revisited* (1995). Commenting on these circumstances, which he witnessed as an *auditor*, wherein the Council Fathers were perceived as "unsympathetic to Thomism,"[8] Swieżawski realized those at the Council were unable "to differentiate between Thomism and St. Thomas," an appreciation he shared with Maritain, another prominent twentieth-century Thomist philosopher whose thought was directly associated with the generation of conciliar humanism. A lack of understanding Swieżawski later addressed in a paper presented at an international conference held at the Catholic University of Leuven in 1974 entitled "On the Distortions of St. Thomas' Thought in the Thomistic Tradition," which informs the background for writing his later *St. Thomas Revisited* (1995). Wherein he claims: "Philosophy is a necessary condition of humanness; in order

---

8. Swieżawski, *St. Thomas Revisited*, 4–12.

to be a human being, in order to develop our humanity, we must be *friends of wisdom*" (emphasis added).[9]

The *sapiential* nature of conciliar humanism is found within an essentially *synthetic* interactive process of Catholic thought, generated during an extended moment of infused Christian wisdom guided by the work of the Spirit, structured around a complex network of three original philosophical ideas which direct the Council's understanding of our shared humanity, human person, community of persons, and human solidarity, thought which unalterably changed the landscape of contemporary Catholic discourse. Summarily expressed in words from *Gaudium et Spes*: "the need to create a synthesis, or to preserve among men and women capacities for contemplation and wonder which lead to wisdom," *quae ad sapientiam adducunt*. Of a philosophical orientation, the "balanced cultivation of the entire '*integram*' human person" is set against the contemporary "this worldly humanism" (para 56). Wherein we find the influence of Maritain's original use of the word integral which captures the essence of his thought. Whereby he introduced "integral" within contemporary philosophical discourse to reflect an integrative way of thinking which brought together the realms of traditional Aristotelian-Thomist metaphysical realism and contemporary ethical personalism and philosophical anthropology. A way of thinking later adopted by Wojtyła through the influence of his colleague Swieżawski as an original way of integrating the various trends of philosophical thought, metaphysical, anthropological, and ethical, employed by the various members of this School.

Sapiential to its core, the pope's message on behalf of the Council recalled these inspired words of Augustine, "let us seek with the desire to find, and to find with the desire to seek still more."[10] Taken from *The Trinity*, Book IX, Prologue, a remarkable treatise on the distinctive doctrine of Christianity written between 400–420, it was directed by a philosophical scrutiny of the idea of "the divine image in man,"[11] the first instance of an emergent Christian philosophical anthropology. Inspired by Augustine's *sapiential* consciousness wherein we find three distinctive interconnected elements, theological, anthropological, and philosophical brought together; this laid the foundation of an integral way of thinking used in conciliar humanism and its Christ centred integral philosophical

9. Swieżawski, *St. Thomas Revisited*, 4.
10. Augustine, *Trinity*, 271.
11. Augustine, *Trinity*, 18–19.

understanding of our shared humanity. Original Augustinian thought previously used by the German philosopher Max Scheler, known among contemporary German Catholics as "the second Augustine,"[12] reflected in the title of his book *On the Eternal in Man* (1921), a compilation of essays on "philosophy of religion" approached from the perspective of Scheler's original use of phenomenology.

Over the millennia, operating within the tradition of lived Catholic Christianity, this distinctive awareness of wisdom has informed European philosophical and theological discourse for more than twelve centuries, wherein ideas are viewed as being interconnected within a whole, marked by a metaphysical awareness with a propensity to synthesise, especially directed towards understanding our shared humanity. This desire "to be wise" directed a pattern of philosophical thought which was God centred, disposed towards humanity, and which employed an integral or *synthetic* approach, wherein our ideas are viewed as being interconnected within a whole. Succinctly expressed in the thought of the Australian theologian Paul Morrissey: "God as source of all wisdom, human person as being ordered to this wisdom, and wisdom as source of unity."[13]

A pattern of philosophical thought established by formative millennial Catholic thinkers over the course of history, themselves infused with *sapiential* consciousness, namely, Saints Augustine of Hippo Regius (354–430), Thomas Aquinas (1225–74), and Karol Wojtyła (1920–2005). Referring to the latter's "*sapiential* vision," especially found in the original pre-papal thought of this leading Council father from Poland, the Swiss Cardinal George Cottier OP (1922–2016), former secretary general of the International Theological Commission (1989–2003), describes Wojtyła's philosophical orientation as "one which envelops all human beings and events in God's light, where their ultimate reason for existing is to be found,"[14] namely, within his original philosophy of the "human person."

Operating within this broad Catholic intellectual ethos infused with *sapiential* consciousness, we can appreciate the significance of Pope Paul VI's concluding "brief message" to "men of thought and science," wherein he recalls the words of Augustine. Rather than quoting from one of the many remarkable intellectuals thinking within this ethos, especially the

12. Nota, "Development of Max Scheler's Philosophy of Religion," 257.
13. Morrissey, *Examination*, 69.
14. Cottier, "Faith and Reason."

foremost medieval thinker, the Italian Dominican Aquinas, characterized as "Augustine's great pupil" by Erich Przywara (1889–1972),[15] the Polish born German Catholic Jesuit philosopher from Munich, the pope returns to the original thought of one of the most important Church fathers and prolific authors. A formative influence used by the Council Fathers in the genesis of conciliar humanism, a consequence of the resurgence of interest among early twentieth-century Catholic thinkers in Augustinian thought, broadly initiated by Pope Leo XIII's "prophetic intuition" which informed the renewal of Christian philosophy.

Writing on the particular relationship between these two millennial figures, formative Catholic philosophers in their own right, Maritain observed in an essay "St. Augustine and St. Thomas" published in *A Monument to St. Augustine* (1930), while approached from a historical context there are fundamental differences between "a bishop of the fourth-century" and "a schoolman of the thirteenth century," between the "infused wisdom" of Augustine and Aquinas' "theological wisdom," however, both are commonly recognized as "friends of wisdom," thinking within the philosophical ethos of Christian wisdom, drawing inspiration from Augustine's *City of God* (VIII, i) which employs "reason and discourse,"[16] a comparative study Maritain later revisited in his *The Peasant of the Garonne* (1968).

---

15. Przywara, "St. Augustine," 253.
16. Maritain, "St. Augustine and St. Thomas," 221–22.

9

Christian Wisdom

MOVING INTO THE FIRST centuries of Christianity, in what came to be known as the 'Patristic Era,' leading church fathers and theologians, like Saints Ambrose of Milan (c. 339—c. 397) and Augustine of Hippo, equally infused with this distinctive form of human consciousness, understood as *sapiential*, recognized the incarnate Person of Christ as the bearer of divine Wisdom and knowledge. In so doing they ingeniously combined the biblical notion, "Wisdom has built herself a house (Proverbs 9:1)" with the tenets of classical Greek philosophy, especially found in Neoplatonism, an original fusion of Plato's idealist philosophy with the religious mathematical thought of Pythagoras (b. c570 BC) of Samos who emigrated around 532 BC to southern Italy, and other pagan religious ideas. Thinking with this *sapiential* consciousness, the recent convert to Christianity Augustine sought to "lovingly live with wisdom," whereby he brought together "love of wisdom" with "love of God."

This thoughtful philosophical legacy, generated during the early centuries of Christianity, fuelled the ongoing desire for learning throughout Christian Europe. Especially during the Middle Ages under the guidance of appropriately designated teachers, one of whom was Augustine. In 1298 Pope Boniface VIII (1294–1303) recognized him as one of the great 'Doctors of the Church,' from the Latin *doctor* 'teacher,' along with Saints Gregory the Great (c. 540–604), Ambrose of Milan (c. 339–397), and Jerome (c. 342–420). Several years later, Boniface consolidated his promotion of Christian learning with its *sapiential* consciousness when he founded *La Sapienza* (1303), an original *Studium Generale* in Rome dedicated to the pursuit of philosophical and theological study by ecclesiastics.

With no official definition, this expression was first used at the beginning of the thirteenth century to designate a place where students from everywhere were welcome to study. Understood as the foundation for what later became a 'university,' this has been characterized as "a medieval university in medieval Europe." Later, this way of thinking directed by *sapiential* consciousness reflected in the prayerful words of Ambrose, was chosen by Pope John Paul II to conclude one of his regular Wednesday general audiences, spoken at the beginning of the third millennium of the Christian era. Wherein the pope offered a reflection on the *Book of Wisdom*, entitled "True Wisdom is a participation in the mind of God," a unique form of consciousness shared by the influential thinkers of their time, Ambrose, and Augustine, and by the pope himself.

An extraordinarily prolific writer in the Latin church, Augustine is principally known for three books: not only his well-documented autobiographical account of his religious conversion, whereby he offers the first study of consciousness in his *Confessions* (397) which brought humanity to the foreground of philosophical thought, and laid the foundations for Christian anthropology, but also for his *On the Trinity* (400). Commenting on this book Edmund Hill (1923–2010), the English Dominican theologian observed "with a stroke of almost unconscious genius," Augustine offers the "dramatic history of *God*" approached through an "examination of the divine image in man,"[1] wherein he employs his characteristic distinction between *scientia* and *sapientia*. A way of thinking which led the Swedish botanist Carl Linnaeus (1707–78), the so-called "father of modern taxonomy" to designate the human being as *Homo sapiens*. Finally, we see the application of this thought in Augustine's third book, *The City of God* (c. 413–426), a book of Christian philosophy written following the sack of Rome by the Visigoths in 410 in response to the allegation that Christianity had occasioned the decline of Rome with its emphasis on charitable "love of neighbor."

As observed by the renowned Irish historian, Peter Brown, living in a time of "*sapiential* awakening" wherein wisdom was considered a way of life, Augustine may be considered "an excellent example of this vocation and this mentality."[2] Canonized a saint by popular acclaim following his death, Augustine remains in the opinion of Pope John Paul II "one of the best teachers of the Church,"[3] expressed in

1. Augustine, *Trinity*, 18–19.
2. Brown, *Augustine*, 42.
3. John Paul II, *Augustine of Hippo*, 7.

1986 on the sixteenth hundredth anniversary of Augustine's religious conversion to Christianity. A remarkable thinker who was recognized by Henry Chadwick (1920–2008), the British academic and Anglican priest, as "the last of the great Church fathers and in many respects, the first Medieval theologian."[4]

Writing his authoritative biography *Augustine of Hippo* (1967, 2000) Peter Brown drew attention to the popular understanding of Christ at the time of Augustine as "the Great Word of God, the Wisdom of God," quoting one of his numerous sermons.[5] Remarking on a key passage found in *The Wisdom of Solomon*, one of the seven *sapiential* or wisdom books, while not part of the Hebrew Bible, it was included in Catholic thought as being 'deuterocanonical.' Commenting on this biblical text on the nature of wisdom, Augustine observed "for God loves nothing so much as the person who lives wisdom" (7:28f), a way of thinking set against the thought of the Neoplatonist pagan philosopher Plotinus (c. 205–70). Thought which Augustine later used writing *City of God* (c. 413–26) in book eight chapter one wherein he claims, "if wisdom is identical with God, then the true philosopher is the lover of God."[6] Interestingly, apart from the Bible, *City of God* was the most influential book for medieval Christian thought.

Infused with *sapiential* consciousness, the newly baptized convert, the former teacher of rhetoric in Milan, sought to "lovingly live with wisdom" on his return to North Africa and especially during his time as the popularly elected bishop of Hippo Regius (395–430), in the Roman province of North Africa, nowadays Algeria. An extraordinarily prolific writer in the Latin church, Augustine is strategically positioned at the emergence of a new era of Christian thought, well known for his exceptional intellect and wilful personality. Classically educated in Aristotelian rhetoric and logic and Greco-Roman philosophy, Ciceronian scepticism, Roman Stoicism and Neoplatonism, Augustine absorbed ideas from these conflicting pagan worldviews and their essentially religious philosophical insights with the intent to harmonize and integrate these within an original Christian synthesis, characterized by the British scholar John Rist as *Ancient Thought Baptised* for his book (1994).

However, further significance is found in the biblical context of Augustine's original thought quoted by Pope Paul VI during the closing

4. Chadwick, *Augustine*, 1.
5. Brown, *Augustine*, 16.
6. Augustine, *City of God*, 298.

ceremony of the Council on December 8, 1965, which is followed by the words: "For when a man has finished, then it is that he is beginning," taken from The Wisdom of Jesus the Son of Sirach 18:7, which leads to a discussion concerning "what are human beings?" Originally written in Hebrew by Ben Sira of Jerusalem, a Hellenistic Jewish scribe around 190 BC, this Jewish book of ethical teachings, which is applicable to all conditions of life was generated by the Old Testament search for and attainment of wisdom, which in the opinion of Ben Sira is synonymous with "the fear of God," an original form of human consciousness characterized as *sapiential*. Having originated in the biblical genre known as *Logoi Sophon* or "sayings of the wise," this was recently discussed by James M. Robinson (1924–2016), the American New Testament and Nag Hammadi scholar,[7] who recalls the scribal traditions from Mesopotamia and Egypt that merged into Jewish collections, such as the Book of Proverbs.

Writing in *The Birth of Christianity* (1998), the Irish born American New Testament scholar, John Crossan characterized this *sapiential* or Wisdom tradition as the "special ideology of teachers, scribes and bureaucrats within aristocratic states or agrarian empires." However, under the influence of "Hellenistic internationalism and Roman imperialism," the Jewish prophetic traditions absorbed this original form of thought; in so doing, this genre was radicalized as a "double wisdom." Thereby absorbing both the ordinary wisdom of human life and divinely inspired "radical wisdom," as "living divine justice in an evil world."[8] Considered an outstanding example of the *sapiential* orientation which informed the religious literature popular during the Hellenistic period of Judaism around the third century BC, The Wisdom of Jesus the Son of Sirach is now commonly recognized as the deuterocanonical Book of Ecclesiasticus incorporated within the Catholic version of the Bible. Employed in this scriptural context, Augustine reveals his familiarity with this form of *sapiential* consciousness within Jewish thought, probably acquired during his religious instruction preparing for Christian baptism from the *sapiential* consciousness of the renowned preacher Ambrose, Bishop of Milan from 374, which he received during the Easter Vigil in 387, together with his son Adeodatus (372–388), literally "gift from God." A familiarity which subsequently directed the thought

---

7. Robinson, "*Logoi Sophon*: On the Gattung of Q," in Robinson and Koester, *Trajectories through Early Christianity*, 73–74.

8. Crossan, *Birth of Christianity*, 246.

of "friends of wisdom" assembled during the Council which inspired the original thought found in conciliar humanism.

Now on the cusp of the Church's third millennium, there is still much to be learnt from the collective thought of the Council as an extraordinary moment of *sapiential* consciousness, namely, a premodern Christian synthetic philosophical awareness, one which now re-emerged during the twentieth century. Found in these words from *Gaudium et Spes*: "to create a synthesis, or to preserve among men and women capacities for contemplation and wonder which lead to wisdom" (para. 55). An awareness shared by "friends of wisdom" associated with the Council, Catholic philosophers who offered inspiration and guidance during this extended meeting of minds which produced "one of the most remarkable of all councils" in the opinion of Norman P. Tanner, the British Jesuit church historian, author of *The Councils of the Church: A Short History* (2016).[9]

---

9. Tanner, *Councils*, 96.

10

Practical Wisdom

UNPRECEDENTED THOUGHT, CONCILIAR HUMANISM represents a new way of thinking, by which the Council redirected Catholic thinking away from its previous defensive mindset looking inward within a confined place, as in a ghetto, towards a broad inclusive mindset looking outwards, caring for others living in the 'world of today,' understood as an 'act of love.' Well expressed in these words: "In the thoughts of the Holy Father and in their implementation by all the bishops, this Council wants to be an act of love; an act which will weigh upon the history of the contemporary man and will, in some way, tear man away from hatred and push him in the direction of love."[1] These words espouse the Christ centred orientation which directs conciliar humanism approached as an instance of Incarnational soteriology, found in Christ's saving 'act of love.' Spoken by then auxiliary Bishop Karol Wojtyła during a pontifical mass celebrated in the historic old wooden church of St. Szczepan in Mnichów on December 26, 1962 following his return from Rome after attending the first plenary session of the Council, between October 22 until December 8 that year.

Spoken by someone who had never expected he would attend the Council in the first place as Poland's youngest auxiliary bishop. He was enthusiastic about his participation and experience during the Council. Only too pleased to talk about this on his return home, an occasion soon arose when he was invited to speak during a conference held at his *alma mater*, the Metropolitan Theological Seminary in Kraków. During which he

---

1. Boniecki, *Making of a Pope*, 212.

identified the Council as following the "spirit of Pope John XXIII," namely, as an opportunity "to show the truth," in such a manner that it would "captivate the contemporary man and find its way to him," namely, by speaking the universal language of love, which from a Christian perspective, is found in the Person of Christ directed towards humanity.

Writing later in a chapter entitled "the mystery of man: truth" in *Sign of Contradiction* (1978), wherein Cardinal Wojtyla published the twenty-two addresses he gave during the Vatican's Lenten Retreat in March 1976. Now approached as an opportunity to rediscover the whole truth of Christ from the perspective of conciliar humanism, a way of thinking he helped formulate. Whereby he drew attention to the Council's ingenious use of contemporary European philosophical thought, found in *Gaudium et Spes*, behind its evocative expression "in Christ," as he writes in *Signs of Contradiction*: "The mystery of the Incarnation is the focal point in the whole plan of salvation, and its purpose of none other than the salvation of mankind."[2]

Over the course of history, the distinctive relationship between the influence of Christian faith and the use of philosophical reason, sometimes characterized by tension, has directed an original way of thinking. Best expressed in the words of the first Christian philosopher Augustine when he claimed "believers are also thinkers; in believing, they think and in thinking, they believe. If faith does not think, it is nothing." Thought found in his later *Enchiridion (Manual) on Faith, Hope, and Love*, a small treatise which followed his more commonly known books, *Confessions, Trinity*, and *City of God*. Written sometime around 421 as a model for Christian instruction on the three graces necessary for the religious worship of God, following a request by a certain "Laurentius," shortly after the death of Jerome, another well-known Church Father. These words were later quoted by Pope John Paul II in *Fides et Ratio* (1998) wherein he offers an up-to-date systematic discussion of this relationship within Christian thought, building on what was found in the First Vatican Council's *Dei Filius* Dogmatic Constitution "on the Catholic Faith," promulgated on April 24, 1870.

While this Council is commonly associated with the issue of papal primacy and infallibility, defined in its *Pastor aeternus* the First Dogmatic Constitution "on the Church of Christ" promulgated on July 18, 1870, the Council was in fact convened by the pope to condemn

---

2. Wojtyła, *Sign of Contradiction*, 117.

erroneous and prevalent forms of philosophical thought. The so-called "problems" encountered by the Catholic Church with the rationalism inspired by the French philosopher René Descartes (1596–1650), the atheistic humanism of the German philosopher and anthropologist Ludwig Feuerbach (1804–72), the emergent forms of scientific and material positivism inspired by the French philosopher August Comte (1798–1857), and the German philosopher and social critic Karl Marx's (1818–83) revolutionary socialism and communism, all of which were identified by Pope Pius IX (1846–70) in his Apostolic Letter *Aeterni Patris* of June 29, 1868 to convene the Council. Unprecedented in Catholic practice, the title of this Letter was later re-used by Pope Leo XIII for his highly original papal encyclical *Aeterni Patris* "on the restoration of Christian philosophy" published on August 4, 1879. These problems express the emergent twofold denial generated during the nineteenth and early twentieth century in European philosophy, not only concerning the human capacity to think about the idea of God's existence, but also the human capacity for transcendence. Contemporary philosophical problems of a human orientation which challenged Catholic thinking and were subsequently addressed during both ecumenical councils held within the precincts of St. Peters Basilica, Vatican City, as these studied the various dimensions found in human activity.

Set against the "fiercely ambitious ideology of secular humanism," building on the promotion of the human capacity to think about God addressed during the First Vatican Council, the Second Vatican Council sought to consolidate the human orientation of Catholic thought found in the recognition of the 'humanity' of those who think about God, found within a Christ centred integral philosophical vision of our shared humanity. A way of thinking characterized as "both theological and theocentric" in the opinion of Maritain, found in what he calls "a humanism of the Incarnation." Namely, an integral humanism wherein humanity rediscovers its connection with God through the incarnate Person of Christ.[3] Moving into the twenty-first century little seems to have changed living in the postmodern world *where anything goes* which generates similar concerns about 'being human without God,' a situation which prompted the 2003 International Congress on Christian Humanism. Namely, a consolidation of the distinctive human and philosophical

---

3. Maritain, *Integral Humanism*, 197.

orientation of Catholic thought during the Second Vatican Council in response to the question "what is human?"

Original thought expressed in Pope John Paul II's oft quoted words from *Gaudium et Spes*: "it is only in the mystery of the Word incarnate that light is shed on the mystery of mankind" (para. 22). A way of thinking first discussed by Canon Charles Moeller (1912–86), the Belgian diocesan priest theologian in his commentary on the "history of *Gaudium et Spes*" wherein he claims this seminal document was directed "along the axis of Christian anthropology," based on "the mystery of the incarnate Word, the crucified and risen Christ,"[4] original thought captured by van der Weyden's *Descent from the Cross*. Moeller's thought was published in the original five-volume English-speaking *Commentary on the Documents of Vatican II* (1969), edited by Herbert Vorgrimler (1929–2014), the German Catholic lay theologian from the University of Münster (1780), understood as an invaluable resource for ongoing research on Conciliar thought used in this book. This human philosophical orientation of thought was later observed by the German theologian Cardinal Walter Kasper: "for the first time in conciliar history the question of anthropology was raised for discussion."[5]

Following his papal election on April 19, 2005, the former Council *peritus* Joseph Ratzinger, now Pope Benedict XVI addressed these remarkable words to Roman curial officials gathered to receive his Christmas message on December 22, 2005: "With the Second Vatican Council broad new thinking was required. Its content was certainly only roughly traced in the conciliar texts but determined its essential direction," oblique thought, especially coming from a well-known Catholic theologian, which has been given insufficient attention. While the pope identifies the novel, innovative, and tentative though directive nature of conciliar thought found in the Council's sixteen officially promulgated documents, this prompts the question 'why' was broad new thinking required in the first place? A conundrum explored in this book.

Written more than one hundred years after Pope Leo XIII's *Aeterni Patris*, Pope John Paul II took this opportunity to "revisit" the traditional relationship between "faith and reason," now approached in light of the Council's renewal of humanity. As he recalls the concluding thought in *Gaudium et Spes* which refers to the fundamental recognition

---

4. Moeller, "History of the Constitution," 5:89–91.
5. Kasper, "Theological Anthropology," 129–38.

of our shared humanity, namely, what we share in common: "for what unites the faithful is stronger than what divides them" (para. 93). In support of this claim the Council Fathers recall the original thought of Pope John XXIII, "there should be unity in essentials, freedom in doubtful matters, and charity in everything," taken from his first encyclical *Ad Petri Cathedram* published on June 29, 1959. Concluding *Fides et Ratio*, the pope promotes the Conciliar renewal of humanity, which is comprehensive with universal appeal through its use of philosophy: "in which there shines even a glimmer of the truth of Christ, the one definitive answer to humanity's problems" (para. 104), wherein he cites *Gaudium et Spes* para. 10.

Problems which can be addressed, in the opinion of Pope John Paul II, primarily through the recovery of philosophy's *sapiential dimension*: "understood as a search for the ultimate and overarching meaning of life" (para. 81). Based on the recognition of the human capacity "*to know the truth,*" first addressed during the First Vatican Council with its discussion of natural theology, now the Second Vatican Council marks a further stage in this philosophical process of recovery generated by *sapiential* consciousness by offering a unified form of human knowledge and action, a form of practical wisdom, wherein we find the meaning and purpose of human existence, namely, found in the tenets of conciliar humanism. Furthermore, incorporated within the pope's integral vision of philosophy, one which combines *genuinely metaphysical thought* within an anthropological orientation, a way of thinking especially practiced by members of Lublin's "School of Thomist Philosophy." Wherein, in the words of the pope, "the person constitutes a privileged locus for the encounter with being, and hence with metaphysical enquiry" (para. 106).

Envisaged as a way of thinking in continuity with the earlier Leonine program of philosophical renewal, initiated by *Aeterni Patris*, now *Fides et Ratio* represents the contemporary so-called 'Wojtyłan' renewal of Catholic philosophy by the recovery of "its *sapiential* dimension" (para. 105). Years later, writing on the twentieth fifth anniversary of Pope John Paul II's pontificate, Cardinal George Cottier (1922–2016), the Swiss Dominican and theologian, described the pope's "*sapiential* vision" as one which "envelops all human beings and events in God's light, where their ultimate reason for existing is to be found."[6]

---

6. Cottier, "Faith and Reason."

The consequence of *sapiential* consciousness, conciliar humanism represents an original way of thinking among "friends of wisdom," wherein we find God through understanding the mutual relationships found between the individual "human person" lived within "a community of persons." A remarkable understanding of "human solidarity" directed towards God, expressed in the innovative thought of *Gaudium et Spes*: "just as God did not create human beings to live separately but to form a united society" (para. 32). Seminal Ideas first introduced by Pope John in *Gaudet Mater Ecclesia*, during his opening address which inaugurated Council proceedings on October 22, 1962. Wherein we find his modern sociopolitical understanding of the human "subject" as a bearer of rights, ingeniously integrated within a convergence of thought between traditional metaphysics and a contemporary philosophical understanding of humanity.

All of which came together in the Council's original understanding of the human person, found in the person's act of transcendence, in the act of conscience, approached as openness to God and to other persons, a triadic way of thinking which reflects the original thought of Scheler. Furthermore, aspects of this Conciliar approach had been foreshadowed in Pope John XXIII's two encyclicals, *Mater et Magistra* "On Christianity and Social Progress" (1961) and *Pacem in Terris* "on human dignity and equality among all people" (1963) wherein we find a Christ centred integral philosophical understanding of our shared humanity, one he already alluded to during his surprising announcement to convene a general council to discuss the crisis of "humanity at the threshold of a new age." Intended to direct the orientation of Council proceedings, the pope introduced a new way of thinking and related expressions drawn from within these encyclicals which would become synonymous with conciliar humanism, such as the "whole human person, body and soul," our collective identify as "pilgrims" who dwell on earth striving towards heaven, expressed as "the common heritage of humanity" found in the "dignity of the human person" and "community of persons."

A novel approach first recognized by Michael Novak in *A New Generation* (1964), wherein he claims Pope John epitomised Aristotle's "man of practical wisdom" in these two papal encyclicals.[7] While written in the Leonine style of philosophical thinking whereby Pope Leo XIII sought the renewal of Catholic philosophy in the tradition of St. Thomas

---

7. Novak, *New Generation*, 91–104.

Aquinas, known as Thomism, by integrating this philosophical thought within a discussion of social justice issues. Now Pope John, according to Novak, joined this discussion, whereby he sought to renew this current way of Catholic thinking, moving away from the "appalling state of Latin scholasticism," the consequence of "seven centuries of Catholic laziness" in the opinion of Jacques Maritain, by directing attention to the so-called "victories" gained by the thought of other prominent European Catholic laymen, especially French philosophers such as Emmanuel Mounier's (1905–50) Christian personalism, Jacques Maritain's Thomistic personalism and Gabriel Marcel's (1889–1973) Christian existentialism; original thought which informs the philosophical background for understanding the ideas found in conciliar humanism.[8]

Characterized by this original network of foundational ideas, human person, community of persons, and human solidarity, whereby we find the anthropological, sociological, and implicit theological orientation brought together within conciliar humanism. This represents a remarkable way of thinking about humanity generated by the consequent resurgence of philosophical interest among European Catholic intellectuals, especially from France and Germany, in the study of the human being. Namely, understanding the God given nature of human existence as being "personal," as individual human persons living naturally together with other human beings in a "community of persons," wherein we find God through being in community, a Conciliar interpretation of the classic notion of *imago Dei* now based on a Trinitarian understanding of personal and mutual relationships, found in 'human solidarity.'

The first layperson from "behind the Iron Curtain" to be appointed by Pope John XXIII as an *auditor* or observer to attend Council proceedings was another commentator on this new way of thinking, namely, the Polish philosopher Stefan Swieżawski (1907–2004) when introducing his *St. Thomas Revisited* (1995), written as a means "to encounter the thought of St. Thomas Aquinas." Again, one of those remarkable figures very active operating on the sidelines of Conciliar proceedings, though rarely discussed in the English-speaking world. Considered a bright young philosopher of his time, he was one of the founding members of the University of Lublin's (1918) "School of Thomist Philosophy," which was established during the 1950s to counter the prevalent forms of atheistic Marxism. Writing in the opening chapters of *St. Thomas Revisited* he offers

---

8. Novak, *New Generation*, 100–101

invaluable information concerning the philosophical, and specifically *sapiential* orientation of Conciliar thought. While it "is commonly viewed as a pastoral council, one that seemingly forgot all about philosophy," he claims this was not the case. To counter this misguided interpretation he highlights 'the agenda of philosophy,'[9] found in the quoted thought from *Gaudium et Spes* which directed attention to "the need to reconcile contemporary culture *with the preservation in human beings of the capacity for contemplation and wonder, which lead to wisdom*" (para. 56). A moment of *sapiential* consciousness which offers an intellectual environment suitable for the balanced promotion of the entire human person, one independent from a "purely this-worldly humanism."

As a remarkable way of thinking, conciliar humanism was influenced by the so-called "Lublin connection," as an effective collaborative effort working behind the scenes during the Council, especially drafting these final documents. As members of the "School of Thomist Philosophy" they shared a philosophical awareness which Pope John Paul II recognized, addressing the participants of the 2003 International Congress, within the tradition of Christian thought associated with the foremost medieval scholastic theologian, Thomas Aquinas. Whereby in the opinion of the pope we are better equipped to respond to the critical circumstances of the time, seeking guidance from the "teacher of humanity," who he recognized in his Apostolic letter "Inter Munera Academiarum" (1999), especially concerning the promotion of the "dignity of the human person and the use of reason," understood as necessary for the recognition of the human capacity "for contemplation and wonder, which lead to wisdom," found in conciliar humanism.

Finally, another commentator to observe this philosophical orientation found in *sapiential* consciousness, insofar as he possessed this himself was then Professor Joseph Ratzinger, an authority on St. Augustine and active participant during the Council working as a *peritus* advising the German bishops as a theological expert. The subject of his 1953 doctorate in theology, "The People and the House of God in Augustine's Doctrine of the Church" from the Ludwig Maximilian University of Munich (1472), whereby Ratzinger placed himself at "the origin of the European spirit," in the opinion of his contemporary from Munich, the Jesuit philosopher Erich Przywara, another person equally infused with *sapiential* consciousness; in so doing Ratzinger was able to study

---

9. Swieżawski, *St. Thomas Revisited*, 8.

Augustine's remarkable convergence of thought, ideas drawn from classical antiquity and the Christian Gospel. Successful research which Ratzinger continued to pursue when he wrote his 1959 *Habilitation* on the Augustinian influence on the thought of the renowned medieval scholastic theologian, the Italian Franciscan monk St. Bonaventure (1221–74), *The Theology of History in St. Bonaventure*.

Set against this broad European and Augustinian philosophical background, writing as a young professor of dogmatic theology, having witnessed this thoughtful reception during the Council, Ratzinger now drew these ideas together in his 1968 seminal article on *Gaudium et Spes*, "The Dignity of the Human Person."[10] Wherein, within the context of his discussion of the Council's original employment of Augustinian thought, especially its use of the *scientia-sapientia* distinction, he returns to what he considers the document's "guiding idea," namely, understanding the "human constitution" or *humanum*, discussed in sections fourteen and fifteen of this Conciliar document, approached as a unified being of material, social, intellectual, and spiritual components, namely, the human as an integral being to use Maritain's expression. Wherein the Council's original understanding of the "human person" provides access through the exercise of wisdom to "seek and love what is true and good," achieved by means of a thoughtful progression from visible realities to "those which are invisible."

By employing this familiar framework of an Augustinian approach toward understanding humanity, Ratzinger claims the thought of *Gaudium et Spes* offers the means for "the humanization of man" based on wisdom, specially through the use of philosophy. Furthermore, operating within this thoughtful presentation, Ratzinger was one of the first commentators to recognize a common theme, found in "the human connection" which characterizes the thought of both Vatican Ecumenical Councils, namely, the philosophical recognition that the questions asked by human beings concerning the use of metaphysics or the question concerning the idea of God's existence "are fundamentally the same."

Another contemporary Catholic philosopher, similarly confident operating within Augustinian thought as author of *Augustinus* (1934), Erich Przywara was one of the first Catholic thinkers to creatively and critically engage contemporary European thought, thereby initiating a pattern of thoughtful reception among Catholic philosophers of ideas drawn from

---

10. Ratzinger, "Dignity of the Human Person," 132–33.

European philosophy, notably his critical engagement with and use of phenomenology practiced by the German philosophers Edmund Husserl, Max Scheler and Martin Heidegger. One especially gained through his friendship and philosophical collaboration with Husserl's young assistant, Edith Stein who was martyred in Auschwitz 1942.

Returning to Ratzinger's commentary, we find within *Gaudium et Spes*, the recognition of the necessary philosophical cultivation of a form of *sapiential* consciousness for the rejuvenation of humanity, in response to "the present age [which] more than ever requires such wisdom to humanize its new discoveries." A philosophical way of thinking which offers access "penetrating to the truth of reality" living in a world dominated by science and technology, found in a vision of "*sapientia* [which] involves man's very humanity."

11

Awake to God

WHILE ADDRESSING THE 2003 International Congress on Humanism the elderly Pope John Paul II, the famous *alumnus* from Rome's *Angelicum*, drew attention to the foundational claims which had been made in *Gaudium et Spes* inspired by Maritain's integral philosophical understanding of the human being: "man is a unity, made of body and soul" (para. 14), now approached by another "striking insight," namely, that "it is only in the mystery of the Word made flesh that the mystery of man truly becomes clear" (para. 22). A seminal passage frequently quoted by the pope, wherein we find the twofold orientation of conciliar humanism, as a Christ centred integral philosophical understanding of our shared humanity, especially found in two of the Council's final documents.

A documented legacy he acknowledged in his Apostolic Letter *Novo Millennio Ineunte* published on January 6, 2001, wherein the pope claimed "with the passing of the years, *the Council documents have lost nothing of their value or brilliance,*" as he continues, "I feel more than ever in duty bound to point to the Council as *the great grace on the Church in the twentieth century*: there we find a sure compass by which to take our bearings in the century now beginning" (para. 57). Moving into the twenty-first century a sense of perspective that is found in the original network of ideas which constitute conciliar humanism. A new way of thinking about our shared humanity which encapsulates the connection between thought and action, between philosophical and pastoral activities performed by human beings, characterized as "Catholic and open" in the words of Pope Francis.

A BELIEF IN HUMANITY: THE UNTOLD STORY OF CONCILIAR HUMANISM

A way of thinking best expressed in the words of an elderly pope who had been directly involved with its transmission through the Council: "The human person, constituted of body and soul in the unity of the person—*corpore et anima unus*, as the Constitution *Gaudium et Spes* para. 14 says—is called to enter into a personal dialogue with the Creator." As Pope John Paul II continues in his "letter to the President of the Pontifical Academy for Life," addressed to participants in a one-day Congress on the "Quality of Life and Ethics of Health," written on February 19, 2005, only months before his death on April 2, 2005. Wherein he recapitulates his lifelong understanding of the superiority of the "ontological dignity of the person" as a constitutive part of the human being. Ideas which reflect a new way of thinking about humanity which emerged during the Council found in conciliar humanism, the subject of this book. Established in 1994, a consequence of this new way of thinking, the Academy for Life remains a centre for ongoing multidisciplinary research and discussion in the field of bioethics, which deals with contemporary issues, such as embryonic stem cell research, IVF and gene therapy, and Catholic moral theology, another means of dialogue with the 'world of today.' Found in the theme "Roboethics: Humans, Machines and Health" adopted for the 2021 one day conference held by the Academy. One might ask, where is the human being in such circumstances? A situation not unlike that which confronted another elderly Italian pope, well trained in the study of history, seventy years ago as he solemnly convened the Second Vatican Council on December 25, 1961 with his Apostolic Constitution *Humanae Salutis*: "Today the Church is witnessing a crisis underway within society. While humanity is at the threshold of a new age, immensely serious and broad tasks await the Church, as in the most tragic periods of her history."

Approaching this new way of thinking, the Australian Catholic theologian Tracey Rowland observed in the context of the significance of *Gaudium et Spes*, it was a call "to recentre the Church's teaching and pastoral life on Christ," whereby perennial teachings are presented in a "more personalistic, less scholastic idiom." A form of conciliar thought which affirms our human aspirations for freedom and personal development that are embedded within our "relationship with the Trinitarian God," as she writes in "Saint John Paul II: Doctor of Incarnate Love."[1] Celebrating the fiftieth anniversary of this Constitution, the 2012

---

1. Rowland, "Saint John Paul II."

special Spring-Summer issue of *Communio* drew attention to the "challenge of Vatican II: Keeping the World Awake to God." Herein we find another instance where we can learn from the ideas found in conciliar humanism, namely, the integrity of the human person as being 'open' and in the idea of our human solidarity, wherein we find ourselves directed towards God. Whereby the Council affirms our twofold human capacity, not only to think about the idea of God's existence, but within this, our natural capacity for transcendence.

While the first ecumenical councils dealt with theological and especially Christological issues, which generated the concept of 'person,' now the last council to date reversed this way of thinking, whereby the awareness of God was directed by its understanding of our shared humanity from a philosophical perspective, found in its original understanding of the 'human person.' A way of thinking which identifies the Council's indebtedness to Scheler's phenomenological personalism, wherein the human person is defined by the capacity for transcendence, understood as 'openness.' Namely, the capacity of the person to move beyond oneself towards another person, either a finite person, individual or community, or towards God, understood as the Divine or Absolute Person. Hitherto unrecognized, there is merit in Scheler's recognition of a triadic structure between persons, one which avoids any binary reduction of one to another. That is between human persons, as an individual and as a community of persons operating on the horizontal level, simultaneously directed towards God, the Infinite Person through the idea of 'human solidarity' from the vertical level. Approached from this understanding, the absolute transcendence of God is preserved but equally approachable as a Person self-revealed in the act of mutual personal love. From this integrative way of thinking, we can appreciate the Council's original understanding of 'human solidarity,' namely, as human persons living together with God. A radical way of thinking, perhaps out of our 'comfort zone' for those unfamiliar with Wojtyła's appropriation of Scheler's thought; once again a connection hitherto discussed, to which I will return in my discussion of Wojtyła.

Living together in this so-called "post Christian" world wherein everything is permitted, the gauntlet is certainly thrown down to those who share religious faith to rethink our shared humanity, what and who we are as human beings as a first step, an essentially philosophical task, as a means of initiating a conversation with the world of today. Then in the light of this faith filled thinking to recover our awareness of being together with God as human beings. As a new way of thinking, the network of three basic ideas which constitute conciliar humanism offer the theoretical means towards this recovery. While the threat of "atheistic humanism" and "aggressive secularism" which "in a sense defied" the Council, in the words of Pope Paul VI might have receded, the persistence of their two-fold denial of our human capacity to think about the idea of God and the associated "capacity for transcendence" which characterized modern thought and, in a sense 'determined' the original 'human agenda' of the Council which generated conciliar humanism, continues to inform the intellectual ethos of postmodern thought with its Godless and secular orientation.

Found in a radical rethinking of our shared humanity, of what it means to be human, known as 'transhumanism.' Understood as a resurgence of Nietzsche's atheistic humanism in the original thought of the English evolutionary biologist Sir Julian Huxley (1887–1975), and the ethical secularism found in the scientific thought espoused by the World Transformation Movement founded in 1984 by Jeremy Griffith, an Australian biologist from Sydney. While these contemporary scientific ways of thinking about humanity are marked by the absence of God, they nevertheless espouse an ethical orientation in their preference for the word 'choice.' Taking up the gauntlet afforded by these contemporary ways of thinking, we can access the legacy of conciliar humanism. Namely, as an observance of our shared humanity in action, whereby we choose to encounter the person of Christ as we literally "look into" the faces of those around us, recognized as our sisters and brothers.

Approached historically, the question 'what am I' evolved from within Ancient Greek thought, following the interrogative methodology of 'question and answer' devised by the fourth-century BC Athenian thinker Socrates. This was used to understand the makeup of being human, what constitutes our human 'nature' as a biological, material, and social being, as an object of scientific scrutiny, objective thought which informs 'humanism' as a way of thinking. Building on this European tradition of disciplined philosophical interrogation, 'doing philosophy,' which was effectively employed during the so-called Middle Ages, a supplementary question emerged during the Enlightenment. A European intellectual and cultural movement of thought which arose in the seventeenth century, initiated by the scholastic rationalism of the French Catholic philosopher, René Descartes (1596–1650), the so-called founder of modern philosophy.

While the idea of 'person' initially arose within a Christian setting, during the first ecumenical councils at Nicaea (325) and Chalcedon (451), used to address theological issues concerning the Second Person of the Trinity, Jesus Christ, the Son of God, it assumed philosophical significance when the Roman philosopher Boethius (480–524), well acquainted with the thought of the Greek philosopher Aristotle, while writing in a theological context, used the idea of 'person' to define human nature as being a rational substance. This philosophical orientation was taken up by subsequent thinkers, such as the Englishman John Locke (1632–1704) and the German philosopher Immanuel Kant (1724–1804), who sought to understand our being human as a person, in response to the question who am I? Namely, our awareness of a personal identity inaccessible to scrutiny from outside accompanied by the recognition that there is 'something more' about the individual human being as a 'person,' a subjective way of thinking characterized as 'personalism.'

During the twentieth century, it would be one of the salient features of Conciliar thought to ingeniously synthesise these two ways of thinking about our humanity within an original understanding of the 'human person.' While ubiquitous in contemporary discourse, little attention has been given to the specific circumstances as to how this remarkable transition took place. Namely, how to account for the movement from the confined arena of nineteenth- and twentieth-century papal thought, especially on social justice issues by 'champions of humanity,' whereby diverse ideas were drawn from various forms of twentieth-century European philosophy, such as phenomenology, Christian variants of existentialism, humanism and personalism, as well as twentieth-century Thomism, and were ingeniously brought together in the idea of a 'human person,' and its pivotal role within a network of three ideas which makeup conciliar humanism.

While Pope Francis was too young to participate in this seminal and consequential moment of thoughtful reflection for the Catholic Church during the twentieth century, his predecessor was very much involved as another significant figure operating 'behind the scenes' as Professor Joseph Ratzinger (1920–2022) from Munich, directing the implementation of the Council's agenda. Decades later, following his election as pope on April 19, 2005 Benedict XVI assumed the status as another promoter of conciliar humanism, following the example of Pope John Paul II as proponent of the 'human person.' Now Pope Benedict becomes a promoter of the idea of *communio*, used to express a 'community of persons.' Furthermore, as "friends of wisdom" during the Council, their active presence draws attention to the Council as an extended moment of *sapiential* consciousness. Namely, what emerged as conciliar humanism was the consequence of the exercise of Christian wisdom, guided by the work of the Spirit, namely, the result of a *synthetic* and unitary interactive process of conciliar thought.

Herein we find access to a remarkable way of thinking in response to a perennial question, the desire to understand our humanity, one which re-emerged during and came to characterize twentieth-century thought, as when Martin Luther King Jr. (1929–68) asked "What is Man?" The subject of his sermon preached at the first National Conference on Christian Education of the United Church of Christ at Purdue University in 1958. Included with another sermon "The Dimensions of a Complete Life" in a subsequent publication entitled *The Measure of a Man* (1959). Famous for his iconic dream, the thought of this leading activist for the black civil rights movement until his assassination was embedded in his awareness "of harmony and equality for all people" as observed by Pope Francis on Martin Luther King Jr. Anniversary Day in the United States on January 19, 2021. This awareness subsequently inspired the Black Lives Matter (2013), namely that we should value the human being simply because she or he is human.

A decentralised political and social movement organized to combat 'racism,' a long held human mindset over the course of history which assumed the status of a phenomenon during the twentieth century. Namely, an inexcusable prejudiced view of humanity based on social inequality, the recognition of biological or racial differences which generated the mass murder of European Jews or the unjustified killing of a black man George Floyd by a white man Derek Chauvin, a Minneapolis police officer. However, we might ask as many did during the twentieth century what are the circumstances which generated this awareness, namely, the lack of any consideration given to God.

Approached from Rev. Martin Luther King's Christian perspective, the human being is envisaged as God's marvellous creation, as a "spiritual being with 'rational capacity' in possession of a unique capacity for 'fellowship with God.'"[2] However, not everyone thought the same during the 1960s. A perplexing decade characterized by 'crisis,' it was time of change, uncertainty, and widespread political disillusionment, marked in America by the emergence of the civil rights movement and anti-Vietnam War

---

2. King, *Measure of a Man*, 24.

(1955–75) protests, which morphed into the countercultural movements associated with the swinging sixties, free love, and sexual promiscuity among liberated youth. During the 1960s no sphere of human activity remained unaffected, whether philosophical, intellectual, political, economic, social, or religious, even within the hallowed confines of Catholic life, nothing was immune. Responding to the 'signs of the times,' and led by divine Providence, conciliar humanism emerged as a suitable guide, "leading us to a new order of human relations which, by human effort and even beyond all expectations, are directed to the fulfillment of God's superior and inscrutable designs, [whereby] the joy of the gospel fills the hearts and lives of all who encounter Jesus."

The consequence of a Council of faith with a human agenda, conciliar humanism provides those living and thinking in the tradition of Catholic Christianity with the theoretical means for initiating a conversation with the contemporary world. Namely, to implement the Council's novel human, philosophical and pastoral outreach towards humanity in need of salvation.

Written over the course of many years, this book reflects our shared search for wisdom understood as both "Catholic and open" in the mindset of Pope Francis, one which shuns the petty sectarian opposition between "either-or" in favour of "both and," an inclusive methodology wherein differences are integrated, especially when understanding our shared humanity. A concern especially raised by philosophers in a discursive manner, through the human activity of "doing philosophy," traditionally understood as "the love of wisdom." A rational activity which follows the "question and answer" way of thinking initiated by the "engaging and infuriating" Athenian thinker Socrates (c. 470–399 BC), the enigmatic so-called "founder of Western philosophy."

Wherein doing philosophy involves asking the right questions, such as "what is human," critically examining the manner previous thinkers addressed this question, understanding their ideas, where they came from and the reasoning behind them, all of which broadly informs the "context" for this question. Operating "with the text" provides the means to assemble and articulate a cogent response or argument of one's own, achieved in the pursuit of truth. When these ideas are taken together, as found in the generation of conciliar humanism, they constitute the contextual methodology necessary to journey through this book, found in the claim of Alasdair MacIntyre, the Scottish born American Catholic philosopher as he introduces *Selective History of the*

Catholic Philosophical Tradition (2009): "Christian philosophy is best approached historically."[3] An approach the author of this book shares in the mutual pursuit of truth as being inherently worthwhile, wherein the integrity of human life is affirmed as essentially valuable. The consequence of the Council's integral philosophical way of thinking, conciliar humanism, expressed as "human solidarity," offers an original vision of humanity which incorporates the individual "human person" living in a "community of persons" directed towards the natural world, each other, and the Triune God.

Writing "The Pursuit of the Ideal" (1988), the first essay later published in *The Proper Study of Mankind: An Anthology of Essays* (1997), Isaiah Berlin observed: "only barbarians are not curious about where they come from, how they came to be where they are, where they appear to be going."[4] Certainly not barbarians, this interrogative capacity informs the evolution of our ideas which established the tradition of discursive and disciplined rational thought in "doing philosophy," one which inspired the original thought found in conciliar humanism, which began on October 22, 1962 in a world unlike any other. Literally days before the Council's official opening humanity approached annihilation by its own hand during the Cuban Nuclear Missile Crisis between October 16–28, 1962, a consequence of the so-called 'Cold War' (1947–91). A period of ideological and geopolitical tension between the democratic West, the United States and its Western European allies, and the communist socialist East, the Soviet Union, and its Eastern European satellite states. Circumstances which occasioned the iconic words, prompted by a shared awareness "that peace and freedom walk together" spoken by the American president John F. Kennedy (1917–63) during his address to the graduating students from the American University (1893) on 10 June 1963: "Our most basic common link is that we all inhabit this planet. We all breathe the same air. We all cherish our children's future. And we are all mortal," an awareness assuredly shared by the Council Fathers as they gathered in the reconstructed precincts of St. Peter's Basilica in the Vatican City to address this universal issue confronting the contemporary Church and "the world of today," namely, the crisis of "being human." Their thoughtful response to this question set the unprecedented human agenda which generated the Council's original thought, from which emerged conciliar humanism.

3. MacIntyre, *God, Philosophy, Universities*, 1.
4. Berlin, *Proper Study*, 2.

Portrayed by Gerald O'Collins, the Australian Jesuit theologian, as "the 21st Council for the 21st Century," conciliar humanism as a Christ centred integral philosophical understanding of our shared humanity was generated during an extended moment of infused *sapiential* consciousness, the brainchild of one person, namely, Pope John XXIII. Known for his natural humility and jovial humanity, and clearheaded thoughtfulness informed his characteristic pastoral awareness he shared with other Council Fathers. Among these were notable collaborators in implementing the Council's unprecedented human agenda, such as the Italian Cardinal Giovanni Battista Montini who was elected Pope Paul VI on the death of Pope John, Cardinal Suenens, and the German Cardinal Josef Frings (1887–1978), all of whom became 'leading lights' during his Council.

While it is commonly recognized that Pope John's address *Gaudet Mater Ecclesia* which opened Council proceedings on October 22, 1962, as the culmination of three years of extensive consultation and necessary preparation, contains his manifesto for the Council, the impetus for this reformative enterprise and inspiration for its human agenda can be found in Pope John's earlier Apostolic Constitution *Humanae Salutis*, "salvation of humanity." Whereby he officially convened the Council on Christmas Day 1961, a fitting opportunity with Incarnational significance, to introduce the Council's thoughtful response to the perennial question asked by those living in the chaotic and turbulent world of the mid-twentieth century in response to the uncertainty about the identity of being human, the so-called "crisis of humanity," one which initiated a novel way of thinking within Catholic discourse. Which determined the Council's unprecedented human agenda moving "toward a new order of human relationships" under the guidance of Divine Providence. Whose thoughtful influence remains an ongoing source of inspiration for renewal in the Church, one which speaks to the contingencies of living in our time, captured by the colloquial expression "here and now," found in the awareness of our shared humanity.

As such, this Council has been characterized as the most significant event in the history of Roman Catholicism since the 'Protestant Reformation.' A religious movement for reform within the Catholic Church during the 1500s but with disastrous effect, which occasioned the separation of various religious groups from the Church. In response, Pope Paul III (1534–49) convened the nineteenth ecumenical assembly of the world's Catholic bishops and religious leaders in the Italian city of Trent between 1545 to 1563, as a reaction against Protestant teachings. Namely, on Catholic doctrine dealing with faith, grace and the sacraments, the Council sought to identity and reject heretical teachings through the establishment of the Roman Inquisition in 1542. Furthermore, it sought to restore the unity of the Church through the reform of the liturgy, though the publication of the Roman Missal. And finally, it sought to reform the clergy and those preparing for the clerical state by the establishment of a formal system of training, conducted in a 'seminary,' a system which persists to this day. These Tridentine initiatives came to be recognized under the umbrella expression of the so-called "Counter-Reformation." Interestingly, the last ecumenical council to date likewise sought also to enhance these areas of Catholic life and practice, a subject of ongoing discussion and debate moving into the twenty-first century.

Years later Saint John Paul II (1978–2005), the great philosopher pope of the twentieth century, would be canonized together with Saint Pope John XXIII (1958–63) in an unprecedented ceremony in St. Peter's Square on Divine Mercy Sunday April 27, 2014, presided over by Pope Francis. Among over one and fifty Cardinals and seven hundred bishops who were concelebrants with the pope during the Canonization mass was his predecessor Emeritus Pope Benedict XVI. The presence of the former Father Joseph Ratzinger (1927–2022) from Munich, one of the youngest theological experts appointed as a *peritus* to advise during Council proceedings, only heightened the obvious connection between these popes associated with Council, and promoters of the ideas found in conciliar humanism. Further substantiated when the date of the opening of the Council on October 22, 1965 was chosen to celebrate Saint John Paul II's feast day.

As an unprecedented way of thinking addressed to humanity, conciliar humanism represents "the promotion of unity and charity among people," based on the recognition of what "human beings have in common, what brings them together." A way of thinking anticipated in the Council's earlier *Nostra Aetate* Declaration "on the church's relation to non-Christian religions." The shortest of its sixteen documents, promulgated by Pope Paul VI on October 28, 1965. Understood as the recognition of our human solidarity, wherein the individual human person lives within a community of persons, directed towards God, the Divine Person. Extraordinary twentieth-century thought, approached as a "communion of salvation."

12

Living in the World of Today

LATER THAT YEAR DURING his general papal audience on September 9, 2021, Pope Francis' thought reflects the influence of conciliar humanism when he claims: "There is no place for discrimination or divisive distinctions among people who believe in Christ" as he continues, "that everyone is made new and equal in who Christ overcomes all ethnic, economic differences, even between the sexes." Musing on its instructive intent his biographer Massimo Borghesi observed, as for many of us, "the Council would be Bergoglio's greatest teacher, and the single source, of his pontificate," among its many features it has been defined by his use of the ideas drawn from conciliar humanism. Especially found in the pope's call for a "new humanity" and his employment of terminology encompassing original expressions found in conciliar humanism and its network of three mutually connected ideas about our shared humanity. Namely, human person, community of persons, and human solidarity, which were generated in response to the critical circumstances which the Second Vatican Council addressed, wherein we find the thoughtful foundations of conciliar humanism. A Christ centred integral philosophical way of thinking about our shared humanity, found in *Gaudium et Spes* and *Dignitatis Humanae*. Subject matter not included in preparatory discussion material for the deliberation by the Council Fathers, these documents finally emerged after three years of energetic, critical discussion and at times acrimonious debate, with the latter, previously titled *schema XIII*, now renamed with the formal title *Gaudium et Spes*.

Understood as the consequence of what Pope Francis calls "a Council of faith" in his inaugural papal encyclical *Lumen Fidei: On the*

Light of Faith (2013): "The Second Vatican Council enabled the light of faith to illumine our human experience from within, accompanying the men and women of our time on their journey of faith" (para. 6), herein we find his recognition of the legacy of conciliar humanism. As a Christ centred integral philosophical understanding of our shared humanity accessible to everyone, one which informs the purpose and meaning of human existence and experience, enlightened by a faith inspired vision of humanity found in the Incarnate Person of Christ, "a good news story" for Christians and unbelievers alike.

Approached from the perspective of world history, at certain critical junctures Christian thinkers have been infused with *sapiential* consciousness. During his visit to *La Sapienza* (1303), Pope Benedict XVI referred to this venerable institution's ongoing commitment to scholarly collaboration and dialogue when the University sponsored a World Meeting of University Rectors to discuss "a new humanism for the third century," one considered by the pope as a "prophetic and complex proposal." Recalling the thought of Pope Benedict XVI given in his extended interview with Peter Seewald published as *Light of the World* (2010), wherein he claimed the Council provided an opportunity to return "to the question about God." Summarily expressed in the words of Pope Paul VI during his address to the seventh and final plenary session of the Council on December 7: "Our humanism becomes Christianity; our Christianity becomes centred on God; in such that we may say it differently; a knowledge of man is a prerequisite for a knowledge of God." While the first ecumenical council at Nicaea (325) came to an understanding of the personal nature of God, the last to date council in attempting to understand humanity, directed attention to God.

Ever the consummate theologian, Pope Benedict explores this thought through the lens of these words: "God's love can become concrete and can almost be experienced in history with all its painful and glorious vicissitudes," changing circumstances which characterize the enigma of being human. Quoted by his successor Pope Francis on January 27, 2019, during his closing homily World Youth Day (WYD) homily on during the final open-air mass in Panama City's Metro Park. Reflecting on the thought which begins Jesus' public ministry, found in the Gospel of Luke (4:20–21), "today it has been fulfilled," Pope Francis speaks to the "now of God" revealed in the humanity of the person of Jesus, through His face and flesh, "a face that is fraternal and friendly, concrete and familiar," one envisaged within the God-centred legacy of conciliar humanism. Equal to the task, this "synthesis of fidelity and dynamism" offers an original form of thinking generated in a moment of *sapiential* consciousness which brings together theological and philosophical ideas, "new and old" about our shared humanity.

Unlike other Council documents, *Gaudium et Spes* was simply addressed to "humanity," following its publication in 1965 this Pastoral Constitution literally put the Catholic Church on the world stage, receiving global attention and acclaim in identifying the Church's novel "pastoral" outreach to the world at large, moving away from the Church's previous nineteenth-century defensive and 'ghetto' mindset, toward an orientation informed by an unprecedented way of thinking based on a process of universal and mutual "dialogue" with "the world of today," a translation of the Council's Latin *in mundo huius temporis* preferable to the commonly used though misleading expression 'modern world.' Whereby the Council draws inspiration from the twentieth-century Jewish existentialist philosopher Martin Buber's (1878–1965) appropriation of Socratic thought as the foundation for his "philosophy of dialogue."

Whereby the Council addressed the crisis of humanity in need of salvation, to "believer and unbeliever alike," by means of an original Christ centred integral philosophical way of thinking about our shared humanity, based on an understanding of the whole of being human, wherein the various dimensions of human existence, such as material, rational, emotional, spiritual, and personal are respected in the "human person." Operating within this integrative way of thinking, which avoids the traditional binary opposition between a spiritual mind and a physical body, we find the originality of Scheler's understanding of the human person as being dimensional, made up of various connecting sphere or dimensions, as the basis for his original philosophical anthropology; as he observed in his early essay "On the Idea of Man" (1914): "man is a thing so broad, variegated and diverse that all definitions turn out a little too concise. He has too many ends!"[1]

Written while a practicing Catholic, this was Scheler's only philosophical publication which directly addressed the question of being human, a way of thinking inspired by Augustine's commentary on the Book of Genesis, *De Genesi ad litteram* VII, 12, which uncharacteristically for Scheler he quotes directly to introduce this essay. Thereby fulfilling our human destiny as "beings created in the image and likeness of God," who

---

1. Scheler, "On the Idea of Man," 185.

possess the capacity to know the complete truth about our origins, nature, and destiny found in "relation to God," approached "*in lumine Dei*," an expression Max Scheler attributed to Augustine. Writing in "Problems of Religion," published in his compilation of essays on philosophy of religion, *On the Eternal in Man* (1921), a title which supposedly employed another Augustinian idea about our God centred humanity. Wherein Scheler identifies the revelatory and insightful character of religious activity, through his phenomenological study of religious experience, which is embedded within his early personalist and sociological thought written as a Catholic philosopher.

While the Council's legacy, found in its documented thought and especially in these two final documents, remains a watershed for contemporary Catholic thought and action, as the subject for further studied reflection it's time to go a little deeper, insofar as little attention has been given to the overall background concerning the Council's philosophical understanding of the human being as a 'human person.' Namely, thinking about the nature of the "person" who performs such activity as a human being, and our constitutive orientation as human persons towards "God," the Divine Person; thought which formulates the Council's "belief in humanity" found in conciliar humanism. An original philosophical way of thinking about humanity generated in response to the perennial question "what is human" and to counter the two-fold denial which characterized modern thought; the denial of the human capacity to think about the idea of God, the foundation of modern atheism, constructed on the denial of the human "capacity for transcendence" found in secular humanism. Brought together within the Council's original understanding of the human activity and capacity for "choice," the exercise of our free will.

Every generation strives to interpret the time it lives in, living in "the world of today," wherein we try to move towards something better, relying on our best hopes, in the encounter with our present circumstances. Living in a world unlike those before, during a time of global upheaval and violence, of unprecedented social and political confusion which shattered every humanist illusion in the post-best and worst of humanity. As such as when confronting self-annihilation by our own hands during the Cuban Missile Crisis between October 16–19, 1962, an extraordinary period characterized by worldwide tension and anxiety during which the Council opened on October 22, 1962. These last years of the second millennium represent an 'era of apparent contradiction,' an unparalleled period in history during the twentieth century which prompted critical reflection on our human identity brought on by a "human crisis." As a man of his time, Pope John XXIII employed the biblical expression 'signs of the times,' used in the Gospel of Matthew (16:3) to inspire those present during the Council to address this crisis 'head on,' by means of which an original way of thinking emerged and was endorsed, one which transformed the universal Church as "the human face of Christ." Like the Lunar landing, Vatican II emerged from a three-year period of intense preparation which set in motion a new era, transformed by the idea of a "human person."

Wherein we find the Council's "belief in humanity" embedded within a distinctive form of Christian humanism, the consequence of collaborative personal and thoughtful connections generated during an extraordinary extended "meeting of minds," an expression which characterizes Council proceedings. Original thought expressed in the extraordinary introductory words of *Gaudium et Spes*, literally the last words of the Council: "For it is the human person that is to be saved, and human society restored. It is around humankind therefore, one and entire, body and soul, heart and conscience, mind and will, that our whole treatment will revolve" (para. 3.) Words which bear testimony to the innovative use of philosophical ideas which directed the thought of the Council Fathers following their unprecedented human agenda.

What am I? Who am I? In the blink of an eye, we find ourselves living in the twenty-first century returning to these perennial questions, commonly asked by human beings to better understand ourselves, thinking about our humanity living in the world of today. Now characterized as global, nuclear, and digital, one which represents an era of unprecedented uncertainty, wherein *anything goes*, an expression originally used as the title of the American composer and songwriter Cole Porter's (1891–1965) 1934 smash-hit musical comedy to portray American society during the 1920s. Whereby he characterized the "roaring twenties" as "an era of uninhibited excess."[2] Now used to designate the philosophical and cultural milieu of the twenty-first century, labelled "postmodern," "post human," and "post Christian," whereby we identify ourselves in terms of what has been lost, namely, our Christian heritage, as observed by the American Christian author Leslie William's *When Anything Goes: Being Christian Is a Post-Christian World* (2017).

---

2. Moore, *Anything Goes*, 17.

Thinking in these circumstances the traditional understanding of what it means to be human as *Homo sapiens*, as being essentially rational and social, following the Socratic dictum *know thyself*, appears insufficient living in an entertainment "polls driven" world, inhabited by opinionated humanoids, alien beings with a structure generally like that of a human, robots who share human features but do not look convincingly like a real person, or biological mutants who exhibit superhuman abilities, all of which calls into question being human.

Moreover, living in this media driven world influenced more by science fiction than science, how can we address these beings who are "suspiciously human?" Against what criteria is this assessment made: what is reasonable when addressing the issue of humanity and human nature? Basic philosophical issues raised over the course of Western history, now addressed living in a postmodern world wherein the desire to understand our identity as human beings is not shared by all. Moving into the third millennium of the Christian era, the ongoing relevance of conciliar humanism remains a "good news story," a legacy to be shared by all. As observed by the Australian Catholic laywoman theologian Tracey Roland, *Gaudium et spes* was a call "to recentre the Church's teaching and pastoral life on Christ," perennial teachings presented in a "more personalistic, less scholastic, idiom." A form of Conciliar thought which affirms our human aspirations for freedom and personal development are embedded within our "relationship with the Trinitarian God," as she writes in "Saint John Paul II: Doctor of Incarnate Love."[3] Directed to the 'world of today,' this unprecedented way of thinking which emerged during the Second Vatican Council is best approached through the popular expression "back to the future," whereby we find a thoughtful legacy. As such, conciliar humanism remains what I characterize as "a work in progress" accessible to all moving into the twenty-first century.

An interrogative reading of *Gaudium et Spes* by means of which D'Ercole identified three interconnected contemporary issues, based on his discussion of the significance of the social teaching found in Pope John XXIII's encyclical *Pacem in Terris* "on Establishing Universal Peace in Truth, Justice, Charity, and Liberty" published on April 11, 1963, months before his death on June 3 that year. Written by the pope who had convened the Council and whose thought indirectly influenced the genesis of conciliar humanism. Taking up the bishop's

---

3. Rowland, "Saint John Paul II."

thought provides the means for further thoughtful engagement with the "world of today," moving into the arena of twenty-first-century thought which is concerned with anthropological, sociological, and theological issues, a thoughtful means to access the legacy of conciliar humanism discussed in this book. Through an anthropological discussion of the human person found in the exercise of freedom through the use of "conscience," a sociological consideration of our inherent social orientation as human beings towards each other living in a 'community of persons,' approached through the impact of "racism," a phenomenon of the twentieth century, and the theological issue concerning the "absence of God" found in contemporary forms of "atheism." Concerns first raised by the Diocesan priest Josef Ratzinger in his 1966 lecture "Catholicism after the Council" following his appointment as professor of dogmatic theology at the Eberhard Karl University of Tübingen (1477) which he delivered to the annual *Katholikentag*, held in Bamberg, one of Germany's most beautiful towns in the state of Bavaria.

Another extraordinary "behind the scenes" figure during the Council, Ratzinger was one of the youngest *periti* 'theological experts' initially appointed to assist Cardinal Josef Frings (1887–1978), Archbishop of Cologne (1942–69), then later appointed to assist the whole Council. Having witnessed the Council firsthand, Ratzinger recalled its ground-breaking reorientation of understanding the relationship between the Church, now approached as "a pilgrim on this earth" living in the "world of today," discussed in *Gaudium et Spes* and *Dignitatis Humanae*. In so doing, he identifies the legacy of the Council as something to build on, paraphrased as "a work in progress," or quoting thought from his 1966 lecture, "a new milestone on the road," thought he would revisit following his papal election on April 19, 2005 as Pope Benedict XVI offered his 2005 Christmas message to the assembled members of the Roman Curia. Distancing himself from the former mindset of a "refuge," conciliar humanism embodies the "scandal of the Cross" shared by all, an inclusive way of thinking which rejects any sense of the Church's former triumphalism in favour of an ecclesial identity which he characterized as "a scandal for men of all ages."

Taking up this inclusive thought several years later during a 1969 broadcast on German radio, Father Ratzinger claimed the Catholic Church would be a "moral beacon in the turbulent waters of its time." Amid an era "brimming with existential danger, political cynicism and moral waywardness, [which] hungered for an answer," he recalls the timely veracity of Saint Augustine's insightful Christian anthropology which inspired the Christ centred vision of our shared humanity found in conciliar humanism: "man is an abyss; what will rise out of these depths, no one can see in advance. And whoever believes that the Church is not only determined by the abyss that is man, but reaches down into the greater, infinite abyss that is God, will be the first to hesitate with his predictions, for this naïve desire to know for sure could only be the announcement of his own historical ineptitude."[4] Embedded within Conciliar wisdom, the Church of faith understood as a "communion of salvation" was now envisaged "as man's home, where he will find life and hope beyond death," portrayed by van der Weyden's *Descent from the Cross*.

The product of personal and thoughtful connections among the Council Fathers and their advisors during this "meeting of minds," conciliar humanism emerged as an original Christ centred integral philosophical understanding of our shared humanity, documented in *Gaudium et Spes* and *Dignitatis Humanae*, which literally "changed the face of Catholicism." An observation made by one of those persons who contributed to this process, then Cardinal Karol Wojytła, Archbishop of Kraków (1964–78) writing in *Sources of Renewal: The Implementation of the Second Vatican Council* (1979), wherein he outlines the ongoing process of thoughtful reception of this documented legacy from which we have much to learn, "still being received as it is tested in the lives of believers."[5] Universally recognized as having reshaped the way contemporary Catholics worship, pray, and think, little attention thus far has been given to the Council's original understanding of the human being who performs such activity, a major lacuna in the study of Conciliar thought which this book seeks to redress. This original awareness, found in the connection between philosophical ideas and pastoral concern, was shared by Council Fathers such as Montini, Suenens, and Wotjyła, which persisted even after death.

An original awareness which informed an unprecedented canonization ceremony on April 27, 2014, when Pope John Paul II together with Pope John XXIII, who inspired this awareness of our shared humanity, were proclaimed saints of the Catholic Church by the recently elected Pope Francis in the presence of his predecessor Pope Benedict XVI, a former

---

4. "When Father Joseph Ratzinger Predicted the Future of the Church," para. 2.
5. O'Collins, *Living Vatican II*, 171.

Council *peritus*. Contributing further to the significance of this extraordinary moment in Church history, it was announced Saint John Paul II's annual feast day would be celebrated on October 22 each year, rather than the usual custom of a person's date of death. A date on which we celebrate the anniversary of his papal inauguration, one he purposefully chose in recognition of the date when the Council officially opened.

"We believe in God; we believe in human persons. That is, we believe in both with one act of divine faith,"[6] a remarkable creedal formula offered by Ghislain Lafont and inspired by the original thought of the last ecumenical council to date, characterized by Pope Francis as a "Council of faith." Thinking outside the context of the Council's human agenda, these Christ centred words are unimaginable. Namely, their significance is found within the context of an extraordinary extended moment of *sapiential* consciousness, wherein we find the "birth of a new humanism." Concluding his Address to the final plenary session of the Council on December 7, 1965, Pope Paul VI provides an evocative summary of this distinctive way of thinking about our shared humanity, attentive to "the friendly voice of pastoral charity," found in his recognition of the "tears and sorrows on the face of Christ," portrayed in the religious art of the Flemish artist Rogier van der Weyden (1399–1464).

Reflecting on the Johannine exhortation recalling Christ's words, "He who sees me, sees also the Father," (John 14:9), the pope concludes: "our humanism becomes Christianity, our Christianity becomes centred on God; in such sort that we may say, to put it differently; a knowledge of man is a prerequisite for a knowledge of God." A way of thinking which recalls the *sapiential* consciousness of the fourth-century Augustine, Bishop of Hippo Regius as he introduces book one of his *Soliloquies*, a little devotional book "almost unknown."[7] Written in the form of an inner dialogue with himself leading to self-knowledge, found in his awareness of the presence of God directing his life, compiled soon after his religious conversion around 386 and subsequent Christian baptism with his son Adeodatus during the Easter vigil on April 24, 387 by St. Ambrose (c. 339–c. 397), bishop of Milan, another formative Christian thinker infused with *sapiential* consciousness.

"We believe in God; we believe in human persons." Lafont's remarkable creedal formula mirrors the original "profession" used by the

---

6. Orsy, "Divine Dignity," 347–48.
7. Augustine, *Soliloquies*, 3.

world's Catholic bishops assembled for the first ecumenical council held in the Bithynian city of Nicaea in 325 to profess their belief in the Triune God, "God, the Father Almighty," "one Lord Jesus Christ, consubstantial with the Father," and "the Holy Spirit," which settled the Christological issue of the divine nature of Christ, the Son of God and His relationship with the Father in what came to the known as Consubstantial or *Homoousian* Christology: "same in being, same in essence." An original theological approach which emerged in response to contemporary 'Arianism,' living in 'the world of today,' a way of thinking subsequently declared heretical by the Council, inspired by the thought of the Cyrenaic presbyter theologian Arius (250–336) who emphasized the unique status of God the Father, while subordinating that of the Son of God. Whereby the doctrinal teaching of the Greek speaking bishops assembled at Nicaea not only made theological claims concerning the nature of the Triune God as 'person,' but in so doing also spoke about themselves as human beings who make this profession of faith. Wherein they addressed their humanity as being God's people, members of a religious community united by a shared profession of faith, theological ideas taken up during the last ecumenical council through its concept of 'People of God,' 'a community of persons.'

Used as expressions of biblical truth for over nearly two millennia, creeds remind us of our human identity as being Christian, defined as "a fixed formula summarising the essential articles of their religion"[8] in the opinion of the Oxford theologian J. N. D. Kelly (1909–97) as he begins his authoritative *Early Christian Creeds* (1950). Expressed more succinctly by another Englishman N. T. Wright, one of the world's leading Bible scholars and the former Anglican bishop of Durham (2003–10), creeds are "portable narratives"[9] which tell the biblical story of creation of Adam's fall, and of Christ's salvific death and resurrection, literally from "creation to new creation," as portrayed in van der Weyden's religious art. Expressed in the words of a too little-known French Benedictine ecclesiologist, this creedal formula speaks to the synthetic way of thinking which emerged during the twentieth century, bringing together philosophical and theological ideas about our shared humanity which inform the tenets of conciliar humanism, namely the ideas of the "human person," "community of persons," and "human solidarity,"

8. Kelly, *Early Christian Creeds*, 1.
9. Wright, "Reading Paul," 64.

Author of *Imagining the Catholic Church: Structure Communion in the Spirit* (2000), Lafont was not only one of the few remaining octogenarians who witnessed the Council but also "one of its most insightful commentators," a highly original theologian whose thought continues to inspire. Commemorating the golden anniversary of the Council provided the opportunity for another octogenarian, the Hungarian born American Jesuit Ladislas Orsy to creatively engage ideas found in Lafont's *L'Église en travail de réforme* (2011) to introduce his own informative essay "The Divine Dignity of Human Persons in *Dignitatis Humanae*," by someone who also witnessed the Council as a *peritus* advising the Council father Francis Markall (1905–92), Archbishop of Salisbury (1956–76) in then Rhodesia. Characterized as someone "with the courage to remember it," the critical issue of reform within the contemporary Catholic Church has directed the theological thought of this noted French Benedictine monk from Sainte-Marie de la Pierre-qui-Vire Abbey in Burgundy. Writing in *L'Église en travail de réforme* he posed the rhetorical question, "Why has Christ not yet returned, why so long a wait for the end of time," to which he responds, "to give us time to believe in the human person." Namely, "Christ died because he 'believed' in the human person."[10]

Reading Lafont's provocative thought certainly captured my imaginative attention, approaching language which would have been unimaginable nor intelligible halfway through the last century, herein we find an opportunity to creatively explore the legacy of Conciliar thought as Ladislas Orsy sought to achieve. Obviously, the intent of the American Jesuit church historian David G. Schultenover who assembled a series of essays, entitled *50 Years On: Probing the Riches of Vatican II* (2015), whereby he sought to recall his own initial excitement when "Vatican II happened for me personally," namely, his reading the *Documents of Vatican II* (1966), the first English translation edited by Walter Abbott and Joseph Gallagher, which "fired his imagination." An experience I similarly found when reading Orsy's thoughtful engagement, one of the first as an English-speaking theologian to take up the innovative thought of Lafont, a truly remarkable essay which explored the conceptual significance of "the human person" found within Conciliar thought.

Employing the traditional Socratic approach, Orsy sought to further highlight the theological significance of the idea of "the human person," one which emerged from within a philosophical orientation, a

---

10. Orsy, "Divine Dignity," 347–48.

context rarely discussed. Drawing attention to the Council's original use of this expression found in these final two documents, the noted Jesuit canonist remains one of the few commentators to appreciate the broader significance of this concept, not only within *Dignitatis Humanae*, as "latent yet dominating throughout the document," but more significantly, as "the ultimate hermeneutical clue for the interpretation of the Council and for its implementation." A clue I have deliberately taken up in my philosophical reading of the Council's human agenda which informs the genesis of conciliar humanism. Namely, "the human person" represents an original product of the Council, the consequence of a unique confluence of twentieth-century European ideas, generated during a tumultuous era unparalleled in human history, in an era of unprecedented chaos wherein the very basis of understanding our humanity and its inherent personal dignity was being challenged.

A connection interestingly also made by Joseph Ratzinger within his discussion of the Augustinian distinction between *scientia-sapientia* in his seminal essay "the dignity of the human person," wherein he speaks of Christ as "the new Adam" who as the embodiment of "the actual accomplishment of human personal life" functions as the bridge between the theology of the incarnation and that of the cross.[11] Drawing attention to the Council's "discussion between Christian and unbeliever on the question who and what man really is," Ratzinger identifies a theology of the cross as an indispensable feature of a Christian anthropology, found in the New Adam whereby a "theology of the incarnation necessarily leads to a spirituality of the cross." Captured by van der Weyden's positioning of a human skull at the feet of St. John, pointing towards the figure of Christ, a portrayal of Incarnational soteriology.

Approached as an act of ecclesial service, this Christ centred integral philosophical understanding of our shared humanity found in conciliar humanism, a consequence of an infusion of *sapiential* consciousness, "changed the face of Catholicism" in the words of one of its primary proponents, the Archbishop of Kraków. Having witnessed first-hand the atrocious effects of the greatest genocide in recorded history during his days as a child living in this university city, the liquidation of over two thousand Jews in the Kraków ghetto between March 13–16, 1943. And their being relocated to the nearby Auschwitz-Birkenau (1940–45) concentration and extermination camp complex, a

---

11. Ratzinger, "Dignity of the Human Person," 132–33.

consequence of living under the Nazi regime. Furthermore, after 1945 then living under the restrictive and atheistic Stalinist regime imposed on post-war Catholic Poland, the emergent philosopher priest sought to better understand the nature of humanity, using reasonable thought writing as a man of faith. Initially addressed during a series of public lectures he gave in 1949 to Kraków's academic community, following his successful doctoral study in Rome's Pontifical University of Saint Thomas Aquinas (1577), known as the *Angelicum* between 1946–48, later published as *Considerations on the Essence of Man* (2016). Wherein he outlines "the first truth of Christian humanism" within a God-centred philosophical approach, found in "the internal life of God—that in which man by grace receives by filial *participation*" (emphasis added) though "an analysis of our human spiritual *experiences*" (emphasis added),[12] original ideas Wotyła had appropriated from Aquinas and Scheler respectively which were then ingeniously incorporated within conciliar humanism as a new way of thinking for a man of faith.

---

12. Wojtyła, *Considerations*, 197–99.

13

The Denial of God?

IN ITS ELEVENTH EDITION, *A World of Ideas* (2020) remains a popular and invaluable resource for students to engage "the big ideas that shaped society and are reshaping it today," written by Lee A. Jacobus, a retired academic from the University of Connecticut (1881). Such as found in *The Idea of Man* (2021), wherein the American author Mark Aman offers a highly original philosophical discussion of being human, approached scientifically from our innate verticality or "uprightness" found in the earliest form of the human species *homo erectus*. By means of this description Aman proposes a "new ontology," a new study of the nature of "being" human, commonly regarded as referring to existence or reality. A study similarly undertaken at the turn of the last century by the German Catholic philosopher Max Scheler in his small article "On the Idea of Man" (1914), his only philosophical publication which directly confronted the question of being human. In his later years, having repudiated his Catholic faith, he returned to address the metaphysical questions "what is man" and "what is man's place in nature" whereby he revealed the defining question of the twentieth century, "what is human."

Writing in "The Purpose of Philosophy" (1962), the Latvian born British philosopher, Sir Isaiah Berlin (1909–97), draws attention to understanding a person's "general conception of the world" or 'worldview,' through the critical scrutiny of our thought, wherein we discover the influence of our ideas, disclosed in the hidden categories and models, our prejudices used by humans to think; as he concludes: "to assist men to understand themselves and thus operate in the open, and not wildly, in the dark."[1] Writing later in *Power of Ideas* (2000) he recalls the thought of the German poet Heinrich Heine (1797–1856): "Never underestimate the power of ideas: philosophical concepts nurtured in the stillness of a professor's study could destroy a civilization." While this pithy warning was given to the "proud men of action" following the French Revolution (1789–99), a time of radical political and social upheaval, these words paraphrased by Berlin could well be applied to Ricoeur's infamous "school of suspicion," wherein we find the philosophical ingredients for the Godless materialist worldview in the thought of Nietzsche, Marx, and Freud.[2]

Returning to his original thought concerning our ideas. Writing in his introduction to "The Pursuit of the Ideal" (1988), the first essay published in *The Proper Study of Mankind* (1997), an anthology of his formative writings, Berlin identified two basic factors which have "shaped human history in the twentieth century" and which directly influenced the lives of "all mankind." Namely, the development of the natural sciences and technology, and the emergence of the "great ideological storms."[3] A twofold crisis set against the spectre of nihilistic and atheistic thought which emerged during the nineteenth century, especially through the influence of Friedrich Nietzsche and his dysfunctional humanism, circumstances which inform the genesis of conciliar humanism.

Described as "the most brilliant, most challenging and most demanding philosopher of the modern period,"[4] as "a scandal wrapped in layers of enigma,"[5] Nietzsche remains a formative influence in contemporary twenty-first-century thought who, like his Socratic hero, questioned the traditional norms and claims of Western certainty based on a madman running through the streets crying "God is dead. And we have killed him," "a monstrous event" which announced European atheistic nihilism, wherein everything is permitted, perhaps a foreshadowing of postmodernity. While "God is dead" remains one of the most famous sayings in Western philosophy, narrated in *The Gay Science* (1882) and *Thus Spoke Zarathustra* (1883–85), its actual meaning remains remarkably ambiguous, like its author. Obviously, this does not mean God is literally dead, that the Christian God who existed for all eternity has

1. Berlin, *Concepts and Categories*, 14.
2. Berlin, *Proper Study of Mankind*, 191–94.
3. Berlin, *Proper Study of Mankind*, 1.
4. R. J. Hollingdale, *Nietzsche Reader*, xviii.
5. Norris, *Deconstruction*, 56.

now suddenly died, has ceased to exist as with any other finite created being. But rather by means of the madman's claim, our human thought, our capacity to think about God, an Eternal Being omniscient, omnipotent, and all-loving, which has provided the foundations of Western thought has been discredited by this madman, whose existence can no longer be affirmed on rational grounds.

However, and herein lies the crux of Nietzsche's claim, namely, in the absence of the idea of God as the source of Truth, which has traditionally supported the claims of objective knowledge, there are no foundations to support any form of knowledge, what we claim to know; it now becomes a matter of perspective. Namely, the loss of objectivity has been replaced by a philosophy dependent on a human perspective, not the truth. Given the demise of the idea of God, and following the logic of Nietzsche's idiosyncratic thought, these "all too human" foundations ultimately foreshadow the "death of man," the inevitable consequence of Nietzsche's humanism as observed by Michel Foucault (1926–84), the French structuralist philosopher. As Nietzsche introduces *Ecce Homo* (1888), referring to the title of an earlier work, "*Human, All Too Human* [1878] is the memorial of a crisis," the nature of this crisis came in a moment of sudden insight, namely, Nietzsche's realization that with the renunciation of these hitherto recognized God centred foundations of Western thought and human culture, everything which he had revered, even reverence itself, nothing remained, the basis of Nietzsche's nihilism.

Set against the intellectual and spiritual malaise which characterized the twentieth century, what does our life mean when viewed as a whole? What is its purpose and what are the means to achieve this? Questions to which everyone seems to have an answer, such as "what is human" in response to "what am I," a perennial and quintessential question particularly asked by philosophers. During the eighteenth century they broadened their approach asking the related personal question "who am I" about the human 'subject,' studied by philosophers such as the Englishman John Locke (1632–1704) and the German Immanuel Kant (1724–1804). Once again, while a meaning is commonly assumed, presumably shared by all, there is nothing more prone to misunderstanding than a response to these questions. Such as whether there is a shared nature common to being human, and if so, what essential qualities define this nature? Are humans different from other animals or other forms of animate life in response to "what is man?" Considered by the formative figure of the Enlightenment, Immanuel Kant as "one of the most fundamental questions of philosophy." Persistent questions which Scheler sought to address throughout his unconventional and somewhat turbulent personal and academic life, as a figure of some ambiguity. For nearly thirty years, following his 1899 baptism as a Catholic in the parish church of St. Anton in Munich until his repudiation of Catholicism, as a Church way of thinking, detailed in the 1926 Preface to the third edition of his seminal *Formalism in Ethics and Non-Formal Ethics of Values* (1912), he wrote as an avowed Catholic, self-described as a "theist and realist." Wherein basic ideas from his phenomenological ethical personalism, and philosophical sociology found their way into conciliar humanism through the influence of his Polish critic Karol Wojtyła.

Recognized as *a questioning being*, Aristotle first identified the human context for asking these questions prompted by the human experience of "wonder" wherein we ask "why," an experience which generated the thought of future philosophers as he introduced his discussion of "first philosophy" with the claim "all men desire to know." Discussed in one of his most widely, though very difficult books to read, *Metaphysics* (384–322 BC), a later complex compilation of fourteen treatises wherein he discussed "what is being," a claim later paraphrased as "why is there something rather than nothing?" The foundation of Aristotelian realism which informed the thought of diverse philosophers over the course of history, such as the Italian Dominican scholastic Thomas Aquinas, the German polymath Gottfried Wilhelm Leibniz (1646–1716), the German Martin Heidegger (1889–1976), and the Austrian born British Ludwig Wittgenstein (1889–1951). However, thinking within the context of a unified philosophy, the original awareness of the "human" orientation of the person who posed this question receded into the background. Only to re-emerge during the early decades of the twentieth century within European thought, an era of "apparent contradiction" wherein the worst and best of humanity was exhibited, circumstances which inform the genesis of conciliar humanism.

Given the cumulative effects generated by the political, economic, and cultural turbulence and intellectual disenchantment following two world wars between 1914 and 1945, new diverse patterns of philosophical thinking about the truth of human existence, being human, our inherent personal identity and associated use of freedom and rights subsequently emerged. Of particular concern, these were found in diverse ways of thinking especially taken up by European philosophers, whether Christian, atheists, or secular humanists alike, who drew attention to understanding humanity within "the social, cultural and historical conditions of thought and existence," patterns of existential thought characterized as 'continental.' Initially a pejorative expression, understood as a "category of exclusion,"[6] this word was used by English speaking philosophers to identify European ways of thinking which differ from "analytic" or Anglo-American thought. Notwithstanding the absence of a precise definition, continental philosophy refers to these various and disparate philosophical ways of thinking, especially about humanity, found on mainland Europe, which evolved over the nineteenth and early twentieth centuries in response to the traditional classification of "being human" as it came under critical scrutiny, namely, as a member of species of primates known as *Homo sapiens*. An expression coined by Carl Linnaeus (1707–78), the Swedish botanist and taxonomist in *Systema Naturae* (1738) wherein he formalised the modern system of naming organisms.

Characterized scientifically by bipedalism, sexually dimorphic with the use of large complex brains, during these centuries being human was reduced to a one-dimensional biological material being among many, wherein we find the malaise which characterized twentieth-century thought. In so doing, European philosophers sought to overcome the disconnect between the use of traditional philosophy to argue for humanity as being essentially different from other forms of life, and the reduction of humanity to a biological condition one being among many, found in Marx's dialectical materialism, Nietzsche's atheistic nihilism or Comte's scientific positivism. Approached as a human activity which touches all levels of human experience, rational, emotional, communal, personal, and spiritual, twentieth-century European Catholic philosophers like Scheler and Maritain sought to rethink "what is human" through the reappropriation of classical themes found in traditional Western philosophy, such as "existence," "human nature," "person," "consciousness," and "dialogue." In so doing, the "nature" of being human was approached from a broader, philosophical perspective as in the past, set against the current scientific use of the idea of the human "condition," whereby being human was approached as one biological entity among many. Furthermore, the human condition was now approached through an imaginative use of various forms of literature, such as novels and poetry, to explore themes and practical issues commonly associated with the experience of being human, such as the exercise of freedom, individuality, authenticity, choice, dread,

---

6. West, *Introduction*, 3.

and despair which characterized human existence. In so doing, thinkers of an atheistic disposition, like Camus, sought to move beyond the perceived strictures of nineteenth-century abstract thought.

The re-emergence of attention given to understanding our humanity during the twentieth century was taken up by a variety of thinkers approached from these different perspectives. Approached from a Christian perspective, Martin Luther King Jr. (1929–68), the famous American Christian minister and leading activist for the black civil rights movement until his assassination, gave a sermon entitled "What is Man?" This was preached at the first National Conference on Christian Education of the United Church of Christ at Purdue University in 1958, and later published with another related sermon, "The Dimensions of a Complete Life" in *The Measure of a Man* (1959). Contrasting the current issues of totalitarian government and democracy, the Rev. Dr. King claims: "although there is widespread agreement on asking the question, there is fantastic disagreement in answering it." Approached from a Christian perspective, his response was based on the assertion that the human being was essentially "God's marvellous creation," understood as a spiritual being with "rational capacity," in possession of a unique capacity "for fellowship with God," what I describe as our human "capacity for transcendence."

This intellectual ethos which characterized the first half of the twentieth century was captured in literature by Aldous Huxley (1894–1963), the English writer and philosopher, in his *Brave New World* (1931), a thought-provoking *tour de force* account of the enormous pressures placed on contemporary humanity and especially on our social relationships projected within a prophetic fantasy living in a socialist utopian future. Wherein humans are reduced to the status of scientific animate beings, genetically engineered, and chemically anesthetized at the disposal of an omnipotent ruling order, the State: "a satirical prediction of a distant future which quickly became a reality." A way of thinking taken up in the twenty-first century known as "transhumanism," espoused by his older brother, the evolutionary biologist Sir Julian Huxley (1887–1975). This twentieth-century literary genre of political and social fiction was later practiced by George Orwell (1903–50), the pen name adopted by Huxley's fellow countryman, the novelist Eric Arthur Blair writing his exposition of humanity living in a totalitarian state through his signature books *Animal Farm* (1945) and *Nineteen Eighty-Four* (1949).

Writing *Nineteen Eighty-Four*, Orwell further explored the reductive consequences for understanding human life in a Godless totalitarian future with his original expression of an "unperson," a neologism applied to the fictional protagonist Winston Smith who literally lost his name. Portrayed as a diligent and talented "rank-and-file" worker, while remaining secretly resentful of increasing restrictions imposed upon him by Big Brother, the consequence of which meant the ultimate denial of human existence and personal identity, along with its accompanying rights and freedom, erased through the bureaucratic manipulation of the Party: "Your name was removed from the registers, every record of everything you had done was wiped out, your one-time existence was denied and then forgotten. You were abolished, annihilated; vapourised was the usual word." Commonly taken for granted, Orwell creatively draws attention to the significance of the idea of our personal identity and accompanying freedom and rights exercised as 'named' human beings, encapsulated in a person's name, a descriptor of all that is valuable in the life of an individual human being to the world at large.

Normally our ideas, such as belief in God or our understanding of the human person, constitute a framework of assumptions within the realm of consciousness, envisaged as a "world" or intellectual environment in which we can live and think, a perspective or outlook which we adopt, a worldview which informs our thought. Nowhere is this more applicable than understanding the broader philosophical background for the genesis of conciliar humanism, an original way of thinking about humanity which emerged during an extraordinary moment of Catholic thought, during the Second Vatican Council, and its watershed idea of the 'human person,' received as "the most important voice of our age" in the words of Archbishop Karol Wojtyła during his Vatican Radio talk "On the Dignity of the Human Person" on October 19, 1964.

While this idea is ubiquitous within contemporary Catholic discourse and synonymous with conciliar thought, "an element of the doctrine of the Council," this was not always the case. Unheard of within Catholic thought at the turn of the last century, apart from Scheler's ethical personalism and instances of papal teaching on social justice, especially that of Popes John XXIII and Paul VI. This idea was initially found in Pope Pius XII's (1939–58) discussion of "the dignity and rights of the human person" during his 1942 Christmas Radio Broadcast "The Rights of Man. The Feast of Christmas and Suffering Humanity." Wherein he denounced the implementation of the Nazi regime's "Final Solution to the Jewish Problem," the systematic murder of European Jews endorsed at the Wannsee Conference on January 20, 1942, a twentieth-century phenomenon of gross inhumanity, one of universal significance for which there is no name. Now, during the deliberations of the Council, especially over its seven public plenary sessions, the parameters of papal teaching on social justice were significantly broadened, directing attention to understanding the humanity of its recipient, the bearer of these rights and responsibilities, namely, the "human person," an idea which became the *leitmotiv* of conciliar humanism.

While the issue of humanity has been the subject of ongoing thoughtful scrutiny since the emergence of Ancient Greek philosophy, the issue of human "rights" re-emerged during the first half of the tumultuous twentieth century, set against the denial of these experienced in the two-fold human phenomena of racism and genocide, issues of social concern addressed by the popes of the twentieth century, "champions of humanity." Initially discussed by the English philosopher John Locke (1632–1704) in *Two Treatises of Government* (1689) wherein he laid the theoretical foundations for rights, based on "the law of nature and of Nature's God," which informed the claim that all humans are naturally free and equal, later considered "unalienable," as the basis of the American Declaration of Independence (1776) following the American Revolution (1765–83).

Best described as "omnipresent," the awareness of our inherent rights, based on our dignity and value as individual human beings is found in everyday speech, particularly embedded within contemporary political and legal discourse, as observed by Christopher McCrudden, the editor of *Understanding Human Dignity* (2013). The product of a "decidedly multidisciplinary group" of scholars assembled in 2012 under the auspices of the British Academy to discuss this issue,[7] it represents another instance of the resurgence of contemporary interest in our human dignity which brings together insights and ideas drawn from several academic disciplines and various professional specializations, apparent in *The Cambridge Handbook of Human Dignity: Interdisciplinary Perspectives* (2014).

An awareness which initially emerged within the conflictual situation of global violence during the first half of the twentieth century, "a century at war," a situation exacerbated by the presence on the European continent of the Godless totalitarian regimes of Spanish Fascism (1936–39), Italian Fascism (1922–43), German National Socialism

---

7. McCrudden, *Understanding Human Dignity*, 1.

(1933–45) or Soviet Marxist Communism (1922–91). Ideologically driven antithetical systems of political dictatorship, which sought to obliterate any sense of human dignity, the devaluation of being human in favour of the apparatus of an omnipresent State. While "genocide" was first recognized as a crime under international law by the UN in 1946, along with the issue of "crimes against humanity," both commonly used in contemporary discourse, this word was first used by the Polish lawyer of Jewish descent Raphäel Lemkin (1900–1959) in his book *Axis Rule in Occupied Europe* (1944), to designate mass atrocities relating to the Nazi policy of the systematic murder of European Jewish people, it has been more generally applied to the destruction of groups of people, such as the Armenian Genocide (1915–16) by Ottoman military personnel. However, the expression "crimes against humanity" has also been applied to the issue of slavery and the slave trade of late eighteenth and early nineteenth centuries, and to describe European colonialism in Africa and related the atrocities committed by King Leopold II (1835–1090) of Belgium in the Congo Free State. While it remains to be fully codified in a treaty of international law, this expression has been used to prosecute crimes committed in the former Yugoslavia and Rwanda in International Criminal Tribunals.

A remarkable historian of ideas, at the age of six Isaiah Berlin witnessed the political upheaval and social crisis occasioned by the Russian Revolution (1917–23), a series of two revolutions which ended when Vladimir Lenin's (1870–1924) Bolsheviks established the Soviet Union in 1923 under the leadership of the Georgian revolutionary Joseph Stalin (1878–1953). This ideologically driven conflict generated the rise of excessive nationalism, racism and religious bigotry which characterized the first half of the twentieth century. Found in the Godless world of Auguste Comte's scientific positivism and totalitarian regimes, those of the politically right, Spanish Nationalism (1939–75), Italian Fascism (1922–43) and German National Socialism (1933–45), and those of the politically left in Soviet Marxist Communism (1922–91) and the eastern European countries behind the Iron Curtain, ideologically driven antithetical systems of political dictatorship which sought the devaluation of being human, found in the annihilation of individual human dignity and rights in favour of the faceless bureaucratic apparatus of the State.

One of the Young or so-called 'Left Hegelians,' Marx was a member of a radical group of followers of the German philosopher Hegel, who attacked the philosophical basis of religion, such as the German theologian

David Strauss (1808–74) and the German philosopher Ludwig Feuerbach (1804–72). Having studied philosophy at the universities of Bonn (1818) and Berlin (1818), Karl Marx became a political activist, unwelcome in his country of origin he became "stateless" following his exile from Berlin in 1848. Whereupon he relocated to London for the remainder of his tortured life which occasioned his critical theories about society, economics and politics, the foundations of Marxism. Thinking within the confines of the British Museum's "Reading Room," he researched and wrote his monumental and revolutionary *Das Kapital* (1867–94). In asserting the centrality of work in human life, Marx not only challenged the traditional self-understanding of human existence as *Homo sapiens*, but also offered the theoretical means whereby the political landscape of Europe was altered, found in his understanding of the social status of class, modelled on Hegel's innovative use of "dialectic," an atheistic landscape which was eventually transformed by the arrival of another "man of ideas," a Catholic bishop from communist Kraków in Poland.

Set against this competitive atheistic ideological background, found in the promotion of scientific positivism and the political division between right and left which initiated unparalleled global and indiscriminate violence, conciliar humanism emerged as a faith-filled philosophical and thoughtful antidote, the consequence of thinking within the tradition of lived Catholic Christianity, one with a long and illustrious history.

Scarcely one year after his death, Augustine was recognized by Saint Pope Celestine (422–432) as "one of the best teachers of the Church," centuries later he would be universally recognized as "the common father of Christian Europe" by Pope John Paul II on the sixteenth centenary of Augustine's conversion in 386. There is still much to learn from the *sapiential* thought of this first millennial Christian genius, as the British academic and Anglican priest Henry Chadwick (1920–2008) observes: "By his writing, the surviving bulk of which exceeds that of any other ancient author, he came to exercise pervasive influence not only on contemporaries but also on the West since his time,"[8] one recognized by the canons of the second diocesan synod held in 529 at Orange in southern France, convened to condemn semi-Pelagianism. By means of this local assembly, the Christian theology of Augustine came to exercise preeminence within the subsequent medieval mindset and especially that

---

8. Chadwick, *Augustine*, 1.

of Thomas Aquinas. Following the modern focus on human subjectivity found in the "turn to consciousness" initiated by Descartes' well-known claim *cogito ergo sum*, the American Augustinian theologian Michael J. Scanlon (1937–2018) directed attention to the thought of Augustine, who may be recognized as "the first modern man" with his own "turn to interiority."[9] Interestingly, Scanlon also observed the influence of the "effective history of the Augustinian Pascal" when reading *Gaudium et Spes*, a Conciliar document wherein we find definite indications of the phenomenological ethical personalism of Scheler's "philosophy of love," inspired by this particular history.

As a human phenomenon, love is prototypically ambiguous; nevertheless, love informs the very fabric of our human lives as individual and social beings,[10] and lies at the heart of the Christian life. Characterized by the American psychologist Bernard Murstein (1929–2020) as "an Austro-Hungarian Empire uniting all sorts of feelings, behaviors and attitudes, sometimes having little in common."[11] Narrated in sacred scripture as the principle of God's saving action and the believer's response lived in community, a love story wherein humanity is saved. Prior to our being an *ens cogitans* or an *ens volens*, according to Max Scheler writing in his essay "Ordo Amoris" (1914–15), the human is a loving being, an *ens amans*.[12] Considered the *leitmotiv* of his thought, Scheler indicates the direction of his nascent philosophy of love, the driving force behind his critical exchange with Nietzsche with his claim: "*Our heart is primarily destined to love*, not to hate," wherein Scheler reveals the influence of Augustine's "philosophy of the heart." In the opinion of Margaret R. Miles, Harvard Professor of Historical Theology, "Augustine was the first Christian author to begin his thinking and writing with an analysis of human experience,"[13] namely, from the experience of our human restlessness.

A way of thinking later taken up by the French philosopher Blaise Pascal with his foundational insight, his recognition of an *ordre du coeur*, "the heart has its own reasons," devised to counter the prevalent rationalism of Cartesian thought. A way of thinking which informs the religious philosophical background of Scheler's critical engagement with Friedrich Nietzsche's subversive assertion in *Assorted Opinions and Maxims* (1879):

9. Scanlon, "Modern Theology," 825–26.
10. Carroll, "Deceptive Ambiguity,"156–208.
11. Murstein, "Taxonomy of Love," 33.
12. Scheler, *Selected Philosophical Essays*, 110–11.
13. Miles, "Body and Human Values in Augustine of Hippo," 37.

"'*Love*'—The subtlest artifice which Christianity has over the other religions is a word: it spoke of *love*."[14] As Scheler claimed in his essay "Love and Knowledge" (1915): "Augustine expressly made love the *original* power of movement of the divine as well as the human spirit."[15] Expressed in the words of the Prologue to the *Catechism of the Catholic Church*(1994): "God draws close to man. He calls man to seek him, know him, to love him with all his strength. He calls together all men, scattered and divided by sin, into the unity of his family, the Church."

However, philosophically speaking, it is difficult to understand a "new commandment" to love which moves simultaneously in several directions towards God, neighbor, and one's enemies, and by implication oneself, not to mention the difficulty in commanding love in the first place. The more theologically nuanced Johannine claim "God *is* love" only exacerbated this situation, with its distinctive emphasis on 'action' rather than 'being' an entity, employing a verb rather than a noun, in which being is understood as lovingly and purposefully created *ex nihilo* by a loving God who takes the initiative, loving us first and from within this relationship, the one who loves knows God, a spiritual journey narrated by the "greatest Christian thinker" in his famous *Confessions*. The syncretism which informs early Christian thought compounds this scriptural indistinctiveness with the emergence of two competing ideas of love, the Platonic *eros* and the Johannine *agape*. As discussed by the British writer and Oxford lay theologian C. S. Lewis (1898–1963) in his publications *The Allegory of Love: A Study in Medieval Tradition* (1936) and *The Four Loves* (1960), based on a 1958 series of radio talks on the BBC. Beginning with the Johannine claim "God is love," wherein Lewis speaks of "gift-love," epitomized by God's unconditional love for humanity, he then approached the nature of love from Christian and Greek philosophical perspectives, moving from passionate love *eros*, affection or friendship, to "brotherly love" *philia*, and finally to the unique form of Christian love found in charity *agape*.

Herein we find the distinctive movement towards the personal which came to characterize Christian thought, facilitated by the appropriation of terms commonly used at the time, drawn from "two very different realms: that of common sense and that of Christian theology" as observed by the Swiss theologian Hans Urs von Balthasar (1905–88),[16] such as the use of

14. Nietzsche, *Nietzsche Reader*, 172.
15. Scheler, "Love and Knowledge," 149.
16. Balthasar, "On the Concept of Person," 18.

the common expression 'person,' Greek *prosopon* or Latin *persona*, meaning mask, face or role. This expression formed the basis for the elaboration of the Christian doctrine of the Trinity as a relationship between three loving Divine Persons, formalized during the first ecumenical councils of Nicaea (325) and Chalcedon (451), which addressed the theological question concerning the meaning of God, *quid sit Deus?*

14

Human Crisis?

ON MARCH 28, 2016 the American actor Viggo Mortensen delivered a reading of "The Human Crisis" at Columbia University (1754) in the city of New York, a paper which had been written seventy years earlier by the Algerian born French philosopher and author Albert Camus (1913–60). Characterized the "Don Draper of existentialism" by Adam Gopnik, staff writer for *The New Yorker*, also a former member of the French Resistance and political activist for the Left, though he was especially critical of Stalin's totalitarianism. In 1946 Camus was invited to the United States where he read this paper which explores various themes associated with 'existentialism,' an intriguing twentieth-century post Second World War European way of thinking about human existence, a loose expression with many variants, foreshadowed in the thought of the nineteenth-century Danish philosopher Søren Kierkegaard (1813–55). The epitome of an "existentially anguished philosopher" who discussed ethical issues such as individuality, freedom, choice, dread, and despair, in order to better understand human existence and the meaning and purpose of humanity.

Subject matter now approached by this French nihilist and self-characterized "absurdist," whereby Camus drew attention to irrational and passionate dimensions found in understanding "post war" human existence, discussed by William Barrett (1913–92), the American philosopher from New York in *Irrational Man: A Study in Existential Philosophy* (1958). Recounting the reason why he told four short stories in this paper, Camus claimed it was not to answer the question "is there a human crisis" but to emphatically assert "there is a human crisis," namely, living in a world where "the death or torture of a human being" could be dispassionately approached with "feelings of indifference, friendly concern, scientific interest, or simple passivity." Having read this paper seventy years later, the American actor felt little had changed and so "the 'human crisis' drags on."

From a cursory assessment, the first half of the twentieth century represents a remarkable enigma in human history, an era of apparent contradiction which witnessed the best and worst in the story of humanity, coming to the brink of destruction at our own hands at the height of the Cuban Nuclear Missile crisis, between October 16–28, 1960, during the Cold War (1947–91) between the Soviet Union and Unites States of America. Understood as "the worst of all centuries, with more of war, more of 'man's inhumanity to man,' more conflict and trouble than of any other century in the history of the world," few would disagree with this summation offered by Gordon B. Hinckley (1910–2008),[1] the American author and religious leader of the Church of the Latter-Day Saints (1995–2008), taken from *Ensign*, its monthly magazine. Truly "a man of the last century," this American religious figure ingeniously incorporates the well-known phrase from the popular Scottish poet Robert Burns' (1759–96): "Man was made to mourn: A Dirge," (1784) as a realistic dissection of the enigma of humanity encountered during the twentieth century, designated as "a time to mourn."

Circumstances which prompted a radical rethinking and timely reassertion of what it was to be human? Found in two seminal documents of the twentieth century, namely, the Universal Declaration of Human Rights, adopted by the United Nations General Assembly on December 10, 1948 in Paris, the first global expression of the rights to which all human beings are inherently entitled as simply human, and the Catholic Church's response to 'the world of today,' found in an original way of thinking characterized as conciliar humanism, explored in *Gaudium et Spes* and *Dignitatis Humanae* when read together. Documents unanimously approved by over two thousand and three hundred assembled Council Fathers and officially promulgated by Pope Paul VI on the last day of Council proceedings December 7, 1965, wherein we find the Council's "belief in humanity." Namely, its Christ centred integral philosophical understanding of our shared humanity within a network of original ideas. Found in the 'human person' who possesses these rights

---

1. Hinckley, *Teachings*, 47.

equally shared with other human beings within a 'community of persons,' wherein we find our God given meaningfulness, inherent dignity, and value of our shared humanity, expressed in the idea of "human solidarity" as being directed to God. The seismic effect of this thoughtful legacy contained in these documents persists to this day.

Set against this conflictual sociopolitical background of the twentieth century, much can be learnt from the genesis of the seminal Universal Declaration "on human rights," a pattern to approach the untold story of conciliar humanism. Understood as a unique international charter, the Declaration emerged after the Second World War (1939–45), following the establishment of the United Nations in 1945. A consequence of the devastation wrecked amid global conflict, this international organization was tasked to maintain worldwide peace and security, based on the recognition of our inherent "rights" equally shared as human beings. Proclaimed by the United Nations General Assembly in Paris in 1948, the Universal Declaration of Human Rights was a thoughtful and critical response to the consequential circumstances which challenged our preconceptions about humanity arising from the shattering experience of the Second World War (1939–45).

Received as "a warning to humanity" in the words of the French Jurist René Cassin (1887–1976), seconded to the UN Commission on Human Rights in 1946, he was one of the principal architects of a remarkable document for which he would receive the Nobel Peace Prize in 1968. Recognized as the UN Declaration "on human rights" (1948) "at the end of one hundred sessions of elevated, often impassioned discussion, [the Declaration] was adopted in the form of 30 articles on December 10, 1948," it was later used as the basis of the UN's "International Covenant on Civil and Political Rights" (1966): "these [human] rights derive from the inherent dignity of the human person." However, as already mentioned, in preparation for this Declaration, aware of the wide range of opinions, especially during the 1930s and 1940s, concerning "what is human," a preliminary symposium was convened to discuss the philosophical foundations which underpin the bearer of human rights. Held during the first session of UNESCO's General Conference in Mexico during November 1947, wherein our French lawyer Cassin would join the ranks of philosophers, diplomats, and critical thinkers from around the world invited to attend and contribute their thought. Among those who had much to contribute were notable figures, such as the English philosopher writer Aldous Huxley (1894–1963), author of *Brave New World* (1932) and *The Perennial*

Philosophy (1945), along with the Italian idealist and humanist Benedetto Croce (1866–1952), the last Neapolitan philosopher since Aquinas, author of the *Manifesto of the Anti-Fascist Intellectuals* (1925) issued following the vote of no confidence on October 31, 1922 which facilitated the Fascist government of Benito Mussolini (1883–1945), the foremost Italian philosopher of the first half of the twentieth century, and finally, the prominent French Catholic philosopher Jacques Maritain.

Living in a "world of ideas," the twentieth century remains an enigma, characterized by a proclivity for 'ideology,' a systematic organization of ideas and issues relating to our economic and political life, wherein we find the common use of the somewhat pesky suffix "ism." Notably found in its distinctive philosophical orientation to organize our patterns of thought as a means to theorize from an historical perspective. Employing arbitrary though useful expressions, such as rationalism, materialism, atheism, scientific positivism, communism, individualism, humanism, existentialism and personalism, wherein we find a convergence of ways of thinking directed towards understanding humanity during the twentieth century. Furthermore, the contemporary use of expressions "postmodernism," "modernism," and "premodernism," which have been "bandied about freely in academia and in the media,"[2] add a further level of complication understanding the association between our ideas and these various 'isms.' Moving into the digital age of the twenty-first century, the old isms which characterize twentieth-century thought, such as nationalism, liberalism, socialism, and individualism, did not disappear but have been reconceptualized within another sociopolitical format, such as militant religious fundamentalism, or genderism, which questions the traditional classification of gender into two distinct forms, masculine and feminine, and the promotion of eco-terrorism, the use of civil disobedience, sabotage and other forms of disruptive violence to effect environmental policy change, the consequence of an apparent process of readaptation, which demonstrate the resilience of an idea.

Such as the idea that anything created also has an end. Considered axiomatic in traditional Western thought from Aristotle onward, this way of thinking was currently characterized as 'endism.' This view was recently challenged by the American political scientist Samuel P. Huntington (1927–2008) in his essay "No exit: The Errors of Endism" (1989), written for *The National Interest* in response to the thought of

---

2. Connelly, "Modernity," para. 1.

his colleague the Japanese born American political scientist Francis Fukuyama's seminal 1989 essay "The End of History?" This was later published as *The End of History and the Last Man* (1992), which reflected a way of thinking set against the combative ideological clash between the Communist socialist east and Democratic capitalist west, which informed the socioeconomic mindset of the twentieth century. A clash which informed Fukuyama's idea of an "end point" to humanity's ideological struggle which only initiated further ideological threats, again indicative of the ongoing power of "ideas."

First recognized by the Ancient Greek use of 'dialectic,' this way of thinking later formed the foundation of the German philosopher Georg Wilhelm Hegel's (1770–1831) Absolute Idealism. Approached in linear terms as a dialectical process, moving from thesis, antithesis and finally a synthesis, a sequence of thought which then constitutes another higher thesis, all of which informs the continual movement of our ideas without resolution, *ad infinitum*, an absolute movement without an end. Distancing himself from Hegel's adaptation of Aristotelian thought which informs modern thinking, the Algerian born French iconoclastic philosopher of "deconstruction," Jacques Derrida (1930–2004) envisaged the unanticipated "burst of laughter" occasioned by the use of parody, the eventual recognition that something is different through imitative satire, serves to disrupt Hegel's endless rational process in a moment of unanticipated laughter, namely, only humans can laugh, but we can also think doing philosophy.

While the cultural phenomenon known as *Belle Époque* mirrored the heightened expectations which ushered in the last hundred years of the second millennium as a "golden age" of global peace and economic prosperity following the Franco-Prussian War (1870–71), which brought on the indefinite postponement of the First Vatican Council which began on December 8, 1869. However, these soon dissipated amidst the dehumanizing horrors and cultural devastation associated with the Great War (1914–18); regrettably, its characterisation by the prolific English writer H. G. Wells (1866–1946) as "the war that will end war" was not the case. In the meantime, the necessary post-war recovery generated a period of sustained economic prosperity with a distinctive cultural edge among industrialized countries in the Western world, the so-called "Roaring Twenties." Once again, these favorable expectations, wherein everything seemed to be feasible using modern science and industrial technology were confounded following the dramatic stock market crash on Wall Street in October 1929, which prompted various economic imbalances and structural financial irregularities around the world, and in turn initiated the Great Depression, an economic crisis of global proportions over the next ten years.

Approaching the apparent liquidation of our former ideas about humanity, Catholic philosophers like Scheler and Maritain, addressed the pressing issues concerning how we exist as human beings and more significantly as persons living amid social revolution, global armed conflict, and economic crisis. In so doing, they were not alone in responding to these critical times, whereby they learned to cooperate with other European philosophers who might not necessarily share their religious values, in the pursuit of a better understanding of our humanity, the meaning of human identity and existence living with other human beings. This remarkable phenomenon of collaborative thought not only set the agenda for the 1948 Universal Declaration on Human Rights, but also identified the critical, at times combative and collaborative pattern of thought undertaken during the Council's ecclesial "meeting of minds" wherein we find the genesis for conciliar humanism: following its human agenda and distinctive philosophical pastoral orientation.

While any designated period of human history stands for much, there is always an underlying "spirit of the times," found in the word "crisis" used to characterize the twentieth century or "revolution" for the previous century, wherein we find the ingredients for the former. Whether the political revolutions of 1848 throughout Europe, the industrial revolution which began in Great Britain or the Viennese revolution in understanding the mind, the nineteenth and early twentieth century witnessed a critical breakdown of long held certainties about being human accompanied by rapid and innovative expansion in other fields of human endeavour, such as the birth of science as a profession when in 1834 the Cambridge University historian and philosopher of science William Whewell (1794–1866) coined the term "scientist." Perhaps this change in mindset was captured by the English naturalist Charles Darwin (1809–82) in his ground-breaking *On the Origin of Species* (1859), a milestone in both science and philosophy, an attitude of mind found in the expression "hermeneutics of suspicion." Whether Nietzsche, Marx or Freud, as original thinkers who despite their obvious differences of intellectual approach were equally committed to unmasking "the lies and illusions of consciousness," a studied awareness which characterized twentieth-century thought.

As such, the late nineteenth and early twentieth centuries represent an unprecedented era dedicated to the study of humanity, which marks a movement away from the natural sciences, toward the emergence of the so-called "human sciences," such as anthropology, psychology, and sociology, which followed the same scientific methodology and generated the opportunity for what came to be known as 'secular' humanism. However, there was an accompanying downside associated with this thoughtful movement, namely, a level of disenchantment which brought on the "crisis of science." While these human sciences offered a "wealth of facts" concerning being human and human existence approached scientifically, there was a corresponding complication associated with this massive explosion of knowledge about humanity, which generated an array of disconnected and fragmented scientific data, namely, the absence of any conceptual unity underpinning this data.

15

Thinking without Foundations

THE ABSENCE OF ANY theoretical foundations, considered necessary to support the study of natural science, was critically observed by two students preparing for the *licence en sciences* at the University of Paris (1150), known as the Sorbonne, namely Jacques Maritain and his Russian born girlfriend Räissa Oumansov (1883–1960), an awareness also shared by Max Scheler, another young student from Germany as he began his study of natural science at the Ludwig Maximilian University of Munich (1472). Unlike previous generations wherein this sense of connection was provided within the context of an all-encompassing religious and philosophical worldview, now these students of natural science discovered they were thinking within an ethos of 'scientific positivism,' one which not only lacked such foundations but was incapable of providing them—an intellectual environment characterized by Pope John Paul II as "the relativism of the scientists and the scepticism of the philosophers" (*Fides et Ratio*, para. 81).

Confronting what the pope would later characterize as generating "the culture of death," one which informed the oppressive materialism prevalent at the Sorbonne, these two young French university students of natural science, "two lost souls" without any religious faith considered taking their own lives in 1901 as the only alternative to thinking without foundations.[1] Fortunately, they met the noted French essayist Charles Péguy (1873–1914) who directed them literally across the road to the *Collège de France* (1530) to hear the lectures of the French philosopher

---

1. McInerny, *Very Rich Hours of Jacques Maritain*, 15.

Henri Bergson (1859–1941), famous for writing *Creative Evolution* (1907) which offered a critical response to Darwin's "mechanism of evolution." Several years later these students married on November 26, 1904, and with Jacques' successful completion of his *agrégation en philosophie* in 1905, they were both baptized Catholic along with Räissa's sister Vera a year later on June 11, 1906 in the church of Saint-Jean-l'Evangeliste in the Parisian precinct of Montmartre, with the French novelist Léon Bloy (1846–1917) as their godfather. Through the spiritual guidance of the Dominican Père Clérissac, they finally found the certainties and intellectual foundations they were looking for around 1909 when they followed his advice and read Aquinas' seminal *Summa Theologica*.

Thinking without foundations and within Comte's pervasive Godless milieu of positive science, many scientists, emerging sociologists, and psychologists, and of course philosophers challenged the idea that human nature was somehow unique, that the human being was essentially different from other species of animate being and that *Homo sapiens* was just one animal species among many. In other words, that humans are only quantitatively different, possessing a higher degree of intelligence, more organic complexity and greater sophistication in their natural drives, energies, and capacities, found in the processes of natural selection and adaptation. Approached from a philosophical perspective, as a theist and realist, Scheler challenged this broad naturalistic approach which reduced being human to a form of one-dimensional biological material being no different from other forms of animate life, in favour of the idea of the human being as a "person." Envisaged as a multidimensional being Scheler initiated a philosophical conversation with the insights of the related natural, human, and social sciences, which informed the foundation of what he called 'philosophical anthropology.'

The malaise found in the modern scientific reduction of the unique status of being human to a single biological being one among many, which prompted the "human crisis," is best captured by two iconic paintings of the early twentieth century: *The Scream* [of Nature] (1893, 1910) by the Norwegian painter, atheistic nihilist Edvard Munch (1863–1944), and *Guernica* (1937) by the Spanish painter Pablo Picasso (1881–1973), an avowed atheist and anarchist. The agonized resemblance of humanity portrayed by Eduard Munch's *The Scream*, internally screaming, yet strangely familiar bearing human features, wherein no-one seems to be listening, spoke to the frustrating spirit of his time. Wherein the traditional religious and philosophical understanding of humanity as *Homo sapiens*, as being rational and capable of free action, was reduced by scientific scrutiny to an undifferentiated being among many.

Alternatively, this scientific understanding of humanity resembles a cubist painting, fragmented, distorted, and confused. Found in the early twentieth-century avant-garde art movement, pioneered by the Spanish painter Pablo Picasso (1881–1973) and the French painter Georges Braque (1882–1963), wherein the human subject is approached from a multitude of viewpoints. Such as Picasso's famous oil painting *Guernica* (1937), which portrays the April 26, 1937 bombing of Guernica, a Basque town in northern Spain during the Spanish Civil War (1936–39), bombed by forces from Nazi Germany (1933–45) and Fascist Italy (1922–43) at the request of General Francisco Franco (1892–1975), leader of the Spanish Nationalists (1936–75). This powerful anti-war painting portrays the indiscriminate suffering of dismembered humans and animals wrought by violence and chaos, humanity as being indeterminate and fragmented. Each painting in their own distinctive and original artistic manner seeks to capture the human crisis living in the intellectual and spiritual malaise which characterized the first decades of the twentieth century, the philosophical and cultural backdrop for the genesis of conciliar humanism.

Attempting "the study of the variety of ideas about the views of life," based on the Socratic "question and answer" approach, this noted historian of ideas identified two basic factors or what he calls "phenomena," which have "shaped human history in the twentieth century," namely, the development of the natural sciences and technology, which the German born American historian Peter Gay (1923–2015) characterized as the "threat of the machine," the scientific mechanized vision of being human, and the "great ideological storms," a consequence of Gay's "disappearance of God" factor, which emerged during the Russian Revolution (1917–23) and its aftermath, namely the Godless totalitarian regimes which characterized both competing political factions of Right and Left and associated forms of nationalism, racism and religious bigotry, which directly influenced "all mankind" during the twentieth century. Observations Berlin developed during his public address on February 15, 1988 in Turin as the recipient of the inaugural *Agnelli International Prize* "for the ethical dimension in advanced Western societies," known as "the lawyer," the senator for life Giovanni Agnelli (1921–2003) was a prominent Italian industrialist and head of Fiat (1899), an Italian automobile manufacturer.

By means of his comparison Berlin not only highlights the influence of a comprehensive "worldview" or network of ideas and beliefs, within which we perceive and interpret ourselves as human beings, our place within the natural and material world and our social interaction with those living around us, but also the presence of a fundamental dichotomy between two opposing and mutually exclusive philosophical worldviews, namely, the affirmation of the idea of God's existence found in 'theism,' and the alternative found in the denial of the idea of God in 'atheism,' equally influential worldviews which came to characterize late nineteenth and twentieth-century European thought. While theism was pervasive over the course of Western thought, the emergence of atheism in its modern form, as a structured thoughtful and reasoned denial of the idea of the existence of the Christian God is attributed to the critical thought of the German philosopher Ludwig Feuerbach (1804–72) in his *The Essence of Christianity* (1841). Wherein he rejected Hegel's absolute idealism which had found a place for Christian religion within the rationalism of modern philosophy. Having dismissed the latter, Feuerbach proposed an alternative humanistic and scientific "philosophy of the future," wherein religion was reduced to the status of a "dream of the human mind," a distorted projection of our emotional needs as a projection of oneself: "Christian religion is the relation of man to himself, or more correctly, to his own nature (i.e., his subjective nature)."[2]

Furthermore, within his theological writing, Feuerbach was the first to recognize the social dimension found in human consciousness, later understood as being 'intersubjective': "*the mystery of the Trinity is the mystery of participated, social life—the mystery of I and Thou.*"[3] Feuerbach's essential insightfulness, employing the 'I and Thou' relation, was later used as the foundation for the dialogical and relational thought of the Jewish philosopher Martin Buber (1878–1965) and the French Catholic philosopher Gabriel Marcel (1889–1973). This intersubjective orientation was also extensively employed within Scheler's phenomenological ethical personalism to understand the "sphere of being together," found in human consciousness which he characterized as 'I and thou' writing in *The Nature of Sympathy* (1912) and later employed within his phenomenology of religious experience outlined in *On the Eternal in Man* (1921), works which predate Buber's classic study *I and Thou* (1922). Later, Marx would reject Feuerbach's reduction of religion to "the essence of man" in so far as the latter failed to recognize this projection

---

2. Feuerbach, *Essence of Christianity*. 14.
3. Feuerbach, *Essence of Christianity*, Appendix #8, 293.

as another instance of "abstraction," whereas Marx reduced our humanity to an "ensemble of social relations" characterized as 'class,' writing in *Theses on Feuerbach* (1845), wherein he concluded "philosophers have hitherto only *interpreted* the world in various ways, the point is to *change it*" (no. 11): a pamphlet edited by his friend Friedrich Engels (1820–95), the German political and revolutionary socialist who co-authored *The Communist Manifesto* (1848) with Marx.

With the publication of *Cartesian Meditations* (1931), Husserl was the first among his contemporaries to engage the seminal thought of the so-called "founder of modern philosophy," the French philosopher René Descartes' (1596–1650) *Meditations on First Philosophy* (1641), based on a series of lectures he gave in Paris in 1929, wherein Husserl took up the rarely discussed issue of "intersubjectivity," one initially raised within his psychological discussion undertaken in *Logical Investigations*. Namely, how to understand the mechanism of our human social interaction, our awareness of relationships we share with each other. Approached from the perspective of an individual ego, as 'a self' engaging with or relating to other human beings similarly understood as individual selves. Namely, how to account for this human social phenomenon, why, and under what circumstances, does the individual human being approach "another" human being? Writing in his final unpublished *The Crisis of European Sciences and Transcendental Phenomenology* (1939) Husserl seemed to distance himself from his previous idealism. As with his earlier *Meditations*, a "notoriously difficult work" to understand, Husserl's *Crisis*, especially its first part "the crisis of the sciences as expression of the radical life-crisis of European humanity," confronts the contemporary problems of human finitude, history, and culture living in post-war Europe, wherein he develops his original concept of a "life-world," a concept employed by the American private research scholar priest John F. Kobler in his highly original book *Vatican II and Phenomenology: Reflections on the Life-World of the Church* (1985).

The Lithuanian Jewish born French philosopher Emmanuel Levinas (1906–95) will develop Husserl's original thought within an ethical orientation as one of the first French intellectuals during the early 1930s to appreciate the philosophical connection between the existential thought of Heidegger and the phenomenology of Husserl, translating the latter's *Cartesian Meditations* into French. While a prisoner of war, a status which protected Levinas from the horrific life as a Jew confined in a concentration camp, he continued his philosophical activity writing drafts of *De l'Existence à l'Existant* (1947) and *Le Temps et 'Autre* (1948), which form the background to his book *Totalité et Infini: essai sur l'extériorité* (1961) for which he is primarily known. As a Jewish religious philosopher Levinas argues for the moral 'authority' given to the "face of the Other," ethical overtones of an Absolute which he finds within a human context rather than with God, as discussed in Buber's *I and Thou* (1923). Levinas' appreciation of the human encounter with another human being, which forms the foundation of his ethics of Otherness, was later developed writing *Humanisme de l'autre homme* (1972). Wherein he draws these ideas together by means of his claim that our humanity can only be understood through the recognition of the "humanity of others." An awareness prompted by the long history of dehumanization "which reached its apotheosis in Hitler and Nazism," wherein "all respect for the 'human mystery' is thereafter denounced as ignorance and oppression."[4]

Furthermore, embedded within this twentieth-century return to Socratic practice toward understanding our shared humanity in the context of consciousness, the idea 'dialogue' was taken up by European philosophers to better understand the philosophical issue of "intersubjectivity," notably by the Jewish born Viennese religious existentialist Martin Buber (1878–1965), the foundation of his "philosophy of dialogue." Found in his seminal publication *I and Thou*, an expression originally employed by the German philosopher and anthropologist Ludwig Feuerbach (1804–72), writing against the practice of established religion in *The Essence of Christianity* (1846), whereby Feuerbach laid the foundations for atheistic humanism in the "religion of humanity." A philosophical colleague and friend of Buber, Max Scheler will connect these ideas relating to the issue of "intersubjectivity" in his first book, *The Nature of Sympathy* (1913), wherein he used phenomenology to understand our value oriented emotional and religious life as a human person lived in relationships with other finite persons, 'a communal person' and with he calls the "Absolute Person." Whereby he explores the complexity which characterizes humanity within an original multidimensional understanding of human nature, detailed in his early essay "On the Idea of Man" (1914): "Man is a thing so broad, variegated and diverse that all definitions turn out a little too concise. He has too many ends!"[5] Scheler's original phenomenology of sympathy and intersubjectivity was later critically addressed by the

---

4. Levinas, *Humanism of the Other*, 58.
5. Scheler, "On the Idea of Man," 185.

Silesian born German philosopher Edith Stein (1891–1942), writing her doctorate in philosophy *On the Problem of Empathy as It Developed Historically and Considered Phenomenologically* (1916) under the supervision of Husserl at the University of Freiburg, whereupon she became his first personal assistant, a remarkable achievement for a woman within the male dominated ethos of German academic life.

Living in a world unlike those before, during a time of global upheaval, of unprecedented social and political confusion which shattered every humanist illusion in the "modern world," the last hundred years of the second millennium represent an "era of apparent contradiction." An unparalleled period in history wherein "man is more of a problem to himself at the present time than ever before in all recorded history"[6] in the words of Max Scheler, writing in *Man's Place in Nature* (1928). Wherein the philosophical response to the question "what is man," which characterized "the signs of the times," informs the general background for two seminal documents of the Catholic Church, *Gaudium et Spes* and *Dignitatis Humanae*.

Interestingly, in the same year Pope John announced his intention to convene an ecumenical council which would address these contemporary concerns and from which these documents were generated, Hannah Arendt (1906–75), the Jewish German born American political philosopher published her ground-breaking *The Human Condition* (1958). Written as a philosophical reconsideration of being human in the modern world which was characterized as "a work of striking originality," a second edition was published in 2018. Set against the problems of "diminishing human agency and political freedom," she sought to engage the contemporary paradox of a loss of control over the consequence of our human actions living with enhanced means of technology which challenged the characteristic sense of human autonomy. Her insightful analysis of human activity was viewed through the lens of the traditional expression *vita activa*, drawn from the classic Christian spiritual distinction between the active life and the contemplative life. Whereby she opts for the former, understood as the fundamental condition found in "human existence," namely, our active participation in political activity and our social interaction with each other. A way of thinking which offers the theoretical foundations whereby she confronted the denial of this human activity in her seminal study, for which she is primarily known, *The Origins of Totalitarianism* (1951), a tragic

---

6. Scheler, *Man's Place in Nature*, 17.

twentieth-century phenomenon, the consequence of Hitler's "ice-cold reasoning" and Stalin's "merciless dialectics."

While recognized for her acclaimed *The Origins of Totalitarianism* (1951), a complex study of the emergence and features of Nazism and Stalinism, someone who narrowly escaped from Nazi Germany herself, Arendt received criticism for her perceived injudicious observations about the "banality of evil" in her *Eichmann in Jerusalem: A Report on the Banality of Evil* (1963). She was mistakenly accused of suggesting the Holocaust was something commonplace, even ordinary, thereby trivializing what was in fact a "thought defying" atrocity, one equally defining of the twentieth century. A criticism found in *Becoming Eichmann: Rethinking the Life, Crimes, and Trial of a "Desk Murderer"* (2007) by David Cesarani (1956–2015), a British historian and specialist on the Holocaust. Commissioned by *The New Yorker*, Arendt had travelled to Jerusalem to attend and write an account of the trial of Adolf Eichmann (1906–62), following his capture by Mossad in Argentina on May 11, 1960; he was hanged in Jerusalem for war crimes in 1962.

Primarily responsible for the organization and implementation of the *Shoah*, the Hebrew word used for the Holocaust, the "Final Solution to the Jewish Question," this infamous SS-Gestapo officer was a participant during the Wannsee Conference on January 20, 1942. Following the assassination of Reinhard Heydrich (1904–42), chief of the Reich Security Main Office, described by Hitler "as the man with the iron heart," Eichmann assumed overall responsibility during the war for organizing and managing the mass deportation and extermination, the systematic murder of European Jews in a network of death camps throughout Nazi occupied Eastern Europe (1940–44), epitomized in the emblematic words "Auschwitz-Birkenau." While she recognized that the accused himself embodied "the dilemma between the unspeakable horror of the deeds and the undeniable ludicrousness of the man who perpetrates them," to many like herself he looked "so ordinary!" Herein we find the enigma understanding humanity.

While philosophical activity drives our current quest for truth as a means of personal self-transcendence, embedded in the phenomenon of human consciousness expressed in the Greek aphorism, "know thyself," its origins are far more remote as recognized by the German-Swiss Christian psychiatrist turned philosopher Karl Jaspers (1883–1969), someone who appreciated the significance of these words living in the disordered world of post-war Germany. Addressed in a series of lectures, later published as

The Question of German Guilt (1946), Jaspers was one of the leading voices in the reconstruction of a free and democratic Germany after the Second World War. As a prominent alumnus Jaspers was invited to speak at the ceremony to mark the reopening of the School of Medicine at Heidelberg University (1386) on August 14, 1945, which also marked his academic rehabilitation following the Nazi persecution of intellectuals against the regime, Jaspers exhorted those present to feel "confidence and fortitude in the face of a grim reality," to rededicate themselves to the pursuit of truth, found in human existence. Redirecting his attention to philosophy, he became an early exponent of post-war European 'existentialism,' though he disliked the expression applied to his thought because of its association with the atheism of the French philosopher Jean-Paul Sartre (1905–80), the dominant intellectual of his time.

A recognized Christian thinker, notwithstanding his cautious disassociation with French existentialism, Jaspers aligned his way of thinking with this particularly twentieth-century thoughtful reaction, foreshadowed in the philosophy of Søren Kierkegaard. Whereby the Danish philosopher reacted against the prevalent abstract rationalism, found in Hegel's notion of "absolute consciousness," in favour of the original use of the German word *existenz* or 'existence' now applied to designating "the being of man." An employment to be distinguished from the "French literary movement of existentialism" critically discussed by Jaspers' doctoral student, the German born American political theorist Hannah Arendt (1906–75) in her 1946 article "What Is Existenz Philosophy?" written for the American cultural journal *Partisan Review*.

Used in this philosophical context, Kierkegaard understands the 'self' as a distinctive mode of human consciousness, the foundation of "an existing individual." In so doing, the Danish philosopher promotes the irreducibility of the subjective, namely, the personal dimension of human life, found in his discussion of various themes commonly associated with the human condition, such as freedom, individuality, authenticity, choice, dread, and despair. Addressing a variety of themes and issues related to human experience rather than being a unified philosophy, existentialism would reach its heyday in post-war European thought. One of the most intriguing philosophies of the twentieth century, characteristically diverse as its subject matter, existentialism addressed the practical issues associated with human existence living in era of turbulence, as a means of moving beyond the perceived strictures of nineteenth-century abstract thought, as found in Cartesian rationalism or Hegel's absolute idealism.

16

World of a Person

NORMALLY OUR IDEAS, SUCH as belief in the existence of God or the idea of being human, constitute a framework of assumptions in the realm of our consciousness, envisaged as a 'world', as a thoughtful and intellectual environment within which we can live and think, a perspective or outlook which we can adopt. However, during the twentieth century, these ways of thinking assumed further significance in the "era of ideology." Wherein we find a remarkable coalescence of ideas thinking about humanity, being human, human existence and the human person. Characterized during the nineteenth century as a *weltanschauung*: an expression used by the German historian and founding figure in "sociology," Wilhelm Dilthey (1833–1911). Wherein he employed the scientific methodology found in the natural sciences to formulate his comprehensive theory of a worldview within which to better understand humanity.

Writing in his essay "The Purpose of Philosophy" (1962), Isaiah Berlin distinguishes between "the world of a man who believes that God created him for a specific purpose" from that of "the world of a man who believes in none of these," arguing that these ideas differ because "of their general conception of the world."[1] In so doing, Berlin not only drew attention to the prevalence of "ideology" during the twentieth century, systems of ideas about ourselves as human beings and our place in the world, and how we interact with those around us, but in so doing, he identified the fundamental dichotomy found between two opposing world views and related systems of thought, which either recognized the

---

1. Berlin, *Concepts and Categories*, 10–11.

presence of God or the denial of this presence, the absence of God, both became equally influential during the twentieth century. This fundamental polarity between these competing worldviews, came to characterize European twentieth-century thought.

Given the cumulative effects generated by the political, intellectual, economic, and cultural turbulence and disenchantment following two world wars, new patterns of philosophical thinking about our human existence emerged, in response to "what am I?" and our personal identify and associated freedom and rights, and in response to "who am I?" which generated three twentieth-century European forms of thinking about humanity, found in humanism, existentialism and personalism. With its origins in Antiquity, humanism re-emerged as a form of atheistic and secular thought, first discussed by the French atheist philosopher Jean-Paul Sartre (1905–80) in his 1945 lecture *Existentialism is a humanism*, which addressed the perennial question "what am I?" Now accompanied by a way of thinking which drew attention to the personal question "who am I? known as 'personalism.' With a distinctive Christian orientation as a Personal God centred way of thinking about humanity based on the centrality of the concept of "person," this was especially dismissed by Sartre.

While rejecting the spiritual philosophy of his doctoral advisor, Scheler integrated these ideas within his phenomenological ethical personalism. Thereby drawing attention to the centrality of the "human person," an orientation shared within various forms of French and German philosophical discourse. As observed by the French Catholic philosopher Jacques Maritain (1882–1973) in his 1939 paper "The Human Person and Society," wherein he promotes his own version of Thomistic personalism with its distinctive metaphysical orientation: "there are, at least, a dozen personalist doctrines, which, at times have nothing in common than the term 'person.'"[2] Later he would respond to Sartre's atheistic existentialism, which was destructive of the human person, wherein he argued that the "existence" Maritain discussed involved human action, a subject taken up in *Existence and the Existent* (1947), subtitled "An Essay on Christian Existentialism," a publication based on his lecture to the Pontifical Academy of St. Thomas (1879), wherein he argued in favour of a form of Thomistic Existentialism. These novel ways of twentieth-century Catholic thinking about human existence and the individual

---

2. Maritain, *Person and The Common Good*, 13.

person, someone considered free and responsible for their own action, set the scene for the emergence of conciliar humanism.

While there are many variants of personalism, two distinct trends developed independently on different Continents, North America and Europe; however, in its philosophical origins 'personalism' shares a common Christian religious inspiration. Expressed by the Scottish idealist Andrew Seth Pringle-Pattison (1856–1931) as "the person and the relations of persons to one another as the essence of reality." Developed in America by Protestant Christians, especially the "Boston Personalists," inspired by Borden Parker Bowne (1847–1910) the Methodist theologian from the Boston University School of Theology, and in Europe, by the French philosopher Charles Renouvier (1815–1903) who first employed this word in 1903 to describe his social philosophy, later taken up by the Catholic philosopher Emmanuel Mounier (1905–50), author of the seminal *Personalism* (1950), wherein he claims "the universe of the person is the universe of man."[3] While French personalism reflected a broader social, ethical orientation, this was not immediately apparent approaching the thought of the German philosophers Eucken and Scheler who directed their critical attention to the issue of understanding humanity approached philosophically from the perspective of metaphysics, by addressing the human crisis, notwithstanding Scheler's description of his thought as "ethical personalism."

The fundamental polarity, which defined post World War II twentieth-century European philosophy, was outlined by the author of *Being and Nothingness* (1943), the French philosopher Jean-Paul Sartre in a public lecture, later published as *Existentialism is a Humanism* (1946), wherein he differentiated between Christian existentialists, namely the Danish philosopher Søren Kierkegaard (1813–55) and the French philosopher Gabriel Marcel (1889–1973) and the alternative, so-called "atheistic existentialists," such as himself and the German philosopher Martin Heidegger (1889–1976), the author of *Being and Time* (1927), recognized as one of the most important works of twentieth-century philosophy. Approached as a consequence of a Godless and secular epoch, initiated by Feuerbach, Sartre's reactionary manner of thinking about human existence and its related human concerns and experiences, set against the traditional tomes of speculative philosophy, came to characterize French "continental philosophy" following the liberation

---

3. Mounier, *Personalism*, xv.

of Paris from the 1950s onwards, with the discovery of Sartre's idiosyncratic approach to philosophy.

Found in his original use of literature, especially novels, as a means of discussing humanity through our emotional and psychological experiences, in his classic *No Exit* (1944) published with three other plays, "The Flies," "Dirty Hands" and "The Respectful Prostitute." In 1948 Sartre's atheistic thought was officially censored by the Catholic Church, with his *oeuvre* included in the twentieth and final edition of the *Index Liborum Prohibitorum*. Well known for *Being and Nothingness* (1943), wherein we find Sartre's original use of phenomenology applied to the study of being, his phenomenological ontology was initially generated in response to a feeling of powerlessness. An emotional state Sartre had experienced as a young Marxist socialist living under the Nazi occupation of France, wherein he experienced a particular sense of freedom as a former POW and member of the French Resistance, namely, facing the possibility of denunciation and death each day: "we were never more free than during the German occupation." Living under these circumstances he discovered the true "human condition" living in what he calls "the universe of human subjectivity." A way of thinking which informed his "doctrine of action," an original way of thinking generated by the inescapability of freedom and responsibility he had experienced, which informed our human capacity to "choose." In this context he recall's Heidegger's notion of "abandonment," experienced in the absence of God, whereby he sought to discover a truth about the state of being and man's purpose in the world.

These issues were taken up in his 1945 lecture "Existentialism Is a Humanism," wherein Sartre sought to outline the humanistic nature of his thought, defined by the first principle of existentialism, in the absence of God, "man is nothing other than what he makes of himself,"[4] and from the perspective of his existential humanism, "man will realize himself as truly human." Within this ambiguous context, "humanism tends essentially to render man more truly human, and to manifest his original greatness by having him participate in all that can enrich him in nature and in history." Operating within a Christian context the thought of Max Scheler is recalled by the French philosopher Jacques Maritain as he introduces his essay "Integral Humanism. Towards a New Christendom" later published as *Integral Humanism* (1936).

---

4. Sartre, *Existentialism Is a Humanism*, 22.

Set against the conflictual background which informs late nineteenth and early twentieth-century Catholic thought, especially in response to the Catholic heresy of "modernism," Scheler's "life and thought were by no means conventional," words which introduce *Max Scheler, 1874–1928: An Intellectual Portrait* (1967) by his American biographer John Raphael Staude. Perhaps also symptomatic of the times, Heidegger remains an equally problematic though certainly more well-known figure within twentieth-century European philosophy, especially for his existential phenomenology. Having received a traditional Catholic upbringing in the spirit of the First Vatican Council (1869–70), he initially studied theology at the University of Freiburg (1457) with a view towards a religious vocation supported by the Church.

However, thinking within this intellectual milieu, Heidegger's attention was soon directed to the study of philosophy, completing his 1914 doctorate on psychologism viewed through the lens of current neo-Thomism and neo-Kantian thought, a nineteenth-century mainly German philosophical position which directed attention to the use of psychology. Two years later, while preparing for his 1920 *Habilitation* on the Scottish Franciscan friar and scholastic philosopher Duns Scotus (c. 1265–1308), he was introduced to Edmund Husserl's phenomenology; upon successful completion of this writing, he was elected an extraordinary professor in philosophy in 1923 at the University of Marburg (1527). In 1927 he returned to his *alma mater* succeeding Husserl as professor of philosophy at Freiburg where he published his seminal work *Being and Time*; the next year he interrupted his regular lecture on May 21 to offer his "In memoriam Max Scheler" on hearing of his friend's sudden death on May 19, 1928. Following his election as Rector of the University on April 21, 1933 he officially joined the Nazi party on May 1; however, a year later in April 1934 he resigned from this position and withdrew his support for the Nazis. Following the denazification hearings held after the War, he was dismissed from his position at Freiburg and banned from teaching in 1949; while the ban was lifted in 1953, he was never allowed to resume his philosophical activities.

17

Learning from Others

RECOGNIZABLY HUMAN, THE EXERCISE of thought understood as a distinct activity touches all levels of human experience; in the words of the twelfth-century Anglo-Saxon Christian humanist John of Salisbury (c. 1120–80): "Our own generation enjoys the legacy bequeathed to it by that which preceded it. We frequently know more, not because we have moved ahead by our own natural ability, but because we are supported by the [mental] strength of others." Taken as the motto of Google Scholar, the expression "standing on the shoulders of giants" was first used by John of Salisbury writing in his *Metalogicon* (1159), wherein he offers a systematic account of the study of the seven liberal arts of his day, the *Trivium* and *Quodrivium*, taught in tenth and eleventh-century monastic and cathedral schools, which evolved into twelfth-century "universities." Used in Western science, culture and philosophy, this expression is commonly understood as referring to the thoughtful process of a creative reception, whereby "one develops future intellectual pursuits by understanding and building on the research and works created by notable thinkers of the past" as observed by the renowned English theoretical physicist Stephen Hawking (1942–2018) in his Introduction to *On the Shoulders of Giants: The Great Works of Physics and Astronomy* (2002). Referring to its use in the famous 1676 correspondence between two notable English scientists, the physicist Isaac Newton (1642–1727) and the polymath Robert Hooke (1635–1703), Hawking identifies this expressive metaphor as an apt comment on how science, and indeed the whole of Western civilization, represents a series of incremental advances, building on what went before, learning from others.

The Italian semiotician and medievalist Umberto Eco (1932–2016) employs this metaphor in his popular novel *The Name of the Rose* (1983) in the exchange between the fictional characters William of Baskerville and Nicholas of Morimondo, the master glazier at the monastery. In response to the latter's assertion concerning his art, "we no longer have the learning of the ancients, the age of giants is past!" To which William responds: "We are dwarfs but dwarfs who stand on the shoulders of those giants, and small though we are, we sometimes manage to see further on the horizon than they." Later, Umberto Eco offered a lecture in 2001 "On the Shoulders of Giants," wherein he detailed his fascination with the historical polemic about the dwarfs and the giants, and how the literary classics of Western civilization have contributed to our own time and to the mission of intellectual life, published in a collection of recent essays *On the Shoulders of Giants* (2019).

However, such intellectual optimism did not remain unchallenged. Found in the essay "Philosophy in the Tragic Age of the Greeks" (1873) by Christianity's trenchant critic the German philosopher Friedrich Nietzsche, wherein he rejects the notion of intellectual progress when he uses this metaphor in reference to another German philosopher Arthur Schopenhauer's (1788–1860) distinction between "the republic of scholars," identified as the Ancient Greek masters, and "the republic of creative minds, envisaged as "dwarfs" who reduce creative insightfulness to their level of understanding, as in the case of the Persian sage Zarathustra, traditionally dated about sixth century BC. In Nietzsche's provocative discourse "Of the Vision and the Riddle," contained in *Thus Spoke Zarathustra* (1883–85), "A Book for Everyone and No One," his most accessible and influential work, this prophet carries the inquisitive dwarf on his shoulders, moving toward "a thought you could not endure!" In this exchange, Nietzsche anticipates his nihilistic philosophy which would accompany his own decline into insanity.

Unacknowledged by Hawking and these other authors, at least the author of *God's Philosophers: How the Medieval World Laid the Foundations of Modern Science* (2009), the British historian James Hannam recognized the original source of this metaphor in the thought of the medieval humanist John of Salisbury. Wherein he envisages his teacher Bernard of Chartres (died around 1124), a renowned French grammarian and commentator on Plato, who had been a student of the French scholastic logician Peter Abelard (1079–1142) during the early days of the University of Paris (1150) and their contemporaries as "standing on the shoulders of giants," namely on those of the ancient philosophical greats, such as Plato and Aristotle. As recorded by John of Salisbury, Bernard pictures himself and his medieval contemporaries as "dwarfs" positioned on the shoulders of these giants of Antiquity. As such, this image not only identifies the originality of medieval thinkers who could see more and further than the Ancients, but such insight could only be achieved through the thoughtful assistance of these influential predecessors. Alternatively, in the opinion of Sir R. W. Southern (1912–2001) writing in *The Making of the Middle Ages* (1998) the noted English medieval historian, Bernard's phrase well formulates the "aim of a man viewing the world of learning from the greatest of all the cathedral schools."

Celebrating the fiftieth anniversary of the closing of the Council, the University of Notre Dame Australia (Sydney) sponsored the *Tradition Conference 2013*. According to its promotional material, "there is no more Catholic word than 'Tradition.'" Used with a capital T this word indicates one of the two sources of God's Revelation to human beings, defined in the Council's *Dei Verbum*, Dogmatic Constitution "on Divine Revelation" promulgated on November 18, 1965: "Tradition and Scripture together form a single sacred deposit of the word of God, entrusted to the Church" (para. 10). Once the Apostolic faith is delivered, through the ongoing action of the Holy Spirit, the Church under the authoritative leadership of the pope, as successor of St. Peter, and those he entrusts as leaders in the local church or dioceses, assume responsibility for the authentic interpretation of the word of God, whereby ongoing guidance and teaching towards a deeper understanding of the content of faith is offered, a way of thinking Pope Francis describes as "Catholic and open." One which involves the use of disciplined rational thought found in theology, philosophy, and related fields of scientific endeavour as these evolve, such as the human and social sciences during the twentieth century.

Used in the lower case, the word "tradition" has received many meanings over the course of Western history; however, operating within the tradition of lived Catholic Christianity, as it especially informs Catholic philosophy, it refers to a generational transmission of "accepted and desirable patterns of thought and ways of life," drawn from contemporary thought and customs to engage the 'world of today.' Envisaged as a collective and living transmission of thoughtful ideas acquired over time moving into the future, expressed earlier in the words 'back to the future.' As a generative process of 'handing on,' one which naturally involves a process of 'reception,' this speaks to an interactive phenomenon, involving two equally important components which inform the inherent tension between "development" and "conservation" within Catholic thought.

Characterized as 'living in the truth,' this productive interaction was expressed in the title "Retrieving the tradition," used for a regular section of the theological journal *Communio: International Catholic Review*. Established in 1972 by prominent twentieth-century theologians, some were Council *periti*, namely the German theologian Joseph Ratzinger, the French Jesuit Henri de Lubac and the Swiss Catholic priest and theologian, Servant of God Hans Urs von Balthasar, for the purpose of overcoming the characteristic twentieth-century "polarization between 'modernists' and 'traditionalists' in the Church." More significantly, *Communio* was established as a resource for ongoing reflection and renewal "in the spirit of the Second Vatican Council as interpreted by the Pontificate of John Paul II" in the words of von Balthasar, an approach which directs my understanding of the genesis and legacy of conciliar humanism as an instance of the ongoing tradition "living in the truth."

Found in the philosophical legacy of the foremost medieval scholastic Thomas Aquinas which forms an integral part of our Catholic tradition and remains, in the opinion of Polish philosopher Stefan Swieżawski writing in *St. Thomas Revisited* (1995), a source of ongoing guidance; as he writes: "just as the music of Bach never grows old," he continues "neither do the authentic achievements of philosophical thought" found in Thomism, "the philosophy that developed under the banner of St. Thomas over the years."[1] Quoting the thought of the Polish poet Konstanty Gałczyński (1905–53), Swieżawski claims "in Bach you will find everything and for all occasions."[2]

As a recognizable human phenomenon, music soothes the soul, assuredly the case as the American cellist Jo Jo Ma played a powerfully evocative piece of music. Namely, the Sarabande from Bach's fifth suite in C Minor for unaccompanied cello which he chose for the special ceremony to mark the first anniversary of the infamous terrorist attack on the New York World Trade Centre on September 11, 2002; beautiful music to accompany a defining moment of human tragedy perpetrated by fellow human beings which brought in a new millennium; circumstances which speak of the enigma found in our shared humanity.

---

1. Swieżawski, *St. Thomas Revisited*, 11–12.
2. Swieżawski, *St. Thomas Revisited*, 11.

Drawing inspiration from within Scholastic thought, approached as "hints from the past," music represents humanity at its best—nowhere more so than in the extraordinary and unsurpassed musical output of the German Baroque composer and musician Johan Sebastian Bach (1685–1750), characterized by Tim Banning in *The Triumph of Music* (2010) as the "Homer of music." Bach's influence on Western civilization, like that of the epic poems *Iliad* and the *Odyssey*, remains undisputed. However, while immediately recognizable today as summits of musical and spiritual expression, this was not always the case. Until the twentieth century, Bach's music was unknown, outside the narrow confines of Lutheran sacred church music and a few specialists, unpublished, and unperformed.

This recently acquired status inspired a popular biography published at the turn of the century wherein we find these words: "This genius was not an individual, but a collective soul. Centuries and generations have laboured at this work, before the grandeur of which we halt in veneration." This was the appraisal offered by Albert Schweitzer (1875–1965), the Alsatian born Lutheran theologian and great Christian humanist of the time, also an accomplished organist, to introduce his two-volume authoritative *J. S. Bach* (1904); thought which could well have been applied to the genesis of conciliar humanism. Understood as a "symphony of ideas," this remarkable and unique confluence of ideas concerning our shared humanity, drawn from both "outside" and "inside" the philosophical resources of Catholic thought available at the time, conciliar humanism emerged from the "collective soul" of the Second Vatican Council, a remarkable extended "meeting of minds" infused with *sapiential* consciousness. A way of thinking, hitherto unrecognized, which represents the culmination of "centuries and generations" thinking about our shared humanity within the tradition of Catholic philosophical thought.

Until the middle of the twentieth century the music played at the World Trade Centre memorial was unknown to the broader public, until a curious and resourceful young Spanish Catalan boy named Pablo Cassals (1876–1973) walked into a second-hand book shop, to discover edited manuscripts of music which became synonymous with this preeminent twentieth-century cellist. Characterized by commentators as "one of the most renowned movements of the whole set," its wistful tones accompanied the reading in remembrance the names of loved ones who lost their lives on that tragic September day in 2002. The simple melody of this Sarabande has been characterized as "another instance of Bach's taking hints from the past and basing on them structures of the utmost complexity," to recall thought from *The New Bach Reader* (1998). Namely, his innovative use of contrapuntal polyphony, as found in his music for "The Well-Tempered Clavier" (1722). Originally considered "frivolous," this particular style of music emerged during the Avignon papacy (1309–76), considered more suitable for performance before an audience than for Catholic liturgical worship, which incorporated two or more independent melodies played simultaneously, an approach applicable to understanding the genesis of conciliar humanism as a network of ideas. Writing about this chamber music, the well-known English conductor and authority on Bach, Sir John Eliot Gardener observed: "it is obvious how much hinged on Bach's power of *inventio*—his capacity to find the germ or creative spark that would, in large measure, determine the content of a piece."[3]

Employed within Scholastic thought, the technical term *inventio* referred to one of the five classical canons of rhetoric, the others being *disposito, elocutio, memoria,* and *pronuntiatio,* all of which depend on *inventio*. This interdependence generated a systematic process of organized thought, a means of clarification and communication, whereby "invention" or "discovery" was employed as the first step in the search for ideas leading to a compelling argument, discussed by the Athenian philosopher Aristotle in a small treatise entitled *Rhetoric*. Employed in the context of dialectical reasoning, *inventio* provided the mechanism for discovering universal truths, currently defined as "the art of using language so as to influence or persuade others."[4] The issue of invention was taken up by the French philosopher Jacques Derrida in his essay *Psyche: Inventions of the Other* (1987) wherein he asks "why is it that *invention* cannot be reduced to the discovery, the revelation, or the unveiling of truth?" but rather he claims "the invention *of the other* the absolute initiative for which the other is responsible."[5] A claim made in reference to Bach's use of "invention," wherein Derrida employs the plural to highlight the multiple functions found in Bach's original use of "inventions." Not merely didactic but also used as "composition exercises," Bach invites one to think "thoughts of technical virtuosity, didactic exercise, instrumental variations," namely, to think of "the other" in the opinion of Derrida.

3. Gardner, *Bach*, 208.
4. Blackburn, *Oxford Dictionary of Philosophy*, 330.
5. Derrida, "Psyche," 200, 201, 219.

Approached on a broader scale, Bach's St. Matthew Passion (1727) represents an instance of thinking "the other." A monumental portrayal of humanity, suffering, and saved, which was all but buried with him following his death in 1750; however, it is now recognized as one of Bach's most profoundly spiritual, immensely conceived works of sacred music. Once again, due to the efforts of an outsider, a bright young twenty-year-old German music student, Felix Mendelssohn Bartholdy (1809–47) who chose this work for his debut as a conductor at the *Singakademie-Berlin* on March 11, 1829, thereby initiating the nineteenth-century "Bach Revival." Recognizably Lutheran from his baptism on March 23, 1685 in Georgenkirche in Eisenach, the bulk of Bach's sacred music reflected this religious orientation which employed the vernacular German; however, he also produced sacred music in Latin from another tradition of a Catholic orientation. This followed his appointment as Thomaskantor in the Protestant city of Leipzig between 1723–50, then under the control of the King of Catholic Poland, and as Royal composer for the Catholic court of the Prince Elector in Dresden he was called upon to compose suitable music. This "somewhat anomalous situation" generated Bach's Catholic sacred music, such as what is commonly known as his B-minor Mass, a setting of the Kyrie-Gloria parts of the Catholic Mass completed in 1733, his Latin Magnificat or his Cantata *Tilge, Höchster meine Sünden* (BWV 1083), a German paraphrase of psalm fifty-one, "Cancel, Highest, my sins." A form of parody music completed in the 1740s, based on the Italian Catholic Baroque composer Giovanni Battista Pergolesi's (1710–36) well known *Stabat Mater* (1736), one of the Italian's most celebrated sacred works, composed for the Neapolitan *Confraternita dei Cavalieri di San Luigi di Palazzo*.

Given the remarkable ingenuity and flexible brilliance of this German Baroque composer to adapt to the circumstances of his time, it came as no surprise that his music "made the cut." It was chosen as truly representative of the musical achievements of the human race by the organizing committee of NASA scientists and world leaders, tasked to select appropriate music to accompany the Voyage space probe mission in 1977, an ongoing American scientific program into deep space exploration beyond the moon. In fact, two pieces of Bach's music were selected, the first movement of the Brandenburg Concerto No. 2 in F and the *Gavotte en Rondeau* from the Partita No.3 in E Major. Along with other familiar music, such as that of the Austrian Wolfgang Amadeus Mozart (1756–91) and the Russian Igor Stravinsky (1882–1971), this representative collection literally travelled out of this world, into outer space on a "Golden Record" loaded onto the spacecraft.

Like Bach's ingenious integrative capacity to assemble music from various religious traditions, to incorporate "hints from the past" which gave voice to "the other," conciliar humanism, approached as a "symphony of ideas," of human person, community of persons and human solidarity, represents the consequence of a remarkable moment within twentieth-century Catholic thought, found in the retrieval of *sapiential* consciousness. Wherein we find a remarkable "synthesis of fidelity and dynamism," operating from within and without the tradition of lived Catholic Christianity, which represents an original fusion of ideas drawn from traditional sources of thought, biblical, ancient, patristic, and scholastic, brought together with contemporary ideas from twentieth-century European philosophy, such as Christian humanism, Phenomenology, Existentialism and Personalism.

With many variants, the meaning of "retrieval" applied to conciliar thought is taken from the philosophical project found in Martin Heidegger's seminal book of twentieth-century European philosophy *Being and Time* (para. 385). Set against the background of his previous study of the metaphysical thought of Blessed Duns Scotus, the Scottish Franciscan friar who is best known for his philosophical concept of "univocity of being," namely, a concept of being as something universal. Whereby the language used to describe the attributes of God typical for the scholastic thinkers of the time, such as "good," "truth" and "being," meant the same when applied to human beings or things. A philosophical way of thinking which re-emerged during the Council within conciliar humanism, whereby we can understand the nature of the Triune God though understanding our shared humanity in the Person of Christ.

Critical of Scotus, Heidegger pursued an alternative, phenomenological project to return to an understanding of the original idea of "being" found in things themselves, wherein he reappropriated ideas taken from "ontology," the philosophical study of "being," especially found in Pre-Socratic thought. Approached within this Heideggerian perspective, whereby Ancient Greek philosophical thought is revisited as a means of thinking with an eye to the future while accommodating the present, we discover human beings as inherently temporal and world bound, a philosophy of finitude expressed in Heidegger's use of the German *dasein* 'being there.' Interestingly, given Heidegger's sense of "retrieval," his thoughtful appropriation of ideas taken from the past to accommodate the present is also attributed to the Italian *aggiornamento* "bringing up to date" or "renewal," which together with the French neologism *ressourcement* "a return to the sources," are expressions commonly associated with the methodology of pastoral renewal undertaken during the Council, which informs the genesis of conciliar humanism.

Approached philosophically, this way of thinking is received as the gift of Wisdom to discern the "signs of the times," one which energises our continual search for truth and our quest to better understand our shared humanity, our being human, defined in *Fides et Ratio* (1998) as *"the one who seeks the truth"* (para. 28). Expressed in the prayerful intent, "Everlasting Wisdom, come to us: Dwell with us and work in us today"[6] which characterizes the Catholic philosophical tradition of "doing philosophy in the pursuit of truth." An activity which builds on the legacy of conciliar humanism, a thoughtful consequence of the Second Vatican Council, a moment which defined Catholicism in the twentieth century. Seeking the truth infused with *sapiential* consciousness, thinking about ourselves as being a human person, living together in a 'community of persons' directed towards God moving into the third millennium, we are more appreciative than ever of the resourcefulness of philosophical activity as it enhances our shared quest to better understand ourselves, our being together with other human beings and being together with God, wherein we find the legacy of conciliar humanism. The result of a consequential human interaction "taking hints from the past" during an extended "meeting of minds," as together the Council Fathers sought answers to questions held in common, thinking within a philosophical context which offers an opportunity for further conversation. As Pope John Paul II introduces *Fides et Ratio* (1998): *"Who am I? Where did I come from and where am I going?* Perennial questions which direct our shared human quest for meaning, which arise in the human heart."

---

6. Intercession from Tuesday Morning Prayer, 25th Week of the Year.

18

Thoughtful Foundations

"On the threshold of the third millennium of the Christian era, humanity may come to a clearer sense of the great resources with which it has been endowed and may commit itself with renewed courage to implement the plan of salvation of which its history is part" (para. 6)—an expressive thought of one of the proponents of conciliar humanism writing in *Fides et Ratio* (1998). Negotiating this complex philosophical terrain, "a landscape with figures," guidance is received from the thought of Michael Novak, a graduate in philosophy at Stanford University (1891) between 1965–68. The first to recognize this unique synthesis as a "break with the past," an expression with ambiguous significance insofar as this was not literally a break but rather an adaptation of an original way of thinking, "taking hints from the past" within the philosophical tradition of Catholic thought, an invaluable resource which generated conciliar humanism.

"Traditions are defined retrospectively. It is only on looking back that the unity of a project to which over considerable stretches of time there have been many different contributors, each with their own goals and concerns, become apparent,"[1] thought taken from the Scottish born American philosopher Alasdair MacIntyre's remarkable *God, Philosophy, Universities* (2009). From the Latin *trader* 'to deliver,' a tradition is best approached from a distance, like Germany's largest Cathedral in the city of Cologne with its two dominating and inspiring spires, finally completed in 1880, following pressure to resume work from the recently elected Pope

---

1. MacIntyre, *God, Philosophy, Universities*, 35.

Leo XIII. Already familiar with this building when, as a young thirty-four-year-old Church diplomat Vincenzo Pecci (1810–1903) he made regular trips to Cologne, following his appointment as Apostolic Nuncio to the Kingdom of Belgium (1843–46), consecrated titular Archbishop of Damietta with the guarantee of a Cardinal's hat on leaving this position. As Nuncio these responsibilities took him to the northern part of Germany, which was predominantly Catholic, where he took a particular interest in the completion of Cologne's great yet unfinished Cathedral.

Another instance of Pecci's capacity to anticipate the future was his support for Monsignor Aerts' proposal to establish the Belgian Pontifical College in 1844, where a young Karol Wojtyła would reside between 1946–48 while studying at the *Angelicum*. Furthermore, another resident who would also work as college librarian while pursuing doctoral study between 1920–27 in both scholastic theology and continental philosophy at the Gregorian University (1551) was a young Belgian diocesan priest Leo-Jozef Suenens sent by his Archbishop, Cardinal Désire-Joseph Mercier. Both *alumni* of the College, Cardinal Suenens and Archbishop Wojtyła would be extremely influential figures during Council proceedings, directing the human agenda and philosophical thought, especially found in *Dignitatis Humanae* and *Gaudium et Spes*, wherein we find conciliar humanism.

Modelled on Our Lady of Amiens Cathedral (1220) and dedicated to St. Peter and the Blessed Virgin Mary, Cologne's medieval gothic cathedral was "built to impress" as a magnificent setting to accommodate the reliquary of the Three Kings, the intention of the original architect, following their acquisition in 1164 by Rainald von Dassel, Archbishop of Cologne (1159–67) from the Holy Roman Emperor Frederick Barbarossa (1122–90), who took these from the city of Milan. The most beautiful religious buildings the Christian world has created, medieval gothic cathedrals originated in France during the twelfth century when Abbot Suger (1081–1151) decided to rebuild the abbey church of Saint Denis in Paris, remodelling the existing Carolingian church, built in the Romanesque style, by adding a new façade at the western entrance with an elaborate portal and the first "Rose Window." As such, this abbey church provided a veritable manifesto of Gothic architecture, one which represents a unique synthesis of existing technologies merged into a new architectural style, which incorporated the pointed arch, the ribbed vault and flying buttress, emphasizing verticality and light. Utilizing stone and glass, medieval cathedrals with their breath-taking material appearance symbolize living the Christian faith as we literally strive to reach heaven, exemplified by Cologne's imposing spires. Approached as "buildings of faith," their East-West orientation further express our human movement towards God in buildings built by humans.

Visible throughout the city, Cologne's remarkable Cathedral began when its foundation stone was blessed and laid in 1248, the same year a young Italian Dominican friar, Brother Thomas of Aquino arrived in the city from Paris, accompanying his teacher Saint Albert the Great (1206–80), a Dominican friar from Bavaria. Following previous study at the recently established *studium generale* in the city of Naples, founded on June 5, 1224 by Frederick II (1194–1250), King of Sicily from 1198 and the Holy Roman Emperor (1220–50), where Aquinas first encountered the translated thought of Aristotle which was available at the time. On receiving the Dominican habit as a professed religious brother, he was then sent to Paris in 1245 to further his study in the liberal arts under Albert, who held the Chair of Theology at the College of St. James, a *Studium Generale* which was integrated within the recently established University of Paris (1150).

Having completed his humanistic instruction at Naples and Paris, Aquinas would continue his theological formation in Cologne under Albert's guidance, working as a *baccalaureus biblicus*, an "apprentice professor" instructing students on the books of the Old Testament at the newly erected *stadium generale* established by the Dominican Order in that city and where Albert had been appointed Master; Aquinas remained in Cologne for four years, probably being ordained a priest in 1250. As well as scriptural commentaries, Aquinas finished his required writing on the Italian scholastic theologian Peter Lombard's (c. 1096–1160) *Four Books of Sentences*, the set text for any student of theology, and completed his *De Ente et Essentia*, one of Aquinas' few explicitly philosophical works "on being and essence" written to help his students in Paris.

While it took considerably longer to complete than anticipated, what would become Cologne's renowned monument to German Catholic Christianity with its twin spires raised heavenward built on solid foundations, remains "a powerful testimony to the strength and persistence of Christian belief in medieval and modern Europe" and "an exceptional work of human creative genius." While these accolades were offered to mark its inclusion onto the UNESCO World Heritage List in 1996, these equally apply to the philosophical and theological edifice constructed by the young Dominican friar centuries ago. Having lived less than fifty years, Thomas Aquinas died suddenly on March 7, 1274 at the Cistercian abbey at Fossanova in the Papal States, while on his way to attend the Second Ecumenical Council of Lyons (1274), in the Kingdom of Burgundy-Arles, where he was invited to speak on the reconciliation between Eastern Orthodox and Roman Catholic Christians, following the Great Schism on July 16, 1054 with the mutual excommunication between the Patriarch of Constantinople Michael 1 Cerularius (1043–59) and the Bishop of Rome, Saint Pope Leo IX (1049–54), one which was eventually revoked on December 7, 1965 during the final session of the Second Vatican Council. Interestingly, the other great medieval theologian of the day, the Italian Franciscan friar Saint Bonaventure (c. 1218–74) was another invitee, who remained an active participant during Council proceedings, but died soon after these had finished on July 15, 1274 at Lyons. Unfortunately, Aquinas' premature death brought to an end an extraordinary literary output, already numbering more than sixty books on theology and related subjects.

Recalling the image of Cologne's Cathedral, built to impress, when viewing it as intended, one's attention is automatically drawn to the two inspiring and imposing spires and the voluminous light filled building which support these, which represent the medieval philosophical edifice of thought infused with *sapiential* consciousness. Carrying the name of its "towering" originator, the edifice of "living Thomism" represents a distinctive synthesis of original creativity built on the foundations of another towering figure in Christian thought, Augustine of Hippo, the other spire, whose thought encapsulates the notion that "traditions are defined retrospectively." A way of thinking which characterizes the Catholic philosophical tradition, as expressed by Alasdair Macintyre, wherein I find three interrelated components, the use of philosophical reason within an educative environment by human beings to better understand what they believe, expressed in the words, philosophy, university, and faith.

By means of which Macintyre identifies a particular pattern of Catholic thought which has evolved over millennia and has influenced the course of Western thought, one which especially re-emerged during the twentieth century, when in the opinion of the American commentator Alan Vincelette, "Catholic Philosophy comes into its own, and, through the genius of Catholic thinkers," such as the philosophers Max Scheler, Jacques Maritain, and Karol Wojtyła. Understanding their influence concerning the genesis of conciliar humanism can be approached reflecting on the words: "For whom are we philosophizing, unless it be for the men of our times? And what is our object, unless it be to attempt a solution of the doubts which are an obsession in our contemporaries?"[2] Written by the Belgian Cardinal Désirè-Joseph Mercier (1851–1926) former Archbishop of Mechelen-Brussel (1906–26), a noted Thomist of the twentieth century, founder of my *alma mater*, Leuven's famous Institute of Philosophy (1889) and seminary philosophy teacher of Leo Jozef Suenens (1904–96), who as Cardinal Archbishop of Mechelen-Brussel (1961–79) became one of the leading lights of the Council, another instance of personal thoughtful connections which inform conciliar humanism.

While already observed, "Christianity's engagement with philosophy was neither straight-forward nor immediate" in the opinion of Pope John Paul II in *Fides et Ratio* para. 38, the perennial relationship between the presence of Christian faith "and" the use of philosophical reason remains a constitutive feature within our Catholic DNA, as found in the original thought of Maritain, a remarkable proponent of Aquinas during the twentieth century. Wherein our Catholicity is characterized by the presence of philosophical *openness*, as observed by the pope, "the basis and source of this openness lies in the fact that the philosophy of St. Thomas is a philosophy of being, that is, of the 'act of existing' (*actus essendi*) whose transcendental value paves the most direct way to rise to the knowledge of subsisting Being and pure Act."[3] Expressive of papal confidence in the use of philosophy, these words outline the tenets of what the English priest Terence McGuckin refers to as "Pontifical Thomism,"[4] a phenomenon of the twentieth century, wherein we find the great philosopher pope's original appropriation of philosophical ideas taken from Aquinas within his critical engagement with Scheler's phenomenological ethical personalism, a way of thinking "taking hints from the past" later summarily expressed as "Catholic and open." Aspirational thought in the tradition of Catholic philosophy, characteristically open to future ideas, wherein "tradition is something unwritten." Namely, the consequence of a collective and interactive process found in the living transmission of thought acquired over time moving into the future, literally "standing on the shoulders of giants," a way of thinking with a scriptural orientation.

The first-time humans appear in the Bible occurs in the canonical structure of the Genesis creation narratives in chapters 1 and 2.

2. Mercier, *Origins of Contemporary Psychology*, 344.
3. John Paul II, *Whole Truth about Man*, 218–19.
4. McGuckin, "Century of 'Pontifical Thomism,'" 377–84.

Notwithstanding the obvious textual differences found within, they communicate a coherent theological vision about the wisdom of God the Creator, the goodness of creation and God's purposes for humanity, both male and female. Being created "in the image and likeness of God; male and female he created them" (Gen 1:26–27), these words determined the theological concept of *imago Dei* as the source of the dignity found in human life, the basis of Catholic social teaching as it emerged towards the end of the nineteenth century, a way of thinking especially championed by the popes of the twentieth century. Unlike the origins of ancient pagan religions, those of Christianity came to be understood as distinctively personal. The former found in some form of heavenly or spiritual intervention, an intellectual process of enlightenment or infusion of learning as the means of salvation, such as found in *Gnosticism*, a second-century quasi-religious movement and way of interpreting reality. Whereas Christian faith was initiated in response to God's unconditional love, found in a decisive and revelatory event, understood as a personal encounter with the Incarnate Word, the Person of Jesus Christ, wherein the earthly Jesus invited his disciples to follow him, an approach made in love: "I am the way and the truth and the life. No one comes to the Father except through Me" (John 14:6).

Scriptural thought which inspired Christianity's first philosopher, the author of these words: "To believe is nothing other than to think with assent. Believers are also thinkers: in believing, they think and in thinking, they believe. If faith does not think, it is nothing" (para. 79). Writing in *De Praedistinatione Sanctorum*, the saintly north African bishop of Hippo-Regius captures the mindset which informs thinking in the tradition of lived Catholic Christianity: a believing mind. At the end of the twentieth century, Pope John Paul II further characterized this aspirational thought of Augustine as being *sapiential*, one with distinctive metaphysical overtones; writing in his papal encyclical on the exercise of faith "and" reason within our Catholic tradition, which begins with the memorable characterisation, "like two wings the human spirit rises to the contemplation of truth."

Quoting with approval the thought of this first millennial Christian thinker infused with *sapiential* consciousness in *Fides et Ratio*, the pope ingeniously reintroduces this expression within contemporary Catholic discourse as a means of accessing its philosophical orientation. In so doing, the pope seeks to move beyond the traditional binary tensions between "either/or," a very postmodern concern which has challenged philosophers and theologians over two thousand years in the critical engagement between the exercise of faith and the use of reason. Writing his thirteenth encyclical Pope John Paul II drew an unusual amount of news coverage, as it "struck a chord" with the public at large, in a manner unsurpassed by other papal documents, in the opinion of the editors of *The Two Wings of Catholic Thought: Essays on Fides et Ratio* (2003). It was a very personal letter, reflecting the author's own contemplative experience as a professional university philosopher with over twenty years of exemplary papal leadership as shepherd teacher.

In arguing to the reasonableness of faith as a committed philosopher, a topic so often dismissed by his contemporaries, the pope successfully bridges the binary tensions which initially emerged during the transition of first-century Christianity, as it evolved from the Palestinian "Jesus Movement," as formulated by the British Augustinian scholar John M. Rist, "in the beginning Christians did not philosophise." While agreement exists on the centrality of Jesus Christ as the driving force for the emergence of Christianity from this Jewish sect, as recorded in Luke's Gospel "Jesus called the twelve together, and sent them out to proclaim the kingdom of God" (9:1–2), what followed is marked by significant complexity; again quoting the opinion of the pope: "the practice of philosophy seemed to the first Christians more of a disturbance than an opportunity" (para. 38).

Consequences observed by Cardinal Joseph Ratzinger in his seminal *Introduction to Christianity* (1968), which includes a reprint of "The God of Faith and the God of Philosophers: A Contribution to the Problem of Natural Theology," his 1959 inaugural lecture on becoming a professor at the University of Bonn (1777), when he claims: "The choice made in the biblical image of God had to be made once again in the early days of Christianity and the Church."[5] Brought on by the use of contemporary philosophical terminology, through the merging of various influences, such as Greco-Roman philosophical ideas, especially Platonic and Neoplatonic, along with the indirect influence of Jewish and pagan religious practices, to accomplish the missionary task of proclaiming the faith, evident in the compilation of *The Acts of the Apostles* and the subsequent Pauline and Johannine writings, containing considerable linguistic complexity which occasioned unease. A thoughtful evolution succinctly described by John Mark Reynolds, author of *When Athens Met Jerusalem* (2009): "For

---

5. Ratzinger, *Introduction to Christianity*, 137.

centuries these two cities, Athens and Jerusalem, provided the boundaries for intellectual and cultural growth. They formed one new kingdom. Tensions between the rationalism of Athens and the faith of Jerusalem always existed, but each recognized the contribution made by the other. Eventually, however, the citizens of both cities grew restless."

Generated by his own characteristic "restlessness," Augustine's thoughtful pursuit for wisdom as a Christian philosopher, moving away from a life of sensual indolence toward a spiritual life, enabled him to discover that he had in fact been responding to an invitation already offered by God, outlined in the thirteen books of his famous *Confessions*, written between 397 and 400. A way of thinking which informed the human orientation of medieval education, following the so-called 'dark ages,' found in Augustine's *Teaching Christianity* (c. 396), which provides a program of study used as the benchmark for the "complete intellectual formation" undertaken in European monastic and cathedral schools, wherein teaching as a human activity was essentially communicative, one which involves other human beings willing to learn, well expressed in these aspirational words of Josef Pieper (1904–97), the German Catholic philosopher, for anyone who assumes the vocation of teaching, taken from *The Silence of Thomas* (1957): "Thomas was the *teacher* of truth. Teaching is a process that goes on between living men. The teacher looks not only at the truth of things; at the same time, he looks at the faces of living men who desire to know the truth. Love of truth and love of men—only the two constitute a teacher."

Like Aquinas, who was first and foremost a believer who thought and taught within the Catholic *'tradition of schools,'* we meet the challenges of today looking into "living faces eager to know the truth," while positioned on "the shoulders of giants." Found in the thoughtful endowment of Augustine and Aquinas and those who aspire to follow their legacy, especially twentieth-century European philosophers living in the Catholic tradition such as Scheler, Maritain and Wojtyła; their way of thinking informs the genesis of conciliar humanism and its *sapiential* philosophical orientation.

While depictions of these great saints are well known in field of religious art, notably by Italian Renaissance artists Sandro Botticelli's (c. 1445–1510) *Saint Augustine in His Study* (1480) and Filippo Lippi's (c. 1406–69) *St. Augustine's Vision of the Trinity* (1437–38) or Carlo Crivelli's (c. 1430–c. 1495) well known portrait of Aquinas (1476), holding an opened book in one hand, the source of his scholarship, and a church building on the other, the recipient of his talent, or the lesser known but highly innovative art of Bartolomeo degli Erri (1447–82) with his portrayal of Aquinas on a single panel, not only consulting a book while standing beside a library shelf but also seated between Saints Peter and Paul, who have miraculously appeared to help him interpret sacred texts. However, over the course of art history these great Christian thinkers have never been portrayed as working together in a collaborative setting, an exception is found in the painting entitled "Augustinus en Thomas van Aquino." (1776)

An unusual piece of religious art positioned or rather hidden away in one of the side chapels within Sint-Pieterskerk which I first stumbled across during my graduate student days in Leuven's Katholieke Universiteit (1834). It was remarkable in so far as this art seems to refute the common misunderstanding of a bifurcation within Christian thought between Augustinian and Thomistic ways of thinking. On the contrary, this religious art captures a moment of *sapiential* consciousness, which not only characterizes the emergent synthetic tradition of twentieth-century Catholic philosophy, especially found in the pre-papal thought of Wojtyła, but also as it generated conciliar humanism as a particular instance of this way of thinking. Interestingly, and I believe quite remarkably given the obscure location of this painting, the American theologian from Loyola University Maryland, Frederick Christian Bauerschmidt chose this picture to introduce his essay "Augustine and Aquinas," part of a collection of essays entitled *Companion to Augustine and Modern Theology* (2013).[6] This religious art was originally commissioned by Leuven's Faculty of Theology to mark the episcopal consecration of Jacques T. J. Willens as Bishop of Antwerp (1776–84), a graduate of the faculty who was formerly the President and professor of theology at the neighboring Holland College attached to the University. It was painted by the Flemish artist Pieter-Jozef Verhaeghen (1728–1811), the last representative of the so-called "Flemish School of painting," known for his large scale religious and mythological scenes, as an altarpiece for the small chapel attached to the Faculty of Theology, and subsequently removed to its current location, "hardly a masterpiece nor even one of his better works" in the opinion of Bauerschmidt.

Notwithstanding its questionable artistic merit, this constructed scene wherein Augustine and Aquinas are engaged in a collaborative

---

6. Frederick Christian Bauerschmidt, "Augustine and Aquinas," in Pecknold and Toom, *T. & T. Clark Companion to Augustine*, 113.

endeavour represents the theological program undertaken within the faculty. Whereby Augustine is pictured standing, pointing to a passage in scripture on which a seated Aquinas with quill held in hand is ready to write a commentary, both figures inspired by the presence of the Holy Spirit. In so doing, the artist captures the spirit of Leuven theology, the collaborative endeavour portrayed in both figures seen in relation to each other, namely the combined use of sacred scripture and tradition, especially found in the thought of Augustine and Patristic writings, the twofold resources which inform medieval scholastic theology, especially that of Aquinas. Used in this book, this painting captures the thoughtful relationship between these two towering millennial figures within the philosophical edifice of Catholic thought; as expressed by Bauerschmidt, not only "the harmonious relationship depicted between the two doctors of the Church" and the complexity found within their thought, but also the recognition of Aquinas' thoughtful indebtedness to Augustine. As understood by the French philosopher Étienne Gilson (1884–1978), one of the outstanding commentators on medieval scholastic thought, who observed while there were obvious and accountable differences in the philosophical language they employed, when it comes to faith, Aquinas "has nothing to say which has not been said already by Augustine," both in the opinion of Étienne Gilson, *The Christian Philosophy of Saint Augustine* (1960) represent "the outstanding achievements of human reason in its attempt to understand the meaning of divine revelation."

19

A Tapestry of Thought

As QUESTIONING AND THINKING beings, our ideas do not occur in a vacuum but emerge within an interactive process, operating within a "tradition of thought," both receptive and interactive; this is expressed succinctly by Macintyre: "to be outside all traditions is to be a stranger to enquiry; it is to be in a state of intellectual and moral destitution."[1] Mixing metaphors, my earlier description of approaching the genesis of conciliar humanism set against a philosophical "landscape with figures" sits well with Ratzinger's metaphor of a thoughtful edifice, applied to understanding the philosophical tradition of Catholic thought as a "*mysterious fabric of texts and actions*" (emphasis added) which emerged from within the Catholic faith lived over the centuries. Writing in his *Milestones: Memoirs, 1927–1977* (1998), then Cardinal Ratzinger refers to the "Schott missal," a gift he received as a child. Namely, a sympathetic translation of the Latin *Missale Romanum* (1474), one catering for children and lay Catholics, produced by Dom Anselm Schott from the Benedictine Archabbey of St. Martin de Tours in Beuron, a municipality in the district of Sigmaringen in Baden-Württemberg, Germany. While its content was not always presented in a logical manner and "sometimes things got complicated and not easy to find one's way," it was precisely these aspects of the missal which, in the opinion of Ratzinger, "made the whole edifice wonderful."[2]

---

1. MacIntyre, *God, Philosophy, Universities*, 165.
2. Ratzinger, *Milestones*, 20.

Offering these observations about his missal, Ratzinger could well have been referring to the "edifice of philosophy" lived within the tradition of Catholic Christianity, wherein "every century had left its mark." Characterized as "Catholic and open," a lived tradition drawing thought from early Christianity, the church fathers, from medieval schools of theology moving into the modern era of nineteenth and twentieth-century thought, and onwards, whereby this tradition remains a "mysterious fabric of texts and actions." Approached as a tapestry of thought, this is especially applicable to the remarkable confluence of ideas which constitute the genesis of conciliar humanism as a "wonderful" edifice of documented thought about our shared humanity found in *Gaudium et Spes* and *Dignitatis Humanae*.

If Aristotle, in the opinion of the Florentine poet and scholastic philosopher Dante Aligheri (1265–1321), was "master of those who know," then in the opinion of Sir Richard Southern, the renowned English medieval scholar, the Roman politician and philosopher of the sixth century Boethius was "the master of those who wanted to know," which earned him the scholastic accolade "schoolmaster of medieval Europe."[3] A man of his time, awaiting execution for a 'trumped up' charge of treason, Boethius wrote his famous *Consolation of Philosophy* (523), one of the most influential books of the Middle Ages. Raised in the philosophical tradition generated by Augustine, who had absorbed the pagan Neo Platonism of his time, Boethius was considered "the last of the Romans, first of the scholastics." An accomplished commentator on Aristotelian thought which was available on the European continent at the time, having translated Aristotle's *Organon* from Greek, a collection of logical and technical treatises, including *Categories, On Interpretations, Prior Analytics, Posterior Analytics, Topics,* and *Sophistical Refutations*, Boethius was one of the main conduits for Aristotelian thought moving into medieval Europe.

Covering a broad spectrum of European history, between the tenth and fifteenth centuries, the world of the so-called "Middle Ages," or medieval in its adjectival form, represents a rather indiscriminate expression for a period of human history which has been characterized as "an age of faith." The American historian and author Barbara Tuchman, writing her "Foreword" to *The Distant Mirror* (1978) captures the medieval mindset: "The Christian religion was the matrix law of medieval life, omnipresent,

---

3. Southern, *Making of the Middle Ages*, 175.

indeed compulsory. Its insistent principle that the life of the spirit and of the after world was superior to the here and now, to material life on earth, is one that the modern world does not share."[4] Namely, the medieval world was inhabited by men and women of faith, living, and thinking within the Abrahamic monotheistic tradition, wherein "teachers were also thinkers." Whether Byzantine or Latin Christians, Jews, or Muslims, these shared a common religious belief in One God, all knowing, loving, and powerful, who freely created the world "from nothing," as found in the notable figure of St. Hildegard of Bingen (1098–1179), the German Benedictine abbess of Rupertsberg.

Operating within this religious context, medieval thought was built on human foundations laid by faith filled teachers, wherein we find a remarkable convergence of three factors: human, philosophical, and educational. Namely, the recognition of the human foundations for a God centred philosophical way of thinking and the human personalities of those who taught during this "era of faith." Summarily expressed by Stephen Kreiss: "Whereas in an earlier time, man was becoming more Christian, in the 12th century, there were efforts underway to make Christianity more human. That is, 'more oriented toward man,'"[5] captured in van der Weyden's *Descent from the Cross*. The remarkable convergence of these philosophical and educative factors is found within an understanding of the human being. Recalling the thought of Southern in his two volume *Scholastic Humanism* (1972): "the first characteristic of the product of the schools is a strong sense of the dignity of human nature. Without this there can be no humanism of any description, and it is a conspicuous force in the schools of the twelfth and thirteen centuries."[6] Namely, through the philosophical promotion of the God given nature of being human in possession of an immortal soul, and its inherent dignity as being rational and its implied respect for the world as being accessible to human scrutiny, the foundations of medieval humanism were laid.

Approached from a theological context, Boethius offered the first philosophical definition of "person" as being "an individual substance of a rational nature," one which was generally unchallenged until the twentieth century. The predication of rationality found in humanity was later taken up by Carl Linnaeus (1707–78), the Swedish natural scientist, designating the human species as *Homo sapiens* in his zoological taxonomy.

4. Tuchman, *Distant Mirror*, xix.
5. Brague, *Legend of the Middle Ages*, 27–28
6. Southern, *Scholastic Humanism*, 1:22.

However, by drawing attention to our humanity as being God given, we acquired indirect knowledge about the nature of God. Once again recalling the thought of R. W. Southern: "the greatest triumph of medieval humanism was to make God seem human."[7]

An approach which facilitated a development of philosophical thought in medieval philosophy, moving from Aristotelian logic towards his metaphysical way of thinking, especially generated by the recovery of Greek and Arabic manuscripts from Antiquity, held in parts of Greece, North Africa and along the Mediterranean coast. Now appearing on the European continent, especially around Naples and southern Italy, following the sack of Constantinople in 1204. A literary movement which prompted the necessity of Latin translations and commentaries on this thought used by "societies of scholars," namely for those unfamiliar with the original language. Wherein we find the foundations of scholastic thought generated through education which builds on the natural human activity to question prompted by wonder.

Writing his introduction to *An Introduction to Scholastic Philosophy* (1903), Maurice de Wulf (1867–1947), professor of philosophy at Leuven's Higher Institute and one of the pioneers of the histography of medieval philosophy, claims: "Whatever may be its extent and duration, the scholastic revival represents at the present time, and will represent in the annals of the twentieth century, an intellectual movement that may not be ignored,"[8] one which sets the background from which to approach the thought of Thomas Aquinas, and indirectly, the genesis of conciliar humanism. As recognized by his biographer Jean-Pierre Torrell, the French Dominican theologian, "Thomas was, in fact, situated in a specific time and place, marked by precise historical contingencies,"[9] like his forebears, Aquinas was a "man of his time."

An era which began in the year 529, "the *beginning* of the Middle Ages"[10] in the opinion of the German layman and Neo-Thomist philosopher Josef Pieper, author of *Scholasticism* (1960). Not because the Byzantine Emperor Justinian (482–565) issued a decree in that year which closed the eight-hundred-year-old Platonic Academy in Athens, as the German philosopher Georg W. F. Hegel (1770–1831) had claimed in volume two of his *Lectures on the Philosophy of History* (1837) but rather

7. Southern, *Medieval Humanism*, 37.
8. Wulf, *Introduction to Scholastic Philosophy*, vii.
9. Torrell, *Saint Thomas Aquinas*, 1:xx.
10. Pieper, *Scholasticism*, 17.

in the opinion of Pieper, that year marks the foundation of the Benedictine abbey on Monte Cassino (c. 529) by Saint Benedict of Nursia (c. 480–534), the founder of Western monasticism who had previously lived as a hermit at Subiaco, a town in the metropolitan city of Rome. This new location was embedded with significance, established on a mountain rising above the major thoroughfare between Rome and Naples, "one of the highways of the great migrations, the *Volkerwanderung*," where a young five-year-old Italian boy, Thomas from the county of Aquino in the Kingdom of Naples, asked "what is God?" A self-defining question documented by the English writer and Catholic convert G. K. Chesterton (1874–1936) in his biography *Saint Thomas Aquinas* (1986).

Son of Landulf of Aquino, a knight in the service of Frederick II (1220–50), the Holy Roman Emperor, King of Sicily and Italy, the five year old Thomas was probably entrusted to Abbot Landolfo Sinibaldi between July 23, 1230 and May 3, 1231 as an "oblate," a person literally "offered to God" by his family in the service of others, following the usual custom of the offering of the younger sons of nobles, prescribed in the fifty-ninth chapter of the Benedictine *Rule* written at this location. Attending the monastery school, the young boy asked this question to the surprise of his teacher and fellow students. Again, following the traditional custom whereby each monastery established a school to educate the monks to a sufficient level of learning to fulfill their spiritual obligations reading sacred scripture. An educative environment described by the French Benedictine and medieval scholar Dom Jean Leclercq (1911–93) in his seminal book *The Love of Learning and the Desire for God: A Study of Monastic Culture* (1961), "one must, in the monastery, possess books, know how to write them and read them, and therefore, if it be necessary, to learn how to read." Attending this school, Aquinas was educated according to the traditional curriculum in the liberal arts, complemented by his study of Aristotle's logic and natural philosophy.

However, early in 1239, as the armed conflict between Frederick II and Pope Gregory IX (1145–1241) began to impact directly on monastic life, the circumstances of Aquinas' life changed when his parents decided to relocate Thomas to Naples, then under the jurisdiction of the emperor. These broad sociopolitical difficulties were generated by the so-called "Investiture Controversy" over who choose and installed local diocesan bishops, between Pope Gregory VII (1015–85), ruler of the papal states and Henry IV, the Holy Roman Emperor (1056–1105) and King of Germany, Italy, and Burgundy. Whereupon Thomas, the child of someone who supported the latter, was enrolled at the city's *Studium Generale* (1224), the first 'state' institution, established in 1224 by the emperor to educate his court officials and administrative staff. Given the availability of Latin translations from manuscripts of Arabic astronomy, Greek medicine, and Aristotelian philosophy throughout southern Italy, the *studium generale* at Naples gained an international reputation for higher education. Especially following the European recovery of Aristotle's manuscript *Metaphysics*, an assemblage of twelve treatises he wrote on the study of "being."

One of the seminal works of Western philosophy which arrived on the European continent following the sack of Constantinople in 1204 by the Crusaders on their way to Egypt during the infamous fourth crusade (1202–4). Which together with other original manuscripts of notable Greek philosophers made Naples a remarkable centre for European learning, in what would become the oldest secular university on the Continent. With the necessary personnel of Latin translators familiar with the original Greek, these local teaching institutions enabled studied access to invaluable documents by Christian, Jewish and Islamic scholars alike. By means of which the young Aquinas became acquainted not only with Aristotle's *Metaphysics*, but also the Islamic thought of Averroes (1126–98), the Andalusian polymath who wrote several commentaries on Aristotle's philosophy, and that of Maimonides (1138–1204), the Sephardic Jewish philosopher, all of whom would influence Aquinas' original philosophical synthesis.

Furthermore, while studying in Naples, the former Benedictine oblate came in contact with members of the recently established Order of Preachers, especially with the elderly brother John of St. Julian, a popular Dominican preacher. Known as Dominicans, this mendicant order of friars was founded by the Castilian priest Saint Dominic Guzmán (1170–1221) and approved by Pope Honorius III (1150–1227) with his papal bull *Religiosam vitam* on December 22, 1216. Against the objections of his parents, around the age of nineteen Thomas chose to join this Order as a religious novice.

While the twentieth century lays claim to a 'philosopher pope,' during the tenth century there emerged the so-called "Mathematical Pope,"[11] namely Sylvester II (999–1003). Also philosophically trained and inclined, the Frenchman Gerbert (circ. 946–1003) of Aurillac, the

---

11. Hannan, *God's Philosophers*, 25.

location of the Benedictine monastery of St. Gerald which he entered around 963, was the foremost intellectual of his time, a recognized teacher who systematically lectured on the whole range of Aristotelian logical treatises assembled by Boethius. With a natural talent for study Gerbert initially studied mathematics in the region of Catalonia within Muslim Spain, where he acquired a knowledge of Arabic learning. One which he later integrated within his study of dialectic under Gerannus, the archdeacon of the cathedral of Rheims who taught at its cathedral school. Eventually appointed Archbishop of Rheims (991–98), then following one year as Archbishop of Ravenna, Gerbert was elected Pope Sylvester II in 999, whereby he continued to exercise intellectual and philosophical influence through his students, which initiated a new era of learning in France. Especially through the influence of Fulbert of Chartres (952–1028), an accomplished scholar and teacher at the cathedral school, later appointed Bishop of Chartres (1006–28), known as the "patriarch among masters of the great cathedral schools."

Set against this broad intellectual background, the so-called 'dark ages,' occurring roughly between the sixth and ninth centuries when Western Europe seemed submerged in chaos on all levels; this was not so dark as human scholarship, literature, and learning was kept alive and indeed thrived within the religious environment of European monastic and cathedral schools, initiating the so-called "era of schools" and the generation of 'scholasticism.' Rather than a set of doctrines, this latter expression designated a *modus docendi*, a medieval way of teaching philosophy, theology and biblical exegesis used in these schools, based on Aristotelian logic, found in Boethius' translation of the available Greek *Organon*, and used to organize what was being taught; this method was initially practiced by the French logician Peter Abelard (1079–1142) which he acquired at the cathedral school of Notre-Dame in Paris, and taken up by the French theologian Anselm of Laon (died 1117). He was known as *Doctor Doctorum Scholasticus* who established a "school of scholars" at the local cathedral of Laon, where Abelard also taught for a while. Typical for the times, these Latinised accolades were used to draw attention to the characteristic interests associated with the expertise of celebrated 'teachers' of theology or law, from the Latin *doctor*.

Within this educative ethos, scholastic thought employed rational argumentation over the traditional appeal to authority previously used in Patristic thought, employing a rational methodology as a means of instruction. Based on Socratic dialectical reasoning, this was employed to expand knowledge by means of rigorous analysis, using inference and the drawing of distinctions, within a discursive medium of question and answer. As a means of instruction, it had two notable features, the *lectio* and *quaestio*. Namely, an interpretative exposition or lecture was given on the content of a piece of writing by an acknowledged 'authority,' such as Plato, Aristotle, or Augustine. This way of thinking was characterized by the argumentative use of dialectic found in the expression *sic et non*— 'yes and no" originally used by Abelard. A way of thinking which generated the *quaestio disputatio*, the distinctive feature of scholastic thought. Originally used in the faculty of theology as a device to integrate or harmonise the thought of various "authorities" on a previously selected topic, drawn from the tenets of Christian faith. A method of teaching exemplified by the Italian scholastic theologian Peter Lombard's (1096–1160) *Four Books of Sentences*. A literary arrangement of source material from Sacred Scripture and the church fathers which became the standard textbook of theology used in medieval universities, as well as being required reading for students, those preparing for an academic career, such as the great scholastic thinkers, the Italian Dominican friar Thomas Aquinas, his fellow Italian Franciscan friar St. Bonaventure of Bagnoregio, the Scottish Franciscan friar Duns Scotus from Oxford University (1096), and the English Franciscan friar William of Ockham (1287–1347) from Oxford University, who were required to submit a written commentary on the *Sentences* to ensure their appointment as teachers.

However, "by the end of the twelfth century some semblance of order emerged within the turbulent crowds of scholars." Namely, there was a marked transition away from these monastic and cathedral schools as centres of learning towards civic institutions "built on men" in prominent towns and cities. Originally *universitas* referred to these urban institutions which encompassed scholastic guilds or "societies of scholars" in the words of the French lawyer Etienne Pasquier (1529–1615).[12] Mandated by papal authority, these institutions of higher education were responsible for teaching the standard curriculum of the seven liberal arts, replicating the grammatical schools of Antiquity, namely, study of the *Trivium* comprising grammar, logic, and rhetoric, which formed the prerequisite for further study of the *Quodrivium*, arithmetic, astronomy, music, and geometry. Known as the "humanities," these subjects were taught in the Faculty of Arts within medieval schools, as

---

12. Haskins, *Rise of Universities*, 64.

well as incorporating at least one of the higher Faculties of Law, Medicine, and Theology, which morphed into a *universitas scholarium* during the twelfth century. Writing in *The First Universities: Studium Generale and the Origins of University Education in Europe* (1997) Olaf Pedersen (1920–97), the Danish historian, characterized these institutions as a collective educative environment comprising teaching masters who attracted students, both local and international.[13]

Interestingly, while Aquinas subsequently addressed the idea of "the existence of God" at the beginning of his monumental *Summa Theologica* (1220–74), a subject which directed his lifelong theological project with his first question asked at Monte Casino, Aquinas was inquiring as to the nature rather than the existence of a Being who the medieval world took for granted. However, in the 1918 official formulation of Thomistic thought the subject of "God" concludes the assembled theses, with the claim: "God is distinguished from all finite beings" (para. 24). This is indicative of the philosophical approach adopted in twentieth-century Catholic thought which begins with a discussion of the basic distinction found in ontology, the study of being, between "act and potency," the foundation of the metaphysical systems of Aristotle and Aquinas upon which everything else depends. Recognized for his enthusiasm for study and accompanying spiritual zeal, this remains an extraordinary and very telling question coming from the young Thomas, especially given the circumstances of the time. Namely, living and thinking in the medieval "age of faith" wherein the existence of God was presumed, he was searching to understand the nature of being God within a religious environment which gave priority to human learning as being essentially communal.

---

13. Pedersen, *First Universities*, 64.

20

A Search for Learning

"Whatever you may bestow me from your fatherly heart and soul is chosen by wisdom, strengthened by authority and seasoned with love."[1] These words characterize the communal orientation of a medieval mindset in search for learning, as being philosophical, hierarchical, and *sapiential*. As a young Benedictine monk, a budding author approached his former teacher, Blessed Lanfranc of Pavia (c. 1005–89) seeking endorsement for his first book, the *Monologion* (1077–78), wherein Saint Anselm of Canterbury (1033–1109), following encouragement from his students at the monastic school at Bec, spoke about the attributes associated with a Christian understanding of God in the form of a thoughtful meditation about humanity. The first instance of a philosophical formulation leading to an understanding of God's existence, the so-called "ontological argument." The result of "one of the most fruitful and important minds in human history" as observed by Pope John Paul II in *Fides et Ratio* para. 14. Like our contemporary A-list celebrities who are sought out with extravagant and wild enthusiasm by their young fans, medieval scholars known for their wisdom and learning, like Lanfranc, were a similar source of popular attraction among the young, though perhaps approached in a more subdued manner and in places more remote.

Such was the case with a young man named Anselm who was prepared to travel a considerable distance from his home in Aosta in the Italian foothills of the Mont Blanc range to the secluded Benedictine Abbey of Our Lady in Le Bec Hellouin, the most influential abbey in the Anglo-Norman

1. Anselm, "Letter," 3.

kingdom at the time. Here in this remote location, far from the emerging centres of Christian learning in cosmopolitan Paris, Anselm continued his philosophical and theological study in 1059 at the abbey school which its famous prior Lanfranc had established. Recognized for his scholarship as *totius Latinitatis magister*, Lanfranc taught Aristotelian logic and Patristic theology, especially that of Saint Augustine, a preeminent theologian of the Latin Church of the first five centuries. Writing in *The Life of Anselm* (c. 1124), his friend Eadmer (c. 1060–c. 1126), an Anglo-Saxon monk from the Benedictine monastery of Christ Church in Canterbury, recalls: "Anselm came to Lanfranc and recognized the outstanding wisdom which shone forth in him. He placed himself under his guidance and in a short time became the most intimate of his disciples."[2]

A recognized teacher of Catholic thought of a philosophical orientation, Anselm embodied the medieval mindset inspired by Augustine's synthetic way of thinking which was subsequently used by generations of Catholic thinkers equally infused with *sapiential* consciousness as "friends of wisdom," such as the other formative millennial saints, Thomas Aquinas and Karol Wojtyła. As observed by the French Dominican Yves Congar (1904–95), one of the influential theologians during the Council, writing in *The Meaning of Tradition* (1964): "Catholicism is not limited to the catechism and that its present form has its roots in a long past, rich in thinkers, saints and creative minds."[3] Understood by Pope John Paul II as a "process of philosophical enquiry which was enriched by engaging the data of faith," conducted in the search for truth and justice in the "service of humanity," a process exemplified in the thought of Jacques Maritain and Wojtyła, which lies at the heart of conciliar humanism.

Recognized as "the *magna carta* of the Neo Thomist movement,"[4] whereby Pope Leo XIII promoted the Church's return to "the wisdom of St. Thomas," as his two seminal encyclicals generated various forms of Thomism over the twentieth century in response to the Leonine program of reform. Likewise, the papal encyclical *Fides et Ratio* encapsulated the spirit of the Wojtyłan program of *sapiential* reform within Catholic thought moving into a new millennium of the Christian era, found in the genesis of conciliar humanism. While Leo's *Rerum Novarum* (1891) initiated an awareness of social justice as a constitutive feature of subsequent Catholic thought it was a built on the philosophical foundations

2. Eadmer, *Life of St. Anselm*, 8.
3. Congar, *Meaning of Tradition*, 4–5.
4. McCool, "Thomism (1), Modern," 703.

elaborated in *Aeterni Patris* which inspired the promotion and subsequent popularity of Thomism as a way of thinking in search for learning during the mid-nineteenth century and onwards. This so-called "revival" of a philosophical and theological way of thinking attributed to the thought of Aquinas, evolved into further movements within established Catholic thought, found in so-called 'Neo-Scholastic' Thomism and Neo-Thomism. In part as a response to the blight of Catholic "modernism," characterized by "immanentism," understood as a denial of the human capacity for transcendence in preference for the subjective, denounced by Pope Leo XIII's successor Saint Pope Pius X (1903–14) in his encyclical *Pascendi Dominici Gregis* (1907), wherein he defined "modernism" as "the synthesis of all heresies" (para. 39) and his subsequent decree *Lamentabili Sane Exitu: Syllabus Concerning the Errors of the Modernists* on July 3, 1907. However, in continuity with previous papal teaching, Pope Pius X promoted Thomism as a way of thinking by means of the identification of 24 *Theses* (1914) found in the thought of Thomas.

In its heyday nineteenth and early twentieth century Neo-scholastic philosophy appeared overly confident, found in Latin manuals of "perennial philosophy" which sought to stand beyond the rigors of "time and space" as a "philosophy for all time," hardly self-critical, this way of thinking generated a spirit of complacency and over confidence among Catholic thinkers. Operating within the familiar scholastic framework which absorbed the themes of Greek philosophy, and the accompanying Aristotelian categories of being and associated terms, such as actuality and potentiality, matter and form, essence and existence, substance, and accidents, these became much more systematized than in their original context. While Plato explored ideas in a dialogical setting and Aristotle's treatises were not written as formal textbooks or systematic presentations, now the tenets of their thought formed the foundations for the study of theology and theological thought, approached from within the framework of late medieval philosophy—used by the formidable philosopher theologians of the time, such as Aquinas, Bonaventure, Duns Scotus and William of Ockham.

As a disciplined and systematic way of thinking, the spirit of modern philosophy and the emergence of Cartesian Rationalism, was initiated by its so-called "founder" the French philosopher René Descartes (1596–1650), author of *Discourse on the Method of Rightly Conducting One' Reason and of Seeking Truth in the Sciences* (1637). This French polymath was obviously well trained in scholastic thought at the Jesuit College

(1604), established by King Henry IV (1553–1610) in the city of La Flèche in western France "to instruct the young people and make them fall in love with science, honour and virtue, in order to be able to serve." Following the norms established by the ecumenical Council of Trent (1545–63), this way of philosophical thinking was envisaged as a means for transition into the formal study of theology for those preparing for priesthood, an approach the Council Fathers would have been familiar with having read the authorised Latin manuals of philosophy, a thoughtful encounter which certainly challenged the young seminarian from Kraków.

Introducing his informative commentary, *A Reader in Recent Catholic Philosophy* (2020) Alan Vincelette observed "Catholic philosophy has exploded in its amount and variety in the last century,"[5] written as a companion piece to his earlier publications *Recent Catholic Philosophy: The Twentieth Century* (2011) and *Recent Catholic Philosophy: The Nineteenth Century* (2009). In so doing, Vincelette identified the levels of layered complexity which inform the diversity found within the philosophical conversation undertaken by Catholic thinkers during the last century,[6] whereby he highlights two significant statistics, especially concerning the genesis of conciliar humanism. Namely, there have been approximately three thousand Catholic philosophers, including two popes, namely Leo XIII and John Paul II, and at least three converts, Max Scheler, Jacques Maritain, and Edith Stein, who fit into this broad category, all of whom have offered contributions of note, especially when it comes to understanding the background of conciliar humanism.

Moreover, these philosophers can be grouped within seven major movements within Catholic thought, with around sixty percent falling under the broad category of Thomism. As a theological way of thinking with a definite philosophical orientation, Thomism is based on the leading ideas of Thomas Aquinas, a way of thinking which has evolved over seven hundred years from a scholastic mindset operative in the medieval world. Wherein the philosophical giants of the thirteenth century, equally infused with *sapiential* consciousness, such as Aquinas, Albertus Magnus, Bonaventure, John Duns Scotus and William of Ockham, were recognizable theologians who all sought to integrate ideas taken from the pagan philosophy of Aristotle within Christian teachings; in so doing, they used

---

5. Vincelette, *Reader in Recent Catholic Philosophy*, 1.
6. Vincelette, *Recent Catholic Philosophy: The Twentieth Century*, 7.

their natural rational resources to think about the existence and nature of God, a consequence of their search for learning.

During the twentieth century several variants of this Catholic way of thinking emerged, such as Neo-Thomism, Transcendental Thomism, Historical or "existential" Thomism, the latter found in the thought of Maritain and Étienne Gilson. A way of thinking which used traditional scholastic Latin terminology, drawn from the metaphysical systems of Aristotle and Aquinas, and especially followed the interpretation of Thomas Cajetan (1469–1534). This Italian Dominican friar and later a Cardinal (1517–34) was known for his dedicated and disciplined promotion of the thought of Aquinas, especially through his extensive and rigorous commentaries on the *Summa Theologica*, Aquinas' seminal three-part book written as an introduction for students of theology published around 1485. Meant to facilitate reading the original text, Cajetan's widely consulted and popular commentaries proved to be somewhat counterproductive during the twentieth century in supplanting this necessity, with a document typical for the time, *Twenty-four Thomistic Theses*. Published by the Sacred Congregation of Studies which was responsible for oversight of Catholic universities and seminaries, following Saint Pope Pius X's (1835–1914) decree *Postquam sanctissimus* of July 27, 1914.

Beginning with the fundamental Aristotelian axioms of ontology, the study of "being" and its basic division between "act and potency," along with its related principles of non-contradiction and of causality, the philosophical content of this curial document not only identified the basic principles and original thought underlying Thomism, but in so doing, defined the means to differentiate this Catholic way of thinking from other currents of contemporary philosophical thought, indicative of the consolidation of the Leonine programme of philosophical renewal. As such, the compilation of the *Twenty-Four Theses* established what might be considered as being "outside" of the parameters of recognizable 'Catholic' thought of the time, generating Novak's observation "a break with the past": an expression open to interpretation. Whereby this Congregational document sought to consolidate the philosophical foundations of Catholic thought moving into the twentieth century initiated by Pope Leo XIII's seminal *Aeterni Patris* (1879), subtitled "on the restoration of Catholic Philosophy in Catholic Schools in the Spirit of the Angelic Doctor, St. Thomas Aquinas."

A direct consequence of the Leonine program of renewal, the "Higher Institute of Philosophy" was established on November 8, 1889 as an independent institution under the auspices of the Catholic University of Leuven (1425), wherein an alternative school of interpretation of Thomistic thought emerged, based on an integral understanding of humanity. Inspired by the thought of its founder, then Professor Désiré-Joseph Mercier (1851–1926), who directed attention to the usefulness of Thomist thought to critically assess and engage the tenets of contemporary scientific thought, found in his popular *The Origins of Contemporary Psychology* (1918). An original approach later adopted by one of its professors of philosophy, the Jesuit Joseph Maréchal (1878–1944), the founder of Transcendental Thomism. Interestingly, one of the leading figures during the Council, Cardinal Suenens had been a philosophy student of Mercier at the local diocesan seminary in Mechelen, who was later responsible for sending Suenens to Rome for graduate study in both philosophy and theology.

"How can such rapid progressive diversification of particular disciplines be combined with the need to create a synthesis, or to preserve among men and women capacities for contemplation and wonder which lead to wisdom,"[7] remarkable thought taken from *Gaudium et Spes* para. 56, which was used by Stefan Swieżawski in *St. Thomas Revisited* (1995), to identify the philosophical agenda found within Conciliar thought. In so doing, he sought to counter the suggestion that the Council was only pastoral. Furthermore, the philosophical intent underlying these words direct attention to a moment of *sapiential* consciousness within conciliar thought, namely the search for wisdom found in wonder and contemplation in the tradition of Western philosophy. In so doing, the Polish philosopher drew attention to the fundamental human orientation of this thoughtful activity: "Philosophy is a necessary condition of humanness; in order to be a human being, in order to develop our humanity, we must be *friends of wisdom*" (emphasis added).[8] Wherein, he reiterated the claim made by Pope Leo XIII as he introduces *Aeterni Patris* (1879), his papal manifesto on Christian philosophy: "it is in the very nature of man to follow the guide of reason in his actions" (para. 2).

Whereby Pope Leo identifies the human orientation of his Leonine program of philosophical renewal within Catholic thought, the promotion of a way of thinking, suitable to "true faith" and "consonant with the dignity of human knowledge," which offers sound instruction

---

7. Swieżawski, *St. Thomas Revisited*, 8.
8. Swieżawski, *St. Thomas Revisited*, 8.

for any "reasonable person," and in so doing, the pope anticipates the human agenda and philosophical orientation which generated conciliar humanism. Given this human orientation, one might claim the use of philosophical thought constitutes part of the DNA of those thinking in the tradition of lived Catholic Christianity wherein we find "desirable patterns of thought" associated with those living "inside" the Catholic tradition; moving into the twentieth century, one characterized by remarkable diversity among European philosophers who are recognizably Catholic.

A later offshoot of this variant of Thomist thought was found in "Lublin Thomism" or "Transcendental Personalist Thomism" generated within the Catholic University of Lublin's "School of Thomist Philosophy," a connection found in the intellectual bond established between Leuven (Louvain), as one of Europe's oldest Catholic universities and Lublin, one of Europe's youngest Catholic universities established on July 27, 1918. Known for its independent philosophical stance against the prevalent Marxist atheistic materialism and associated political ideology, the "School of Thomist Philosophy" promoted an original understanding of realist metaphysics, "a philosophy of being" found in the thought of one of its founding members, a specialist in the history of philosophy, Stefan Swieżawski's *Being* (1948) and *A Treatise on the Human Being* (1966). Approached as a form of cognitive realism in the Aristotelian Thomistic tradition, outlined by Swieżawski in *St. Thomas Revisited* (1982), this way of thinking brought together an original philosophical anthropology, understood as the study of the nature and destiny of the human person who thinks, and a related understanding of ethics, based on the person who thinkers about the values and principles which guide our activity towards other human beings, achieved through a thoughtful engagement with classical philosophers and their texts, directed towards a more complete "humanism."[9] An original way of thinking which directed the original thought of both Maritain and Wojtyła wherein we find ingredients for the philosophical and pastoral inspiration underlying conciliar humanism. As George Weigel records: "It was Swieżawski who introduced Wojtyła to Maritain's *Integral Humanism*, a key 1936 text that later influenced the Second Vatican Council and its approach to the modern world."[10]

---

9. Krąpiec and Maryniarczyk, "Lublin Philosophical School," 405–22.
10. Weigel, *Witness to Hope*, 139.

During the Council, these members of the School, Professors Stefan Swieżawski and his colleagues Karol Wojtyła and George Kalinowski, would exercise considerable influence in the direction and content of conciliar humanism, the so-called "Lublin connection." Having previously encountered both Gilson and Maritain while in Paris in 1929 studying at the Sorbonne (1257) and the neighboring Collège de France (1530) in preparation for his doctorate on Duns Scotus under the guidance of the former, which he would receive from the University of Lwów in 1932, Swieżawski returned to Poland to become a proponent of Maritain's existential Thomism. Following his appointment to the Catholic University of Lublin (1918), he assumed prominence as one of the founders of Lublin's "School of Thomist Philosophy" as it evolved during the 1950s. Attempting to draw together "the best and brightest young Catholic minds in the country," Wojtyła was invited to join the School following his appointment to teach Christian ethics at the university on October 12, 1954. A friend and professional colleague of Wojtyła, Stefan Swieżawski was not only officially present during the Council as a lay auditor appointed by Pope John, but also functioned as an effective philosophical collaborator, literally speaking the same language with the young Archbishop while working "off site."

Finally, through the historical research of the medieval scholar Étienne Gilson, professor of history of philosophy at the University of Strasburg between 1921 till 1932, a third variant emerged, namely, historical, or existential Thomism. As a means of promoting this approach, Gilson founded the Pontifical Institute of Medieval Studies in Toronto, Canada in 1929. With a mutual interest in original research into the existential thought of Aquinas, especially in his Christian humanism, both Gilson and Maritain were the first recipients of honorary doctorates awarded by the Pontifical Academy of Saint Thomas Aquinas (1879) in 1930. Most recently another variant has emerged, namely "Papal Thomism" of the twentieth century, found in the thought of Pope Leo XIII and Pope John Paul II.

Nevertheless, notwithstanding these variants, the use of Thomism in the opinion of Vincelette "remains particularly rare in continental philosophers born between 1930 and 1960." Namely, among those who looked for alternative resources within contemporary European thought to better engage the "human crisis" in their pursuit of truth, especially philosophers like Scheler who espoused Augustine's Christian anthropology viewed through the lens of Pascal's original thought, which helped in their efforts to address the issue of being human living in the critical and violent circumstances of the twentieth century. In so doing, to articulate the inherent dignity and value found in human existence, its meaning and purpose. All of which is indicative of "a struggle within the Church against the absolute, unchanging fortresses of Latin Scholasticism" in the words of the American Catholic philosopher and journalist Michael Novak (1933–2017), an intellectual struggle which informs a mindset which he calls a "break with the past."[11] Whereby Catholic philosophers like their forebears drew ideas and concepts from diverse contemporary movements of European thought, such as humanism, phenomenology, existentialism and personalism, a situation of particular significance leading up to and during the extended ecclesial "meeting of minds" which generated conciliar humanism.

An original way of thinking which emerged during the Council about our shared humanity, especially inspired by and drawn from the philosophical thought of two converts to the Catholic faith, namely Max Scheler and Jacques Maritain. United in their quest for wisdom, these philosophers took alternative paths towards understanding "what is human," employing ideas found in phenomenology and ethical personalism, and existential Thomism, and a mixture thereof found in the thought of Wojtyła. However, unlike the American poet Robert Frost's (1874–1963) iconic 1915 "The Road Not Taken," wherein we find a multiplicity of meanings applied to the inevitability of making a choice, written as a joke about his friend, the "chronically indecisive" English poet Edward Thomas (1878–1917), these remarkable Catholic philosophers in their own right in the pursuit of wisdom sought to follow a different path towards an integral understanding of our shared humanity, metaphorically standing on the shoulders of two faith filled intellectual giants, Augustine and Aquinas, outstanding students of humanity. A study which came to fruition during the twenty first and last to date ecumenical council, following its unprecedented human agenda and its integral philosophical orientation, which addressed the philosophical question *quid sit homo?*

Wherein the meaning of our shared humanity is found within the Triune nature of God as *communio*, now understood as a 'community of persons' living together in human solidarity directed towards God. This personal and relational way of thinking, which especially characterized the thought of Scheler, was reflected in the Council's human love story,

---

11. Novak, *New Generation*, 93.

that of conciliar humanism. Wherein we find a unique convergence of various patterns of contemporary European thought, an original way of thinking articulated in a new language about the human being as a 'human person,' found in the original thought of one of its major proponents, Archbishop Karol Wojtyła from Kraków. By means of his creative juxtaposition of two fundamental ideas of traditional philosophy, person, and act. The former drawn from the thought of Max Scheler's phenomenological ethical personalism and the latter represents Wojtyła's adaptation of Aquinas' original idea of *actus essendi*.

21

An Outsider?

As a Catholic philosopher of the early twentieth century, Scheler drew particular inspiration from Augustinian resources, viewed through the lens of the French philosopher Blaise Pascal's original adaptation, as someone who addressed the persistent issue of "man's need for renewal" occasioned by the "disappearance of God" and the "threat of the machine,"[1] discussed by the German born American historian Peter Gay (1923–2015) in *Weimar Culture: The Outsider as Insider* (1974). In so doing, Scheler focused attention on the idea of the "human person."

While Scheler was not the first to ask "what is man" and "what is man's place in nature," the title of a posthumous publication,[2] over the duration of his somewhat tumultuous philosophical career he sought a synthesis of thought which embraced "what man is and what metaphysical position and status is which he occupies within the totality of being, world and God,"[3] especially found in his original understanding of philosophical anthropology, based on the idea of a 'human person,' foundations for which were to be discussed in his anticipated book on metaphysics, which never eventuated. In the meantime, he offered a synthesis of original thought about humanity approached from the perspectives of phenomenological realism, ethical personalism and philosophical sociology. As József M. Bochenski (1902–95), the Polish Dominican philosopher observed in *Contemporary European Philosophy*

---

1. Gay, *Weimar Culture*, 8.
2. Scheler, *Man's Place in Nature*, 3.
3. Scheler, "On the Idea of Man," 184.

(1982), Max Scheler deserves special recognition for the "return to man" which was so "characteristic of our age."[4]

"Today we see and experience the powerful pressure of evolutionary naturalism, coloured by the ideology of atheism, which dominates in studies on man and reduces man to a product of nature by stripping him of spiritual and transcendental dimension."[5] Taken from the "Introduction" to one of Karol Wojtyła's earliest works *Considerations on the Essence of Man* (1949) these words were used by the Polish philosopher Andrzej Maryniarczyk, SDB, from The John Paul II Catholic University of Lublin (1918) to characterize the two fold philosophical challenge posed during the first half of the twentieth century. Namely, one which reduced being human to our biological and material status as a political animal, which engaged the thought of European Catholic philosophers, like Scheler and Maritain, and one which sought to respond to the questionable influence of the French atheist and philosopher Auguste Comte's (1798–1857) scientific positivism or "evolutionary naturalism," discussed by Scheler in his essay "On the Positivistic Philosophy of the History of Knowledge and Its Laws of Three Stages." (1921)

This philosophical way of thinking generated the aggressive ideology of "atheistic humanism," which in the opinion of Scheler originated from Comte's scientific thought, wherein he substitutes "'mankind' as '*Grand-Etre*' in the place of God" writing in his early essay "Concerning Ressentiment and the Value Judgement of Morals: A Contribution towards a Pathology of Culture," later published as *Ressentiment* (1912).[6] Whereby Scheler subverted Nietzsche's original analysis of the sublimated effects of the human phenomenon of ressentiment, literally a "re-feeling" of an experience of impotence. Written from a Christian perspective, inspired by the thought of Augustine, for which Scheler received the somewhat ironic epithet "The Catholic Nietzsche" from his friend Ernst Troeltsch (1865–1923), the German philosopher and sociologist of religion. Set against a critical examination of "the existence and organization of the *genus Homo*," Scheler confronts the contemporary "blindness" found in scientific positivism as a means to access the broader dimensions found within human experience, namely, being personal and spiritual. As he writes in his essay "Christian Love and the Twentieth Century" (1917): "humanitarianism rebels against the first principle of the Christian

---

4. Bochenski, *Contemporary European Philosophy* 153.
5. Wojtyła, *Considerations on the Essence of Man*, 11.
6. Scheler, *Ressentiment*, 73.

commandment of love."[7] A way of thinking he later addressed in his 1921 essay "On the Positivistic Philosophy of the History of Knowledge and Its Law of Three Stages." Understood as a philosophical movement generated by the thought of Comte, which in the opinion of Scheler replaced 'the Divine,' his preferred reference to the personal God, in favour of humanity, wherein we find the ingredients for the re-emergence of humanism. Now approached as an atheistic and secular variant within twentieth-century European philosophy, generated by the thoughtful influence of the so-called "masters in the 'school of suspicion,'" namely, the disruptive and toxic thought of Nietzsche, Marx, and Freud.

Notwithstanding the inherent ambiguity arising from Scheler's unorthodox personal life and complicated philosophical thought, recent years have witnessed a rehabilitation of his status within Catholic circles, mentioned favorably as a Catholic philosopher by Alan Vincelette in *A Reader in Recent Catholic Philosophy* (2020) and *Recent Catholic Philosophy: The Twentieth Century* (2011). However, while difficult to read due to Scheler's unusual and disorganized style of writing, his thought remains relatively unknown to a contemporary readership, especially in the English-speaking world. Largely unread, Scheler remains a figure of ambiguity due to several factors. As a prominent German philosopher thinking within the milieu of Catholic thought for nearly two thirds of his life, following his very public rejection of Catholicism around 1923, his thought was considered suspect; with his major books *The Nature of Sympathy* and *Formalism in Ethics and Non-Formal Ethics of Values*, both published in 1913, *On the Eternal in Man* (1920) and *Man's Place in Nature* (1928), automatically placed on the *Index Librorum Prohibitorum*. Established by the Congregation for Doctrine of the Faith around 1560, this list identified publications to be blacklisted as deemed suspect by Catholic authorities because they contained either heretical content or material considered detrimental to morality which Catholics were forbidden to read. Following a change of mindset during the Council, the *Index* was formally abolished on June 14, 1966 by Pope Paul VI. Compounding this complex situation was Scheler's Jewish heritage which prevented the publication of his books during the Nazi regime in Germany due to its anti-Jewish policies. While this situation changed after the War, with Scheler's books readily available to read in German, the persistence of suspicion remained within Catholic circles regarding his published

---

7. Scheler, *On the Eternal in Man*, 367.

thought. Difficult enough to read in the first place given his idiosyncratic style of writing, this was further complicated by a lack of reliable translations within the English-speaking world.

Given these circumstances, Scheler's original ideas have been primarily accessible through their use by other prominent Catholic European thinkers, such as the German philosopher, Saint Edith Stein (1891–1942) in her doctoral dissertation *On the Problem of Empathy* (1916), a critical study of Scheler's *The Nature of Sympathy*, and especially her autobiographical study *Life in a Jewish Family 1891–1916* (1986). Wherein she recalled Scheler's positive influence during her participation in the University of Göttingen's "Philosophical Society," which also included another student Dietrich von Hildebrand (1889–1977), wherein she claimed she encountered in the person of Scheler a "phenomenon of genius" who was prepared to engage the question of religion as a serious issue worth consideration, but also someone who was also capable of seductive and dazzling thought, "scattering about ingenious suggestions without pursing them systematically."[8] Also coming under the influence of Scheler's thought, von Hildebrand would become a prominent German Catholic philosopher, recognized by Pope Pius XII (1939–58) as the so-called "twentieth century Doctor of the Church." Considered a leading proponent of phenomenological realism and ethical personalism in the style of Scheler, von Hildebrand was recognized as "one of the great ethicists of the twentieth century" by Pope Benedict XVI,[9] someone he knew as a young priest while working in Munich. The influence of Scheler's Christian personalism is especially evident in Hildebrand's classic *On the Nature of Love* (1965), recently translated *The Heart: An Analysis of Human and Divine Affectivity* (2007).[10] Building on his 1912 doctoral dissertation supervised by Husserl, wherein Hildebrand indicates his indebtedness to Scheler, especially in the final chapter entitled *Amare in Deo*, while attributed to Augustine, this expression was originally employed by Scheler.

Furthermore, through the influence of the Kraków born philosopher Roman Ingarden (1893–1970), who was trained in phenomenology, Karol Wojtyła was introduced to Scheler's original phenomenological approach to the study of ethics and the hierarchy of values. Initially trained

---

8. Stein, *Life in a Jewish Family*, 259–60.

9. Thought taken from a letter written in 2000 by Cardinal Ratzinger to Alice von Hildebrand, quoted by John Henry Crosby, Introduction to Hildebrand, *Heart*, x.

10. Hildebrand, *Heart*, 173–82.

under Husserl as a member of Göttingen's "philosophical Society," where Scheler offered seasonal lectures on contemporary philosophy, Ingarden then relocated to the University of Freiburg (1457) where he completed his doctorate under Husserl in 1918. After which Ingarden returned home to teach at Kraków's Jagiellonian University (1364), where he encouraged a recently appointed young lecturer in Christian Ethics at the university to study Scheler's philosophical thought, whereby Wojtyła successfully wrote his Habilitation, *Revaluation of the Possibility of Founding a Christian Ethic on the Ethical System of Scheler* (1953)

Not for the first time this young priest and graduate philosopher confronted the challenge of serious reading, let alone understanding a difficult book which he eventually translated into Polish: "look what I've got to cope with"[11] he exclaimed to his lifelong friend Mieczyslaw Malinski (1923–2017), the Polish theologian from Kraków, when confronted with reading Scheler's *Formalism in Ethics and Non-Formal Ethics of Values* (1913), written during Scheler's "explicitly Catholic phase."[12] Circumstances which mirror Wojtyła's earlier confrontation reading another difficult book, *Ontologia czyli metafizyka* (1926) by the Thomist philosopher Professor Kazimierz Wais (1865–1934). As with his previous efforts to read *Ontologia*, Wojtyła's critical engagement reading Scheler in the original German were extremely productive: "It opens up a new world; a world of values, and a fresh view of mankind," especially "Scheler's theory of values and of human nature" which he now sought to reconcile with the tenets of Thomist philosophy he first encountered in Wais' *Ontologia*,[13] brought together in his idea of a 'human person.'

While Scheler died in 1928, well before the Council, ideas drawn from his phenomenological ethical personalism and philosophical sociology, especially found in these personal connections, inform the genesis of conciliar humanism and its original network of ideas, human person, community person, and human solidarity. Original thought which emerged while a Catholic philosopher between 1900 till 1921 in response to the contemporary "human crisis," ingeniously integrated within Scheler's original understanding of the essential and constitutive triadic structure which informs his phenomenology of religious activity. Namely, one which includes the individual believer who performs religious activity, such as acts of personal prayer and liturgical worship,

11. Malinski, *Pope John Paul II*, 127.
12. Williams, *Mind of John Paul II*, 115.
13. Malinski, *Pope John Paul II*, 130.

together with the religious community wherein this activity is enacted, all of which is simultaneously and independently directed to the Divine Person, as the source and inspiration for this activity, both individual and communal. Regrettably, as observed by Wojtyła, Scheler's highly original descriptive analysis of this human phenomenon, found in his phenomenological ethical personalism and philosophical sociology, lacked the necessary support of a form of philosophical language, which Wojtyla found in the metaphysical realism of Aquinas' original idea of *actus essendi*. Ingeniously rehabilitated and appropriated by Wojtyla, Scheler's ideas were subsequently used in conciliar humanism, understood as a form of nuanced thought which can be easily detected, though not specially referenced within Council documents for reasons previously indicated. Whereby ideas generated from 'outside' the traditional 'empire of twentieth-century Catholic Thomism,' to paraphrase the thought of Winston Churchill, would re-emerge as an 'insider' within contemporary Catholic discourse found in conciliar humanism.

Scheler's remarkable synthesis of original thought, at times clouded with ambiguity, was generated by his "endless search for God along ever new paths" in the words of his friend Martin Heidegger speaking "in memoriam Max Scheler."[14] However, until his death Scheler never doubted the existence of God, though how this was to be understood in his final years very much deviated beyond the boundaries of traditional Catholic thought, towards 'panentheism.' Words delivered while Heidegger was lecturing on Monday May 21 having been informed of Scheler's unexpected death on May 19, 1928, following Heidegger's recent appointment as professor of philosophy at the Albert Ludwig University of Freiburg (1457), when he succeeded Edmund Husserl. A philosophical search unexpectedly interrupted by Scheler's sudden death from cardiac arrest while relocating from Cologne, a predominantly Catholic city where he was regarded with suspicion by its Archbishop, Cardinal Karl Joseph Schutte (1920–41), moving to the city of Frankfurt to take up a new professorial appointment teaching at the recently established citizen's University at Frankfurt am Main (1914), where he could pursue his special philosophical interest in sociology of religion and comparative religion, later named in 1932 after one of the city's famous "native sons," Johann Wolfgang von Goethe (1749–1832). This relocation also afforded Scheler with an opportunity for further collaboration with Rudolf Otto

---

14. Heidegger, "In memoriam Max Scheler," in *Metaphysical Foundations*, 51.

(1869–1937) author of the ground-breaking *The Idea of the Holy* (1917), the German Lutheran theologian and specialist in comparative religion who was teaching at the Philipps University of Marburg (1527), which were not met due to his untimely death. One which brought to an end a life characterized by ambiguity, like the times he lived in.

Max Ferdinand Scheler was born on August 22, 1874 in Munich, the capital city of so-called 'Catholic' Bavaria, during the reign of Kaiser Wilhelm II (1859–1941), the last emperor of Germany, characterized as "the land of the Reformation" wherein religious affiliation informed all aspects of German consciousness. The child of a Protestant father and Jewish mother, the aspiring Doctor Max Scheler was eventually baptized a Catholic on September 20, 1899 in the Capuchin parish of St. Anton in Munich. What is fascinating about Scheler lies in the fact that his most productive philosophical activity was conducted while outside the confines of formal University life, operating from within the 'spirit' of Roman Catholicism, understood as a religious philosophical orientation, found in the thought of St. Augustine and the seventeenth-century French philosopher Blaise Pascal, an orientation which he eventually renounced. As such, Scheler might be considered "a philosopher of his time" in so far as his thought is clouded with ambiguity; difficult to pin down, he sought to engage contemporary ways of thinking, including the emerging field of phenomenology and the practice of social analysis, to assume the status as one of the founding figures in sociology.

As a philosopher, Scheler was recognizably 'catholic,' understood as a "universal-historical-human" oriented way of thinking, rather than Catholic "in the sense of the Church," consistent with his lifelong rejection of all forms of indoctrination by what he disparagingly referred to as "Church philosophy." According to his friend Martin Heidegger, as he offered a memorial reflection on hearing of Scheler's death, "Augustine and Pascal acquired new meaning—new answers to and against Nietzsche." Answers initially found in Scheler's second piece of writing, an essay entitled "Concerning Ressentiment and Value Judgement of Morals: A Contribution towards a Pathology of Culture," (1912) whereby he received universal acclaim not only from local Catholics but also from the intellectual community at large. Especially from Germany's leading sociologists from Berlin's Friedrich Wilhelm University (1810), the world's preeminent institution for the study of natural science, with whom he had previously worked while a student.

AN OUTSIDER?

Scheler's decision to relocate to this modern industrial city in 1894 was strategic, with far reaching consequences, whereby he was introduced to the study of philosophy, following an uneventful year at the medical faculty at Munich's Ludwig Maximilian University (1472) in 1893. The subsequent publication of *Ressentiment* received acclaim from Berlin's leading sociologists, Georg Simmel (1858–1918), Max Weber (1864–1920) and Werner Sombart (1863–1941), who gave a warm welcome to "the Catholic Nietzsche" in their midst. Following this initial success, Scheler wrote his first book entitled *The Nature of Sympathy* (1913) which documented his original application of the phenomenological method to the analysis of the diverse forms of human emotions found in the experience of "fellow feeling." Namely, the sense of identity that humans experience in relationships with other human beings, including "empathy," and through the experience of love and hatred. Original thought concerning the nature of intersubjectivity, which Scheler developed within his original philosophical sociology, and his appropriation of two patterns of socially based thought. Namely, Ludwig Feuerbach's philosophical discussion of *I and Thou* and the sociological distinction between two forms of social organization, between *gemeinschaft* 'living community' and *gesellschaft* 'society,' first used by the German philosopher Ferdinand Tönnies (1855–1936), cofounder of the German Society for Sociologists, along with Max Weber (1864–1920) and Georg Simmel (1858–1918).

The latter served as the basis for Scheler's study of the various forms of social and communal groups, namely, the family, nation, and church, from which emerged his original idea of a "communal person" and his unique approach to 'solidarism,' discussed in *Formalism* and *On the Eternal in Man*. Writing in the 1921 Preface to the former wherein Scheler recognized the contribution of "the well-founded 'principle of solidarity' and the interrelated 'theory of essential forms of human groups." The significance of these connections inform Scheler's Christian understanding of what he calls 'human solidarism,' a way of thinking expressed in the observation of his Jesuit biographer John Nota: "Aloneness with God is necessarily a togetherness with others in the Church."[15]

Ideas which comprise Scheler's so-called "sociological proof for God," namely, as genuine evidence for understanding the idea of God's existence, based on Scheler's idea of a community of finite personal,

---

15. Nota, *Max Scheler*, 86.

spiritual human beings, characterized by the "tendency for transcendence," leading to the "discovery of God" as Divine Person. Approached through the sphere of the Absolute, an integral dimension of being a human person, discussed in his essay "Christian Love and the Twentieth Century" (1917). This Christian orientation, which informed Scheler's original thought, is especially found in his phenomenological ethical personalism discussed in *The Nature of Sympathy* and in *Formalism in Ethics and Non-Formal Ethics of Values*, both published in 1913. These were seminal publications which brought Scheler international recognition, which remains so today. The latter received critical attention, chosen by Wojtyła as the subject for his *Habilitation*. However, notwithstanding their successful reception, Scheler remains an enigmatic figure within European thought, living in Weimar Germany (1918–33) during "an age of collapse," according to another biographer John Raphael Staude, writing his informative *Max Scheler, 1874–1928: An Intellectual Portrait*. (1967), Scheler was "a mirror of many intellectual and political tendencies in early twentieth-century Germany."[16] A person of considerable philosophical vision and genius, according to Staude, "Max Scheler was a remarkable and historically significant figure."[17]

Given the religious divisions which constituted German national consciousness, Munich's religious ethos and its distinctive Catholic *Weltanschauung* exercised a significant influence on Scheler's personal, religious, and eventual philosophical formation; for two thirds of his life Scheler wrote as a "catholic philosopher." Especially through his personal association with the Benedictine Archabbey of St. Martin (1863) at Beuron in the Black Forest near Freiburg, where he would retreat from his duties as a visiting lecturer at the philosophical societies at Munich and Göttingen, to join the religious activities of this monastic community. Often he would be joined by other emerging young phenomenologists, Catholic such as Martin Heidegger and Dietrich von Hildebrand, and the young agnostic Jewess Edith Stein, in what I refer to as their "Beuron experience" of Catholicism, namely, one which is essentially communal, intellectual, and united in bonds of loving friendship, which informed Scheler's idea of a "community of persons."

Already "thoroughly assimilated into German Catholic culture" by 1894, in the opinion of his friend the Jewish philosopher Martin Buber

---

16. Staude, *Max Scheler*, 256.
17. Staude, *Max Scheler*, 257.

(1878–1965),[18] Scheler took the decision to move from Munich and continue his study of natural science in the modern industrial city of Berlin. While only there for a year, Berlin provided Scheler with an opportunity to significantly broaden his intellectual formation through the influence of the city's social scientists, Wilhelm Dilthey (1833–1911), who pioneered the development of the human sciences and the social economic political theorists Georg Simmel (1858–1918), Max Weber (1864–1920) and Ferdinand Tönnies (1855–1936), founders of the German Society for Sociology. As a leading social philosopher, Scheler drew particular inspiration from Tönnies original 1887 distinction between *Gemeinschaft* 'living community' and *Gesellschaft* 'society' in his discussion of "essential forms of human togetherness" in a section of *Formalism* entitled "Individual Person and Collective Person." Interacting with Berlin's intellectual "leading lights," we find the ingredients for Scheler's lifelong interest in bringing together the fields of philosophy and sociology within his original philosophical sociology.

A further significant piece in what would be the characteristic "jigsaw puzzle" found in Scheler's evolving thought occurred when he made another strategic decision to relocate to the predominantly Protestant city of Jena in 1895. Jena is the second largest city in Thuringia, a state in central Germany which borders Bavaria. A move inspired by the presence of Rudolf Christoph Eucken (1846–1926) and his Christian personalism. He was well-known as a Christian idealist and moral philosopher who promoted the thought of Augustine, Eucken was one of two professors of philosophy teaching at the small Friedrich Schiller University (1558) in Jena, under whose supervision Scheler wrote his doctoral dissertation *Contribution towards the Establishment of the Relationship between Logical and Ethical Principles* in 1897, and his *Habilitation, The Transcendental and Psychological Method: A Fundamental Discussion in Philosophical Method* in 1899, whereupon Scheler received his first university appointment as a *privatdozent* in 1900 under the supervision of Eucken, as an unsalaried lecturer of philosophy.

Referred to as "the philosopher of the spiritual life"[19] by Baron Friedrich von Hügel (1852–1925), the Austrian Catholic layman and modernist theologian when writing to his friend George Tyrrell (1861–1909) on June 4, 1902, the excommunicated modernist Jesuit theologian. Namely,

---

18. Staude *Max Scheler*, 2n2.
19. Cited by Kelly, *Baron Friedrich*, 140n60.

Eucken espoused a distinctive form of personalism, a "spiritual type of philosophy," which sought the promotion of "a sense of responsibility" together with an increased awareness of the "significance of the individual person" through "the recognition of a spiritual world" approached from within an historical context, writing in his seminal *The Problem of Human Life* (1909).[20] Subtitled "As Viewed by the Great Thinkers from Plato to the Present Time," Eucken employed the traditional approach of a discursive dialogue with other thinkers to address the question, "what does our life mean when viewed as a whole?" A conversation set against the current impoverishment of humanity wherein human beings have become "mere tools and instruments of an impersonal civilisation." Later writing in *The Meaning and Value of Life* (1913), Eucken claims: "Man is a spiritual being, and his membership of a spiritual order gives him a position that is quite unique."[21]

Eucken's philosophical reputation was based on his seminal work, *The Unity of the Spiritual Life in the Consciousness and Action of Mankind* (1888), wherein he sought to establish the systematic foundations for "personal idealism" by drawing attention to the contemporary "neglect of personality" in the current philosophical movements of European materialist naturalism and rational intellectualism. Whereby Eucken sought a "philosophy of experience" based on his "search for new solutions" by means of a particular methodology which he refers to as being "noological," namely a study of the processes found in human thought wherein the idea is understood within the context of an encompassing whole, what he calls 'life,' understood as a 'creative energy.' A way of thinking very similar to the thought of the French philosopher Henri Bergson (1859–1941), though they never met. Writing *The Problem of Human Life* (1909), Eucken offered a historical examination of the various changing perspectives from which the human being has been understood by the major philosophers. Whereby he arrives at the philosophical conclusion that the presence of the "Person of Christ" represents the "climax of a world-historical movement," insofar as "Jesus began the complete union, the 'interweaving' of divine and human." A union not only found in the nature of Christ but "in all who accept and manifest the life revealed in him," especially found in the thought of St. Augustine,[22] who in the opinion of Eucken "possesses a unique value to

20. Eucken, *Problem of Human Life*, 566–67.
21. Eucken, *Meaning and Value of Life*, 80.
22. Eucken, *Problem of Human Life*, 197.

the comprehension of every kind of tendency, inasmuch as in him all kinds show in the most distinct manner how they originate from the totality of human nature."[23] Scheler would absorb this philosophical understanding of the Incarnation within his own phenomenological ethical personalism, wherein he considers this fundamental Christian doctrine as the paradigmatic event for Catholicism, the foundation for his original understanding of religious activity which eschews the traditional "either/or" in favour of the "both/and."

While Scheler repudiated Eucken's spiritual idealism, having encountered the phenomenology of Husserl, the Christian orientation of his personalist insights left a permanent impression on Scheler's philosophical evolution. In the opinion of József Maria Bocheński (1902–95), "history will continue to regard him as a personalistic and theistic thinker." Furthermore, according to the Polish Dominican philosopher, "Eucken introduced Scheler to St. Augustine and Pascal and to 'the philosophy of spirit.'" Once again, Scheler made a strategic decision in 1906 to relocate to the familiar precincts of his home city and to the Ludwig Maximilian University (1472) which afforded another introduction, into the world of phenomenology, and an opportunity to consolidate the orientation of his philosophical thought, summarized in his December 1906 formal letter of application for the position of *privatdozent* to Baron Georg von Hertling (1843–1919), professor of philosophy at the University, wherein he described himself as "a theist and realist following the thought of Augustine and Pascal."[24]

Following his successful appointment as a lecturer, Scheler's philosophical formation continued under the direction of Theodor Lipps (1851–1914), the German philosopher, psychologist, and aesthetician; an early proponent of phenomenology, he was an influential figure well known for integrating this philosophical thought within the framework of the concept of *Einfühlung*, literally 'in-feeling' or 'feeling into,' translated as "empathy." A concept he modified using the original thought of the German philosopher Robert Vischer (1847–1933), found in his 1873 doctoral thesis *On the Optical Sense of Form: A Contribution to Aesthetics*. In what were to be his "most formative years"[25] in the opinion of Herbert Spiegelberg, Scheler became actively involved in Munich's "independent" philosophical circle as a 'leading light' of its phenomenological realism,

23. Eucken, *Problem of Human Life*, 246.
24. Mader, *Max Scheler*, 34.
25. Spiegelberg, *Phenomenological Movement*, 169.

however, and not for the first time, personal difficulties necessitated his resignation from the university in 1911.

While his philosophical talks with Husserl generated initial interest in phenomenology, Scheler's interaction with those inspired by Husserl proved more productive. Especially through his engaged participation in a reading group of likeminded academics and students to discuss Husserl's *Logical Investigations* (1900–1901) at the university, in the so-called "Munich philosophical society." A school characterized by phenomenological realism under the direction of the psychologist Theodor Lipps, including young philosophers Alexander Pfänder (1870–1941) and Adolf Reinach (1883–1917). A philosophical environment within which Scheler not only excelled but one which enabled him with the necessary resources to engage the fundamental issue of the early twentieth century, the so-called "human crisis," which he first addressed in his small, seminal essay entirely given to this subject, "On the Idea of Man." (1914) Wherein we find Scheler's philosophical response to the dilemma of humanity occasioned by the contemporary scientific and atheistic worldview which reduced being human to a biological organism, one among many.

Such was the notable presence of Scheler, whose Catholic thought had been initially influenced by an Augustinian priest, his high school chaplain and teacher, that now as a recognizable Catholic philosopher from Munich he similarly exerted his personal influence on the young Jewish born Silesian student Edith Stein and her Protestant student friends from Berlin, also converts to Christianity, Hedwig Conrad-Martius (1888–1966) and her husband Theodor Conrad (1881–1969), young phenomenological realists who came together in Göttingen's Philosophical Society. Invited to speak on his recent book *Phenomenology and The Theory of the Feelings of Sympathy* (1913), which Stein would later critique in her 1916 doctorate *On the Problem of Empathy*, Stein records her initial encounter with Scheler in her autobiography *Life in a Jewish Family 1891–1916*: "This was the time when he was quite full of Catholic ideas, which he knew how to propagate with all the brilliance of his mind and the power of his oratory. It was my first contact with this world, which till then remained completely unknown to me,"[26] their subsequent philosophical careers were stalled by the rise of Nazism.

This quest to understand the complexity found in our humanity would remain a lifelong pursuit for Scheler, leading to his original notion

---

26. Stein, *Life in a Jewish Family*, 260.

of philosophical anthropology. As he later observed in *Man's Place in Nature* (1928), following his rejection of Catholic faith, "man is more of a problem to himself at the present time than ever before." Posthumously published in the year of his sudden death, this book marked the abrupt termination of a philosophical study of humanity, a new way of thinking which Scheler called *Philosophischen Anthropologie*, found within north European thought until the 1940s. This field of scientific study sought the philosophical elucidation of being human through dialogue with contemporary science especially the emergent human and social sciences, to identify the basis qualities and conditions humans share with other living beings as natural organisms, along with the elucidation of what essentially distinguishes us as human beings, as "persons."

Writing in part two of *Formalism in Ethics and Non-Formal Ethics of Values*,[27] Scheler sought to elucidate what he calls a "*theomorphous* idea of Man" wherein "the unique *value* of humanity lies!" Having shunned all forms of indoctrination, especially the prevalent forms of Catholic Neo-Thomism or "church philosophy," Scheler passionately engaged the issue of humanity, inspired by Eucken's Christian thought which he appropriated within his own ethical personalism, an original God centred "integral" vision of humanity, which recognized our inherent human "capacity for transcendence" found in the exercise of our personal freedom. Interestingly, though familiar with Scheler's thought, Maritain would employ this word within a different social political context, writing his *Integral Humanism* (1936), as a "Christian manifesto" on humanism. Thinking within different contexts, the thought of these two influential Catholic philosophers set the broad philosophical background which informs the genesis of conciliar humanism: brought together through the thoughtful influence of a third person. Namely, Kraków's Archbishop Karol Wojtyła's original and critical use of ideas taken from Scheler's phenomenological ethical personalism found in *Formalism*, which he critically studied writing his 1954 *Habilitation, Evaluation of the Possibility of Constructing a Christian Ethics on the Basis of Max Scheler's System*.

While regularly attributed within Scheler's Catholic thought, his early essay "On the Idea of Man" (1915) remains remarkable as the only instance wherein Scheler directly quotes the thought of Augustine, used to introduce this essay, referring to Augustine's all-encompassing vision

---

27. Scheler, *Formalism in Ethics*, 288–89.

of humanity "within the totality of being, world and God."[28] Drawing inspiration from Augustine's *On the Literal Interpretation on Genesis: A Work in Twelve Books* (415), whereby the great Christian philosopher of the first millennium promoted a unified understanding of humanity. One which incorporates the biological, rational, social and spiritual dimensions of being human to counter the influence of contemporary Manichaeism, a dualistic religious way thinking proposed by the Persian prophet Manes (c. 216–c. 276). By aligning his own thought with this great Church Father, Scheler sought a philosophical response to the dilemma of humanity occasioned by the contemporary scientific and atheistic worldview, typified by Munch's "The Scream."

Interestingly, the renewed interest in the philosophical study of consciousness, found in phenomenology, especially practiced by twentieth-century European philosophers, was matched by the revival of interest in Augustine's Christian anthropology and his understanding of humanity, found in Scheler's *On the Eternal in Man* (1921) and the German born American Jewish political philosopher Hannah Arendt's (1906–75) doctoral dissertation *Love and Saint Augustine* (1929) at the University of Heidelberg (1386), Germany's oldest university, directed by Karl Jaspers (1883–1969).

Scheler's quest to understand the complexity found in our humanity would remain a lifelong pursuit leading to his notion of philosophical anthropology. As he later observed in *Man's Place in Nature* (1928), "man is more of a problem to himself at the present time than ever before." However, this book marked the abrupt termination of a philosophical study of humanity understood as philosophical anthropology. A critical way of thinking which engaged ideas drawn from contemporary science, especially those from the emergent human and social sciences. Whereby Scheler sought to defend the integrity of human nature against Comte's reductionistic scientific positivism with an understanding of being human as multidimensional. Namely, an essentially natural and social being, whose material, rational, emotional, and spiritual dimensions must be respected. This counter cultural way of thinking was expressed in the idea of a 'human person,' who was defined by a "capacity for transcendence." Writing as a Catholic philosopher, Scheler claims in *On the Idea of Man* (1914) this capacity makes us uniquely human, "[as] that being which can *transcend all life* and can *transcend* himself."

---

28. Scheler, "On the Idea of Man," 187.

Approached from this wholly new sense, the human being as a "person" is understood as "the intention and gesture of 'transcendence' itself." Within the context of Scheler's personalist philosophy, there is significance in the word "gesture" applied to the human being as being a person, envisaged as a directional being, as a dynamic movement directed towards God, whereby the human being as "person" assumes the status of a "God-seeker." While an original Christian concept used within theological discourse during the fourth century, the concept of "person" re-emerged during the first half of the twentieth century within the European thought within a human context, as the central concept of 'personalism,' a way of thinking with many variants.

Following the withdrawal of his *venia legandi* for moral turpitude which deprived Scheler of a formal academic career within the National University system, a consequence of the "Scandal-trial" initiated by his estranged wife Maria Scheler in 1910 which brought to light her husband's extra marital affairs, Scheler continued to give external seminars and invited lectures, travelling on numerous occasions to address the Philosophical Society established at the Georg August University of Göttingen (1734), which similarly espoused a form of phenomenological realism, where he impressed the Jewish Silesian born Edith Stein (1891–1943). Scheler's participation in these activities provided opportunities to further explore his use of phenomenology within his ethical personalism, characterized a "café and soirée intellectual"[29] in the dismissive opinion of George Huntston Williams (1914–2000), an American Unitarian theologian. Known to Pope John XXIII he was invited to attend the Council as a Protestant representative when he met Archbishop Wojtyła, later writing the first English biographical account of *Pope John Paul II* (1981), wherein he gives particular attention to the development of his philosophical thought.

While September 20, 1899 marks his formal reception into the Catholic Church, Scheler's actual adherence to the tenets of Catholic practice remains clouded by ambiguity; in the words of his Dutch Jesuit biographer Jan Nota, "it is another question whether he always lived in harmony with the teachings of the Catholic Church."[30] Nevertheless, for two thirds of his adult life he wrote from an "avowedly religious standpoint" inspired by the Catholic thought of St. Augustine and the

---

29. Williams, *Mind of John Paul II*, 119.
30. Nota, *Max Scheler*, 10.

French philosopher Blaise Pascal (1623-62) rather than by the prevalent scholastic neo-Thomism; while not adhering to Catholic Ultramontanism, he was regarded with suspicion by both sides. Finally, while a new academic opportunity emerged following the recent foundation of the Institute for Adult Education within the University of Cologne (1388), where in 1919 he was appointed to teach philosophy and sociology; the ambiguity which characterized his personal life remained, having repudiated his Catholic faith "as the Catholic Nietzsche withdrew into the mists of Schellingian pantheism" in the words of his biographer Raphael Staude.[31] Interestingly, while the locations of Munich, Jena and Berlin might characterize the evolution of Scheler's personal religious background, unlike many of his contemporaries, at no time did he actually reject the idea of God's existence.

Adding another level of complexity when approaching Scheler's evolving thought, he lived and thought as a Catholic during the turbulent years of "modernism" and its intellectual environment operating within the Catholic Church of the late nineteenth and early twentieth centuries. A topic addressed by the so-called "founder of modernism," Alfred Firmin Loisy (1857-1940), the French Catholic priest and theologian, who was dismissed in 1893 from teaching at the *Institut Catholique de Paris* (1875), known as the "Catholic University of Paris," when he observed that while Catholic intellectuals of the time commonly rejected *scholasticism* as a rigid form of Church thinking and agreed on the necessity for "a reform of Catholic teaching" this was approached from different perspectives and "through varied experiences."[32] This was nowhere more evident than in Catholic Germany, where it had acquired its own traditions following the negative experience of *Kulturkampf* (1872-78). A cultural power struggle initiated through the conflict between the Kingdom of Prussia led by the conservative politician Otto von Bismarck (1815-98) who actively opposed the Catholic Church under Pope Pius IX (1846-78), the last pope to rule over the Papal States.

Against this conflictual background we can better understand the emergence of *Reformkatholizimus* (1899) as a broad intellectual and political movement among German Catholics which sought reform "from within Catholicism," without the heretical aspects of modernism. Namely, through the eradication of the contemporary *ghetto mentality*

---

31. Staude, *Max Scheler*, 243.
32. Reardon, *Roman Catholic Modernism*, 11.

which characterized contemporary German Catholic intellectual life, by means of promoting a positive intellectual engagement with contemporary issues, which inspired the Munich journalist Carl Muth (1867–1944) to establish the *Catholic Literary Revival* in 1899, which sought to "create a literature informed by the spirit of faith." A mindset which informed the founding of *Hochland* (1903–41) as a religious, cultural, and political journal for the dissemination of the Catholic thought, such as through the faith filled political activity of the Munich university students Sophie Scholl (1921–43) and her brother Hans Scholl (1918–43), friends of Muth and founders of the non-violent intellectual resistance group known as "White Rose."

While there is no textual evidence of Scheler's direct involvement with *Reformkatholizimus* other than through his personal friendship with Muth and the numerous articles he contributed to *Hochland* during the War, Scheler certainly shared a similar mindset. Namely an openness to alternative directions found within Catholic thought which directed his attention towards a "genuine medieval Thomism" of a definite Augustinian orientation, and the influence of the French Catholic philosopher Blaise Pascal (1623–62), as discussed in the Preface to the second edition of *On the Eternal in Man* (1922).[33] Whereby he sought to move away from the "thoroughly rationalization of Thomism in the Age of Enlightenment" which had evolved into "the school-philosophy of German neo-Thomism" or simply "Church philosophy." An approach consistent with his intellectual restlessness which rejected all forms of dogmatism, "closed" or systematic thinking in favour of a fundamental "openness" to new directions which would eventually lead him to posit a form of "panentheism."

Indicative of "the totality of his questioning," seeking "new possibilities and forces opening up," Scheler was a philosopher whose thinking was always "on the move," reflected in his idiosyncratic style of writing. In these circumstances, his eventual break with Catholicism in his later years came as no surprise to his contemporaries, such as the Munich philosophers, the Jesuit Erich Przywara (1889–1972) or the neo-Thomist historian Joseph Geyser (1869–1948), professor of ancient and medieval philosophy, who would have readily characterized Scheler as an "outsider," to employ Gay's expression, from the traditional parameters of Catholic thought, namely scholastic Thomism. Certainly, his provocative

---

33. Scheler, *On the Eternal in Man*, 20.

claim, "the birth of man and the birth of God are, from the outset, reciprocally dependent upon each other," during his extended lecture at the School of Wisdom in Darmstadt in April 1927, posthumously published as *Man's Place in Nature* (1928), would have raised a few eyebrows should any Catholics had been present. A way of thinking Maritain later critically engaged while introducing his seminal *Integral Humanism* (1936), wherein he criticized Scheler's later "concentration of the world in man" by "diluting man to the world."[34]

---

34. Maritain, *Integral Humanism*, 153.

22

A Definite Insider

Given the recognizable pestilence of twentieth-century atheistic humanism as it informed the intellectual ethos of European thought, Maritain joined the ranks of contemporary Catholic philosophers who addressed this issue "head on," such as the French Jesuit Henri de Lubac's *Drama of Atheistic Humanism* (1944). However, unlike other forms of Christian humanism, Maritain adopted a different approach, "a new style" when writing his "Christian manifesto" which had evolved during the early 1930s, whereby he coined the original expression "integral humanism." Used as the title for his seminal book on this subject *Integral Humanism: Temporal and Spiritual Problems of a New Christendom* (1936), a book for which Maritain is commonly known, it was popular reading among Catholics around the world, laypersons, and clergy alike, especially among those Council Fathers responsible for their documented thought. A subject he initially addressed in a compilation of six lectures given in 1934 while teaching at the *Institut Catholique de Paris* (1875) based on a way of thinking which Aristotle and St. Thomas call "practical philosophy," insofar as it deals with the whole philosophy of human action, an approach which informs Maritain's original awareness of the profound connection between philosophical thought and socio-pastoral issues.[1]

Set against this particular orientation, *Integral Humanism* should be read in conjunction with an earlier essay, "Freedom in the Modern World" (1936), wherein Maritain engages the twentieth-century human

---

1. Maritain, *Integral Humanism*, 150.

crisis, as he begins this essay referring to Scheler's later thought wherein he "concentrated the world in man." Following the human orientation of this German philosopher, Maritain likewise sought to engage the "human milieu" but thinking within the tradition of Catholic thought. Set against the background of Ricoeur's "masters of suspicion," Maritain critically engaged the current forms of atheistic humanism associated with Nietzsche and especially Marxist "dialectical materialism" and "revolutionary materialistic dialectic," which he considered self-destructive forms of humanism. Whereby Maritain claims there is no quarrel between humanism and Christianity, but rather between two conceptions of humanism,[2] which he identifies as *theocentric*, found in Christian thought and based on the central truth of Christianity, the dogma of the Incarnation, and the *anthropocentric* version, inspired by the intellectual spirit of the Renaissance.

By means of this comparison, Maritain drew attention to the original *theocentric* orientation of his own thought, namely, that of two of his Catholic forebears, "the great doctors of integral humanism." A way of thinking he understands as a "service to man and to human interests" wherein the human being is approached in "the wholeness of his natural and supernatural being."[3] Thought especially found in two of the foremost medieval thinkers in the scholastic tradition, namely the Italian Dominican friar Thomas Aquinas, recently discussed by the American Catholic theologian Dominic F. Doyle from Boston in *The Promise of Christian Humanism: Thomas Aquinas on Hope* (2011) and the Spanish Carmelite friar and mystic St. John of the Cross (1542–91). Considered proponents of "a humanism of the Incarnation," the scholastic thought of these two saints was based on the "image of a man," namely, the redemptive image of the suffering and risen Christ, thinking which sets the background of conciliar humanism, captured by the religious art of van der Weyden.

Fifty years on from the start of the Council, during the opening mass of the Synod of Bishops on *The New Evangelization for the Transmission of the Christian Faith* on October 7, 2012, which included bishops who had participated as Council Fathers, Pope Benedict XIV recalled the intuitive sense which informed Pope John's clarion call for *aggiornamento*, now found in Pope Benedict's "call for conversion" which

---

2. Maritain, *Integral Humanism*, 45.
3. Maritain, *Review of Politics*, 8.

grounds the work of evangelization, namely, the spiritual impulse generated in the Council's universal call to holiness, as "the ideal in Christian life." Reflecting on the Christ centred spirit of the Letter to the Hebrews (13:8), "Jesus Christ is the same today as he was yesterday and as he will be forever," the pope drew attention to what he called a "three stage Christology." Namely, one focused on Christ's "pre-existence, humanity and exaltation," who in the words of the pope "loved us with a faithful love, even to the cross," a constant theme in Pope Benedict's personalist and relational anthropology. However, reading these quoted words from the Letter, their context can sometimes be overlooked, found in the preceding verse, "remember your leaders, imitate their faith." Namely, the affirmation of Christ's identity is found in the faith-filled advocacy of evangelical witness on the part of those who follow Christ, namely, the human foundations of lived Catholic Christianity within what the Council refers to as a "community of persons."

Interestingly, the pope used this occasion to "invoke the intercession of great evangelisers" by proclaiming two additional "doctors of the Church." Namely, the so-called "Apostle of Andalusia," the Spanish priest St. John of Avila (1499–1569), a scholastic specialist on sacred scripture who penetrated the redemptive mystery "worked by Christ for humanity," envisaged as the means for the "fruitful reform of the Church." And the German Benedictine abbess, a scholastic philosopher and polymath, St. Hildegard of Bingen (1098–1179), whom the Lord granted "a prophetic spirit and fervent capacity to discern the 'signs of the times.'" A scriptural expression, which along with two other words of uncertain origin are commonly associated with the Council: namely, the Italian word *aggiornamento* and the French neologism *ressourcement*. The latter is primarily associated with the claim *Ad Fontes!* understood as a "return to sources," which referred to the historical recovery of Patristic thought during the twentieth century as a means for religious revitalisation and spiritual renewal living in the present: moving towards "a new and deeper sounding of ancient, inexhaustible and common resources" in the opinion of the French essayist Charles Pèguy (1873–1914), a mindset which he shared with his friend Jacques Maritain.

Recognized in *Fides et Ratio* as one of the recent "masters" whose "process of philosophical enquiry was enriched by engaging the data of faith" (para. 74), Jacques Maritain remains an exemplar in this way of thinking "in the service of humanity," a definite "insider" within the tradition of lived Catholic Christianity in his lifelong pursuit for truth. First awakened to Maritain's intellectual prowess as a young diocesan seminarian, Michael Novak (1933–2017) was determined "to read every word that he wrote," writing in his journalistic review of Maritain's final book *The Peasant of the Garrone* (1965). Characterized as an innovative commentator on the thirteenth-century thought of Aquinas and a student of the history of recent Catholic thought which, according to the critical observation of this French octogenarian and "inveterate layman," whereby Maritain learnt "that 'seven centuries of laziness' must be ended and fresh intellectual strides taken. The Church is not what it is today, it is what it must be tomorrow: our loyalty is to the Church reformed," observations of someone whose thought directly informs the genesis of conciliar humanism. Ideas drawn from this prominent figure midway through the twentieth century, "that golden period for Catholicism," when Maritain assumed the status as a recognizable Catholic philosopher. An opinion expressed by Ralph McInerny (1929–2010), the American Catholic philosopher from the University of Notre Dame (1842), author of *The Very Rich Hours of Jacques Maritain: A Spiritual Life* (2003).

Like many others of his generation Maritain came to Catholicism through the personal example of others who shared the recognition that philosophy "is just as much a social form of existence as a theoretical enterprise" in the opinion of the editors of *Philosophers at the Front: Phenomenology and the First World War* (2017). A way of thinking which, like the medieval "schools" typical of the times, generated European philosophical societies, such as those held at the Universities of Munich and Göttingen, and discussion groups, such as Gabriel Marcel's regular weekly philosophy group wherein a young generation of French philosophers found inspiration, such as Paul Ricoeur (1913–2005) and Emmanuel Levinas (1906–95). Or Maritain's *Les Cercles D'Études Thomistes*, a series of regular meetings which began in 1919 focused on the thought of Aquinas, held at the Maritain home in Meudon, a municipality outside Paris. Unusual for the time, these were led by laypersons rather than clerics, by a married couple Jacques and his wife Raïssa, who structured these meetings like a Parisian literary "salon." Interestingly, the French Catholic philosopher Emmanuel Mounier (1905–50), the founding figure of French personalism, author of *The Personalist Manifesto* (1938), was a regular participant during these meetings at Meudon, herein we find the source of Maritain's initial interest in personalism.

Catholic recognition of the scholastic philosophical tradition as a means of thoughtful guidance and critical instruction has a history within conciliar thought, notably its promotion of the 'Christian philosopher' during the Fifth Lateran Council (1512–17). The last ecumenical council held before the Protestant Reformation, a tumultuous period in human history which splintered Catholic Europe, the consequence of a religious, intellectual, and cultural movement for reform within the Western Church during the 1500s. While this Council, held for the fifth time within the precincts of the Papal Archbasilica of St. John at the Lateran, the cathedral church of the Diocese of Rome, was initially convened by Pope Julius II (1503–13) on July 18, 1511 in response to a quasi-council convened by a group of schismatic cardinals at Pisa (1409), to condemn the teachings over papal jurisdiction proposed by the various claimants to the papal office in Avignon and Rome, and to end the Great Western Schism (1378–1417), this Lateran Council was eventually reconvened in May 1513, following the election of Pope Leo X (1513–21). Following a broad agenda, the council was held over twelve sessions, which included the establishment of peace among Christian rulers on the European continent, the promotion of internal church reform and the suppression of heresy; the latter was addressed during the eighth session on December 19, 1513. Namely, the "condemnation of every proposition contrary to the truth of the enlightened Christian religion" wherein the Council detailed the activities of the Christian philosopher, especially the use of human philosophy "flavoured by divine wisdom and the light of revealed truth."

Understood as a means of opposing "propositions contrary to the truth of the enlightened Christian faith," Catholic philosophers teaching in universities and local colleges should "clarify the truth of Christian religion" supported by "convincing arguments." This original Conciliar thought was quoted by Renè Descartes, the creative French mathematician and scientific thinker, writing to the Dean and members of the Faculty of Sacred Theology in Paris, to introduce his forthcoming book, *Meditations on First Philosophy* (1641), wherein he explicitly refers to this Conciliar vision of Christian philosophy and its endorsement of a methodology based on explanation and clarification. Adhering to this Conciliar vision, Descartes sought "to refute arguments contrary to the faith and to employ all their powers in making known the truth."[4] Till then the terrain of clergymen, perhaps this represents the first instance of a Catholic philosopher who was a lay person, someone who sought

---

4. Descartes, "Dedication" to *Meditations on First Philosophy*, in *Philosophical Works*, 1:134.

to identify the influence of an ecumenical council in directing their thought, or was this simply an instance of speaking to his audience? No matter what, there remains no doubt that the so-called "father of modern philosophy" was a God centred practicing Catholic, as recognized by the British philosopher A. C. Grayling in *The Life of René Descartes and Its Place in his Time* (2005): "Given Descartes' lifelong adherence to the Catholic faith and to the Jesuit interest, he counts as a signal example of the success of their methods."[5]

Referring to his training in the rigors of scholastic thought through Jesuit manuals of instruction, Descartes later recalls writing *Rules for the Direction of the Mind* (1701): "we ourselves rejoice that we in earlier years experienced this scholastic training."[6] Having systematically applied critical distrust to everything we claim to know by means of a methodology of relentless doubt, Descartes eventually identified a solid foundation for knowledge in thought, "a clear and distinct idea" found in the first person, who he identified in the proposition *cogito ergo sum*; as he writes in *Principles of Philosophy* (1644): "this proposition *I think, therefore I am* is the first and most certain which presents itself to those who philosophize in orderly fashion."[7] By means of this radical claim Descartes initiated a Copernican Revolution, repositioning the primacy of the mind and the use of reason as the intellectual centre of gravity, moving away from the sphere of traditional Aristotelian and Thomist metaphysical realism found in medieval scholastic thought. In this philosophical transition from metaphysics to epistemology, which lies at the core of what came to be known as Cartesian rationalism, we find the ingredients for the re-emergence of the philosophical issue of "immanence," which informed the thought associated with Catholic modernism during the late nineteenth century, described as "an abortive and self-destructive attempt at adaptation and rejuvenation."

While the canon *Cum Adolescentium Aetas* (1563), adopted during the twenty third session of the ecumenical Council of Trent (1545–63), initiated the diocesan seminary as the location for the education of those preparing for the diocesan priesthood, by the nineteenth century the use of scholastic thought had become *passé* within Catholic circles. Recalling a critical observation made by John Baptist Hogan (1829–1901), an Irish Sulpician priest writing in *Clerical Studies* (1898), teaching

---

5. Grayling, *Descartes*, 2:29.

6. Descartes, *Rules for the Direction of the Mind*, no. 2, in *Philosophical Works*, 1:4.

7. Descartes, *Principles of Philosophy*, principle X, in *Philosophical Works*, 1:222.

dogmatic theology for over thirty two years at the Seminary College of Saint Sulpice (1637) in Paris, employing the educational methods of its former student, the diocesan priest from Reims Saint John Baptist de la Salle (1651–1719), Hogan identified the gradual ossification of Catholic philosophy into an assemblage of thought, characterized by "a sort of eclecticism, neither profound, nor systematic, nor powerful." Wherein scholastic concepts and axioms, drawn from Aristotelian-Thomist thought, were encrusted within little used dusty manuals, an unfashionable form of thought which had been gradually replaced by an over reliance on current Cartesian rationalism.

Speaking at the dawn of the third millennium, Pope John Paul II highlights the many cultural circumstances which continue to challenge our understanding of humanity in response to this perennial question "what is human?" Addressing "the human being's condition in relation to God, to other human beings and to all creation" the pope recalls the thoughtful assistance offered by Aquinas, the "teacher for our time," approached as "the apostle of the truth." Insofar as Thomistic thought with its pervasive "metaphysical realism of *actus essendi*" which deals with humanity envisaged in relation to God through his promotion of "the dignity of the human person and his use of reason," the pope recalls the epithet he previously gave to Aquinas in 1980 as *Doctor Humanitas*. Set against the creative and at times tense interaction between adherence to tenets of Christian faith and the use of reasonable thought, "taking hints from the past" remains a perennial issue wherein our shared humanity is currently best approached in a way of thinking generated during an extended moment of *sapiential* consciousness, found in conciliar humanism. A way of thinking inspired by the ingenious synthesis offered by Pope John Paul II for the third millennium.

Sixty years on, we are in a better position to appreciate the integral unity found in conciliar humanism, and to especially recognize the thoughtful influence of the "right people" approached as "friends of wisdom," European Catholic philosophers of the twentieth century like Jacques Maritain thinking in a tradition, whose thought was ingeniously integrated by the Council Fathers within their original Christ centred integral philosophical understanding of our shared humanity. The foremost Thomist philosopher of the twentieth century, Maritain chose these words *philosophandum in fide*, "one should philosophize in the ambience of the faith" for his personal motto as indicative of his philosophical approach. Originally used by John of St. Thomas (1589–1644), the Portuguese

Dominican friar, a graduate in scholastic theology from my alma mater, the faculty of theology of the Catholic University of Leuven, and like Maritain, he was a specialist in the thought of Aquinas.

Characterized as a "new humanism" for the twentieth century, found in the content of *Gaudium et Spes* and *Dignitatis Humanae*, wherein "the human is defined above all in terms of our responsibility to our sisters and brothers and to history." A way of thinking which Pope Paul VI exhorted the Council Fathers, on behalf of the Catholic Church, "to recognize our own type of humanism." Advice taken up by Cardinal Justin Rigali, the Archbishop of Philadelphia (2003–11) on September 26, 2005 speaking at the prestigious Villanova University (1842) to celebrate the fortieth anniversary of *Gaudium et Spes*, one of the first prelates to do so since the Council. While years later he wrote of the continued relevance of Council documents wherein he recalled his "minor role" during the Council as a newly ordained priest from the Archdiocese of Los Angeles living in Rome for graduate study, during his 2005 Address he recalled the thought of Pope Paul who recognized the "birth of a new humanism" announced in *Gaudium et Spes*. Speaking at a location with significance as one of America's preeminent Catholic institutions of higher education, named after the Spanish Augustinian friar St. Thomas of Villanova (1488–1555), the oldest and largest Catholic university in the Commonwealth of Pennsylvania USA, the Cardinal explored the inherent connection between "the new humanism of Vatican II" and the identity and activities undertaken by Catholic higher education. In so doing he recalled the Council's understanding of "the mystery of man" as an invaluable resource to meet the enormous challenges of our time, one accessible to all found in "true and just responses."

Namely, a form of thinking he calls "humanism of solidarity," in which being human, approached as an individual human person, is defined in relationship towards other human beings within a "community of persons," whereby the entire human family is directed towards God. Observing the human orientation found in Catholic education from the Middle Ages on, the Cardinal asked rhetorically, "is not a Catholic university a powerful forum for this solidarity [shared responsibility to others] to be realized and this humanization [of the world] to take place?" Approached from this perspective, education remains essential when understanding our human nature, built on the living synthesis between faith and reason. A human connection identified earlier by R. W. Southern (1912–2001), the noted English medieval historian, in his commentary on Catholic education during the twelfth and thirteenth centuries: "The first fundamental characteristic of the products of the schools is a strong sense of the dignity of human nature. Without this there can be no humanism of any description."[8]

Interestingly, the role of education is embedded within the twofold Conciliar program of renewal, prompted by "examining the signs of the time" and "interpreting them in light of the Gospel," which occasioned the necessary renewal within the Church and promotion of thoughtful engagement with the "world of today." Embarking on the renewal of Catholic thought initially envisaged by *Aeterni Patris*, Catholic higher education is promoted as a suitable midwife to assist the birth of this "new humanism," providing access to the philosophical means and disciplined training to better understand and promote our new humanism. It is noteworthy, two months prior to the promulgation of *Gaudium et Spes*, the Council's *Gravissimus Educationis*, the *Declaration on Christian Education* was promulgated on October 28, 1965. A document worthy of attention in so far as its opening sections, which reflect a distinctively human and personalist orientation, address the "supreme importance of education in human life and its ever-greater influence on the social progress of this age." Building on the right to education found in the 1948 Declaration of Human Rights, the Council now claims this as "inalienable," based on its understanding of "the dignity of persons," namely, "true education aims at a formation of human persons which is directed towards their final end and at the same time towards the good of society." This Conciliar vision identifies the close, productive, and successful collaboration between "humanism" and "education" over the course of Western history, one which persists to this day, especially in promoting the Catholic philosophical tradition.

However, the Cardinal's expectations for a positive reception to his Address were quickly abated, generated by the earlier publication of the Philadelphia Grand Jury Report "on Child Sex Abuse in the Archdiocese" on September 17, 2005. As observed by Ashley Augellio, this address turned into "an open forum" in response to anger aroused among members of the Catholic laity in the audience. In the words of one observer, "it wasn't pretty." One member of the audience, Judy Gray, raised the most contentious of the questions concerning Rigali's repeated reference to "human dignity," a key concept of *Gaudium et Spes*, used thirty-seven

---

8. Southern, *Scholastic Humanism*, 1:22.

times during his address. Namely, for him to explain how this expression could be applied to his support for what she called "criminal cardinals who have protected oral and anal rape?" To which he responded, "I will have to leave that judgement up to God." While this Report "pales in comparison" to the Australian Royal Commission "into Institutional Responses to Child Sexual Abuse" (2013–17), in the opinion of Marci Ann Hamilton, CEO and Academic Director of CHILD USA, "an interdisciplinary think tank to prevent child abuse and neglect," the Report remains the benchmark for "responsible prosecutorial initiative" taken on clerical sexual abuse in the United States.[9] This is shameful conduct which speaks to the enigma found in humanity and understanding our human propensity towards good and as well as evil behavior, an ongoing concern which requires a considered response from the Catholic community living in the "world of today."

---

9. Hamilton, "On the Tenth Anniversary."

23

In Need of Recovery

NOTWITHSTANDING THE LEONINE INNOVATIVE program of philosophical reform, overcoming the lazy mindset which had characterized twentieth-century Catholic philosophical thinking was not easily relinquished, as James Daniel Collins (1917–85) observes: "even after the turning point of 1879, many Thomistic manuals continued to employ the modern rationalist framework in terminology, statement of principles, division and organization of materials, and mode of inference."[1] A critical observation made by the former president of the Metaphysical Society of America and a recipient of the Cardinal Spellman—Aquinas Medal, taking up the philosophical diagnosis made by Jacques Maritain, a prominent figure in the twentieth-century revival of Thomist thought in response to what he claimed were "seven centuries of laziness," wherein Catholic philosophers preferred novelty over rigor, superficiality over foundations.

A mindset beset with ambiguity which informed the innovative thought of the German philosopher Martin Heidegger (1889–1976) in his ground-breaking *Being and Time* (1927), a former Catholic seminarian who had studied theology at the University of Freiburg (1457). A teaching environment wherein the emergent philosophical movement known as phenomenology flourished, notably through the presence of its founding figure, the Jewish born Edmund Husserl (1859–1938) and its journal *Yearbook for Philosophy and Phenomenological Research* (1913–30). Following his retirement as Professor of Philosophy in 1928, partly through the influence of *Being and Time*, Heidegger replaced

---

1. Collins, "Leo XIII," 192.

his friend as professor of philosophy, a position he would retain until retirement around 1967, notwithstanding the serious consequences of his controversial collaboration during the Nazi regime (1933–48). As well as the notable presence of Husserl and Heidegger, this educative environment nurtured the aspirations of other prominent twentieth-century European philosophers, such as the Jewish born Hannah Arendt (1906–75) and Edith Stein (1891–1942) and later the French Jewish philosopher Emmanuel Levinas (1906–95); the Catholic Jesuit theologian Karl Rahner (1904–84) attended Heidegger's lectures between 1934–36. All these thinkers are part of the broad philosophical landscape which informs the genesis of conciliar humanism.

Arguably dismissed "as a charlatan or as the celebrated end of metaphysics," Heidegger remains another twentieth-century figure of ambiguity in the appraisal of the Canadian philosopher Sean McGrath introducing *The Early Heidegger and Medieval Philosophy: Phenomenology for the Godforsaken* (2006), which builds on the innovative research found in Theodore Kisiel's *The Genesis of Heidegger's Being and Time* (1993). Against this background of medieval thought, these contemporary authors represent a renewed interest in understanding the thoughtful background of Heidegger's philosophical originality, namely, found in the legacy of the Scholastic tradition. Whether approached through Kisiel's recognition of the influence of Augustinian thought or the early Heidegger's quest for a "synthesis of Scholasticism," based on his study of the concept of "univocity of being" in the metaphysics of Blessed Duns Scotus (1266–1308), the Scottish Franciscan philosopher from Oxford. Who together with Aquinas, Bonaventure, and the English Franciscan philosopher William of Ockham (1287–1347) remain the source of contemporary inspiration for twentieth-century philosophers as the foremost medieval representatives of the tradition of Aristotelian Scholastic thought.

Set against this philosophical background which subsequently generated the Cartesian rationalism of his day, this forms the context for understanding Heidegger's original phenomenological project to re-engage the study of the question of Being, traditionally the God centred understanding of being found in Aristotle's "onto-theology," which necessitated the creation of a new philosophical expression as part of this audacious project, found in the German word *dasein*. By means of which, Heidegger along with his friend Scheler reject the current Cartesian bifurcation of humanity, between mind and body and its preferential treatment given to the former, by means of an original study of being human, found in Scheler's multidimensional understanding of the "human person" as the foundation of his philosophical anthropology or Heidegger's radical idea of *dasein*, humanity lived as 'being there.' Regarding the latter, this represents a movement away from philosophical abstraction about "what is human" towards an answer based on what it means to be human approached as an activity, 'being there.' Whereby humanity is viewed as a unitive phenomenon through an observation of the ordinary and mundane experience of simply "being-in-the-world," the experience of "facticity." However, as Heidegger later acknowledged this original project was an exercise in futility insofar as answering the question of being, the intent of his project, would ultimately objectify being, an unintended consequence, as he wrote in "Letter on Humanism" (1947): "It is everywhere supposed that this attempt ended in a blind alley."[2]

Fortunately, the tenets of conciliar humanism, generated by the Council's unprecedented use of a human agenda, represent an alternative approach to understanding our shared humanity, the consequence of a change of mindset characterized by Michael Novak as a "break with the past" or "a new way of thinking" in the opinion of Ratzinger in his seminal commentary *The Dignity of the Human Person* (1969) on *Gaudium et Spes* (1965). Wherein Ratzinger finds "a dynamic account of man," approached from historical and biblical perspectives within what he characterized as "a mosaic of basic statements," rather than a "static philosophical doctrine of man" found in neo-scholastic thought.[3] While coming to the same conclusion, Novak's initial appreciation of this redirection within Conciliar thought concerning the issue of humanity was disclosed writing his appraisal of the two great social encyclicals of Pope John XXIII, *Mater et Magistra* (1961) and *Pacem in Terris* (1963), published in *A New Generation* (1964),[4] wherein he claims: "Pope John's program, like the Council's thus, is different in style from Latin Scholasticism; and the differences are hard to characterize in a single descriptive phrase," characterized by Ratzinger as a "mosaic of basic statements." Writing elsewhere Novak identified the source of this difference of approach when he claimed: "Pope John introduced the victories won by Emmanuel Mounier, Jacques Maritain, Gabriel Marcel and others into the most authoritative ordinary

---

2. Heidegger, "Letter on Humanism," in *Basic Writings*, 222.
3. Ratzinger, "Dignity of the Human Person," 119.
4. Novak, *New Generation*, 91–104.

teaching of the Church," especially addressing the pressing issue of understanding our shared humanity.

A redirection in thinking on the part of the Council Fathers Novak had personally witnessed during the Council's second plenary session as a correspondent for the recently established *National Catholic Reporter*, a religious newspaper with worldly interests, between September 29–December 4, 1963, the subject of two journalist essays, printed as *A New Generation* (1964) and *The Open Church: Vatican II Act II* (1964). Novak's insightful commentary is supported by his own theological background, having earned a Bachelor of Sacred Theology in 1958 from the Pontifical Gregorian University (1551) in Rome. Following the closure of the second session of the Council on December 3, 1963, Novak returned to America where in 1966 he gained a Master of Arts degree in history and philosophy from Harvard University (1636). While intending to pursue a doctorate in philosophy of religion, he became increasingly dissatisfied with the "analytic" orientation of its philosophy department which he felt impeded the study of religion and he decided to continue his employment in journalism.

Interestingly, given the necessary philosophical background to study Catholic theology, while Novak coined the expression "the era of the laity," he made little reference to the distinct philosophical orientation found in Conciliar thought, though identifying the notable influence of these French Catholic lay philosophers. An era which officially began with the Council's innovative *Apostolicam Actuositatem* "Decree on the Apostolate of the Laity" promulgated on November 18, 1965, one foreshadowed by Pope John's unprecedented appointment of Catholic laymen as *auditors*, official witnesses to the Council. Following the reopening of the Council on September 23, 1963, Pope Paul VI on the advice of Cardinal Suenens, also appointed forty women, lay and religious. Furthermore, in another unprecedented moment embedded with significance, again witnessed by Novak occurred when Pope Paul VI invited the first two *auditors* appointed by his predecessor to address a plenary session of the Council, namely, the philosopher Jean Guitton (1901–99) and the Italian bureaucrat Vittorino Veronese (1910–86), the former Director General of UNESCO (1958–61). This occurred in St. Peter' Basilica on December 3, 1963 in the presence of the pope, on the second last day of the second session of the Council during the solemn commemoration of the Council of Trent (1545–63) following an address by Cardinal Giovanni Urbani (1900–1969), who had replaced

Giovanni Roncalli as Patriarch of Venice. During the final ceremony to close the Council on December 8, 1965, Guitton's presence would again be recognized, along with his compatriot and fellow philosopher Jacques Maritain by the pope as Maritain received the Council's message addressed "to men of thought and science."

Traditionally the domain of ecclesiastics, the involvement of these Catholic lay persons in the field of philosophy marks a feature of twentieth-century French Catholic intellectual life, one which informs the genesis of conciliar humanism. During the 1930s Maritain was involved with several other French Catholic and secular philosophers in a debate concerning the possibility of a "Christian philosophy?" A discussion initiated by the French Catholic philosopher Maurice Blondel (1864–1949), author of the seminal *L'Action: Essay on a Critique of Life and a Science of Practice* (1893), his doctoral thesis which became synonymous with his original thought, a way of thinking which subsequently influenced Wojtyła and the genesis of conciliar humanism. Blondel's original "philosophy of action' was inspired by Augustine which allows for "*the* Catholic philosophy, but also the fully human one,"[5] a way of thinking which informs the background to Blondel's study of human existence in action. Based on the premise "humans are born into the world without choice," Blondel drew attention to the significance of human activity found in our capacity to make free decisions; in so doing, Blondel reintroduced the concept of 'act' within contemporary European philosophy.

A term originally used by Aristotle and later taken up by medieval scholastic thinkers such as Aquinas with his innovative metaphysical idea of *actus essendi*, an 'act of being' approached as act of existence, a subject recently discussed in *Actus Essendi and the Habit of the First Principle in Thomas Aquinas* (2019) by Orestes J. González, an American diocesan priest ordained by Pope John Paul II in 1981. Blondel's original understanding of the significance of action forms the background for Wojtyła's innovative fusion of Thomistic thought with ideas taken from Scheler's phenomenological ethical personalism, found in his highly original *Person and Act* (1969). A seminal book Wojtyła began writing around 1964 while participating as a Council father, whereby he came to appreciate the necessity of a solid philosophical foundation for conciliar thought. Citing the influence of Blondel, Wojtyła wrote in his "Introduction," "*this study will concern the act that reveals the person; it*

---

5. Blondel et al., *Monument to Saint Augustine*, 353.

will be a study of the person through the act."⁶ Prior to Maritain's "integral" understanding of humanity, Blondel adopted a similar approach viewing human nature as a whole, not through abstract and dispassionate thought but by means of a studied awareness of human action. As he introduces *Action*: "It is a question of the whole human; it is not then in thought alone that we must look for the human. We must transport the centre of philosophy to action."⁷

Returning to the 1930s debate, set against this European philosophical background, Blondel sought to establish the correct relationship between the use of autonomous philosophical reasoning and Christian belief. A discussion joined by other philosophers such as the Christian existentialist Gabriel Marcel, the specialist in medieval philosophy Étienne Gilson and Maritain, who share an intellectual background which informed the thought of the Council, especially found in conciliar humanism in the opinion of Gregory B. Saddler, editor of *Reason Fulfilled by Revelation: The 1930s Christian Philosophy Debates in France* (2011). While Scheler died unexpectedly in 1928, the thoughtful influence of this so called "outsider" who turned to the spiritual personalism of the Lutheran philosopher Rudolf Eucken, re-emerged during the Council in another original form, brought together with ideas taken from these French philosophers, through the influence of Wojtyła. Having shunned all forms of indoctrination, especially what Scheler dismissed as "Church philosophy" which he found in scholastic Thomism, now Maritain who was familiar with Scheler's thought, approached this way of thinking following his Catholic baptism, whereby he together with Gilson sought the revival of contemporary Thomism from "within," a tradition in need of recovery. Namely a reappraisal of Thomism approached from a historical and cultural perspective, what Maritain called "lived Thomism."

An original way of thinking inspired by Maritain's friend the French essayist Charles Péguy (1873–1914), who was eventually baptized Catholic in 1908 after years of intellectual agnosticism. An approach which sought "the real St. Thomas" viewed through the lens of a historical context whereby Péguy moved away from the rigid Thomism he found in the sixteenth-century manuals of traditional scholastic philosophy, wherein "buried under five centuries of deposits, ignorance of itself is the most serious ill from which Scholasticism is suffering. To cure it, let us listen to the counsel

---

6. Wojtyla, *Person and Act*, 103n2.
7. Blondel, *Action*, 13.

of history."[8] Following the historical Thomism of Péguy and Gilson, the French Dominican theologian Jean-Pierre Torell, introducing his two volume biography *Saint Thomas Aquinas* (2005) sought "to read Thomas' works in their true context and discover something of his face," as Torell continues: "Thomas was, in fact, situated in a specific time and place, marked by precise historical contingencies."[9] A way of thinking inspired by another Dominican biographer Marie-Dominique Chenu's (1895–1990) *Toward Understanding Saint Thomas* (1964), one which counters the claim that Thomas is "presented as a timeless thinker."

Following the thought of these twentieth-century commentators, this book in hand pursues a similar undertaking, namely, to understand the broader historical and philosophical background which informs the genesis of conciliar humanism from within the tradition of Catholic philosophy. Identified by Pope John Paul II in *Fides et Ratio*: "The intimate bond between theological and philosophical wisdom is one of the Christian tradition's most distinctive features in the exploration of revealed truth" (para. 105). An approach associated with *Nouvelle Théologie*, a French theological movement of the early twentieth century, a derisive label used by its opponents. Characterized as "inheritor of Modernism, Precursor of Vatican II," this movement was viewed with suspicion within Catholic intellectual circles because of its critical reaction to the prevalent mode of Scholastic thinking. However, this way of thinking was later rehabilitated through the active participation, by invitation, during the Council of two prominent French Catholic thinkers, the Jesuit Henri de Lubac (1896–1991) and the Dominican Yves Congar (1904–95), especially in their participation in the preparation of the Council's final documents, *Dignitatis Humanae* and *Gaudium et Spes*, wherein we find conciliar humanism. A collaborative activity which included Archbishop Wojtyła, who as Pope John Paul II created these men cardinals in 1994 and 1983 respectively, in recognition of their efforts during the Council.

Thinking within the intellectual ethos of European thought during the late nineteenth and early twentieth centuries, which was infected by Comte's atheistic scientific positivism and aligned secular humanism, following his religious conversion as a Catholic, Maritain sought the rehabilitation of the innovative thought he found in Aquinas: "Rescued

---

8. Quoted by D'Ambrosio, "*Ressourcement* Theology," 54.
9. Torrell, *Saint Thomas Aquinas*, 1:xx.

from an intellectual and spiritual wasteland."[10] Schooled in traditional Thomism, Maritain was especially influenced by the combined efforts of his spiritual director, the French Dominican Humbert Clérissac (1864–1914) and the French essayist and socialist Charles Péguy. Both of whom encouraged the young convert around 1910, having distanced himself from the metaphysical thought of the French philosopher Henri Bergson (1859–1941), to read Aquinas' *Summa Theologica*. This was undertaken through the thoughtful guidance of the French essayist Léon Bloy (1846–1917), another Catholic convert from agnosticism and a passionate proponent of Catholicism, and the prominent French Dominican theologian Reginald Garrigou-Lagrange (1877–1964), the foremost proponent of traditional Thomism in the twentieth century. A well-known professor of theology at the *Angelicum* who directed Wojtyła's doctorate in sacred theology on St. John of the Cross which he received on June 19, 1948.

Through their guidance, in the words of his American biographer and Catholic philosopher Ralph McInerny (1929–2010), Maritain encountered "the living reality of Catholicism,"[11] an encounter similarly experienced by a young agnostic philosophy student from Silesia, Edith Stein, through the example of Christian witness by members of Göttingen's Philosophical Society. However, through his disciplined and thorough reading of Aquinas' *Summa Theologica*, required reading for any philosophically inclined convert to Catholicism, the trained philosopher soon recognized the great disparity between the original thought he found in the *Summa* and its contemporary use, what he recognized as the appalling state of contemporary Catholic philosophy. Namely, what Maritain found in contemporary forms of Latin Scholasticism and neo-Thomism, exemplified in what he denigrates as "memorized definitions and logical manipulations" which had replaced authentic philosophy, found in engaging the innovative thought he had encountered reading Aquinas' original thought, in preference for the use and reliance on "scandalously inept textbooks."

Namely, the traditional manuals of scholastic philosophy, such as those prepared for Catholic seminarians, which included an arbitrary selection of quoted thought of questionable *provenance* found in Latinisms such as *nemo dat quod non habet*, which I became familiar with, rather

---

10. McInerny, *Very Rich Hours*, 2.
11. McInerny, *Very Rich Hours*, 210.

than being encouraged to read and consult the original source, the consequence of what Maritain categorized as "seven centuries of Catholic laziness." As he introduces *A Preface to Metaphysics* (1962), a compilation of seven lectures on the subject of "being" he gave during his second visit to North America in 1934 when Maritain claimed: "Thomism is not a museum piece," but rather a premodern way of thinking relevant to every epoch, with the capacity for synthesis "which transcends all its components,"[12] one which answers "modern problems, both theoretical and practical," a philosophical approach adopted by Maritain infused with *sapiential* consciousness as a friend of wisdom. An integrative way of thinking found in his personal experience which he described as "relating my discoveries in the medieval world to the contemporary world; a theory of art, of politics, of social reform."

12. Maritain, *Preface to Metaphysics*, 9.

24

A Return to Metaphysics

CONCERNING THE PERSONAL CIRCUMSTANCES of Maritain, it was his friend Charles Péguy (1873–1914), the French essayist and himself a student of Bergson, who literally directed these students of natural science across the road to attend the "celebrated" afternoon philosophical lectures of his teacher, Henri Bergson (1859–1941) at the *Collège de France* (1530), where he had been installed as professor in Greek and Roman philosophy in 1900. Conducted between 1900 until 1914, Bergson established in these lectures an original philosophical approach, one which incorporated a traditional understanding of Aristotelian metaphysics through his intuitive recognition of "the transcendent beyond the material," whereby he sought a rapprochement between metaphysics and science, as discussed by the American educator Paul Michael Cohen in his article "Reason and Faith: The Bergsonian Catholic Youth of Pre-War France."[1] Of an Aristotelian metaphysical orientation, these philosophical lectures inspired a remarkable period of convergence within French Catholic thought, an intellectual engagement between philosophy and faith, which generated a series of religious conversions to Catholicism, generated by Bergson's original intent to convert himself, which was deferred "in solidarity with the Jews then being persecuted in Europe."[2] While not documented, these conversions took place having already been introduced to Bergson's philosophical thought, generating a "spiritual renaissance" among French intellectuals who

---

1. Cohen, "Reason and Faith," 473.
2. Vincelette, *Recent Catholic Philosophy: The Nineteenth Century*, 9.

were "young and restless" in the opinion of the American Salesian philosopher Thomas L. Gwozdz (1929–2007).[3] This was a way of thinking whereby these young students could find adequate answers to the issues of meaning and purpose in life which they sought, to counter the prevalent mood of philosophical positivism at the Sorbonne.

After years marked by intellectual agnosticism, Péguy was eventually baptized Catholic in 1908, and exercised a formative influence in the philosophical and spiritual formation of both Jacques and Raïssa Maritain. Characterized as "a natural metaphysician," Bergson was considered "as much showman as academician" due to the animated lectures of this London born philosopher which "provided inspiration, irritation and challenge to a generation of French intellectuals" in the opinion of the Maritain commentator William J. Fossati, author of *Out of the Shadow* (2002). At the forefront of French philosophy over the first thirty years of the twentieth century, Bergson's way of thinking particularly inspired three of the most impressive Catholic lay philosophers of the era, namely, Maurice Blondel, Gabriel Marcel, and Jacques Maritain.

Following the thought of another friend, Ètienne Gilson (1884–1978), the French layman and scholar of medieval philosophy, especially in the thought of Aquinas, who founded existential or historical Thomism, Pèguy sought "the real St. Thomas" moving away from the Thomism found in the sixteenth-century manuals of Catholic philosophy, a critical approach which similarly informed Maritain's "existential" approach to Thomism, one found in the attention Aquinas gave to his metaphysical understanding of "existence" through his original idea of *actus essendi*, an understanding which similarly inspired Wojtyła.

Initially inspired by Bergson's metaphysical thought, Maritain engaged this as the subject of his first book in 1913, *La Philosophie Bergsonienne*, wherein he offered an incisive criticism of the thought of the philosopher who had brought him, together with his Russian girlfriend, Raïssa Oumansov, literally from the brink of suicide. Now translated as *Bergsonian Philosophy and Thomism* (2007), published as the first volume in the series *The Collected Works of Jacques Maritain* (2007), wherein the editor claims, "it would be difficult to overestimate Bergson's role in extricating French philosophy from the deadening materialism that dominated the Sorbonne." Of Jewish origin, Bergson was a natural scientist who favoured the theory of evolution, wherein

---

3. Gwozdz, "Young and Restless," 549.

he based his understanding of the processes of immediate experience, intuition and his original concept of *elan vital*, discussed in his third book *Creative Evolution* (1907), a way of thinking set against the prevalent abstract rationalism and scientific positivism. Having then moved to the study of humanities, Bergson directed his attention to the study of philosophy, found in his essay "Introduction to Metaphysics" (1903) which was accepted for the prestigious French philosophical journal *Revue de métaphysique et de morale* (1893), wherein Bergson offered a rigorous defence of traditional metaphysics, "of the transcendent beyond the material" from which these students could seriously address the fundamental issues they encountered in their lives.

Thinking within the Catholic philosophical tradition, the young auxiliary bishop from Kraków became a noticeable participant as a Council father, one of the leading figures during the Council, who made a significant contribution to the direction and evolution of Conciliar thought, especially its original understanding of our shared humanity found within the Council's original "humanism." An ambiguous though persistent expression to this day, with many ideological variants used over the course of western thought, well recognized by Maritain; however, whether approached from pagan, Christian, atheistic or secular perspectives, "humanism" represents a philosophically oriented study of being human, based on the recognition of the human being as inherently valuable, the bearer of dignity. A way of thinking which directed the novel Christ centred integral philosophical way of thinking about our shared humanity generated during the last ecumenical council to date, conciliar humanism.

With an acquired international reputation as a Catholic philosopher, one of the foremost proponents of Thomism during the twentieth century and an "insider" within the tradition of Catholic thought, Maritain was personally greeted by Pope Paul VI at the end of the Council. While understandably his thought was unacknowledged within Council documents, given the collective nature of Conciliar thought, nevertheless the significance of the influence of Maritain's *Integral Humanism* (1936), which addressed "the problem of man" and the underlying tragic circumstances of contemporary atheistic and secular humanism, can't be underestimated. Especially through the activity of leading figures within the Council, such as Montini, Suenens, and Wojtyła, who were active promotors of Maritain's thought which inspired conciliar humanism.

Furthermore, Maritain's short essay, "On the Meaning of Contemporary Atheism" (1948),[4] also influenced the Council's original approach to this subject documented in *Gaudium et Spes*, one which informed the "present agony of the world," a subject embedded within conciliar humanism. Found in its promotion of the human capacity to think about the idea of God's existence and the human capacity for transcendence, as a response to their denial within contemporary forms of thought. A connection first discussed by Ralph McInerny in *The Very Rich Hours of Jacques Maritain* (2003) wherein he claims Maritain considered the philosophical foundations of modern atheism were found in the denial of the human person's twofold capacity "for choice" and "for transcendence," a subject directly addressed in part one of *Gaudium et Spes*, "the forms and foundations of atheism" (paras. 19–21).

"We hold these truths to be self-evident, that all men are created equal, that they are endowed by their Creator with certain unalienable rights, that among these are life, liberty, and pursuit." Remarkable and seminal words which open the United States "Declaration of Independence" (1776), which espouse a God-centred, truthful vision of humanity and its inherent value and resourcefulness, a celebration of what we share in common as human beings, which remains as relevant as ever. Adopted by the Second Continental Congress meeting in Philadelphia, Pennsylvania on July 4, 1776 which severed official connections between the thirteen former American colonies at war with the Kingdom of Great Britain, based on specified grievances.

While the contribution of the Declaration's principal author Thomas Jefferson (1743–1826), an American Founding Father, who used the tenets of contemporary social philosophy, such as the ideal of "individual liberty," found in the English philosopher John Locke's (1632–1704) *Second Treatise of Government* (1690) and the French philosopher Jean-Jacques Rousseau's (1712–78) *Discourse on the Origin and Basis of Inequality among Men* (1754) and *On the Social Contract* (1762). While his thoughtful contribution is well recognized, he remains a somewhat puzzling thinker, according to the American historian and educator, Paul K. Conkin, who claims it is impossible to determine Jefferson's world view because he "always ended up with such an eclectic mix of ideas as to defy systematic ordering."[5]

---

4. McInerny, *Very Rich Hours*, 158.
5. Conkin, "Religious Pilgrimage of Thomas Jefferson," 35.

A similar dilemma confronted a group of Catholic scholars, mainly philosophers, following the long anticipated death of Pope John Paul II, as they assembled in West Hartford, Connecticut USA between March 21–23, 2006 to discuss the pope's "philosophical legacy," their lectures were published as *Karol Wojtyła's Philosophical Legacy* (2008). This group included two speakers who had personally known Karol Wojtyla "both before and after he became John Paul II," namely, Han Köchler, an Austrian philosopher from Innsbruck, and George F. Mclean (1929–2016), the American Oblate priest from the Catholic University of America (1887). During this conference participants engaged a 'what if' question, namely had Wojtyła not been elected pope, given his already extensive philosophical activity in Poland, how would his philosophical contribution have been assessed, especially in the area of phenomenology? Reflecting on this "ambiguous legacy," the American Jesuit John J. Conley observed, while there might be widespread agreement on his status as "a philosophical Pope, there is little consensus as to what sort of philosopher he was and how this philosophy shaped his pontifical teaching."[6] I believe a possible answer is found within the story of conciliar humanism.

---

6. John J. Conley, "Philosophy and Anti-Philosphy," in Billias et al., *Karol Wojtyła's Philosophical Legacy*, 33.

25

A Person Who Thinks

KNOWN AS A RIGOROUS and systematic thinker, the issue of an "eclectic mix of ideas" remains problematic when attempting to bring coherence to the thought of this extraordinary person, Karol Wojtyła, later Pope John Paul II. Perhaps coming to know "the truth about the human person" remains the hallmark of thought of the author of *Fides et Ratio* (1998), another extraordinary God centred document which sought to re-establish a thoughtful conversation with "the world of today." One initiated by the Second Vatican Council but under the thoughtful umbrella of Pope Leo XIII's seminal thought. Expressing his indebtedness to both Council and pope, as a teacher infused with *sapiential* consciousness, a human person who thinks, Pope John Paul II assembled what was already known in our Catholic tradition, notably drawn from its patristic and scholastic resources, used over the centuries to address perennial issues such as understanding human nature and the relationship between faith "and" reason.

The consequences of the thoughtful encounter between Christian faith and the use of reason were observed by then Cardinal Joseph Ratzinger in his seminal *Introduction to Christianity* (1968), which includes a reprint of his 1959 inaugural lecture on being appointed a professor of theology at the Rheinish Friedrich Wilhelm University of Bonn (1818), one of the leading research institutions in Germany. Entitled "The God of Faith and the God of Philosophers: A Contribution to the Problem of Natural Theology," wherein he claims: "the choice made in the biblical image of God had to be made once again in the early days of Christianity and the Church,"¹ by means of which he foreshadowed the Council's reappraisal of the idea of 'person' within its distinctive human context. This level of complexity and tension within the transition to an ever expanding Christian community sets the background for the emergence of the first ecumenical councils of the Church and their decidedly theological orientation, convened to discuss major doctrinal issues, such as the nature of the Trinity during the first ecumenical Council of Nicaea (325), incorporated into the Nicene Creed, a Christian statement of belief, and the nature of the Person of Christ, the Son of God, discussed during the fourth ecumenical Council of Chalcedon (451).

During these councils, serious tensions emerged in discussions between Greek and Latin approaches concerning the issue of translation of theological terminology and political differences between the East and West, which culminated in the Great Schism of 1054 within Christianity. Acting on the threat of excommunication, documents of mutual anathema were simultaneously sent by Michael 1 Cerularius, the Greek Orthodox Patriarch of Constantinople (1043–58) and Saint Pope Leo IX (1049–54) in 1054, which subsequently divided Christianity between the Roman Catholic Church and members of the Orthodox Church. While efforts by the Catholic Church towards reconciliation were discussed during the fourteenth ecumenical council, convoked for the second time in the city of Lyon, in the Kingdom of Aries, in modern France on March 31, 1272. These remained unresolved until 1965 when the mutual anathemas of 1054 were finally revoked, bringing about reconciliation between Pope Paul IV on behalf of the Catholic Church and Athenagoras I, the Ecumenical Patriarch of Constantinople on behalf of members of the Orthodox Church of Constantinople on December 7, 1965, the last day of Vatican II, the last ecumenical council to date.

However, there was another perennial issue addressed during the Council, namely, to understand the human capacity "to do good and avoid evil," understood as the elementary precept of "human praxis" found in the human person, as Karol Wojtyła writes in his seminal essay "The Person: Subject and Community" (1976),² published in *Person and Community* (1993), a book I received as a generous gift from the translator, the American Servite sister Theresa Sandok. As one might expect from my rereading of *Gaudium et Spes* during my sabbatical leave,

---

1. Ratzinger, *Introduction to Christianity*, 137.
2. Wojtyła, *Person and Community*, 234.

many questions were raised, especially concerning the influence at the time of the Council of a little known Polish Catholic philosopher Karol Wojtyła, circumstances which took me to Milwaukee in 2010 to meet this religious sister from whom I learnt much. Unable to read the original Polish, I found reading the translation of Wojtyła's foundational work, *The Acting Person: A Contribution to Phenomenological Anthropology* (1979) offered by his friend, the Polish philosopher Anna-Teresa Tymieniecka (1923-2014) rather problematic, especially the use of conceptual language which I found confusing, whether from Thomism or from phenomenology, which took me to the States to consult a specialist in Wojtyla's pre-papal thought. In so doing, I received answers to my questions by someone very familiar with his thought as the English translator. The recent publication of *Person and Act and Related Essays* (2021) as the first volume of the English critical edition of the collected works of Karol Wojtyla/John Paul II marks a welcome access to his original thought, which might be approached as a thoughtful "service to humanity" as he quotes this expression found in *Gaudium et Spes*.

In a sense Wojtyla's original way of thinking, like the subject he thinks about, represents a conundrum, but a quandary capable of resolution. One found in the following characterisation, thinking "as a humanist deeply concerned with the secret of the human heart," like accomplished philosophical forebears, Augustine, Pascal and Scheler. Expressed in the words: "The better to understand the human being and himself, Karol Wojtyla sought reasons in a philosophy illumined and supported by Christian faith."[3] Someone who focused on the question of the human being, and on understanding the nature and reality of the person, wherein we find access to the legacy of conciliar humanism as these are brought together within Wojtyła's original synthesis, inspired by his understanding of a 'Christian *personalismus*.'[4] Namely, an understanding of the human person in relation to the personal God, understood as "the participation of the Divine nature and intimate life of the most Exalted Trinity."

Approached as the "basis of ethical teaching," this way of thinking was given priority as the first of nine items suggested in his letter of December 30, 1959 as possible subjects for the forthcoming Council, written to Lucian Bernacki, auxiliary bishop in the Archdiocese of

---

3. Acosta and Reimers, *Karol Wojtyła's Personalist Philosophy*, 2.
4. Congregationes Generales, *Acta et Documenta*, Series I, Volume II, 741-48.

Gniezno. Which was then forwarded onto Cardinal Domenico Tardini (1888–1961), the Vatican secretary of state, who as President of the Ante preparatory Commission sent a consultative letter dated June 18, 1959 to the world's bishops whereby he sought "opinions and suggestions" concerning possible subjects for discussion. Obviously, these "submission letters" initiated an enormous project of preparing documentation for the Council over the next three years, especially collating the immense documentary response into eighteen folders organized into various subject areas, whose content was eventually reduced to seventy *schema*, prepared documents by the Council's Preparatory Commission and curial officials for discussion during the Council; none of Wojtyla's items 'made the cut.' Later published along with the thousands of other prepared statements collated in the *Acta Synodalia Sacrosancti Concilli Oecumenici Vatican II* (1970–96). Submitted by Wojtyła for discussion in the Council "which is awaited by all with the utmost anticipation, especially by those separated from unity with the Church by reason of heresy or schism. They too seem to possess some love of Christ the Lord, hence there is hope of their reconciliation with the true Church of Christ; *for love gives birth to unity*" (emphasis added), such was the mindset of the young professor of Christian ethics.[5]

During another of his many interventions he makes two interesting observations about their shared orientation. Concerning *Dignitatis Humanae*, he felt it should be entitled, "Doctrine of religious freedom derived from the dignity of the human person,"[6] and secondly, concerning *Gaudium et Spes*, while commenting on the 'pastoral' character he felt it should be approached as a "consideration" rather than a "constitution' insofar as the latter relates to "doctrine," whereas the present schema under discussion proposes a "certain review of ideas for consideration in theory and practice." Furthermore, while he finds merit in the idea of 'dialogue,' "it is important in dialogue to affirm with whom the dialogue is engaged" found in the affirmation of the meaning of 'world' and should reflect a "sense of Christian realism."

"I am at the end now, and this is the positive side of the coin— that a man of religion should not be estranged in his intimate relationship towards God but conversely should be at home with himself and with the world from this very relationship *towards God*. And this is

---

5. Congregationes Generales, *Acta et Documenta*, Series I, Volume II, 742–43
6. Congregationes Generales, *Acta et Documenta*, Series I, Volume II, 292–93.

the aspect, nay conclusion of great moment, for the schema DEIMHT. I have finished my address. Thank you."[7] These are the final words of Archbishop Karol Wojtyła as he finished his fifty seventh and final intervention to the Council. Someone who witnessed the Council literally from the very beginning, who was directly involved with the preparation of the documented thought found in both *Gaudium et Spes* and *Dignitatis Humanae*, and who became one of its foremost proponents, another significant figure in the story of conciliar humanism, which follows a "before, during and after" strategy.

While the greeting "ladies and gentlemen" is an expression commonly taken for granted in the English-speaking world, used as Catholic communities gather in small discussion groups, parish and diocesan assemblies. However, this was not always the case, as observed by the Italian Jesuit theologian Archbishop Roberto Tucci (1921–2015),[8] a member of the preparatory commission on the lay apostolate and *peritus* during the Council, later created a cardinal by Pope John Paul II on February 21, 2001. Spoken in Latin, *Venerabiles Patres, Fratres et Sorores*, the official language of the universal Church, these were unprecedented words within ecclesiastical discourse spoken by the Archbishop of Kraków during the one hundredth and seventh general session of the Council, held in St. Peter's on October 8, 1964 and presided over by the Belgian Cardinal Suenens to discuss the issue of 'dialogue' in the draft document on the lay apostolate, namely, "true and faithful dialogue." Something Wojtyła had previously expressed keen interest in as item number three in his 1959 letter.

A new way of thinking modelled on ideas found in Pope Paul VI's recent encyclical *Ecclesiam Suam* "on the Church" published on August 6, 1964 wherein he addressed the issue of "dialogue" living in the "world of today." Ubiquitous in contemporary Catholic discourse, ideas such as 'people of God,' 'laity' and 'dialogue,' originated during one of the most consequential moments in the recorded history of the Church, expressions which became synonymous with the Council, examples of its broad new thinking. These speak to our communal identity found as a 'community of persons,' in this instance, referring to the involvement of Catholic laity.

---

7. Wojtyła, *Acta*, Series I, Volume II, 359–50.
8. Tucci, "Proper Development of Culture," 261.

An involvement certainly taken seriously by Archbishop Wojtyła who espoused the Council's seminal teaching about the necessary participation of laity as "People of God." Not only through their physical presence, found in his active collaboration with colleagues from Lublin, Stefan Swieżwaski and George Kalinowski, especially in drafting the final documents discussed in this book, on the laity, religious freedom and the Church in the "world of today," wherein we recognize the philosophical orientation which characterized conciliar humanism. But also, his recognition of the presence of laypersons as necessary in the evangelical mission of the Church moving into the future. Later he would be characterized as someone who "tapped laity to reveal Vatican II's power" by the editor of Edmonton's *Western Catholic Reporter*, an independent journal established during the Council, wherein the editor claimed Wojtyła "learned that a zealous, educated laity was essential to implementing the council's teachings," exemplified in the Synod of the Archdiocese of Kraków he convened in 1972.

Promulgated by the pope after over two thousand three hundred bishops voted in favour with two against, documented in *Vatican II: The Complete History* (2015), these extraordinary numbers not only speak to the significant level of agreement in this "meeting of minds" in approving the unprecedented document *Apostolicam Actuositatem: Decree on the Apostolate of the Laity*, but also highlight the essential activities conducted outside St. Peter's. Namely, given the enormity of participants from around the world this generated the operational necessity for the formation of numerous language-based groups and sub-committees made up of Council Fathers, assisted by suitably qualified experts and lay witnesses, formed to prepare sections of written material or drafts of these documents for subsequent discussion and approval during the plenary session, detailed in the *Acta*. Of particular significance was the collaborative effort observed by Tucci between then Bishop Wojtyła and his colleagues from Lublin's School of Thomist Philosophy, Stefan Swieżawski and George Kalinowski (1916–2000), an auditor during the second session between September 29–December 4, 1963, the so-called "Lublin connection." Later these Catholic laymen published an account of what they observed during the first two sessions of the Council, entitled *Philosophy During the Second Vatican Council* (1965), republished by Peter Lang in 2006 for the series "Catholic Thought from Lublin."

26

The First Truth

INTERESTINGLY, IN THE CONTEXT of his discussion of "integral humanism," Maritain identified Aquinas and John of the Cross as proponents of this original thought approached within the scholastic tradition; both these thinkers were studied by the young Polish graduate priest, Karol Wojtyla, who became another formative twentieth-century Catholic philosopher. Drawing on their thought within his original synthesis, Christian humanism remained a lifelong interest for "the pope who rescued Western humanism" in the opinion of his acclaimed biographer the American George Weigel, during an interview on ABC Radio in 2011. Inspired by his reading of Maritain's seminal work, following encouragement from Stefan Swieżawski, his colleague from Lublin's "School of Thomist philosophy," who had worked with Maritain at the *Institut Catholique de Paris* (1875) while on sabbatical leave in 1936. Interestingly, the young bishop had envisaged the connection between this form of humanism and his appreciation of 'Christian personalism' as a suitable topic for the forthcoming Council.

Wojtyła's initial philosophical interest in the specific background of theocentric humanism began as a young priest when he was sent for further study at Rome's Pontifical University of Saint Thomas Aquinas (1577), known as the *Angelicum*, following his ordination on November 1, 1946 by Cardinal Adam Stefan Sapieha (1867–1951), Archbishop of Kraków (1946–51). This is where he successfully completed his doctorate in sacred theology on June 19, 1948, *Faith according to St. John of the Cross* (1981), based on his metaphysical and psychological understanding of the nature of faith through a descriptive analysis of the personal experience of those who believe, based on the writings of this Discalced Carmelite. Whom he had previously studied with a small group of friends at Kraków's Jagiellonian (1364), the oldest university in Poland, where he returned as a lecturer in Christian ethics in 1948, following his study at the *Angelicum* and where he wrote an article "humanism in St. John of the Cross" published in the 1950 volume of the Polish journal *Znak*.[1] Following his appointment as parochial vicar of the University parish of St. Florian's, the young philosopher was able to pursue his interest in humanism when in 1949 he began an annual series of lectures to Kraków's academic community, professors and students alike, entitled *Consideration on the Essence of Man* (2016), which finished with a discussion of "the first truth of Christian humanism."

Originally declared a "Doctor of the Church," it was one of the last accolades given to Aquinas by his fellow Dominican Pope St. Pius V (1504–72) shortly after the conclusion of the Council of Trent (1545–63). Now addressing participants in the eight International Thomistic Congress on September 13, 1980, his successor the recently elected Pope John Paul II added a further scholastic accolade which he gave to Aquinas, namely, *Doctor Humanitatis*, which complemented *Doctor Angelicus* and *Doctor Communis*. Recognized in Conciliar thought in the documents *Optatam Totius: Decree on Priestly Formation* (1965), and in *Gravissimum Educationis: Declaration on Christian Education* (1965), the ongoing influence of Aquinas was observed on January 28, 1999, when Pope John Paul II during his address to members of the Pontifical Academy of Saint Thomas Aquinas (1879) recalled the reason behind this recent accolade, originally given in his Apostolic Letter *Inter Munera Academiarum* while addressing participants to the 1980 International Thomistic Congress. As he asserts: "*Doctor Humanitatis* is the name we give St. Thomas Aquinas because he was always ready to receive the values of all cultures." Given "the cultural conditions of our time" the pope thought it was appropriate to recall Aquinas' integral understanding of humanity, found in his recognition of "the dignity of the human person and the use of his reason," a way of thinking which had inspired Maritain's original thought.

A vision of humanity well expressed in the words: "Man is created to love as well as to think. Man's most exalted position is on bended knee with eyes uplifted to the Cross of the Crucified." Thought which reflects my understanding of Incarnational soteriology, these words begin *The*

---

1. Jordan Aumann, Translator's Preface to Wojtyła, *Faith according to St. John of the Cross*, 13.

Life and Labours of St. Thomas of Aquin (1875), one of the first biographies written in English by Roger Bede Vaughan (1834–83), the English Benedictine and second Archbishop of Sydney (1877–83).² Writing this book between 1871–72, when Vaughan was teaching metaphysics and moral philosophy at the recently established Belmont Abbey (1859) in Herefordshire, following his ordination in Rome in 1859, having graduated from the Roman College (1551) where he studied philosophy in the tradition of Aquinas. Established as a "free school of grammar, humanism and Christian doctrine" by St. Ignatius of Loyola (1491–1556), the Basque priest and scholastic theologian, eleven years after he founded the Society of Jesus, during the eighteenth century this College became a bastion for the promotion of Thomistic thought. Following his relocation to Sydney Australia, the Benedictine monk Roger Bede continued to teach these subjects while Rector of St. John's College within the University of Sydney (1850) between 1874 till 1877 when he succeeded another Benedictine John Bede Polding (1794–1877) as Archbishop of Sydney.

While Archbishop Vaughan was unable to return to the Roman College as he had planned, soon after his papal election Pope John Paul II was able to return to his *alma mater* the *Angelicum*, Rome's Pontifical University of St. Thomas Aquinas (1577) where he studied between 1946–48, to participate in the celebrations on November 17, 1979 to mark the hundredth anniversary of Pope Leo XIII's ground-breaking encyclical *Aeterni Patris* (1879) "on the restoration of Christian philosophy," especially that of the "golden wisdom of St. Thomas." A Catholic way of thinking which drew "hints from the past" and inspired generational change and innovative adaptation moving into the future, a philosophical position characterized by Pope Leo XIII: "to complete the old by the aid of the new."³

As with the city of *Kraków*, the *Angelicum* represents a remarkable coincidence between "location and thought," wherein, like previous generations of European students following in the tradition of the young scholastic Anselm, now at the request of his Archbishop of Kraków, Cardinal Adam Sapieha (1867–1951) a newly ordained priest travelled from Poland to Rome to sit at the feet of a master "in thought," namely as the pope later recalled, "to deepen my knowledge of the teaching of the Common Doctor, St. Thomas of Aquin." As recognized by the Dominican

---

2. Vaughan, *Life and Labours of Saint Thomas*, vi.
3. Collins, "Leo XIII," 201.

Cardinal Christof von Schönbrun, Archbishop of Vienna, Aquinas was "the first, and perhaps only, man ever canonized simply for thinking."[4] As men of ideas, these reforming popes of the twentieth century, Leo XIII and John Paul II, were not only trained in the philosophical tradition which this scholastic thinker established, namely Thomism, but also envisaged the resourcefulness of this tradition as a means for reforming and revitalizing contemporary Catholic thought, especially through education, as proponents of twentieth-century "Papal Thomism." Approached from the perspective of Pope John Paul II's thought, this program of philosophical renewal was achieved by the recovery of its distinctive *sapiential* and metaphysical way of thinking.

While there is much in the claim of Gerard McCool (1918–2005), the Fordham University professor of philosophy as he concludes *The Neo-Thomists* (1994), "the history of the modern Neo-Thomist movement, whose magna carta was *Aeterni Patris* (1879), reached its end at the Second Vatican Council."[5] Pope John Paul II adopts a more cautious approach in *Fides et Ratio* as he suggests "the Church has been justified in consistently proposing Saint Thomas as a master of thought" (para. 43). More than one hundred years since the promulgation of Pope Leo XIII's seminal encyclical *Aeterni Patris*, Pope John Paul II used this as an opportunity to revisit the perennial issue between the exercise of faith "and" use of philosophy in "a more systematic way" in *Fides et Ratio*. Reasserting the claim, "the Church has no philosophy of her own," taken from *Humani Generis* (1950), the encyclical written by Pope Pius XII (1939–58) "concerning some false opinions" which undermine Catholic doctrine, such as found in "existentialism," a new "erroneous philosophy," whereby Pope John Paul II recognized the ongoing legitimacy and the importance of "a Christian way of philosophizing," namely "philosophical speculation conceived in dynamic union with faith." In so doing, he promotes a way of thinking "in organic continuity with the great tradition," one which envelops thought from "the past, Ancient, Patristic and Scholastic" but also includes "the fundamental achievements of modern and contemporary thought." Furthermore, this appeal to tradition reflects a mindset which not only incorporates "a mere remembrance of the past" but a thoughtful awareness of our ongoing cultural heritage shared by humanity. Namely, an intellectual

---

4. Schall, *Mind That Is Catholic*, 187.
5. McCool, *Neo-Thomists*, 230.

openness guided by a willingness which "meets the needs of our times," a way of thinking which generated conciliar humanism.

While not entirely "a break with the past," this thoughtful approach was in line with the original Leonine program of philosophical renewal initiated with *Aeterni Patris*, namely, the acquisition of a new perspective, "a new way of thinking" in the words of Pope Benedict XVI, which builds on the thoughtful patrimony of Catholic philosophical thought in the manner of Jacques Maritain, rather than a complete rupture from the former philosophical tradition. As such, conciliar humanism represents a remarkable confluence of ideas drawn from various traditions within twentieth-century European Catholic philosophy. Approached as a "symphony of ideas," this way of thinking takes inspiration from the patrimony of Catholic thought as it evolved over the centuries, brought together through the pope's creative retrieval of a mindset characterized as *sapiential* consciousness which occurred during the Second Vatican Council.

During his inaugural homily as pope in St. Peter's Square on October 22, 1978, the anniversary of the opening of the Council and as he assumed the Chair of St. Peter, he claimed: "Christ knows 'what is in man' and is able to serve the human person and the whole of mankind." Wherein the new Bishop of Rome clearly identified the orientation of his thought which would determine his pontificate, a Christ centred understanding of the "human person" revealed in the "mystery of the Cross and Resurrection," words which summarize conciliar humanism. Original thought which not only inspired the first Polish pope during his fourteen years on the See of Stanislaus of Szczepanów (1030–79), the first bishop of Kraków and first Polish-born Saint but also informed his academic apostolate teaching moral philosophy and Christian social ethics, first at that city's famous university, the Jagiellonian (1364) then at the University of Lublin (1918) which now bears his name, following a resolution of the Senate of the Polish Episcopacy on October 16, 2005. A Christ centred integral philosophical way of thinking, prompted by "wonder" at the human being, he had already identified in the "Introduction" to his seminal work *Person and Act* (1969), wherein he not only recognized his participation "in the work of the Second Vatican Council" while preparing this work, but also the "impulse to reflect on the theme of the person," especially found in one of the Council's main documents, *Gaudium et Spes*, and the conviction of the person's transcendental character, as he quotes with his particular emphasis: "The Church, by reason of her role and competence, is not identified in any way with the political community nor bound to any political system. She is at once *a sign and a safeguard of the transcendent character of the human person*" (para. 76).[6] Approached as the *actus personae*, characterized as "the vision of the transcendence of the person in the act" this informs the philosophical framework of Wojtyła's thought moving into his pontificate as he builds on foundations already laid.

"In the thoughts of the Holy Father and in their implementation by all the bishops, this Council wants to be *an act of love*; an act which will weigh upon the history of the contemporary man and will, in some way, tear man away from hatred and push him in the direction of love."[7] These words and their obvious human orientation found in "an act of love" were spoken by then auxiliary Bishop Karol Wojtyła of Kraków, during a Pontifical High Mass celebrated in the historic old wooden church of St. Szczepan in Mnichów on December 26, 1962 following his return from Rome after attending the first plenary session of the Council between October 11–December 8 that year. Spoken by someone who had never expected he would attend the Council in the first place as Poland's youngest bishop.

In this sermon he identified the human orientation of what would be his defining idea, the "human person," found in Christ's saving "act of love," thought which encapsulates conciliar humanism expressed as an instance an of "Incarnational soteriology." On his return home, the young bishop was invited to speak about his experience of the Council during a conference held at his *alma mater*, the Metropolitan Theological Seminary in Kraków, wherein he identified the Council as following the "spirit of Pope John XXIII," namely, an opportunity "to show the truth" in such a manner that it would "captivate the contemporary man and find its way to him," speaking the universal language of love, found in the Person of Christ directed toward humanity. Writing years later in the chapter entitled "the mystery of man: truth" in *Sign of Contradiction* (1978) Wojtyła develops this topic addressed to "contemporary man" appraised from the perspective of conciliar humanism. Namely, the Christ centred integral philosophical vision of our shared humanity found in *Gaudium et Spes* (para. 22), and its ingenious use of the evocative expression "in Christ," namely "in the mystery of the incarnate Word." The foundation

---

6. Wojtyła, *Person and Act*, 117n9.
7. Boniecki, *Making of the Pope*, 212, emphasis added.

of this Conciliar way of thinking with its original philosophical anthropology, was summarily expressed in *Sign of Contradiction*: "The mystery of the Incarnation is a focal point in the whole plan of salvation, and its purpose of none other than the salvation of mankind,"[8] found in the Council's use of the idea of "human person."

Writing earlier, in his introduction to *Love and Responsibility* (1960), Wojtyła claims: "it is not enough to define a man as an individual of the species *Homo* (or even *Homo sapiens*). The term 'person' has been coined to signify that a man cannot be wholly contained within the concept 'individual member of the species,' but that there is *something more* to him (Emphasis added), a particular richness and perfection in the manner of his being, which can only be brought out by the use of the word 'person.'" A book written while he was a professor teaching Christian social ethics at the Catholic University of Lublin's (1918) "School of Thomist philosophy" wherein he defends the traditional Catholic understanding of marriage though approached from a new philosophical perspective which informs the "something more" found in humanity, elaborated by his understanding of "Christian personalism."

While recognizing the traditional definition of "person" as "an individual substance of a rational nature" by the early sixth century Roman statesman and philosopher Boethius (477–524), the young Polish philosopher now argues for a broader appreciation of "the something more," as essentially associated with the whole human being, individual and social, rather than simply as a rational thinking being, which he finds in the human person's "capacity for transcendence." Whereby Wojtyła sought, through his reading of Maritain, to integrate the ideas drawn from traditional Aristotelian metaphysical realism with those found in contemporary forms of Thomism along with ideas taken from Scheler's phenomenological ethical personalism. An integral way of thinking which engaged the broader philosophical context of "personalist" and "utilitarian" views of marriage and sexual life, within his comprehensive study of "the human person." A distinctive way of thinking which anticipates Wojtyła's thoughtful involvement drafting *Gaudium et Spes* and *Dignitatis Humanae* and their original use of ideas 'human person,' 'community of persons' and 'human solidarity.'

Like previous generations of students living in the tradition of Catholic thought, such as the young Anselm from Aosta in the north

---

8. Wojtyła, *Sign of Contradiction*, 117.

of Italy, who travelled to learn from his fellow country man Blessed Lanfranc from Pavia (1005–89) teaching the liberal arts at the remote Benedictine abbey of Bec in Normandy, Wojtyła travelled a considerable distance to Rome as a graduate priest to encounter the "human face of learning" found in the thought of Aquinas. Following his ordination to the priesthood on November 1, 1946 by Cardinal Adam Stefan Sapieha (1867–1951), Archbishop of Kraków (1911–51), having completed his initial theological formation at Kraków's Jagiellonian University, the newly ordained Father Karol Wojtyła travelled to Rome on November 14, 1946, at the request of his Archbishop, to continue his theological study at the Pontifical University of Saint Thomas Aquinas (1577), known as the *Angelicum* in honour of its patron *Doctor Angelicus*, to sit at the feet of this master "in thought."

Years later on his return to the *Angelicum* as Pope John Paul II he recalled this thoughtful encounter, whereby he sought "to deepen my knowledge of the teaching of the Common Doctor, St. Thomas of Aquin," and especially his original metaphysical thought based on Aquinas' "philosophy of being, that is, of *the act of existing (actus essendi)*."[9] A profoundly humble and spiritual man, a man of prayer, Aquinas was a towering figure of medieval learning, who envisaged his teaching in very personal terms. Quoting from Aquinas' *Commentaria in Dionysii (Pseudo-Areopagitae) De Divinis Nominibus* (4.4) Josef Pieper recalls wherein the "teacher of humanity" looked into the human faces of those eager for truth: "to lead a man from error to truth, was the greatest service which one man can render another."[10]

Already interested as a final year seminarian in the scholastic thought of Saint John of the Cross, the great Spanish Carmelite mystic and a major figure of the Counter-Reformation in Spain, the young student Karol Wojtyła chose this figure as the subject for his major essay, a requirement for participating in the final seminar of dogmatic theology at the university, entitled "The analysis of faith according to St. John of the Cross."[11] A subject he later chose for his doctoral research at the *Angelicum* which he submitted two years later at the end of 1948, "on faith according to St. John of the Cross," written under the supervision of the French Dominican Réginald Garrigou-Lagrange (1877–1964), the leading twentieth-century proponent of neo-Thomism and professor

---

9. John Paul II, *Whole Truth about Man*, 219.
10. Pieper, *Silence of Thomas*, 23.
11. Boniecki, *Making of the Pope*, 106.

of theology between 1909–60 at Rome's Pontifical University of Saint Thomas Aquinas (1222). With a formidable intellect, this famous French theologian was characterized as "the sacred monster of Thomism" in *Le Figaro* May 26, 1966, in an unflattering obituary written by François Mauriac (1885–1970), the French novelist, a lifelong Catholic and member of the French Resistance. Someone who fell out with another member, the philosopher Albert Camus (1913–60), over the treatment of French Nazi collaborators following the liberation of Paris on August 19, 1944, which Mauriac felt should be deferred in favour of promoting post-war national reconciliation. Interestingly, both Mauriac in 1952 and Camus in 1957 were laureates of the Noble Prize in Literature, the former awarded "for the deep spiritual insight and the artistic intensity with which he has in his novels penetrated the drama of human life," the latter known for his atheistic nihilism.

While Wojtyła expressed a keen interest in the study of Christian ethics and moral philosophy, his pre-papal thought sought to integrate this philosophical interest within his ongoing study of Thomism together with his studied awareness of Scheler's phenomenology directed towards understanding the nature of the human being, through his lecturing activities commuting between the universities at Kraków and Lublin. Having already identified this interest drawing attention to the human orientation in the act of faith approached as a human experience, successfully writing his doctorate in sacred theology at Rome's *Angelicum* in late 1948, he returned home early the next year to teach Christian social ethics in the Faculty of Theology at Kraków's Jagiellonian University (1364), where again he took up this subject in a series of lectures to the broader academic community living in this university city, "to the young intelligentsia" entitled "considerations on the essence of man." Wherein we find traces of his evolving thought based on the premise "man is a rich, complex and multifaceted being"[12] later published as *Considerations on the Essence of Man* (1949).

Thinking in response to the prevalent reductive understanding of humanity, diminished to a one-dimensional biological being in atheistic evolutionary naturalism and Marxist materialism, Wojtyła now sought a comprehensive or integral understanding of the human being, as possessing a rich, complex, and multifaceted nature, one which incorporated "the something more" found in "the human person"

---

12. Wojtyła, *Considerations*, 23.

approached from a Christian perspective. Whereby the young lecturer in Christian ethics creatively engaged Boethius' old definition of person 'as an individual substance of a rational nature' *rationalis naturae individua substantia*, with a view to extending this traditional philosophical understanding within a contemporary human context through his use of the concept of a 'human person,' and in so doing Wojtyła engaged the ongoing influence of this early sixth-century Roman philosopher. Known for his numerous commentaries on the formative philosophers of Antiquity, the Athenians Plato and his student Aristotle, Boethius assumed the status as the main conduit for their thought moving into the medieval world. In a similar fashion, Wojtyła sought to highlight the connection between Christian humanism and Christian personalism, which informs the Council's philosophical appreciation of our shared humanity, the basis of conciliar humanism.

An integrative way of thinking the young priest first discussed in his conclusion to *Considerations*, based on the recognition "[that] the spiritual human soul is able to take into itself *'participation'* in the life of God."[13] A technical expression "participation" used in Neoplatonic thought, it was then appropriated by Aquinas to better understand the loving connection and particular relationship between God the Creator and the human creature, while appreciating the fundamental difference between God and His creation. Unlike Scheler whose later thought following his rejection of Catholic faith plumbed the depths of pantheism, Wojtyła recognized this fundamental difference between the Christian God and the human creature, now employed in the context of conciliar humanism by the idea of "human solidarity." Used to designate the social nature of humanity as being personal and participatory, ultimately directed towards God through the sphere of the Absolute, a constitutive dimension of the human person in the thought of Scheler, which informs the human "capacity for transcendence." A capacity which had been denied by twentieth-century French proponents of scientific positivism, such as Auguste Comte (1789–1857) and Jean-Paul Sartre's (1905–80) atheistic existential humanism, thought which generated Wojtyła's original idea of "alienation" as the denial of this fundamental capacity.

Approaching Wojtyła's understanding of "participation," I find a definite resonance with Scheler's appropriation of Augustine's Christian anthropology and its seminal idea of a human "person," as a God centred

---

13. Wojtyła, *Considerations*, 209, emphasis added.

idea of humanity, one being "open to the Transcendent." In the words of Scheler: "Thus man's intention beyond himself and all life constitutes his *essence*. And precisely this *is* the essential concept of 'man'"[14] as he writes in his *Formalism in Ethics and Non-Formal Ethics of Values* (1913). Another book which posed significant difficulties for Wojtyła to read but one which he well researched for his *Habilitation* (1953–54) and translated from the original German while living in Kraków. Published around the same time as *The Nature of Sympathy* (1913), together with *Formalism* these brought the Catholic Scheler, "a theist and realist," international recognition which remains so today, wherein we find the ingredients of his original phenomenological ethical personalism, notwithstanding its lack of a metaphysical foundation, effectively used by Wojtyła.

Attempting to broaden "Boethius' old definition" of the person as "an individual substance of a rational nature," Wojtyła sought to incorporate the spiritual dimension of being human, that "something more" found in the human capacity for transcendence, wherein he refers to the spiritual and especially Christian perspectives associated with "so-called personalism" in the claim: "that man is a person, an unrepeatable value that does not pass away."[15] Having discussed the theological significance of this thought, wherein according to revelation, "man is admitted by grace to 'participation' in the Divine Nature," Wojtyła concludes his *Considerations* with a discussion of "the first truth of Christian humanism," namely, that "the spiritual human soul is able to take into itself 'participation' in the life of God,"[16] a key concept for both Aquinas and Wojtyła, later used in *Gaudium et Spes*. While undertaking pastoral activities at the parish of St. Florian, Archbishop Baziak granted Wojtyła sabbatical leave on September 1, 1951 until 1953 to undertake formal post-doctoral work, preparing for his *Habilitation* on one of the foremost moral philosophers of the twentieth century, Max Scheler. Following its successful completion on October 9, 1953, with the recommendation of Professor Stefan Swieżawki, the Academic Senate at the University of Lublin (1918) invited Wojtyła to join the Department of Philosophy; several years later, on November 27, 1956 the Senate officially appointed him an Assistant Professor and Chair of Ethics in the Department of Philosophy, a position he held until his election to the papacy in 1978.

14. Scheler, *Formalism in Ethics*, 288–89.
15. Wojtyła, *Considerations*, 159.
16. Wojtyła, *Cosndierations*, 209.

With the rigorous suppression of the well-established academic life in Catholic Poland, by both Nazi and Stalinist occupational regimes, following World War II "a very distinctive spiritual and intellectual situation existed in Poland" which in the opinion of Swieżawski generated a remarkable "hunger for philosophy,"[17] circumstances which gave rise to "Lublin Thomism" at the Catholic University of Lublin. Established on July 27, 1918 under the leadership of the philosopher Father Idzi Radziewski (1871–1922), it was later the only private institution of higher education behind the Iron Curtain, the others being subject to the prevalent Marxist ideology. A graduate from the Catholic University of Leuven, where he studied between 1898 till 1900 completing his doctorate in philosophy "on the genesis of the idea of evolution in Darwin and Spencer" written under the supervision of Professor Désiré-Joseph Mercier, Radziewski returned to Poland with first-hand experience of the particular ethos of a Catholic university, which he then cultivated at Lublin. An intellectual ethos which re-emerged with a new generation of enthusiastic young Catholic philosophers following the reopening of the Department of Philosophy in 1946, under the enlightened leadership of its young Dean, George (Jerzy) Kalinowski (1916–2000), together with Stefan Swieżawski and the Dominican Mieczyslaw Albert Krapiec (1921–2008), foundational figures who inspired a new program of philosophical studies in the "School of Thomist Philosophy," to counter the prevalent Marxist atheistic materialism imposed by the Communist regime. A way of thinking essentially integrative, which brought together the core subjects of traditional Aristotelian Thomist realistic metaphysics under Swieżawski, the emerging field of philosophical anthropology developed by Krapiec, and following the appointment of Wojtyła to the university, the addition of philosophical ethics, a distinct way of doing philosophy which came to be known as "Lublin Thomism."[18]

Set against this broad intellectual background, we can better understand the evolution of the integrative nature of Wojtyła's philosophical thought, which as a Council father informed the genesis of conciliar humanism. An approach which began when Wojtyła was accepted into the clandestine Metropolitan Theological seminary in Kraków in October 1942 to begin his studies in preparation for the diocesan priesthood by taking secret courses at the Theological Department of the Jagiellonian

---

17. Stefan Swiezawski, Introduction to Wojtyla, *Person and Community*, ix.
18. Stefan Swieżawski, Introduction to Wojtyla *Person and Community*, ix–xvi.

University as a theology student. While continuing to work full-time in the boiler room at the Solvay chemical works in Borek Falecki in 1944 as required by the Communist government, this underground seminarian undertook his priestly formation outside normal working hours, when he was asked to read a very difficult book, *Ontologja czyli metafizyka*, *Ontology or Metaphysics* (1926). However, as Wojtyła later observed, reading this book while challenging it proved very productive, which obviously stimulated his later philosophical interests and career.

A manual of philosophical instruction written by Rev. Professor Kazimierz Wais (1865–1934), the product of an accomplished Thomist philosopher, Wojtyła was ill prepared for this serious reading, having been admitted in 1942 to the "underground seminary" by Cardinal Sapieha, living alone and working during the day in the Solvay Chemical works in Krakòw, with no particular background in philosophy having pursued the study of Slavic Polish literature and trained in philology at the Jagiellonian University in Kraków, and without access to the resources of a library, formidable circumstances which Wojtyła successfully overcame. As he recalls the considerable difficulty understanding the unfamiliar content and difficult terminology found in reading this book: "For a long time I couldn't cope with the book, and I actually wept over it. But in the end it opened up a whole new world to me. It showed me a new approach to reality and made me aware of questions that I had only dimly perceived."[19] For the first time, reading this book Wojtyła encountered the classic scholastic theses and Latinized formulas as he sought "to negotiate a trail through the thick briars of concepts, of analyses and axioms, without ever being able to identify the terrain over which I was making my way." Wherein he found a presentation of the basic degrees of being, act, potentiality, existence, and essence presented within their historical context, ancient, medieval, and especially nineteenth-century Catholic thought, found in the tradition of transcendental Louvain Thomism espoused by Cardinal Désiré Mercier and Joseph Maréchal (1878–1944). An approach initiated by Pope Leo XIII's *Aeterni Patris* which inspired the tradition of neo-scholastic thought. Having been trained in scholastic Thomism at Rome's Pontifical Gregorian University (1551), Wais was appointed professor of Christian philosophy and fundamental theology between 1909 till 1929 at the Faculty of Theology of the University of Lviv, established by Polish King Jan Zazimierz (1609–72) in 1661 in Ukraine.

19. Maliński, *Pope John Paul II*, 47, 159.

Writing this difficult book Wais was simply repeating the ideas taken from the well-known booklet as intended, namely, *The Twenty-Four Thomistic Theses* (1914), a distillation of Aquinas' philosophical metaphysics, composed and endorsed as suitable reading for the instruction of seminarians like the young Wojtyla which had been approved by the Sacred Congregation of Studies. A pontifical organization responsible for Catholic universities and oversight of the teaching seminaries established in 1824 by Pope Leo XII (1823–29). This booklet reflected the contemporary Catholic philosophical mindset with its list of propositions suitable for discussion within Catholic institutions of education. A way of thinking which addressed traditional subjects of Western philosophy, dealing with ontology, cosmology, psychology, and the study of God. The significance of this reading for Wojtyła's subsequent career was later observed by one of his early biographers, George Huntston Williams (1914–2000),[20] the American church historian, professor of Unitarian Theology. Appointed as a Protestant observer during the second session of the Council in 1962 and especially fluent in Polish, Williams soon became acquainted with the young bishop from Kraków.

As I once observed, "it is worth noting that a theological concept of person was unknown to ancient pagan philosophy" and only acquired significance as Christians, people of faith began to reflect on the mystery of the Christian God and the uniqueness and value of each human being redeemed by Christ,[21] namely what I call, Incarnational soteriology. Commonly used in the Greek speaking world for a theatrical mask used by an actor, the Greek word *prosopon* translated as 'person' was appropriated by the world's Greek speaking bishops during the first ecumenical councils held at Nicaea (325), Ephesus (431) and Chalcedon (451) to better understand the nature of the Triune God.

This theological orientation received its philosophical determination during the early sixth century when the Roman philosopher Boethius, a specialist in Aristotelian philosophical logical thought, defined "person" as "an individual substance of a rational nature" in his theological treatise *De Persona et Duabus Naturis Contra Eutychen et Nestorium*; the thought of both these theologians was condemned during the third ecumenical council at Ephesus (431). Reacting to the thought of Nestorius (386–450), the Patriarch of Constantinople who

---

20. Williams, *Mind of John Paul II*, 86–87.
21. Carroll, "Human Activity," 44.

rejected the Second Person of the Trinity, the Son of God Jesus Christ's complete hypostatic union, of two natures, human and divine, which the ecumenical council at Chalcedon defined as "one person and two natures." A definition which was rejected by Eutyches (c. 380–c. 456), the archimandrite of a monastery outside Constantinople, who asserted that Christ only possessed a single nature, which was "a fusion of human and divine elements" which constitute the Incarnate Word, a stance which inevitably informed his subsequent rejection of the special title, the first of many, given to Jesus' Blessed mother Mary as *Theotokos* 'God-bearer' by the Council at Ephesus.

While this philosophical definition of person was slightly adapted by Aquinas, wherein "individual substance" becomes philosophically broadened as being something that is complete, subsists by itself and essentially separated from other forms of being, writing in his *Summa Theologica* (3a. 16. 12 ad 2), Boethius' definition remained unchallenged, only to be slightly modified in modern thought with its emphasis on self-consciousness and personal identify. A way of thinking best expressed by the famous axiom of the so-called "father of modernity," the French philosopher Renè Descartes (1596–1650), *cogito ergo sum* 'I think, therefore I am.' Eventually this way of thinking came to inform the eighteenth-century Enlightenment's celebration of the potential found in the use of human reason, and the English philosopher John Locke's (1632–1704) understanding of the person as a "thinking thing," which transformed the existing world of thought and culture, moving into the twentieth-century philosophical turn to "consciousness."

27

What If?

WRITING HIS INFORMATIVE ACCOUNT, *The Ecumenical Councils of the Catholic Church: A History* (2009), Joseph F. Kelly, the American Catholic professor of religious studies from Ohio, recalls one of church history's great 'what ifs.'[1] A question which concerns the probable influence exercised by one of the medieval world's leading theologians, the Italian Dominican friar Thomas Aquinas, had he been able, as he had planned, to attend the Second Ecumenical Council of Lyons (1274). An interesting way to approach the contribution of another Council father, Karol Wojtyła, the forty-two-year-old junior auxiliary bishop from Kraków who was not expected to attend the Second Ecumenical Vatican Council.

With an established theological reputation, the career diplomat Blessed Pope Gregory X (1271–76), who had known the formidable intellectual rigor of Aquinas when he held the Dominican chair of theology at Paris, invited his former teacher to participate during the Council to address the issue of reconciliation with Greek Christians, the so-called "eastern question." Another theological invitee to the Council was the recently appointed Cardinal Bishop of Albano, Bonaventure of Bagnoregio, the previous holder of the Franciscan chair of theology at Paris; both Aquinas and Bonaventure were appointed "Masters of Theology" in Paris in 1257. Unfortunately, any possible reunion in Lyons between these scholastic theological powerhouses did not occur, as Aquinas unexpectedly died while travelling to the Council on March 7, 1274 at the Cistercian abbey at Fossanova in the Papal States, carrying his *opusculum*

---

1. Kelly, *Ecumenical Councils*, 96.

or 'small treatise,' *Contra Errores Graecorum* (1263); Bonaventure died on July 15, 1274 soon after the Council closed.

Convened during a period of sociopolitical turmoil on the European landscape, Pope Gregory X sought unity within the Christian world by addressing this issue through a proposed treaty between the Latin speaking Roman Catholic Church of the West and the Greek speaking Orthodox Christians of the East under Michael VIII Palaeologus, the co-emperor of the Empire of Nicaea and Ecumenical Patriarch of Constantinople (1259–82), which was not achieved. This critical issue for Christian unity arose due to the earlier mutual declarations of anathema issued in 1054 by Saint Pope Leo IX (1049–54) and Michael 1 Cerularius, the Greek Orthodox Patriarch of Constantinople (1043–58), which divided Christianity between the Latin West and the Greek East. Circumstances which can be traced back to the sociopolitical complexity arising from linguistic tensions as Christianity evolved following the era of the Apostles. A transition characterized by theological differences over language which occasioned the first ecumenical councils conducted in Greek, convened to address the nature of the Trinity at the Council of Nicaea (325), expressed in its "Filioque clause" in the Nicene Creed, and the nature of the Person of Christ, Son of God, discussed during the Council of Chalcedon (451) with its *Homousian* 'of one substance' Christology.

While the first seven ecumenical councils were conducted in Ancient Greek, wherein we find the initial theological use of the everyday expression *prosopon* 'person,' meaning one's human face or a theatrical mask, now applied to the Son of God Jesus Christ, the Second Person of the Trinity, the remaining ecumenical councils up to and including the twenty first held in the Vatican, were conducted in Latin, the official language of the Roman Catholic Church. Circumstances which inform the accompanying linguistic tensions between Greek and Latin speaking approaches, such as the translation of theological terminology and related sociopolitical differences between East and West.

The small treatise *Contra Errores Graecorum* was written eleven years before the Council, when Aquinas was a papal theologian and conventual lecturer in the Dominican *Studium Generale* at Orvieto where the pope lived for a time, as a resource commissioned by Pope Urban IV (1261–64) to facilitate reunion with Eastern Orthodox Christians; while not intended for Lyons, in the opinion of the French theologian and Dominican friar Yves Congar (1904–95), this treatise was nevertheless influential in the absence of its author during the Council. Perhaps best known as another "behind the scenes" influential figure during the Second Vatican Council, Congar was later officially recognized for this involvement when Pope John Paul II appointed him a cardinal-deacon on November 26, 1994. According to Congar, Aquinas wrote in defence of Catholic doctrine against what appeared to be Eastern linguistic misunderstandings, demonstrating there was in fact theological harmony between the Greek church fathers and those of the Latin Church.[2] Centuries later this conflictual situation was finally resolved during the Second Vatican Council, when on the last day of council proceedings on December 7, 1965, a Joint Catholic-Orthodox Declaration was read, approved by Pope Paul VI and the Ecumenical Patriarch of Constantinople Athenagoras 1 (1948–72) rescinding the previous excommunications between Rome and Constantinople.

A climactic moment during the Council which was immediately followed by the official promulgation of the Council's final four documents by the pope, having been unanimously approved by the Council Fathers, including *Dignitatis Humanae* and *Gaudium et Spes* wherein we find conciliar humanism. One of those Council Fathers particularly active in drafting these documents, present in St. Peter's Basilica on that momentous day was Archbishop Karol Wojtyła, having been recently appointed to the See of Kraków on January 16, 1964, an unexpected presence during the Council. Circumstances which prompt another "what if" situation, namely, what if this relatively unknown Polish auxiliary bishop, though well recognized within Polish Catholic philosophical circles, especially as a teacher of Christian ethics and for his promotion of the idea of 'human person' had not been present, as he expected not to be, during the Council. Someone certainly familiar with the tenets of philosophical Thomism, he was a last-minute invitee to the Council following his recent election as *Vicar Capitular* or Temporary Administrator by the Metropolitan Chapter of local clergy on July 16, 1962, following the unexpected death of Archbishop Eugeniusz Baziak (1890–1962) on June 15, 1962.

Later that year the young Professor Bishop Karol Wojtyła arrived in Rome to take his nominated seat closest to the main doors of St. Peter's on October 22 for the official opening of the Council as one of the youngest bishops in attendance. Obviously given the extraordinary numbers in attendance for the Council, held in the specifically reconstructed interior of

---

2. Kerr, "Yves Congar," 88.

St. Peter's Basilica, seating for the Council Fathers was strictly organized according to levels of seniority, by year of episcopal ordination and by hierarchical status, with Cardinals, Patriarchs, and Archbishops seated closest to the Papal high altar. Out of the sixty-three Polish bishops at the time, he was the youngest of the twenty bishops who were given permission by the Polish Communist government to travel to Rome to participate during the Council: a virtual "nobody" outside the university cities of Kraków and Lublin in his native Poland. However, after three years operating on this international ecclesiastical world stage, he emerged as a leading figure during the Council, having taken the floor during plenary proceedings whereby he offered numerous "interventions," a twenty-minute address in Latin on a particular subject under discussion, especially of a philosophical orientation, as well as other numerous occasions during committee meetings documented in the *Acta*. Either speaking for himself and on other occasions for the Polish bishops, Wojtyła certainly impressed those present, "There are not many council Fathers who would speak out at the General Assembly as frequently as did the bishop of Krakow," and elsewhere, "the intervention by Archbishop Karol Wojtyła of Kraków was more subtle and philosophical."[3]

Recognized for his numerous activities during the Council, especially with the redaction of *Dignitatis Humanae* and *Gaudium et Spes*, complemented by WoJtyła's obvious spiritual qualities and especially his philosophical prowess, which were there to be observed by all, especially by Pope Paul VI, it came as no surprise when the pope subsequently appointed him Metropolitan Archbishop of Kraków on January 13, 1964, whereupon as archbishop he acquired "a new seat," one appropriate to his higher ecclesiastical status closer to the pope's high altar, a sacred location covered by Bernini's famous bronze *Baldacchino*, where one day in Divine providence he would stand. More significantly, this recent appointment facilitated his further direct involvement, especially in the drafting of these final documents, whose content he immediately sought to implement on his return to Krakòw. Three years later his philosophical and pastoral resourcefulness was recognized when Pope Paul VI appointed him Cardinal priest of *San Cesareo in Palatio* (1967–78). An appointment which would eventually lead Karol Wojtyła, to the surprise of many, to assume the Seat of St. Peter at the age of fifty-eight, following his papal election as Pope John Paul II on October 14, 1978.

---

3. O'Malley, *What Happened at Vatican II*, 217.

"The truly great Pope is thus one who is able to confront the world without denying it, to confront it by asserting the values of the gospel and the mystery of the Church, to affirm it by proclaiming and defending *the sacredness of every human person*" (emphasis added), original thought which encapsulates the philosophical legacy of Pope John Paul II, as a value laden confrontation with the "world of today" in the philosophical promotion and defence of the 'human person' and 'community of persons.' Exceptional qualities identified by William Oddie (1934–2019), the English Catholic author and journalist, which he finds in the "maker of the post-conciliar Church,"[4] the subject of his biographical assessment written soon after the death of *Johannes Paulus Magnus* on April 2, 2005. A former self-styled atheist and secular humanist, you might say "someone of his time," the aspiring journalist converted to Christianity aged thirty-three and was received into Full Communion with the Catholic Church in 1991 to become a leading Catholic writer and broadcaster. An advocate of what he described as "orthodox realism," this recent convert personified the spirit of the person he was writing about when he claimed Catholics should be "subversive" rather than "harmless," committed to a Church which "tells the truth," and in so doing, it will be "unpopular" at times, as the truth is often highly inconvenient.[5]

A way of thinking characterized as "a message of Christ-centred fearlessness in the Church," which is embedded in the seminal thought of this "figure of historic consequence," especially found in Pope John Paul's landmark encyclical *Fides et Ratio* (1998). Written more than a hundred years after Pope Leo XIII's landmark *Aeterni Patris* (1789) to better understand the relationship between faith "and" philosophy operating within the tradition of Catholic thought, with an emphasis on the "value of philosophy for understanding of the faith" (para. 100).

How this philosophical vision of our shared humanity, an instance of Conciliar generosity towards the "world of today," was to be approached was later indicated during Pope Benedict XVI's homily at the opening mass to introduce "the Year of Faith" (2012) which marked the fiftieth anniversary of the Council's official opening by Pope John XXIII on October 22, 1962, wherein Pope Benedict explored the merits of a textual approach, what he understands as "a return, as it were to the 'letter' of the Council, that is to its texts," by means of what he calls a "hermeneutics

4. Oddie, *John Paul the Great*, 20.
5. Phillips, "William Oddie."

of reform and renewal" rather than one of "discontinuity and rupture." By employing this papal methodology to the rereading and critical study of the Council's sixteen officially promulgated documents, whereby both "extremes of anachronistic nostalgia and running too far ahead" could be avoided, access is thereby opened up for the attentive reader to appreciate the Council's true legacy, found in its vision of our shared humanity embedded within conciliar humanism, understood as "a synthesis of fidelity and dynamism" in the words of Pope Benedict XVI. Wherein we find the Council's belief in humanity which is accessible to everyone and from which there is still much to be learnt. Especially from a philosophical reading and historical commentary on the background information and circumstances which generated conciliar humanism, documented in *Gaudium et Spes* and *Dignitatis Humanae*.

While every council remains an ecclesial assembly of Catholic bishops and religious leaders "from around the world," approached as a human phenomenon, this "meeting of minds" has the potential to surprise as a gathering of diverse human beings, occupying various levels of responsibility within the Church, speaking different languages and from diverse cultural backgrounds, whereby the Council "exceeded almost all expectations." Held midway through the chaos and the political, cultural, and social turbulence which characterized the twentieth century, whose cumulative effect marked the "dangerous times" recognized by Pope John; these circumstances posed a significant challenge to our sense of humanity, and which set in motion the Council's human agenda, first outlined *Humanae Salutis* (1959). As observed by Walter Kasper, the prominent German Cardinal theologian "for the first time in conciliar history the question of anthropology was raised for discussion."[6] Confronting these circumstances, the twenty first ecumenical council was to be of a different kind of council, understood as "a council so unlike any other that it redefined what a council does" in the opinion of John W. O'Malley, the noted American Jesuit church historian, whereby the Council "was called to proclaim to the world its sublime vision for humanity. This is new. This is a paradigm shift."[7] Writing in *The New York Review of Books* (November 19, 2019), the celebrated American Catholic journalist and historian Garry Wills in "Changing the Changeless Church," his critical review of John O'Malley's *When Bishops Meet: An*

---

6. Kasper, "Theological Anthropology," 129–38.
7. O'Malley, *When Bishops Meet*, 34, 24–25.

Essay Comparing Trent, Vatican I, and Vatican II, the Catholic journalist observed that in 1959 there was no obvious crisis for the church to deal with which would have necessitated convening an ecumenical Council, as he claimed "Catholics seemed happy in the 1950s, it was a period characterized by 'bubbling religiosity,'" a rather derogatory expression. Sixty years later after the Councill, much has changed, especially under the leadership of Pope John Paul II.

Interestingly, someone who was not surprised with his papal election was George Huntston Williams (1914–2000), the American Unitarian, Harvard professor of Divinity and church historian. Appointed an official Protestant observer during the second session of the Council, between September 29–December 4, 1963, with a shared interest in ecumenical dialogue and fluent in Polish, the American theologian communicated regularly with the young bishop from Kraków outside formal sessions of the Council, which afforded him the "unique distinction of having been the only person in the United States to predict the election of Pope John Paul II,"[8] several years later he wrote one of the first English biographies, well documented *The Mind of John Paul II: Origins of His Thought and Action* (1981).

Especially known for his active participation during the Council and his subsequent promotion and original interpretation of Conciliar thought, it was in fact the Council which provided the necessary setting for the culmination of Wojtyła's pre-papal philosophical thought, found in his effective promotion of the ideas of "human person," "community of persons," and "human solidarity," found within conciliar humanism, in the shared content of *Dignitatis Humanae* and *Gaudium et Spes*. Recalling the thought of the Flemish Jesuit theologian Piet Fransen, Wojtyla was the right person, whose philosophical and pastoral thought directed this right moment. This characteristic connection between philosophical ideas and pastoral concerns was apparent as Archbishop Wojtyła over the four years of Conciliar proceedings wrote and prepared for the publication of what would be his defining book; originally translated as *The Acting Person: A Contribution to Phenomenological Anthropology* (1979), it has been republished and correctly entitled *Person and Act* (2020), following the original Polish title.

Unlike Aquinas, who had an international reputation as one of the accomplished theologians of the time, the young junior auxiliary bishop

---

8. Mace, "Williams, George Hunston (1914–2000)," para. 10.

from Kraków on joining the Council was a relative "nobody" outside his native Poland. However, sixty years on from this momentous event in Catholic history, as Saint John Paul II he is universally recognized as one of the Council's "leading lights," a person of remarkable intellect and faith who I consider primarily responsible for conciliar humanism. Inspired by the great insight of Aquinas, paraphrased "to speak the truth in a mode which the receiver can receive it," this remarkable Christ centred integral philosophical way of thinking about our shared humanity remains accessible to all, a truthful and loving exchange understood in a common language. Expressed in the aspirational words of then Cardinal Karol Wojtyła: "Defend your humanity. This is the great heritage of Christianity, the great heritage of our faith: that we maintain high regard to mankind."[9] Words he addressed to the young people gathered for his pastoral visit to the village of Wiśniowa in southern Poland on September 25, 1970. Assertive language whereby this leading Council father not only took up the challenge of his predecessor, Pope Paul VI to take seriously the original form of humanism which emerged during the Council, conciliar humanism, but more importantly, invites future generations to recognize its thoughtful legacy wherein we discover "looking back to the future" that "we are not alone" when rereading *Gaudium et Spes* and *Dignitatis Humanae*.

"On the threshold of the third millennium of the Christian era, humanity may come to a clearer sense of the great resources with which it has been endowed and may commit itself with renewed courage to implement the plan of salvation of which its history is part" (para. 6). These aspirational words, taken from *Fides et Ratio* (1998), were written by John Paul II, the great philosopher pope of the twentieth century, who like previous Catholic intellectuals and academics envisaged this process of clarification as an essentially ongoing philosophical task, one Wojtyła "enthusiastically" took to as he introduced this seminal encyclical, from the Greek *enthous* 'possessed by God.' A philosophical way of thinking which inspired the original thought generated during the Council following its human agenda which informs the genesis of conciliar humanism, a vision of our shared humanity expressed as "the human face of Incarnate truth," captured by the twentieth-century religious art "In His Image."

---

9. Boniecki, *Making of the Pope*, 407.

As a Christ centred integral philosophical way of thinking about our shared humanity, conciliar humanism represents the Council's thoughtful response to the twentieth-century "crisis of humanity," the critical background which prompted the extraordinary and consequential decision of Pope John XXIII to convene an ecumenical council of the Catholic Church as he writes in his Apostolic Constitution *Humanae Salutis* published on Christmas Day 1961, the traditional day we celebrate the birth of Jesus Christ, "the Word made flesh." Addressing the signs of the times, as well as the "danger of nuclear war," the pope sought to counter "the ongoing dehumanization of men" which he finds in the prevalent forms of "atheistic materialism, affluent hedonism and abject poverty," essentially philosophical and social issues confronting humanity which he diagnosed as "painful considerations." Generated by the prevalent scientific atheistic worldview and its inherent devaluation of being human found in the twofold denial which characterize the twentieth-century European mindset, the denial of the human capacity to think about the idea of God and the associated denial of the human "capacity for transcendence."

A way of thinking which informs the human, philosophical and sociocultural background for approaching conciliar humanism, living in a tumultuous century. Understood as an invaluable resource to better understand the integrity of human existence and our inherent dignity and resourcefulness, set against the background of unparalleled global and indiscriminate violence, during an era of consciousness, desperate yet renewed, wherein competing ideas about humanity dominated the world stage. Thinking within the intellectual milieu of twentieth-century European Catholic philosophy for over six decades, and guided by his exceptional *sapiential* consciousness, the Polish philosopher, a specialist in Christian social ethics, Archbishop Karol Wojtyła of Kraków became the pope who inspired conciliar humanism and its philosophical promotion of the "human person," thereby initiating "the era of the human person" within contemporary Catholic discourse.

A remarkable synthesiser for a new millennium, this young Polish philosopher from Kraków ingeniously adapted ideas from Scheler's original phenomenological ethical personalism and philosophical sociology within his own way of thinking, as he "built on the foundations" of the tenets of contemporary "lived Thomism" he initially learned as a diocesan seminarian at Kraków and later as a graduate priest at Rome's *Angelicum*. Background information he discussed prior to the Council on February

17, 1961 in his talk "Thomistic Personalism" given during the Fourth Annual Philosophy Week at the Catholic University of Lublin (1918), published in *Person and Community: A Selection of Essays* (1993).[10] "Taking hints from the past," Wojtyła's original thought is best understood within the tradition of Catholic philosophy, inspired by Pope Leo XIII's promotion of the philosophy and theology of Thomas Aquinas in *Aeterni Patris* (1879), a formative figure in medieval scholasticism, now envisaged as a means for the revival of contemporary Catholic thought, which came to be known as Neo-Thomism or Neo-Scholasticism. A way of thinking originally espoused by two French philosophers, Jacques Maritain, and Étienne Gilson, who were infused with *sapiential* consciousness, a remarkable achievement of doing philosophy within a Catholic ethos which lies at the heart of Wotjyla's innovative philosophy of the "human person" within a network of original ideas, "community of persons," and "human solidarity," wherein we find the tenets of conciliar humanism.

In so doing, the Polish philosopher builds his philosophical vision of humanity for the future on the Christological and anthropological ideas which informed conciliar humanism, namely the Incarnate person of Christ and the human being created in God's image as *communio*, in the oft quoted words: "it is only in the mystery of the Word incarnated that light is shed on the mystery of mankind" from *Gaudium et Spes* (para. 22). Words taken from what the Pope described as "the Council of the century," which Providence allowed him "to participate in all the sessions of the Council."[11] Whereby he draws inspiration from Conciliar thought to introduce his inaugural encyclical *Redemptor Hominis*, "The Redeemer of Man, Jesus Christ, is the center of the universe and of history" (1979). Under the umbrella of this network of remarkable ideas, the pope was able to further explore his understanding of philosophy as a human activity, one distinctively personal, rational, and *sapiential*, one "consonant with the word of God."

Writing soon after his papal election on October 16, 1978 in his "Foreword" to the Apostolic Constitution *Sapientia Christiana* "on Ecclesiastical Universities and Faculties" (1979) Pope John Paul II claimed: "Christian wisdom, which the Church teaches by divine authority, continuously inspires the faithful of Christ zealously to endeavour to relate human affairs and activities with religious values in *a living synthesis*

---

10. Wojtyła, *Person and Community*, 165–75.
11. Frossard and John Paul II, *Be Not Afraid*, 26.

(italics added). Under the direction of these values all things are mutually connected to the glory of God and the integral development of the human person, a development that includes both corporeal and spiritual well-being." In so doing, he endorsed a biblically inspired faith filled philosophical consciousness, both theistic and realistic in the Aristotelean-Thomistic sense, which sought to assemble various, and sometimes competing ideas within a "living synthesis," philosophical thought which he characterized as *sapiential*. Wherein "all things are mutually connected to the glory of God and the integral development of the human person, a development that includes both corporeal and spiritual well-being."

Inspired by the thought of the great millennial Christian synthesisers, Augustine, the great church father who brought together ideas from prevalent pagan Platonism and Graeco-Roman philosophy with thought drawn from sacred scripture and the tenets of Christian doctrine, and his indebted student Thomas Aquinas, the Dominican friar and foremost theologian of the middle ages, who used the ideas drawn from the recently discovered pagan thought of Aristotle, recognized as "the philosopher" together with the principles of Christian doctrine. Now, imbued with a similar integrative *sapiential* consciousness, Pope John Paul II would emerge as the synthesiser for the third millennium, who brought together insights gained from his participation in Lublin' "School of Thomist Philosophy," which sought to combine the original thought of Aquinas found in Thomism, not to be confused with Neo-Scholasticism, with traditional Aristotelian Thomistic metaphysical realism, contemporary philosophical anthropology and Christian social ethics, integrated with contemporary philosophical ideas drawn from contemporary European thought, especially from the phenomenological ethical personalism of Scheler and the French social personalism of Jacques Maritain into what emerged as an original Wojtyłan program of philosophical renewal for the twenty-first century. Drawing "hints from the past," a way of thinking Pope John Paul II purposefully reintroduced when he referred to Aquinas as *Doctor Humanitatis* 'teacher of humanity,' who possessed a remarkable capacity to draw insights from and connect with the thought of others, especially the Church Father Augustine and the Greek philosopher Aristotle, which informed the intellectual and cultural milieu of his time.

Set against this broad philosophical cultural background, we can better understand the profound originality of Wojtyła's synthetic way of thinking inspired by his *sapiential* consciousness which directed his philosophical thought, well expressed by his American biographer, "foundations were meant to be built upon,"[12] whereby Wojtyła offers another thoughtful edifice on which future generations can build, especially by Catholic philosophers into the twenty-first century. One like the renowned spires of Cologne's Cathedral, a synthesis between German Catholicism and Gothic architecture, which was eventually completed during the nineteenth century on August 14, 1880 to its original medieval plan of 1248, the year a young Italian Dominican novice Thomas Aquinas arrived in Cologne accompanying his teacher Saint Albert the Great.

Recognized as millennial synthesizers from afar, like Cologne's famous towering spires, Aquinas and Augustine remain foundational figures for future generations of Catholic scholars, the Council father Wojtyła was similarly infused with *sapiential* consciousness. Whereby he offered a philosophical way of thinking about our "human solidarity," our shared humanity found in the "human person," individual and communal, within a "community of persons," generated by his Catholic awareness of our inherent human dignity as God's creatures *imago Dei*, and our thoughtful resourcefulness in response to the twofold denials generated during twentieth century within European thought, namely, the atheist denial of our human capacity to think about the idea of God, to exercise our freedom to choose to think about God, and the denial of our human capacity for personal transcendence, shared by Catholic Modernists of the time, which informed the phenomenon of twentieth-century racism based on the denial of our shared human dignity and equality, wherein we find the legacy of conciliar humanism as a thoughtful opportunity to counter these denials.

Like many believers thinking in the tradition of lived Catholic Christianity, Pope John Paul II had identified the spiritual inspiration for his philosophical resourcefulness which informed his original thought during his inaugural papal mass celebrated on October 11, 1978: "to serve Christ and with Christ's power to serve the human person and the whole of mankind"[13] original thought inspired by the Council. The means of achieving this thoughtful response were summarily expressed in March 1976, when Pope Paul VI invited the man he recently appointed a Cardinal, Archbishop Karol Wojtyła from Kraków, to lead the Vatican's Lenten

---

12. Weigel, *Witness to Hope*, 87.
13. Spinello, *Encyclicals of John Paul II*, ix.

Retreat, a series of twenty-four addresses he gave on the theme of Saint Bonaventure's spiritual classic *Itinerarium mentis in Deum* (1259). The famous Italian medieval Franciscan scholastic theologian and philosopher, who died on July 15, 1274 soon after participating in the Second Ecumenical Council of Lyon. Known as the "Seraphic Doctor," Bonaventure was an exemplary model of scholastic thinking in the Catholic tradition who drew particular attention to our human resourcefulness to receive God through his discussion of *our* shared "minds' journey towards God." Inspired by the Christian anthropology of Augustine, which informed his "logic of discovery," Bonaventure's thoughtful progression moved from a consideration of our human senses, using our God given capacity to reason, found in our intelligence and other spiritual faculties, moving towards an awareness of the presence of God.

An affirmation of our shared human resourcefulness to think about and thereby receive God which was reaffirmed during the First Vatican Council's promotion of natural theology in *Dei Filius* Dogmatic Constitution "on the Catholic Faith" promulgated on April 24, 1870, written as a means to counter the many variants of contemporary rationalism. A promotion supported by Cardinal Wojtyła, found in this series of addresses later published as *Sign of Contradiction* (1979).[14] Employing this title, he drew inspiration from the Gospel of Luke's (2:34) account of the prophesy, given by the Holy Spirit to Simeon, "the God-receiver." An elderly man considered "just and devout" from Jerusalem who had spent his entire life preparing to receive the Messiah and was informed in this vision that he would not die until this had occurred, during the Presentation of the child Jesus in the temple. An infant who would grow to become "a sign of contradiction" through the saving witness of "his own blood," captured by van der Weyden's religious art.

Returning to another 'what if' question, it might be asked what if Archbishop Baziak had not died and Wojtyła had not been elected as his temporary replacement, thereby negating any possibility of his participation during the Council as he would not have been invited to attend as only a junior auxiliary bishop, where would he be then—living in and commuting between the university cities of Kraków and Lublin? Fortunately, with God's grace this did not occur; nevertheless, these two locations are significant when accessing the evolution of Wojtyła's original pre-papal thought, a "tale of two cities." Recognized years later as "a

---

14. Wojtyła, *Sign of Contradiction*, 123–24.

figure of world historical significance," in the words of his acknowledged biographer the American George Weigel, the great philosopher pope of the twentieth century had infused this unique moment in Church history through his notable participation during Council proceedings from beginning to end, operating with a particular mindset, characterized as a pre-modern philosophical awareness of which he regularly spoke. In fact, Pope John Paul II was singularly responsible for the twentieth-century 'retrieval' of *sapiential* consciousness and its metaphysical orientation of philosophical thought within contemporary Catholic thought, so necessary for his time. A way of thinking which directed the innovative thought which emerged during the Council, one he would be primarily associated from beginning to end, especially his philosophical promotion of conciliar humanism.

28

A Generous Service

"Christians can have nothing more at heart than to be ever more generous and effective *service to humanity* in the modern world" (para. 93, emphasis added). Received with enthusiastic applause following a near unanimous vote in favour, the Council Fathers spoke with "a unified voice" saving the best till last; these are not only the final words of *Gaudium et Spes*, but of the Council itself, the most philosophical of ecumenical councils. Commenting on the evolution of this unprecedented document in his essay "Finishing the Work Begun: The Trying Experience of the Fourth Period,"[1] Gilles Routhier, the Canadian priest theologian, draws attention to the protracted reception of Schema XIII over the four years of council proceedings which eventually culminated in what came to be known as the unprecedented Pastoral Constitution, *Gaudium et Spes*. The result of a thoughtful confrontation between Council Fathers thinking from within different and at times competing mindsets, which Routhier variously labelled as "reactionaries," who maintained the doctrinal *status quo* and "progressives," who wanted change: "some preferred a more notional and dogmatic approach, others one more experiential or more existential." From within this conflictual ecclesial "meeting of minds," emerged "one of the most anticipated documents of Vatican II." By means of which, in the opinion of Routhier, the Council Fathers were "trying to say something more than business as usual."

Perhaps inspiration was found in the original use of this expression by Saint Pope Gregory the Great (c. 540–604) for his seminal *The*

---

1. Routhier, "Finishing the Work Begun," 59:49–96.

Book of Pastoral Rule (590), which he wrote as required reading for all future Church leaders in "caring for others." Now the purposeful use of this expression received global significance when the Council Fathers chose this as the title for Schema XIII, their thoughtful outreach to our broken humanity "in need of salvation" living in the "world of today." A program of philosophical and pastoral renewal undertaken in response to the contemporary "crisis of humanity," which generated conciliar humanism. The tone of which was initially set out in Pope John's Apostolic Constitution *Humanae Salutis*, issued on Christmas day 1961, whereby he convened the Council to begin in 1962.

The words spoken in frustration by the Council Fathers in mid-October 1962, which set in place the Council's original human agenda, now came to fruition following their unanimous approval of both *Dignitatis Humanae*, and *Gaudium et Spes*, the Council's final documents. Approached as literally its final words, implementing Cardinal Suenens' *ad extra* understanding of the nature of the Church found in its pastoral social outreach to the "world of today" in need of salvation, simply addressed to "humanity," wherein we find the birth of "a new way of thinking" about our shared humanity. Namely, thinking about our human solidarity as individual human persons, lived within a community of persons, directed towards the Triune God in the Person of Christ, following a lengthy gestation, namely, conciliar humanism, understood as the human face of Incarnate Truth. A way of thinking expressed in colloquial language, "we are not alone," summarily expressed in the oft repeated final words of Pope Paul on December 7, 1965: "Our humanism becomes Christianity; our Christianity becomes centred on God; in such that we may say it differently; a knowledge of man is a prerequisite for a knowledge of God. This is our hope at the conclusion of the Second Vatican Ecumenical Council."

Characterized by Pope Benedict XVI as "innovation in continuity,"[2] the Council represents a decisive moment in the history of the Catholic Church, wherein we find a remarkable way of thinking, conciliar humanism, and its remarkable network of original ideas. Generated by the Council's insistence on the twofold recognition of the human person's capacity for transcendence, which is necessarily found within a community of persons, and by implication, the recognition of our human capacity to think about the idea of God's existence, a consequence of

---

2. Shaw, *Eight Popes and the Crisis of Modernity*, 89.

our human solidarity. Wherein we find hints of Scheler's original phenomenological understanding of the personal triadic structure within religious activity, a way of thinking now embedded within the Council's Christ centred integral philosophical understanding of our shared humanity. Again, summarily expressed in the seminal statement from section twenty-two of *Gaudium et Spes*. "The truth is that only in the mystery of the Incarnate Word does the mystery of man take on light." Now driven by philosophical and pastoral orientation towards understanding our broken humanity living in the "world of today." Understood as a Christ centred "knowledge of man" disposed towards God through the Person of Christ, expressed in the words of the Third Acclamation from the *Roman Missal* (2008): "Save us, Saviour of the world, for by your Cross and Resurrection you have set us free."

Like European Catholic philosophers living during the twentieth century, the young philosopher from Lublin was a "man of his time," a thinker who addressed the political concerns and social issues arising from the twentieth-century "crisis of humanity," in response to "what is being human?" An issue which informed Wojtyła's philosophical career which began in 1948 as an assistant lecturer teaching Christian social ethics in the Faculty of Theology of the Jagiellonian University (1364) in Kraków, following his return from Rome, with the completion of his doctoral thesis in sacred theology on "the understanding of faith in the works of St. John of the Cross (1542–91)," published as *Faith according to Saint John of the Cross* (1981). Moving into the third millennium of the Christian era how is this great yet equally ambiguous moment in our human history to be approached?

More than sixty years on, the idea of "human person" remains the "ultimate hermeneutical clue" for the interpretation and implementation of conciliar thought in the opinion of Ladislas Orsy, SJ, the Hungarian born American theologian and canonical jurist writing in his seminal article "The Divine Dignity of Human Persons in *Dignitatis Humanae*," published in *Probing the Riches of Vatican II* (2015).[3] Understood as "an ecclesiological Council," in the opinion of Orsy, concerned with the truth about the universal Church, this way of thinking was embedded in what Cardinal Wojtyła later calls a "dialogue of salvation" writing in *Sources of Renewal*.[4] However, given this span of time, a failure to discuss

---

3. Orsy, "Divine Dignity," 347–64.
4. Wojtyła, *Sources of Renewal*, 37–39.

the Council's "new humanism" remains an Achille's heel within contemporary Catholic discourse and scholarship, namely, to take ownership of this unprecedented original thought about our shared humanity which evolved during the Council and wherein we find the Council's "belief in humanity." In so doing, to better understand the broad personal, cultural, and especially philosophical circumstances which inform the genesis of conciliar humanism as a unique consequence of an extended moment of *sapiential* consciousness, and in so doing, to recognize its ongoing legacy as a "good news story" for everyone. Elaborated within this original network of three interrelated basic ideas, the consequence of an integrative way of philosophical thought which sought to rejuvenate a Catholic understanding of our shared humanity as the human face of Incarnate truth in the human person.

Approached as an ingenious fusion of philosophical ideas about being human during the twentieth century, conciliar humanism represents an original convergence of ideas drawn multiple sources, used by European Catholic philosophers thinking outside the traditional circles of contemporary Neo-scholastic Thomism. Especially used by Council Fathers, such as Montini, Suenens, and especially Wojtyła, who were familiar with this thought from their seminary formation; furthermore, these philosophers came from Catholic cultures who purposefully engaged the politically secular or communist environments living in post-war Europe, employing the Thomistic social personalism of Jacques Maritain, Étienne Gilson's historical Thomism and the German phenomenological realism of Edith Stein, all of whom were acknowledged in *Fides et Ratio* as being "masters" in the service of humanity, contemporary examples of "a process of philosophical enquiry which was enriched by engaging the data of faith" (para. 74).

A way of thinking which also absorbed ideas drawn from the Christian existentialism of Gabriel Marcel, the Thomistic humanism of Karol Wojtyła, the phenomenological ethical personalism of Max Scheler, along with the closely aligned theistic thought of the Austrian born Jewish philosopher Martin Buber's philosophical appropriation of "dialogue." Broadly approached, these philosophers not only sought to rejuvenate twentieth-century Catholic thought by "a return to the ancient sources," "taking hints from the past," especially found in the patristic thought of St. Augustine and scholastic thought of St. Thomas Aquinas, but also drew ideas from their critical engagement with contemporary forms of Thomism along with ideas drawn from other forms of twentieth-century

European philosophy, such as Edmund Husserl's phenomenology and Martin Heidegger's phenomenological existentialism. This integrative way of thinking is well expressed by Jacques Maritain regarding his personal experience "of relating my discoveries in the medieval world to the contemporary world; a theory of art, of politics, of social reform."

However, circumstances were not so "bubbly" thinking outside the nineteenth and early twentieth-century Catholic mindset, characterized as "a ghetto," as it confronted the "crisis of humanity" which informs the first half of the twentieth century in Europe. Circumstances well understood by Pope John, as a period of particular interest in understanding humanity, one which required a collective response from the Church which he led, generated by the increasing awareness of the inadequacy of various contemporary forms of collectivism and individualism, which prompted the "crisis of civilization." Namely, to address "a complex combination of social, cultural, and philosophical questions,"[5] summarily expressed in the question "what is man?" Set against this broad sociocultural background, we can understand the resurgence of interest among Catholic philosophers on the European Continent in a form of humanism as a way of thinking about humanity and the emergence of Christian personalism on the European Continent as a thoughtful response.

The former came to especially characterize the thought of French Catholic philosophers, such as Maritain, in response to the social and economic turbulence generated by the Great Depression and the emergence of the great totalitarian regimes in the sphere of world politics, notably, German National Socialism, Italian Fascism and Soviet Communism. From which emerged a remarkable manifesto, "For the Common Good," written by Jacques Maritain and members of the Thomist circle who met regularly at his house in Meudon. Signed by fifty-two leading French Catholic intellectuals, including philosophers Étienne Gilson, the historian of medieval thought, the Christian existentialist Gabriel Marcel, Yves Simon (1903–61), the political philosopher and a student of Maritain at the *Institut Catholique de Paris*, and Emmanuel Mounier, the person primarily responsible for the resurgence of interest in personalism on the European continent.

While humanism remains an expression characterized by levels of ambiguity, "personalism" with its distinctive Christian orientation drew attention to the individual person's self-identity found in the

---

5. Burgos, *Introduction to Personalism*, 1.

human "capacity for transcendence," whether American or European, from France, Germany, Poland or Italy, "the great majority of the great personalists have been convinced and committed Christians,"[6] converts from Judaism, such as philosophers Franz Rosenzweig (1886–1929), Max Scheler and Edith Stein, and several Jewish personalists such as the philosophers of dialogue Martin Buber (1878–1965) and especially Emmanuel Levinas (1906–95). A Lithuanian born Jewish religious philosopher, Levinas was one of the first French intellectuals during the early 1930s to draw attention to Husserl's phenomenology, under whom he had studied at Fribourg, and offered a translation of Husserl's *Cartesian Meditations* (1931), and to Heidegger's atheistic existentialism found in *Being and Time* (1927).

Set against this philosophical background of early twentieth-century European thought, as well as incorporating ideas drawn from the French philosopher Jean André Wahl (1888–1974), a proponent of Søren Kierkegaard's Christian existentialism, Levinas creatively engaged the dialogical philosophy of the German Jewish theologian Franz Rosenzweig (1886–1929) and the Austrian philosopher Martin Buber's appropriation of the expression "I and Thou," the title of his well-known 1923 book, all of which Levinas ingeniously incorporated within his original appreciation of the philosophical significance of the "other." A way of thinking well recognized by Pope John Paul II, which was initially elaborated by Levinas in his seminal *Totality and Infinity: An Essay on Exteriority* (1961), wherein employing the method of phenomenology, he argues for the foundation of ethics based on the primal confrontation with an "other," one with whom we interact concretely "face to face," such as having a conversation wherein the other person's proximity and distance are simultaneously experienced in this encounter. A concrete way of thinking which leads to his abstract notion of an irreducible encounter with the Other or Buber's *Thou*, wherein we experience both the transcendence and heteronomy of the Other: "The Other precisely *reveals* himself in his alterity not in a shock negating the I, but as the primordial phenomenon of gentleness."[7] This way of thinking marks the contemporary revival in the recognition of the natural human disposition towards each other as human beings, identified as the "other" in Levinas' *Humanism of the Other* (1972).

---

6. Burgos, *Introduction to Personalism*, 212.
7. Levinas, *Totality and Infinity*, 150.

Adopting this philosophical thought directed towards "the other," the French theologian Ghislain Lafont writing his Heideggerian inspired *God, Time, and Being* (1998), identifies Christ as "the man for others," understood as "the embodiment of our personal and collective struggles for humanity."[8] Inspired by the Council's "discussion between Christian and unbeliever on the question who and what man really is?" as observed by Professor Joseph Ratzinger in his seminal essay "the dignity of the human person," wherein he speaks of Christ as "the new Adam," the incarnation of "the actual accomplishment of human personal life," someone who in His Person functions as the bridge between the theology of the Incarnation and that of the Cross.[9] A seminal essay published in the authoritative five volume *Commentary on the Documents of Vatican II* (1969), edited by the German lay theologian Herbert Vorgrimler (1929–2014) from Münster, wherein we find a Christ centred approach based on the philosophical recognition of the human movement towards an "other," namely, our human "capacity for transcendence" found within an integral and holistic understanding of humanity. Whereby Ratzinger highlights "a theology of the Cross" as an indispensable feature of a Christian anthropology, one based on the awareness of the New Adam "whereby a theology of the Incarnation necessarily leads to a spirituality of the cross." A way of thinking found in conciliar humanism, and later appropriated by Pope John Paul II with his claim: "the cross is the cradle of the New Man."[10] Remarkable thought addressed by the pope in *Salvifici Doloris*, his Apostolic Letter "on the Christian Meaning of Human Suffering" (1984), wherein the mystery of *Redemption* is understood as being accomplished *through the Cross of suffering Christ* (para. 3). Approached by the pope as an expression of God's love through the person of Christ as the "human face of Incarnate Truth" to a broken world, the essence of what I call "Incarnational soteriology."

While "every ecumenical council occurs at a unique point in history, Vatican II took place in a world unlike that of any of its predecessors."[11] Held for the second time within the hallowed precincts of St. Peter's Basilica, Vatican City, it was a council without precedent, the largest such gathering in the history of the Church. One which brought together

8. Lafont, *God, Time, and Being*, vii–xi.
9. Ratzinger, "Dignity of the Human Person," 115–63.
10. Kobler, *Vatican II and Phenomenology*, 172.
11. Kelly, *Ecumenical Councils*, 179.

over two thousand and three hundred Roman Catholic bishops and religious leaders coming from one hundred and sixteen countries "around the world," assembled in the reconstructed *Aula Santa Concilii*. Not to mention the thousands of theological "experts" advising these Council Fathers, as well as the unprecedented appointment of official Catholic laypersons as *auditors* as witnesses to Council proceedings. Initially these were laymen, however in response to an inspiring address to Council on October 22, 1963 when Cardinal Léon-Joseph Suenens, the recently appointed Archbishop of Mechelen-Brussels (1961–79), a member of the Council's Central Commission and a leading voice advocating reform in the Church, called for an increase in the number of lay auditors to include women who "make up half of humanity." Advice well received by Pope Paul when he named a total of twenty-three women, including ten from religious orders, as official observers; such as notable laywomen already recognized proponents of the lay apostolate, like Marie-Louise Monnet from France, the Italian Constatina Baldinuci who was a close friend of Pope Paul and the Australian Rosemary Goldie, another already known to him, who was appointed undersecretary of the Pontifical Council for the Laity in 1966. The presence of these laywomen as observers,[12] the so-called "Mothers of the Council," were also active contributors in the preparation of the Council's seminal documents, *Apostolicam Actuositatem*, the Decree on the laity, promulgated on November 18, 1965 and *Gaudium et Spes* on December 7, 1965, which incorporated earlier thought on the laity found in Schema XIII, which marked an instance of the Church "opening its windows." The recognized presence of these lay observers was indicative of what Michael Novak, the American Catholic journalist and a graduate in sacred theology from Rome's Gregorian University, calls "the Age of the Laity" in the Catholic Church.[13]

Along with these official Catholic witnesses were representatives from other Christian communities as well as from the world religious traditions. In addition to these, there were extraordinary numbers of media representatives from around the world to report daily on Council proceedings. Given the numbers of persons involved, the Second Vatican Council was a truly extraordinary "ecumenical" gathering, which required accompanying enormous levels of organizational, staffing, and logistical demands, all of which ensured this ecumenical assembly

12. Well documented by Henold, *Laywoman Project*.
13. Novak, "Achievement of Jacques Maritain."

was a unique global, multilingual, and multicultural ecclesial moment in world history, one equally seminal and consequential. Convened in surprising circumstances in a changing world, it was the right moment midway through the twentieth century for an extended moment of thoughtful reflection, directed by "right persons," to consider the fundamental issue which confronted the Universal Church, the challenge to understand human existence. As outlined in *Gaudium et Spes*: "faced with today's evolving world, an increasing number are asking the really basic questions or feeling them with a new urgency: What is man and woman? What is the meaning of suffering, evil and death, which persist even in the midst of such progress?" (para. 10).

Unlike previous councils, there appeared no particular crisis which prompted the twenty first ecumenical council, such as the first five councils held in the Greek speaking world to address theological concerns understanding the nature of Jesus Christ, the Son of God, wherein we find the original use of the idea of "person." Or the nineteenth council held in the Italian city of Trento between 1545 and 1563, convened to define Catholic doctrine and revitalize the Church, known as the Catholic Counter-Reformation, in response to the doctrinal challenges occasioned by the Protestant Reformation during the sixteenth century, initiated in part by the German theologian Martin Luther's (1483–1546) publication of his *Ninety-five Theses* (1517) in Wittenberg.

This unprecedented ecumenical council broke new ground in confronting the twentieth-century forms of racism and atheism, found in its philosophical and pastoral orientation, taking "hints from the past." While approached as "champions of humanity," the popes of the twentieth century had often addressed the sociopolitical problems and philosophical errors associated with the modern world, now following its original human agenda inspired by Pope John XXIII, the Council broke new ground by directly speaking to "humanity" living in the "world of today," by addressing the concerns shared by all. Expressed in the words of *Gaudium et Spes*: "Believers and unbelievers are almost at one in considering that everything on earth is to be referred to humanity as its centre and culmination. But what is humanity?" (para. 12).

An awareness of concerns arising from our shared humanity, which informed the Council's unprecedented human agenda, which only emerged ten days after the Council began, amid growing dissatisfaction with the preparatory material organized for discussion by the Roman Curia, as the Council Fathers began to take ownership of proceedings.

Namely, when they delivered their own message "to the world": "We urgently turn our thoughts to the problems by which human beings are afflicted today. As we undertake our work, we would emphasize what concerns the dignity of the human person, whatever contributes to a genuine community of peoples."[14] Words which in the opinion of John O'Malley, proved "an adumbration of the Council's future direction." A way of thinking which eventually informed "Schema XIII—*The Pastoral Constitution on the Human Condition in Today's World.*" Understood by an "old French Thomist," the philosopher Jacques Maritain as "a document of great wisdom," "one impregnated with the spirit and the basic views of the Angelic Doctor."[15]

Building on previous papal social justice teaching which had evolved over the twentieth century, these basic issues which engage "the dignity of the human person," informed the Council's original twofold rejection of "atheism" and "racism." Specifically addressed in *Gaudium et Spes*, as the denial of the human capacity of think about God which directed twentieth-century atheism, in the opinion of the Council Fathers, had definite sociopolitical consequences pertaining to the denial of our shared humanity, found in the twentieth-century blight of "racism," which I characterize by the colloquial expression "dark matter." Moving into the twenty-first century, this phenomenon of human inequality perpetrated by human beings against other human beings of a different ethnic, racial orientation remains an adverse feature of our human "universe," one resistant to definition, which continues to exert a strong influence on the evolution of understanding our shared humanity and its sociopolitical structure. Recognized as a worldwide phenomenon during the twentieth century wherein separation of human beings according to their ethnicity or "race" emerged as a sociopolitical issue; used to describe the racial ideology and the horrific consequences directed towards European Jews, perpetrated during the Second World War (1939–45) and associated with the atheistic, political, and social ideology of Nazism; inspired by the Austrian born German politician Adolf Hitler (1889–1945) in his manifesto *Mein Kampf* (1925). On the American continent, this issue was especially associated with the treatment of black Americans which was addressed by John LaFarge Jr. (1880–1963), the American Jesuit sociocultural activist writing against racism and

---

14. O'Malley, *What Happened at Vatican II*, 99.
15. Maritain, *Peasant of Garrone*, 50.

anti-Semitism in his seminal *Interracial Justice: A Study of the Catholic Doctrine of Race Relations* (1937) and *The Race Question and the Negro* (1943), wherein he argues that racial division within the human community is contrary to natural law and revealed truth.

This twentieth-century way of thinking based on the denial of our shared humanity, discussed in the seminal *Interracial Justice*, subsequently engaged the attention of Pope Pius XI (1922-39) and informed his encyclical *Mit Brennender Sorge* 'With Burning Concern' (1937), and the papal denunciation of the racial policies of Nazism. A somewhat neglected figure in contemporary Church history, the former Milanese academic and seminary professor Ambrogio Achille Ratti (1857-1939), holding canonical doctorates in theology, philosophy, and canon law from the Pontifical Gregorian University (1551) was well equipped to implement the Leonine program of philosophical and social renewal, writing thirty-four encyclicals. Among these were *Studiorum ducem* (1923), written on the occasion of the sixth centenary of the canonization of St. Thomas Aquinas in 1323 by Pope John XXII (1316-34), one which also identified the *Angelicum* as the preeminent institution for the teaching of Thomism, along with *Quadragesimo Anno* (1931), his social justice encyclical, written to mark the fortieth anniversary of the groundbreaking *Rerum Novarum* (1891). Towards the unexpected end of his pontificate, Pope Pius XI sought the American Jesuit's assistance in preparing an encyclical on "racialism," which the pope considered one of the "most burning" issues of the time. Their subsequent interaction has been characterized as "the stuff of spy novels" by Garry Wills, the American author and specialist on Catholic Church history, as the American priest makes an unscheduled visit to Rome while travelling Europe during the Nazi persecutions, to prepare a draft document over the summer of 1938. Subsequently given to the pope, whose regrettable death on February 6, 1939 prevented the publication of the encyclical, supposedly titled *Humani Generis Unitas*, "The Unity of the Human Race." (1939), thereafter relegated to "the silence of the [Vatican] archives." Circumstances which the former full-time librarian at the Ambrosian Library in Milan, between 1888 till 1911, might appreciate.

However, the appearance of several articles in the *National Catholic Reporter* (1964), an independent news source located in Kansas City Missouri, between December 1972 and January 1973 entitled "unpublished encyclical of Pius XI attacking anti-Semitism" drew the attention of two Belgian researchers, Father Georges Passelecq, a Benedictine monk from the Abbey of Maredsous (1872) in the French speaking municipality of Anhée, Wallonia, and the Jewish historian and sociologist Bernard Suchecky, author of "Jewish Resistance to Annihilation, 1939–40," who together then produced the well documented *The Hidden Encyclical of Pius XI* (1997).[16] Building on twentieth-century papal teachings wherein we find the philosophical means to address racism and racial prejudice, approached as a consequence of living in a Godless ethos, generated by the denial of the human capacity to think about God, were taken up through the Council's original use of the concept of the "human person," discussed in *Dignitatis Humanae* and *Gaudium et Spes* (1965). Previously used in the Council's unprecedented document, *Nostra Aetate* Declaration "on the Church's relation to non-Christian religions," promulgated on October 28, 1965 by Pope Paul VI, and especially directed to "the descendants of Abraham" (para. 4).

Approached as a "synthesis of fidelity and dynamism," conciliar humanism emerged during and in response to a remarkable period in human history, described by the French philosopher Jacques Maritain as "an epoch when all in man's heart seems grown cold, when the absence of the prophetic spirit adds singularly to the misery of the world,"[17] writing in his Foreword to *Walls are Crumbling* (1953), circumstances which conditioned the failure to recognize the inherent human "capacity for transcendence." Wherein his colleague, Monsignor John M. Oesterreicher (1904–93), another convert to Catholicism, offers a representative account of a unique phenomenon of the twentieth century, "the Christian thought of Jewish thinkers," who challenged these conditions and in so doing, appear as prominent figures on this philosophical landscape of Catholic thought, including members within the phenomenological movement, such as Edmund Husserl, Max Scheler and Edith Stein.

Characterized by Maritain as "an outstanding witness to the great movement he studies," Oesterreicher was Jewish born of Moravian descent, who became a Catholic theologian, following his conversion to Catholicism and subsequent ordination as a priest for the Archdiocese of Vienna in 1927. A prominent anti-Nazi activist during the 1930s, he fled Austria following the German invasion of France in 1940 and emigrated to America. Where in 1953 he founded the Institute of Judaeo-Christian Studies at Seton Hall University (1856), a Catholic

---

16. Passelecq and Suchecky, *Hidden Encyclical of Pius XI*, 1.
17. Maritain, Foreword to *Walls Are Crumbling*, ix.

university in South Orange, New Jersey, for which Pope John XXIII appointed him a Papal Chamberlain in 1961 in recognition of his advocacy promoting Jewish—Catholic reconciliation. An issue close to the heart of Pope John XXIII, who appointed Oesterreicher, along with other notable figures in interfaith relations, such as Bruno Hussar (1911–96), the Jewish born Egyptian Dominican priest, and Gregory Baum (1923–2017), the German born Canadian Augustinian priest and theologian, as well qualified *periti* to assist the German Jesuit Cardinal Augustin Bea (1881–1968), the first president appointed by Pope John XXIII to the Secretariat for Promoting Christian Unity (1960–68) during the Council. Especially in the preparation of *Nostra Aetate*, the Council's unprecedented Declaration "on the church's relation to non-Christian religions," promulgated on October 28, 1965.

The shortest of the Council's sixteen documents, which literally speaks "in our time" for the necessity of a new way of thinking, one less adversarial: namely, as Catholic "pastoral" approach to the monotheistic religious traditions of Judaism and Islam, as well as to Eastern religions, such as Buddhism and Hinduism. A monumental statement which emerged from within a moment of *sapiential* consciousness of our shared humanity during the Council, namely, the recognition of what we have in common as rational and social human beings, our shared humanity as "human persons."

29

A Work in Progress

As a new way of thinking, the tenets of conciliar humanism represent a "symphony of ideas," found in the Council's "belief in humanity," namely, its Christ centred integral philosophical understanding of the integrity of our shared humanity, directed by the perennial questions "what am I?" and "who am I?" As a "leading composer" later observed in *Fides et Ratio*: "the Second Vatican Council offers a rich and fruitful teaching concerning philosophy. One chapter of the Constitution *Gaudium et Spes* amounts to a virtual compendium of the biblical anthropology from which philosophy too can draw inspiration" (para. 60).

Approached as an original phenomenon of twentieth-century Catholic thought, conciliar humanism represents a remarkable convergence of various original ideas ingeniously brought together. By means of a return to traditional sources of philosophical thought about being human, "taking hints from the past" from ancient, patristic, and medieval sources, creatively drawn together within an assemblage of diverse ideas from various sources of contemporary European philosophy. An original network of ideas characterized by Joseph Ratzinger as a "mosaic of basic statements; rather than a philosophical doctrine of man on the lines of the neo-scholastic tradition."[1] The consequence of a thoughtful process expressed by the words "the human face of Incarnate truth," captured by religious art of the twentieth century, "In His image." Viewed from a distance this picture represents the human face and shoulder of the crucified Christ; however, on closer scrutiny, this is found to

---

1. Ratzinger, "Dignity of the Human Person," 119.

be the product of an ingenious arrangement of different human faces variously and indiscriminately placed together, individual components which together constitute this remarkable religious art. Commenting on *Gaudium et Spes*, Ratzinger draws attention to the "dynamic" doctrine of being human which informs the "structure of the entire schema," approached as "a mosaic of basic statements."

A pattern of philosophical and pastorally orientated thought which not only characterized the thinking of the two popes directly involved with the Council, John XXIII and Paul VI, but also the thought of some of the Council's leading lights, Cardinal Frings and his *peritus* Professor Joseph Ratzinger, also Cardinal Suenens as well as the Archbishop Karol Wojtyła, who drew ideas from current trends of European philosophy found in existentialism, humanism, phenomenology, and personalism, along with thought drawn from variants of contemporary Thomism. All drawn together in a remarkable "synthesis of fidelity and dynamism" which occurred during one of the most consequential and *sapiential* moments in the history of the Catholic Church.

Employing Pope Benedict's understanding of a "synthesis," this composition was a Christ centred philosophical integral way of thinking about humanity which emerged during the Council, one which initiated "a break with the past," to use the American Catholic commentator Michael Novak's original thought, an ambiguous expression filled with meaning. As observed by Pope Benedict XVI: "With the Second Vatican Council broad new thinking was required. Its content was certainly only roughly traced in the conciliar texts but determined its essential direction." Words addressed by someone who as Professor Joseph Ratzinger influenced the direction of conciliar thought working collaboratively as *peritus* to the German Cardinal Josef Frings (1887–1978), Archbishop of Cologne, a significant figure during Council proceedings, which informed the so-called "Frings-Ratzinger" connection. Spoken by the recently elected Pope Benedict XVI to his former colleagues in the Roman Curia during his Christmas Address on December 22, 2005. As Cardinal Prefect of the Congregation for the Doctrine of the Faith (1981–2005), and one of the youngest *periti* appointed to assist during the Council, Ratzinger was well positioned not only to identify the novelty which characterized conciliar thought, especially found in its "belief in humanity," namely, its original understanding of our shared humanity, but was also to recognize its equally tentative yet determinative character of its documented thought in *Gaudium et Spes* and *Dignitatis Humanae* as being "a work in progress."

While the Council took place in a "changing world which changed the Church" to paraphrase the thought of Joseph Kelly,[2] initiating changes in how Catholics worship and pray, it also changed the way we think philosophically and theologically.

The year 1961 was very significant in the life of Most Rev. Doctor Thomas William Muldoon (1917–86), a prominent Australian Catholic theologian, variously described as "colourful or intimidating," with the nickname "bull." Consecrated an auxiliary bishop for the Archdiocese of Sydney in Rome on May 8 of the previous year by Pope John XXIII with the Venerable American Archbishop Fulton Sheen (1895–1979), a recipient of the *Cardinal Mercier Prize for International Philosophy* (1923) as a co-consecrator. This former professor of dogma was appointed the first Dean of the recently established Pontifical Faculty of Theology (1954) on the site of Saint Patrick's College, the local Archdiocesan seminary in Manly, NSW Australia, where I subsequently taught. After many years of lecturing in theology Muldoon finally published his *opus magnum*, a five-volume manual in the tradition of scholastic theology, *Theologiae Dogmaticae Praelectiones* (1958–61).

Typical for the time, it was written in ecclesiastical Latin and offered a comprehensive survey of theology annotated with quotations drawn from disparate theological sources, characterized as "anti-historical in character."[3] Known for his "combative style" and "patriarchal orthodoxy," Bishop Muldoon was a robust participant during Council proceedings, favouring the so-called "conservative group" in debates. However, by the end of the Council on December 8, 1965 his literary efforts were of little consequence: "just as Vatican II changed the teaching language at St. Patrick's to English, so his books became instantly redundant."[4] Such was the impact of the changes effected by the Council and its requisite *broad new thinking*; even in the antipodes, things would change.

As already observed, humans are questioning and thinking beings who operate within a broad tradition of thought; as thinking Catholics, this is to be approached retrospectively in the opinion of Alasdair Macintyre: "to be outside all traditions is to be a strange to enquiry; it is to be in a state of intellectual and moral destitution."[5] Within the circumstances of ecumenical conciliar thought, understood as a collective

2. Kelly, *Ecumenical Councils*, 179.
3. Walsh, *Yesterday's Seminary*, 266.
4. Scanlon, "Bishop Thomas William Muldoon," 17.
5. MacIntyre, *God, Philosophy, Universities*, 165.

thoughtful enterprise within an extended "meeting of minds," conciliar humanism may be characterized as consequential, found in a change of mindset among the Council Fathers from which emerged their final documents, *Dignitatis Humanae* and *Gaudium et Spes* wherein we find the source of such thinking. Philosophical thought in response to the perennial questions asked about our humanity; the existential question "what am I" directed to understanding being human, as thoughtful, and naturally social, inclined to other human beings, and the personal question "who am I" asked by human beings as persons. Within this human context of Conciliar thought, following the thought of Scheler, human persons are defined by their capacity for transcendence, found in the activity of love understood as a personal movement, both towards other persons or being the recipient of love from other persons, whereby personal love is relational, freely drawn out of oneself towards another person, either finite or Divine.

As such, the ideas of conciliar humanism emerged as the consequence of a remarkable moment of philosophical reflection about our shared humanity in response to the critical circumstances of the time. Namely, in response to the contemporary twofold denial of our natural capacity to understand and think about the nature of God through the use of reason found in natural theology, discussed during Vatican I, and the recognition of our human capacity for transcendence, found in the "human person," discussed during Vatican II, through the recognition of its use by our individual "conscience," approached as an act of the human person in the exercise of free choice, and the decision to freely associate with other human beings. Critical issues which now directed the attention of the Council Fathers, especially the Polish philosopher from Kraków, Karol Wojtyła, ably assisted by the thought of notable laypersons actively involved on the sidelines of the Council, notably Catholic philosophers like Maritain, Guitton, and Swieżawski. Wherein we find their thoughtful presence as indicative of the Conciliar process of reengagement with "the world of today."

This personal network of thoughtful connections among Catholic European philosophers which informed the genesis of conciliar humanism was best exemplified in the unprecedented moment when Pope Paul VI greeted his personal friends, the French philosophers Jacques Maritain, author of the seminal *Integral Humanism* (1936), and Jean Guillot, "a friend of popes and presidents," during the official closing ceremony of the Council on December 8, 1965. The latter was one of two laymen, along with the Italian Vittorino Veronese (1910–86), someone closely associated with UNESCO (1952–61), to be invited by Pope Paul to "intervene," to formally address the plenary session of the Council held on December 3, 1963, speaking the official language Latin, assembled for the solemn commemoration of the Council of Trent (1545–63).

During the final ceremony to mark the official closure of Council proceedings on December 8, 1965, Pope Paul VI, to the surprise of those present, invited these Catholic laymen, acknowledged Catholic philosophers in their own right to join him on the dais following the reading of the Council' message on behalf of the pope "To Men of Thought and Science," another instance of "the human face of Incarnate truth." Inspired by the thought of Saint Augustine, Bishop of Hippo Regius and an intellectual powerhouse of the first millennium, the pope exhorted those present, with words worth repeating: "Let us seek with the desire to find and find with the desire to seek still more." Among the thousands assembled in the Square to witness this extraordinary moment were three Polish philosophers from the University of Lublin's "School of Thomist Philosophy," Stefan Swieżawski, his colleague George Kalinowski, and Archbishop Karol Wojtyła, the so-called "Lublin connection."

Understood as a "synthesis of fidelity and dynamism" employing a phrase of Pope Benedict, conciliar humanism represents a contemporary Catholic understanding of our shared human existence which emerged within the perennial relationship between faith and reason, a constitutive feature of Catholic thought, now understood as the relationship between "the Church and her faith" and "man and the contemporary world." This thoughtful engagement informs the genesis of conciliar humanism, which is received with gratitude employing a "right hermeneutic," through the promotion of a spirit of "renewal" and "openness to the world." A helpful approach towards understanding the meaning of what Pope Benedict XVI labelled as "content roughly traced in the conciliar texts." Wherein the Pope opens the door for some detective work in the identification of the broad philosophical resources available to the Council Fathers in following their human agenda to better understand the "perilous frailty of human nature."

Operating within the distinctive relationship between the presence of faith "and" the use of reason, "*Openness*" remains a distinctive mark of the Christian faith, found in its "catholicity," as observed by Pope John Paul II: "*The basis and source of this openness lie in the fact that the philosophy of St. Thomas is a philosophy of being, that is, of the 'act of existing' (actus essendi) whose transcendental value paves the most direct way to rise to the knowledge of subsisting Being and pure Act, namely to God.*"[6] Expressive of papal confidence in the use of philosophy, these words outline the tenets of "Pontifical Thomism" of the twentieth century which characterizes Pope John Paul II's original appropriation of philosophical ideas taken from Aquinas, a way of thinking summarily expressed by his successor Pope Francis as "Catholic and open." Wherein we find the foundations of twentieth-century Catholic philosophy well expressed in these aspirational words which encapsulate the seminal thought of its author.

Ladislas Orsy, an octogenarian who witnessed the Council as a theological expert, *peritus* appointed to the English Jesuit Francis Markall (1905–92), Archbishop of Salisbury (1956–76), now Harare, Zimbabwe, engaged the innovative thought of someone else who could well remember the Council, one of its "most insightful commentators" the French Benedictine theologian Ghislain Lafont (1928–2021) who explores anew the meaning of this foundational concept of "human person" within Conciliar thought now incorporated in his original creedal formula: "We believe in God, we believe in human persons. That is, we believe in both with one act of divine faith." While this concept is ubiquitous in contemporary Catholic discourse, synonymous with Conciliar thought, there is more to be found in this interpretative clue, namely its philosophical connection found in Scheler's thought, with two other determinative ideas found in conciliar humanism, namely the "community of persons" and "human solidarity," until now, connections little discussed. Furthermore, found within Orsy's remarkably insightful article is the recognition that this concept provides the thoughtful connection between the Council's final documents, *Dignitatis Humanae* and *Gaudium et Spes*. To date these have not been read together, wherein we move "from the conceptual realm of philosophical reflections into the luminous world of faith," a movement which directs conciliar humanism.

While alluding to Pope John's social encyclicals *Mater et Magistra* (1961) and *Pacem in Terris* (1963) along with Pope Paul's *Ecclesiam Suam* (1964), perhaps the archbishop from Kraków might have been thinking of Pope John's earlier encyclical *Paenitentiam Agere*. Published on July 1, 1962, only months before the official opening of the Council, while addressing the need for the practice of penance, the pope took

---

6. John Paul II, *Whole Truth about Man*, 218–19.

the opportunity to recall his Apostolic Constitution *Humanae Salutis* which solemnly convoked the Council, "to reaffirm God's rights over mankind, whom Christ's blood has redeemed, and to reaffirm the duties of the redeemed mankind towards its God and Saviour" (para. 4). Operating within the context of conciliar humanism, the legitimate espousal of human rights we share presupposes an awareness of our shared dignity as "human persons," expressed in the Council's recognition of personal participatory reciprocity within a "community of persons," and our "human solidarity" in the words of *Gaudium et Spes*: "all human beings are equal in status and dignity, they all have the right to be free and self-actualise" (para. 7). Set against the background of twentieth-century thought, a synthetic way of thinking emerged during the Council, incorporating ideas drawn from papal social teaching, wherein the concept of "human person" was first used, along with ideas drawn from twentieth-century Thomism, Christian humanism and personalism, in response to the perennial questions asked by every human being, regardless of religious affiliations, what am I? And who am I?

While Karol Wojtyła was an unknown person on the world stage, though highly respected within Polish circles as an energetic and pastorally oriented auxiliary bishop and an accomplished philosopher, over the three years of Council proceedings and amid intense conciliar deliberations, he would emerge on the final day well recognized as one of the Council's leading voices. Having acquired an impressive international reputation, it came as little surprise when Pope Paul who obviously heard his voice, announced Wojtyła's promotion to the College of Cardinals on June 26, 1967. The rest they say is history. However, within the context of understanding the genesis of conciliar humanism, Wojtyła's pre-papal thought which he developed while teaching at Kraków and Lublin, stands centre stage with his promotion of the "human person."

Having learned Thomism while a seminarian for the diocesan priesthood at Kraków and later as postgraduate student priest at Rome's *Angelicum*, the young philosopher from the University of Lublin's "School of Thomist Philosophy" certainly engaged "hints from the past" in his original appropriation of the thought of St. Thomas Aquinas, the foundations of medieval scholastic humanism. However, as observed by his acclaimed biographer George Weigel in *Witness to Hope* (1999), "foundations were meant to be built upon."[7] A way of thinking with

---

7. Weigel, *Witness to Hope*, 87.

robust and multidirectional foundations afforded in "the golden wisdom of St. Thomas Aquinas," "teacher of humanity": a way of thinking which inspired Wojtyła's conviction that the human mind could grasp the fundamental truth of "being, what exists" through a disciplined reflection on the world as it is. As he revealed on November 17, 1979, soon after his papal election, when he returned to his *alma mater*, the Pontifical University of Saint Thomas Aquinas (1577), where he had been a graduate student from 1946–48, to participate in a celebration to mark the hundredth anniversary of Pope Leo XIII's ground-breaking encyclical *Aeterni Patris* "on the restoration of Christian philosophy," (1879) doing philosophy lived within our Catholic identify along with its characteristic *openness*. Established in 1885, as a Catholic institute for teaching and research, the *Angelicum* was a means, like Leuven's Higher Institute of Philosophy, to implement this encyclical; situated in the historic centre of Rome, Italy, it represents a remarkable coincidence between "building and location."

Both Polish philosophers were present at the closing ceremony of the Council held on December 8, 1965, the Solemnity of the Immaculate Conception and the anniversary of the opening of the First Vatican Council (1869), in St. Peter's Square to hear the words of Pope Paul VI. Addressed on behalf of the Council Fathers, he greeted one of these philosophers, Jacques Maritain, one of the major proponents of twentieth-century Thomism, his personal friend and thoughtful collaborator, "the man who loved wisdom," to receive the pope's message "to men of thought and science," "Let us seek with the desire to find and find with the desire to seek still more." Words which recall the scriptural spirit and sapiential thought which opens Saint Augustine's autobiographical masterpiece: "'And they shall praise the Lord that seek him,' for they that seek him find him, and finding him they shall praise him." A source of inspiration for Catholic thinkers with diverse philosophical backgrounds who shared a personal commitment to the "search for truth" in the "service of humanity": "a process of philosophical enquiry which was enriched by engaging the data of faith" to quote the words of *Fides et Ratio*, para. 76.

A way of thinking especially found in the proponents of phenomenological realism, such as the German Catholic philosophers Max Scheler and Edith Stein, associates of the Göttingen school of philosophy, wherein a study of consciousness presupposes both a subject and an object within a unified human experience: "Every act of consciousness has a reference to something that is not itself or that is not its own activity."

Herein, following Scheler's original philosophical anthropology, we find his distinctive understanding of the human person's openness to reality in all its forms, especially towards the reality of other persons, and in Scheler's words "openness to the sphere of the Absolute," found in his original recognition of the human "capacity for transcendence," namely, that "something else" which Wojtyla found in being human. In these circumstances of contemporary phenomenology, understanding the nature of the human person is to be found in his or her personal action, through our activity of thought, our use of intelligence and the exercise of freedom, and especially through our personal engagement with other persons. Taking up this thought, Karol Wojtyła argues that it is the free moral act, understood as the *actus humanus*, rather than the rational animal's self-consciousness, wherein we reveal ourselves as human persons in our action,[8] wherein Wojtyła turns to the influence of contemporary French philosophy.

Writing his 1893 doctoral dissertation entitled *Action: An Essay on the Critique of Life and a Science of Practice*. The French Christian philosopher Maurice Blondel (1861–1949) challenged the tenets of late nineteenth and early twentieth century "Life philosophy," *Lebensphilosophie* in German speaking countries, which promoted the meaning, value and purpose of life as a philosophical category. A way of thinking indirectly connected with the French philosopher and evolutionist Henri Bergson's (1859–1941) subjectivist philosophy of vitalism based on his understanding of an original impetus of life understood as *elan vital*, developed in his seminal *L'Évolution créatrice* (1907), written to counter the current scientific and mechanistic philosophies of the time. Set against this broad philosophical background, Blondel sought to establish a correct understanding between the legitimate use of philosophical reason and Christian belief through the methodology of what came to be associated with phenomenology, which leads him to the category of "action." An approach which later enabled Wojtyła to introduce his concept of the *acting person* (1979), title of his foundational book, or rather his original synthesis between *act* and *person* whereby he directed attention away from the human being as a rational animal, towards the whole human person who is defined by an act of transcendence found in the human person's exercise of "conscience," namely, the human capacity to move beyond the constraints of what is given in our ordinary experience.

8. Wojtyła, "Intentional Act," 269–80.

Written during the Council, Wojtyła's *The Acting Person: A Contribution to Phenomenological Anthropology* (1979) represents a unique synthesis of universal significance, especially found in basic ideas drawn from Scheler's phenomenological ethical personalism and his original understanding of the triadic structure between "human person," "community of persons," and Absolute Person, an unchallenged way of thinking which characterize his phenomenology of religious activity. When taken together with traditional Aristotelian-Thomist thought, and especially Aquinas' innovative understanding of *actus essendi* 'act of being,' this offers the background to understand Wojtyła's original discussion of major issues "concerning life, nature and the existence of man," wherein we find the ingredients for this original synthesis.

Soon after the publication of what would become his acclaimed biography of Pope John Paul II, *Witness to Hope* (1999), the prominent American Catholic writer George Weigel was invited to speak on this subject during his keynote address to the twenty third annual convention of the Fellowship of Catholic Scholars, held in Atlanta, Georgia between September 22–24, 2000, to address "the achievement," or more precisely "only *some* of the *many* achievements" of this extraordinary twentieth-century pope, expressed as *Witness to Truth* (2001). Established "in the wake of the Second Vatican Council which stirred the still and deep waters of theological opinion in the Church," this group of faith filled concerned American scholars from diverse backgrounds who were united in their commitment to the Catholic Church's teaching office met between May 7–8, 1977 in the city of St. Louis, Missouri. In response to "a sense of intellectual alienation" they experienced from both within the Church in America and coming from the broader academic world of universities and colleges at large. As then Father Donald Wuerl reported, himself having observed the proceedings of Vatican II while a student in Rome, who eventually gained a Doctorate in Sacred theology from the *Angelicum* in 1974, these scholars sought a disciplined academic witness to the Catholic faith expressed in the Church's teaching office: however, as he cautioned: "Witness does not exist in a vacuum. Neither can theological studies be carried on disconnected from the mainstream of Catholic teaching, theological investigation and thought."[9] Wuerl's thought could well describe the pope's philosophical legacy, found within his personal and intellectual commitment to the tradition of Catholic philosophy as a *witness to truth*.

---

9. Wuerl, "Fellowship of Catholic Scholars," 11.

30

Being without God?

As we move into the twenty-first century, the continued "popular polemic against theism" initiated by the thought of Feuerbach, which directs his atheistic and secular humanism, remains our critical opponent, namely, to account for human life without God? A persistent way of thinking about humanity of a definite philosophical orientation, humanism remains a feature of this contemporary thought, as found in *The Little Book of Humanism: Universal Lessons on Finding Purpose, Meaning and Joy* (2020). A compilation of stories, quotes, and meditations on how to live an ethical and fulfilling life, "grounded in reason and humanity," assembled by Alice Roberts, an English biological anthropologist and president of the charity Humanists UK and her colleague Andrew Copson, chief executive of Humanists UK. Typical of current postmodern "feel good" literature, while this way of thinking moves away from previous twentieth-century forms of "in your face' aggressive atheistic and secular humanism, it remains equally devoid of any religious orientation.

While the proponents of aggressive atheism and secular humanism, forms of thought which in a sense not only "defied" the Council but also defined its human agenda, might have been muted, the underlying polemic remains, the absence of God, discussed in a series of essays written by a group of philosophers and theologians at "the frontiers of faith and reason" published in *Philosophers and God* (2009). Notwithstanding the extraordinary though typical claim, "we are on the same page," made by the American Humanist Association, identified as "good without a god," in its provocative pamphlet, "Humanism Common Ground: Catholicism" (2021). Namely, these secular humanists attempt to find common ground with Catholic thought based on a superficial comparison with "ten principles of Catholic Social Teaching," which generated the Council's original Christ centred understanding of our shared humanity, found in conciliar humanism's three constitutive ideas, 'human person,' 'community of persons,' and 'human solidarity.' A way of thinking about our shared humanity living with God in the Person of Christ, whereby a comparison may be offered as implied by the Association. Based on its identification of "key principles of Humanism" characterized as "a progressive philosophy of life, that without supernaturalism, affirms our ability and responsibility to lead ethical lives of personal fulfilment that aspire to the greater good of humanity." Writing this document, the authors observe that Catholicism and humanism share a common ground focused on humanity, through the recognition of the "inherent dignity of all people, rights and responsibilities" in the pursuit of the common good, herein lies the nexus of comparison.

While offering a selective assessment of current Catholic literature on social justice issues, the authors fail to acknowledge the original source of such Catholic activity found in the recognition of God, found in a real person, in the Person of Jesus Christ, the Son of God, as the ultimate source of our human dignity and our subsequent human rights. The inherent ambiguity found in this publication is symptomatic of a twenty-first-century malaise, which moves beyond aggressive atheism toward a benign, broad based popularist appeal found in a form of secular humanism approached as a "feel good" intellectual and ethical way of thinking, through the use of "sweeping statements" rather than the pursuit of organized and researched critical thought, which generated conciliar humanism. This contemporary approach informs an ever-widening global disparity between what is claimed in official systems and what is actually experienced in so-called reality, "on the ground" so to speak. A challenging situation addressed by Ana Maria Vega Gutiérrez, a Spanish State Ecclesiastical lawyer and consultant to the United Nations headquarters in Geneva, in her *Building a New Humanism for a Globalised World: The Contribution of Religion* (2021). One might ask, compared to what, where is the novelty?

Pope Benedict XVI offers an answer in a personal interview on May 6, 2020 with his biographer Peter Seewald, wherein he discussed modern society's "anti-Christian creed," returning to thought which first generated conciliar humanism. Set in circumstances not too dissimilar to those which not only defied the Council, namely the prevalent forms of atheistic and secular humanism antagonistic to Catholic thought, but also equally defined the circumstances which conciliar thought sought to address, found in conciliar humanism. Now sixty years later Pope Benedict XVI claimed the "real threat to the Church" originated in "the worldwide dictatorship of seemingly humanistic ideologies." Especially found in the current "dictatorship of relativism" wherein exclusive attention is given to the isolated human "'I' and its whims [which] serve as the ultimate measure." An expression he first used in his homily on April 2, 2005, when as Cardinal Joseph Ratzinger he claimed "Jesus Christ is the measure of true humanism," during the Mass in St. Peter's Basilica "for the election of the Roman Pontiff" which he presided over as Dean of the College of Cardinals. Two weeks later he would be elected pope on April 19.

Moving into his pontificate Pope Benedict XVI took up this Christ centred way of thinking about our humanity in his ongoing quest, informed by the "signs of the times," to respond to "the eruption of violence around the world," such as "global terrorism," all of which requires in his opinion, "a new humanism," found in "the Son of God, true man. He is the measure of true humanism." A way of thinking initially found in Pope Paul VI's social encyclical *Populorum Progressio* "on the development of peoples" (1967), written two years after he closed the Council with the challenge to take up its "new humanism," wherein the goal of human improvement, whether social, economic, cultural, or spiritual, is ultimately found in "a full-bodied humanism." Namely, in conciliar humanism, a Christ centred integral philosophical understanding of our shared humanity, wherein "man is not the ultimate measure of man. Man becomes truly man only by passing beyond himself" (para. 42) Years later Pope Francis used the fifth anniversary of this encyclical, to promote what he calls a "civilization of love" built on the foundations of "fraternal humanism" which he writes in his introduction to the Curial letter from the Congregation for Catholic Education on April 16, 2017. Ideas he previously developed within the context of promoting the idea of "an integral ecology," wherein he critiques rampant consumerism and irresponsible environmental degradation found in global warming, all of which calls for a unified global and human response, found in his second encyclical *Laudato Si* "On the Care of Our Common Home," published on May 24, 2015, understood as the foundational document for a new humanism.

Celebrating the fiftieth anniversary of Pope John XXIII's formal convocation of the Council with his apostolic constitution *Humanae Salutis*, as already mentioned a much neglected document, which sets the orientation for conciliar humanism, the 2012 special Spring-Summer issue of *Communio* drew attention to the "challenge of Vatican II: Keeping the World Awake to God," wherein we find the legacy of conciliar humanism as a thoughtful answer for those living with God in a postmodern world, found in its original network of three interconnected ideas. Namely, the anthropological question, addressed by the "human person," the related sociological question of how we live together, found in a "community of persons" and finally, the theological question concerning our human access to the presence of God, found in "human solidarity," the shared recognition of the human person's "capacity for transcendence" in our communal "openness to God" found in the Person of Christ.

Herein we find the overarching issue, what is human? From a shaky start, with poor reviews of its pilot episode (2008), the announcement that the fifth series *Being Human*, the British supernatural television show, would be its last with the final episode to be broadcast on March 10, 2013, prompted a massive online petition: but to no avail. One of the most popular shows on the BBC's iPlayer, this series offered "a curious genre mash-up drama," wherein various types of supernatural beings, such as a ghost, werewolf, and vampire, exist alongside human beings rather than apart. It was acclaimed by the journalist David Belcher as "the supernatural drama that's super in its depiction of human nature,"[1] perhaps reflecting the expectations of twenty-first-century transhumanism? Symptomatic of an age characterized *when anything goes*, approached as a remarkable form of original thought, conciliar humanism offers a necessary corrective as a form of stability in thinking about being human set amid the constant "shifting tides and currents" which constitute postmodern thought, more broadly characterized as "the world we live in is changing. Rapidly. For the worse."[2] Amid these circumstances, how are we to make sense of these words, what does it mean to be human? A question addressed and answered in conciliar humanism in dialogue with several proponents of contemporary ways of thinking, such as "transhumanism"

---

1. Belcher, "When Comedy Gets Better with Age."
2. Williams, *When Anything Goes*, xiv.

and the World Transformation movement, which may be characterized as beyond humanism, but again, being without God.

What is human? An open question to which everyone seems to have an answer. Strictly speaking being "human" is a scientific term, relating to "humanity as a species." Roughly three hundred thousand years ago, human beings emerged as a member of the biological species of mammals known as *Homo sapiens*, referring to the idea of "clever apes," whereby human beings eventually replaced rival Neanderthals, Denisovans, and other species of the genus *homo*, to emerge as a naturally thinking animal within the biological process of evolution. Characterized by erect posture and bipedalism, with larger and more complex brain functioning, with the ability to communicate through language, with the skill to use tools and implements, and the social awareness to form groups of human beings or societies.

Furthermore, these human beings were considered essentially different from other forms of animate life by their biological, intellectual, linguistic, and social features, discussed by the Scottish physician and writer Gavin Francis in *Adventures in Human Being: A Grand Tour from Cranium to the Calcaneum* (2015). Drawing from his professional experience as a medical practitioner, he assumes the approach of a geographer mapping out the evolutionary path of our biological animate being, perhaps unfamiliar territory for many of us. Moving from a popular party board game called *Cranium* (1998) "for your whole brain" to a discussion of the *calcaneus* or heel bone, the biggest of the seven tarsal bones in the human foot. However, during the late nineteenth and twentieth centuries this status as being qualitatively different from other species was challenged by the scientific mindset of modern rational thought, practiced by the "masters of suspicion," a catchy expression coined by Paul Ricoeur the French existential philosopher in *Freud and Philosophy: An Essay on Interpretation* (1970), for Karl Marx, the founder of revolutionary communism, Friedrich Nietzsche, the controversial nineteenth-century German philosopher, cultural critic, the proponent of the "death of God" and Christianity's trenchant protagonist, and Sigmund Freud, the Viennese founder of psychoanalysis, who called into question the distinctive character of human nature as being essentially different. A way of thinking about humanity which has re-emerged during the twenty-first century, with ongoing developments in biotechnology and nanotechnology, which have produced "new forms of hybridity beyond our imagining" arising from the "human-machine interaction." Wherein we find the ongoing significance of transhumanism.

Addressing this fundamental philosophical question about being human, to which everyone seems to have an answer; objectively speaking, human beings are "nothing of consequence." Approached as biological beings we are simply "clumps of atoms" or "particles of dust" living in a universe "with more galaxies than people," wherein we are "present for an instant in eternity." Challenging thought from the English physicist Brian Cox as he conducts an internal dialogue with himself to introduce his acclaimed *Human Universe* (2014), recognized by the *Sunday Times* as a "best seller," obviously his self-described "love letter to humanity" struck a chord with someone! Underlying the popularity of his book was the implicit awareness found in the enigmatic confrontation between the persistent scientific explanation of being human as "clumps of atoms" with the physicist's cautionary "and yet," wherein we find the recognition there might be "something more" to being human other than our biological genetic makeup, characterized more of the same.

Given the claim "much has been written over the millennia about human beings and human nature" Christian Smith, the American sociologist from the University of Notre Dame (1842) explored this issue of "something more" which he finds in the human being as a "person" by *rethinking* humanity in a postmodern world, the subject of his book *What Is a Person? Rethinking Humanity, Social Life, and the Moral Good from the Person Up* (2010), an all-inclusive and exhaustive title for this literary narrative about humanity. Wherein he concludes, that of the many mysteries found in the universe, "we humans are perhaps the most mysterious of all to ourselves."[3] Living in the postmodern world, it seems little has changed since the time of the enigmatic Socrates. The so-called "founder of Western philosophy," when he ingeniously used the Ancient Greek aphorism "know thyself," inscribed on the portal of the Temple of Apollo at Delphi, to direct attention to our consciousness, namely understanding ourselves and our human search for meaning and purpose using an interrogative "question and answer" approach. An infuriating figure self-characterized as a "gadfly" or a thoughtful nuisance, Socrates established a critical way of thinking about ourselves and how we live and act with each other which persists till this day. Quintessentially philosophical, during the twentieth century these questions about

---

3. Smith, *What Is a Person?*, 8.

humanity, "what am I" and "who am I" were addressed by European Catholic philosophers operating with ideas, such as "human person," "act of being," "conscience," "participation," and "solidarity." Taken from several contemporary movements of thought, such as living Thomism, existential Christian humanism and two variants of Christian personalism, German and French, all of which were employed to great advantage during the last ecumenical council in thinking about being human and our shared humanity, which generated conciliar humanism, characterizing this council as the most philosophical of ecumenical councils.

Unpacking the thought behind the nature of being human, like the foundational figures in the emerging discipline of sociology who were first trained as philosophers, such as Scheler, Émile Durkheim (1858–1917) or Max Weber (1864–1920), Christian Smith employs the critical methodology of philosophy to analyze and interpret the processes underlying the various forms of social action, in what might be called "philosophical sociology," as found in Scheler's thoughtful alignment with his original understanding of philosophical anthropology. Likewise, Smith's so-called "ontological turn" enables movement beyond the limits of his chosen discipline as a sociologist to address the foundational issues of being human through a study of personhood within its human context, approached from the perspective of philosophy, found in the human person. In so doing, Smith offers a valuable contribution "given a century of philosophical underdevelopment in the discipline," whereby he attempts to "rethink" the purposes and meaning of ourselves as human beings, "what we are, our constitution and condition."[4] An underdevelopment critically observed by the last popes of the twentieth century, John Paul II and Benedict XVI, by means of which in their own particular manner, as a Catholic philosopher and a philosophically trained systematic theologian, sought to redress this situation thinking within the tradition of Catholic philosophy.

Approached chronologically, the issue of being human has been approached from three perspectives, religious, philosophical, and scientific. Beginning with the biblical claim: "God created man in his own image, in the image of God he created him, male and female he created them." Found in the book of Genesis 1:27 this passage represents the first-time humans appear in the Bible, wherein they are envisaged as being created "in the image of God," as the concluding part of an account of creation

---

4. Smith, *What Is a Person?*, 1.

that God continually calls "very good," which carries the implication that being human is something inherently valuable and worthwhile from the perspective of God. Theologically approached, this God centred religiously inspired thought initiated the idea of *imago Dei* which has provided the linchpin for a Catholic understanding of human nature, of being human, a way of thinking characterized as "pre-modern" used by millennial figures such as Augustine and Aquinas.

Moving into the twentieth century this idea was explored and developed in the Council's final document *Gaudium et Spes* wherein we find the claim that the human being alone is "able to know and love his creator" (para. 12). Now approached within a distinctive social orientation envisaged within the context of the Christian understanding of the Triune God as Being personal. Furthermore, as the Pastoral Constitution continues, as a created being, naturally rational and social according to Aristotle, humans are the "only creature on earth that God has willed for its own sake" (para. 20). Herein we find the inherent value of human nature.

An understanding which began to be challenged during the eighteenth-century within the intellectual ferment known as Enlightenment. Which initiated a way of thinking which marks a change of mindset, away from a medieval God centred religious and metaphysical understanding of humanity, wherein we find the source of the dignity being human, towards an understanding which may be characterized as ethical. One informed by the modern appreciation of the heightened resourcefulness found in the human use of reason liberated from the "shackles of religious dogma and tradition," well expressed in the words of Immanuel Kant "*Dare to be wise!* Have courage to use your own reasoning."[5] In so doing, this German philosopher laid the foundations which led to the tentative demise of the former understanding in favour of an ethical orientation, based on the human use of critical reasoning, as a rational and conscious being. One characterized by the human "capacity for moral choice" in the exercise of free will, discussed in his seminal *Groundwork of the Metaphysics of Morals* (1785), one of the most important works in moral philosophy. Whereby Kant employs his original idea of a categorical imperative to argue that ethical activity reflects the distinctive feature of being human, found in our capacity for freedom. Namely, an ability to choose which determines the foundation between good and bad

---

5. Kant, "What Is Enlightenment?," 54.

behavior by human being, based on the assessment of moral principles which govern such activity as being reasonable found in the exercise of freedom. Whereby establishing the ethical orientation for a philosophical foundation of human dignity, based on the famous Kantian categorical imperative "human beings are always to be treated as ends and not as means." An ethical orientation found in the human activity "to choose" which has assumed renewed significance during the twenty-first century, as foundational for the World Transformation movement.

However, while considered a "necessary postulate of pure practical reason about the nature of morality," the Kantian account of human dignity nevertheless implies in the opinion of Francis Fukuyama, the American political scientist and researcher, the acceptance of a "form of dualism," found in the presence of a realm of human freedom through the exercise of choice, one unrelated to the biological realm of nature that is not determined by the latter, as discussed in *Our Posthuman Future: Consequences of the Biotechnology Revolution* (2002). Furthermore, he claims most scientists in their study of the human condition would challenge the presence of free will, now understood as "an illusion and that all human decision making can be ultimately traced back to material causes," a scientific way of thinking found in late nineteenth and twentieth-century thought. This modern ethical understanding and its underlying scientific orientation was challenged by Scheler, a former student of natural science, in his seminal *Formalism in Ethics and Non-Formal Ethics of Values: A New Attempt toward the Foundation of an Ethical Personalism* (1913–14).

A book for which he is primarily known which was critically studied by Wojtyła for his *Habilitation*; while critical of the absence of metaphysical foundations, he appropriated elements of Scheler's phenomenological ethical personalism, within his novel analysis of the "personal structure of self-determination" and "self-determination and fulfillment" in *Person and Act* (1969), which he was writing during the Council. Wherein Wojtyła claims, approached as a "reality," the use of "freedom is identified with self-determination," whereby we discover "the will as a property of the person."[6] Namely, we discover the natural disposition of the human person, whether being individual or as communal, in the exercise of free will found in human activity, generated by the moral activity of choice. This philosophical recognition of the

---

6. Wojtyła, *Person and Act*, 217.

human person's capacity "to choose" encapsulates what Brian Cox understands as "something else." Thought which directs his recognition of the fundamental difference between a biological organic view of "being human" and the "human being" as capable of ethical and religious activity, a distinction well appreciated by the Catholic Scheler thinking as a "theist and realist." Approaching this suggestive "gap" has generated ongoing interest in this subject matter, the so-called "dualism" found in being human, over the course of recorded history, especially by philosophers thinking within the tradition of Western thought.

On the cusp of a new millennium of the Christian era, humanity's story remains a concern shared by all. Nowhere more so than in the thoughtful attention given to understanding the meaning of being human, the nature of our existence and the origin and destiny of humanity, topics which have long fascinated thinkers over the course of human history. Recently Pope Francis offered an aspirational characterisation: "Human life is like an orchestra that performs well if the various instruments are in harmony and follow a score shared by all." Spoken by the pope on April 4, 2017 as he addressed participants attending a conference to celebrate the fiftieth anniversary of Pope Paul VI's encyclical *Populorum Progressio* (1967), these words and the musical metaphor offer a thoughtful means to engage the original network of ideas, "human person," "community of persons," and "human solidarity," which constitute conciliar humanism, wherein we find the Council's "belief in humanity."

Understood as a "symphony of ideas" these facilitate the means for discussion of our shared humanity, approached through the exercise of the human person's "conscience," the awareness of "participation" we share being members of a community of persons, within which our human solidarity directs our shared humanity towards God in Christ. Remarkable thought found within conciliar humanism, a generous act of service given in love by the Catholic Church to the "world of today. " Found in the introductory words of *Gaudium et Spes*, expressive of our shared awareness as human beings, found in "feelings of oneness, concern and love towards the whole human family," original thought based on the premise "that it is the human person who is to be saved and human society to be restored." Sentiment expressive of a "beacon of hope," offered by the Church under the guidance of the Holy Spirit infused with *sapiential* consciousness concerning "the noble calling of humanity."

While these individual ideas carry a certain familiarity, especially human person, and community, they have never been approached as originally intended within the context of a network of ideas, found in conciliar humanism. A harmonic composition, wherein various instruments are being played together about our shared humanity. Taking ownership of this thoughtful legacy, speaking on December 7, 1965 during the final plenary session of the Council Pope Paul VI found inspiration in Jesus' response to the disciple Phillip's request to "show us the Father" recorded in John's Gospel (14:9), which the pope extended to understanding humanity: "to remember how in everyone we can and must recognize the countenance of Christ." Whereby he endorsed the Council's invitation to rediscover God through the recovery of a Christ centred integral philosophical understanding of our shared humanity found in the narrative of fraternal love between human persons, to lovingly follow a score read in the pursuit of wisdom, "which gently draws the human mind to seek and love what is true and good" in the words of *Gaudium et Spes*, para. 15, which leads to an appreciation of the human person.

By means of this thoughtful pursuit "humanity may come to a clearer sense of the great resources with which it has been endowed and may commit itself with renewed courage to implement the plan of salvation of which its history is part," aspirational words from *Fides et Ratio*, para. 6 equally infused with *sapiential* consciousness. Whereby Pope John Paul II affirms his ongoing commitment to the philosophical promotion of our God given human resourcefulness, one shared by the author of this book, which informs "the plan of salvation," namely, our human solidarity found in "being together with God," whereby as human persons we look back to the future. Extraordinary thought which emerged from within the tradition of lived Catholic Christianity of a theological orientation, based on an integral philosophical understanding of our shared humanity, which informs the hitherto undiscussed legacy of conciliar humanism in the twenty-first century.

31

Living in Uncertain Times

BEGINNING ON JANUARY 1, 2001, the first century of a new millennium thus far has been characterized as an unintended "perfect storm of crises" which threaten to wipe out humanity, a series of interlinked emergencies. Such as the rise of a global economy generated by the emergence of so-called "Third World" consumerism, the unabated concern over the threat of nuclear war and international terrorism, the human generated climate breakdown found in global warming, the loss of biodiversity, and the emergence of new forms of biotechnology following the completion of the Human Genome Project in 2003, expectations shattered during the 2013 COVID-19 pandemic. Approached as "existential risks," the sum of which are greater than their individual impact, these threaten to wipe out humanity and inform the ongoing awareness of the sociopolitical consequences of living in the so-called "the Anthropocene Epoch." Namely, the human induced "anthropogenic" effects on our environment, human and natural, discussed by Fiona Harvey, an environment correspondent for *The Guardian*, February 7, 2020. Described as "big disasters" that could end history generated by the so-called "intelligence explosion," the enhancement of human "superintelligence" and processes of decision-making concerning future biotechnology and nanotechnology, and finally, the most unsettling possibility, her recognition that there is something as yet unknown, very deadly, and unavoidable even when known, the "unknown unknowns." Problematic circumstances which were discussed in *The Conversation* published on May 29, 2014 by Anders Sandberg, the Swedish senior research fellow at the University of Oxford's Future of Humanity Institute (2005). A multidisciplinary organization which addresses these "big-picture questions about humanity and its prospects," founded by Professor Nick Bostrum, the Swedish specialist on existential risk, the anthropic principle and human enhancement ethics.

Currently approached within an ethical secular orientation which directs the ongoing awareness that the actions of being human have consequences, especially on the planet, an international team of scientists and intellectuals proposed a new geological epoch, the so-called "age of humans." Marked by the presence of global ecological changes and their related environmental impact caused by human activity, culminating in the end of the Earth's Holocene epoch. Documenting these circumstances, how humans change the Earth more than all the planet's natural processes combined, the critically acclaimed Canadian film *Anthropocene: The Human Epoch* premiered at the 2018 Toronto International Film Festival, characterized as a "cinematic meditation." Namely, as a "colossal eco doc [which] prettifies disaster," a sobering and visually ravishing look at the horrific ecological havoc humans have wrought on the environment. Later discussed in a series of "mind-expanding essays on modern life and the human experience" compiled by the New York Times best-selling author John Green in *The Anthropocene Reviewed: Essays on a Human-Centred Planet* (2021).

Thinking in this century, conciliar humanism, and its original network of philosophical ideas, hitherto discussed, offers an invaluable resource toward understanding our shared humanity, intended as a beacon of hope. As such, this original way of thinking based on the Council's seminal idea of the human person within a network of ideas, represents a love story, expressed in the pivotal thought that as human persons, whether individual or communal, we are, to again quote the inspirational words of Leslie Williams, "beggars for love, with our hands outstretched, clasping a cup, hoping for contributions from passers-by." Where by as human persons capable of love, as we give each other what we can, relying on what we have been given from each other, but "only when God walks by is the cup filled to overflowing."[1] Remarkable thought coming from someone thinking in an age which she claims has yet to come up with a new label for itself, defining itself from what it has lost, namely the influence of Christianity and its awareness of our human capacity to think about God living in a post-modern world. Based on this claim Leslie Williams wrote remarkable *When Anything Goes: Being Christian*

---

1. Williams, *When Anything Goes*, 53.

in a Post-Christian World (2016), based on her previous *Night Wrestling: Struggling for Answers and Find God* (1997), wherein she offers a *tour de force* guide to the interaction between understanding humanity and thinking about God over the course of history, whereby she concludes with a personal observation on the billboard slogan "Jesus Saves": namely, "He saves us from ourselves."[2] But I would add, "He shows us who we are" as found in conciliar humanism.

Inspired by our human search for wisdom, during an extended moment of *sapiential* consciousness, conciliar humanism offers what Pope Benedict XVI referred to as an instance of "broad new thinking" about what constitutes our humanity shared with Christ, a thoughtful approach which offers foundations to build on, to better understand the meaning of this slogan, "Jesus saves." Like *The Human Predicament: A Candid Guide to Life's Biggest Questions* (2017) written by the South African philosopher David Benatar, though without his advocacy of "antinativism," Williams seeks to elaborate a novel approach when thinking about humanity, built around the fundamental paradox which informs understanding the nature of humanity as a "predicament," summarized in her words: "He saves us from ourselves." Namely, thinking about ourselves as being human paradoxically provides an opportunity to retrieve a Christ centred understanding of our shared humanity. While this expression "predicament" is generally connected with a difficult, a somewhat unpleasant, or an embarrassing situation we experience as human beings, wherein we need to make a choice or a decision, colloquially expressed: "I'm in a bit of a predicament because I've accidentally accepted two invitations to dinner on the same night." Wherein, the predicament is not found so much in the accidental acceptance of something but rather the awareness of something else, a better offer after accepting the first. As such, the use of "predicament" speaks about our human capacity to choose, and herein lies the enigma of humanity.

Defined as "the sum of the behavior and characteristics that are typical of the human species, arising from genetic rather than environmental factors" by Francis Fukuyama, the American political scientist who trained as a minister in the Congregational Church, best known for his book *The End of History and the Last Man* (1992) wherein he looks beyond the typical species oriented explanations for being human, which revolve around the "boundary line between nature and

---

2. Williams, *When Anything Goes*, 137.

nurture" moving into what I call "the sphere of 'nutrition'" wherein we encounter the "predicament" of being human, characterized by our human capacity to choose or by the presence of what Fukuyama calls "Factor X,"[3] namely, the purposeful recognition that there is "something more." There is something special about being a human person, found in the ethical exercise of free will approached as an act of transcendence, which he defines as "the actual ability to transcend natural determinism and the normal rules of causality."[4]

Fukuyama's original thought engaged the philosophical heritage of Wilhelm Friedrich Hegel (1770–1831) and his left-wing proponent Karl Marx, who envisaged a twofold nature found within being human, approached from within a scientific evolutionary and material context as a biologically oriented "species-being," one altruistically directed towards other such beings, and as a socioeconomic entity, a "subject," within an ongoing process of linear adaptation. This broad Godless scientific approach elaborated by one of the "masters of suspicion," emerged towards the end of the nineteenth and into the twentieth centuries, wherein many scientists challenged the traditional idea of *Homo sapiens* which envisaged human nature as essentially different from other species, now approached from this naturalistic scientific perspective, relying on the insights of genetic psychology and the processes of natural and social evolution the status of being human was reduced to one animal species among many.

Understood as a recent product in the process of natural evolution over millennia, human beings were considered only quantitatively different, possessing a higher degree of intelligence, with more organic complexity and great sophistication in their drives, energies, and capacities, evident in the process of natural selection and adaptation. However, towards the end of the twentieth century our suspicions were once again aroused. Recalling the thought of European Catholic philosophers like Max Scheler who challenged the adequacy of the contemporary scientific biological explanations in response to the maxim *know yourself*, whereby we were only offered a "wealth of facts" without the philosophical foundations necessary for understanding this information, let alone making the necessary connections within an ordered whole, found in Scheler's phenomenological ethical personalism from

3. Fukuyama, *Our Posthuman Future*, 151.
4. Fukuyama, *Our Posthuman Future*, 129–30.

which emerged his original philosophical anthropology. Therein we appreciate the subtle but important philosophical distinction between being human and the human being; on face value, the former disclosing aspects associated with the latter, namely as a member of the species *Homo sapiens*. But is this all to be said?

This question addresses the adequacy of scientific explanations as an integral understanding of being human, a concern raised by Fukuyama, a leading academic Hegelian, who rose to prominence with his radical claim: "humanity has reached the end of history as such." First made in his essay "The End of History?" published in the summer of 1989, months before the fall of the Berlin Wall, Fukuyama later used his book *The End of History and the Last Man* (1992) to expand these ideas within his critical reception of the use of emerging biotechnologies for "transhumanist" ends, a distinctive way of thinking which emerged during the twenty-first century. Approaching the events of recent history, the political philosopher finds these symptomatic of a larger process "which gives coherence and order to the daily headlines,"[5] namely, "the unabashed victory of economic and political liberalism." Understood as the end of humanity's ideological evolution, following the end of the Cold War between March 12, 1947 until December 26, 1991 and the demise of Stalinist socialism, with the universalization of Western liberal democracy.

Drawing attention to *our posthuman future*, in a section entitled "what to fight for," Fukuyama outlines what he calls "Factor X." While every member of the human species possesses a genetic biological framework common to all, he claims there is a fundamental difference, an endowment that distinguishes "a human in essence from other types of creatures." One which Fukuyama finds within the complex interactions found in our ethical existence, in "uniquely human characteristics like moral choice, reason and a broad emotional gamut of responses," which come together within a "human whole," who is irreducible to the mechanisms of biotechnology, approached as "the sum of simple parts."[6] Moving into the posthuman world of the twenty-first century, while "human nature is very plastic," according to Fukuyama we share basic features which enable our potential connection with other human beings through the exercise of "true freedom" which ensures as he concludes, "the freedom of political communities to protect the values

---

5. Fukuyama, "End of History?," 3.
6. Fukuyama, *Our Posthuman Future*, 171–72.

they hold most dear" and the ethical means to engage "the biotechnology revolution today."

Interestingly, in his discussion of "human dignity redux," an unusual word meaning restored or revived, from the Latin *reducere* 'to bring back,' the second generation Japanese born Christian political scientist, recognizes the contribution made by the Catholic Church at the end of the twentieth century towards understanding the theory of evolution; more specifically, that of Pope John Paul II in his seminal message to the Pontifical Academy of Sciences (1936)[7] wherein he expanded on critical ideas about evolution initially detailed by the Venerable Pope Pius XII (1939–58) in his encyclical *Humani Generis*, "concerning some false opinions threatening to undermine the foundations of Catholic doctrine" published on August 12, 1950. In celebrating the sixtieth anniversary of the re-foundation of the Pontifical Academy by Pope Pius XI (1922–39) in 1936 "to promote the progress of the mathematical, physical, and natural sciences, and the study of related epistemological problems," Pope John Paul II now used the occasion to "reflect on science in the shadow of the third millennium."

An original way of thinking found in Fukuyama's use of redux, whereby to approach the legacy of conciliar humanism as a thoughtful means to accommodate the Church's pastoral outreach to the "world of today." On the cusp of a new millennium, our human story remains a concern shared by all, when once again, like our forebears we search for an answer to the "mystery of humanity," found in conciliar humanism. A thoughtful means to ease our natural suspicions and unravel the primal paradox of being human, to better understand our human predicament wherein we can choose to think about God, and in so doing to recognize our God given resourcefulness living in the twenty-first century. While "the explosion of scientific understanding and technological capability in modern times has brought many advantages to the human race, it also poses serious challenges": so begins the International Theological Commission's statement *Communion and Stewardship: Human Persons Created in the Image of God*, published in July 2004, a summary of numerous meetings held in Rome between 2000–2002. Suitable words in response to the radical claim, "intervention in biotechnology is a necessary step to make, not because there is a human nature to save but precisely because there is no such nature," made by Carl Packman, the London based

---

7. Fukuyama, *Our Posthuman Future*, 160–61.

Australian freelance writer in his critical review published in the journal *Rethinking Marxism*[8] of Fukuyama's *Our Posthuman Future: Consequences of the Biotechnological Revolution* (2003).

There is much behind the use of "predicament," as it informs conciliar humanism as a way of thinking which moves beyond the traditional paradigms of thought about humanity, as between the philosophical orientation of "nature" with its emphasis on our use of intellect and sociability towards others as human beings, and the scientific orientation of "nurture" with its emphasis on instinctive biological forms of behavior, moving towards the integrative idea of "nutrition," namely, the recognition there is "something more," found in the Council's understanding of the whole "human person," a product of *sapiential* consciousness. While referring to the biochemical and physiological process whereby an organism instinctively uses food to support life, which includes ingestion, absorption assimilation and biosynthesis, this scientific orientation found in "nutrition" has been broadened with the establishment of the Society for Implementation Science in Nutrition (SISN) in 2016 to facilitate collaboration between the various "stakeholders in nutrition implementation" and the collective experience of scientists and practitioners in "taking up the challenge of scaling-up nutrition globally." Similarly operating at the interface between "knowledge" and "action," this expression is applicable to the synthetic and integrative process which generated the Council's understanding of the human person, a consequence of taking in and assimilating a variety of philosophical ideas considered necessary to sustain and enrich an understanding of the whole of human life, characterized by Scheler as "multidimensional."

The publication *Beyond Versus: The Struggle to Understand the Interaction of Nature and Nurture (Life and Mind: Philosophical Issues on Biology and Psychology)* (2014) written by James Tabery, the American specialist on philosophy and applied ethics teaching at the University of Utah (1850), represents an attempt to better understand this "soul-hungry creature." Namely, to overcome the traditional debate when thinking about humanity between a biological "nature" and the sociologically oriented "nurture," as a means to recognize that these human traits arise from the simultaneous interaction between nature and nurture, wherein we discover its potential resolution through the novel idea of "nutrition." Approached as a typical postmodern response with a Hegelian twist, wherein we find the emergence of "a new normal"

---

8. Packman, Review of *Rethinking Marxism*, 317–23.

applied to a nutritional understanding of humanity. Set against the background of the COVID-19 pandemic, this expression first appeared during the Global Financial Crisis, following the bankruptcy of the US financial firm Lehman Brothers on September 15, 2008, in reference to the dramatic economic, cultural, and social transformations precipitated by the subprime mortgage crisis. Concerning the ongoing quest to better understand our humanity, "can there be a more important subject than human nature?"

Asked and answered by E. O. Wilson (1929–2021). in the 2004 Preface to the revised edition of his ground-breaking *On Human Nature* (1978), wherein the renowned American biologist, secular humanist, and the "father of biodiversity," tries to explain human nature, society, and the various forms of social behavior in terms of evolutionary science, through his understanding of "socio-biology." Defined as "the extension of population biology and evolutionary theory to social organization" in his book *Sociobiology: The New Synthesis* (1975) as Wilson attempts to complete the Darwinian revolution by combining biological thought with ideas taken from the social sciences and humanities. Written during the 1970s wherein two concepts of being human dominated Western thought, namely, a religious philosophical oriented understanding of human "nature," commonly used to refer to the way in which things naturally happen by themselves without "interference" from external factors, as being essentially different from other forms of animate life, and an alternative atheistic, scientific, and naturalistic one-dimensional view of the human "condition," wherein there is no essential difference with being human, recognized as one among many forms of biological life.

A debate of ancient lineage between "nature" and "nurture," one currently found in philosophy, psychology, and science as to whether human behavior is primarily determined by our biological genetic constitution which we have inherited, or by external environmental factors conditioned by instinct, such as what we have learned, whereby the former therapeutic approach drew attention to the "healing power of nature" and adopted by the so-called "Father of Medicine," Hippocrates (c. 460–c. 370 BC) from the Greek island of Kos. Taken from the Latin *natura*, 'birth,' nature was a philosophical term derived from the verb for birth, used by Greek philosophers to translate pre-Socratic thought regarding the natural world, especially their study of natural growth based on observation, reflected in Aristotle's lifelong interest in the study of nature. Found in a compilation of manuscripts "on nature," based on the theoretical observation of things that are self-moving and self-developing discussed in Aristotle's ground-breaking *Physics*. A series of lectures regarding the principles of natural or moving things, both living and non-living, namely those of causation, motion, place and time, this treatise provided the conceptual apparatus for the scientific study of natural phenomena, which served as the basis for the first philosophical scrutiny of being human as a rational animal with a natural social orientation towards other humans and established the pattern for the disciplined study of human activity. Undertaken in the fields of anthropology, politics, and ethics whereby life's big "existential" questions asked by human beings are explored through the use of ordered thought and abstract ideas found in philosophy.

A way of thinking which later governed the medieval thought of followers of the Abrahamic religions who envisaged human nature as a God given paradox. Namely, the enigma of a biological embodied living finite being with an immortal immaterial spiritual 'soul,' created in the "image of God" as an intelligent human being with a capacity to perform both good and evil actions, an instance of the so-called "human predicament." A philosophical conundrum addressed by the "teacher of humanity" in the first part of the *Summa Theologica*, in questions 75–89, his so-called "Treatise on Man," recently discussed in *Thomas Aquinas on Human Nature* (2002) by Robert Pasnau, the American philosopher teaching at the University of Colorado (1876). Wherein Aquinas approached the predicament of being human as a paradox, namely, as a socially inclined "rational animal," who was the only member of a biological species that straddles the divide between matter and spirit, between "body" and "soul," whereby possessing the latter, human beings alone possess the intellectual capacity to transcend our material being living in the world through the exercise of freedom, a human situation later discussed by Wojtyła through his phenomenological study of consciousness, found in his seminal work *Person and Act* (1969).

As observed recently in the *National Geographic* magazine, it was probably the pre-Socratic thought of Anaximander (c. 610–c. 546 BC) who lived in Miletus, a city of Ionia, in modern day Turkey, which constituted the original study of humankind with his claim: "humans are born helpless." One of the founding members of the Ionian school of natural philosophy, he was a student of Thales of Miletus (around 585 BC), arguably the founder of the philosophical study of the natural world, who according to Aristotle, applied his study of the natural world to speculate that humans must have descended from some other form of created life who could survive without any help, unlike the human infant, who learnt to adapt. Based on his observation that fish hatch from eggs, popularly understood as an animal that has fins, scales, and lives in water, which emerge immediately as full formed living beings without help from their parents, Anaximander drew the remarkable conclusion that life began in the sea, an idiosyncratic way of thinking which foreshadowed the idea of evolution. A scientific way of thinking about being human taken up by twenty-first-century proponents of "transhumanism" and those of the World Transformation Movement's biological approach to the "human condition."

As a philosophical opportunity to rethink our human identity, rather than being a "situation" with its circumstantial orientation, there is merit in the use of "predicament." Found in the suggestive title *The Human Predicament: Towards an Understanding of the Human Condition* (2013) by Max Malikow, the American scholar "who seamlessly combines philosophy and psychology" by means of his original employment of this word as depicting something "difficult, troubling and, perhaps, perplexing."[9] Wherein "predicament," approached in a theological context, is expressive of the enigma which informs being human "in need of salvation." Namely, as a human person with a recognizable capacity to choose to think about the idea of God or not, to choose to interact with other human beings or not, and to choose to perform acts that are understood as being good rather than ones which are considered bad, herein we find the predicament of being human. Employed as a means to avoid the traditional Western philosophical bifurcation associated with understanding our humanity as being embodied with a spiritual soul, between matter and soul, approaching humanity as a "predicament" enables access to the integrative legacy of conciliar humanism, found in the human person's God given capacity to exercise freedom, "to choose," in the person's act of transcendence. Based on the Council's Christ centred integrative idea of the human person as a multi-dimensional being, following the thought of Scheler, wherein we find an invitation to better understand ourselves by bringing together within a unified whole the constitutive features of being human, the biological, physical, psychological, emotional, intellectual, social, spiritual, and personal spheres, individual dimensions which constitute the human as being multidimensional, found in the idea of human person.

---

9. Malikow, *Human Predicament*, 1.

32

Beyond Categories

WHILE *BEING AND NOTHINGNESS* (1943), the major work of Jean Paul Sartre, supposedly marks the end of the modern world, philosophically speaking the final decades of the twentieth century represent an "unprecedented phenomenon of uncertainty" generated by a new reactionary manner of thought characterized as "post-modern." Approached historically, this expression was initially used by the German philosopher Rudolf Pannwitz (1881–1969) in *Die Krisis der Europaeischen Kultur* (1917) to describe the philosophical and ethical crisis occasioned by 'nihilism,' associated with the thought of Camus, which characterized twentieth-century European culture.[1] However it is more commonly associated with the thoughtful diagnosis offered by the French philosopher Jean-François Lyotard (1924–98) in his classic *The Postmodern Condition: A Report on Knowledge* (1979) wherein he defines "*postmodern* as incredulity towards metanarratives."[2] Namely, as a critical diagnosis on the traditional use of "grand narratives" of historical progress, such as evolution, and of concepts of universal moral value, such as Good or Truth, which informs the condition of contemporary thought with its rejection of the notion of universal reason. One which questions the foundational stories about the whole of life, which had assumed the status of absolute truth in modern thought.[3] Such as the critique of the story of natural evolution in the rhetoric of Darwinism and its paradigm of natural selection regarding the human species,

1. Cahoone, *From Modernism to Postmodernism*, 3.
2. Lyotard, *Postmodern Condition*, xxiv.
3. Smith, *Who's Afraid of Postmodernism?*, 59.

"the human condition," thereby utilizing a broader understanding of the word "condition" within contemporary discourse.

A century which began with "modernism," a nebulous expression which designates a priority given to the scrutiny of consciousness, found in modern thought and the emergence of phenomenology which swept across the European continent, now finished with a resurgence of intellectual interest in subjects previously discounted or dismissed by major figures in modern philosophy, such as theorizing about the possibility of thinking about the idea of the existence of God and the practice of religion, discussed by the Enlightenment philosopher Immanuel Kant in *Religion within the Limits of Reason Alone* (1793) and *Lectures on Philosophical Theology: A Study of the Rational Justification of Belief in God* (1821), interests commonly associated with factors effecting the way people think of themselves and others which inform the so-called "human condition." A rather broad expression which encapsulates the characteristics and major events considered essential to human existence, such as birth, education and the intellectual life, our emotional and moral life, and social interactions and aspirations, approached philosophically in *The Human Condition* (1958) by Hannah Arendt (1906–75), the German born American political philosopher, a Holocaust survivor, and one of the most influential sociopolitical theorists of the twentieth century.

Engaging unprecedented levels of intellectual uncertainty about what we know, which generated the "crisis of relativism" in the words of Pope John Paul II, and the accompanying disturbance effected by levels of dramatic socio, economic, and political change, we are confronted with moments of thoughtful ambiguity living in the world of today, but also with new opportunities to address the perennial question about our humanity? While not espousing the relativist tenets of postmodernism, as a cultural and intellectual phenomenon it has occasioned the dismantling of many of the earlier rationalist prejudices which generated a "narrow" scientific understanding of the being human, our condition, which negated the human capacity to think about the existence of God and the consequent distrust of religion, wherein living in a postmodern context we find new opportunities to think about the predicament of being human, a means to explore the legacy of conciliar humanism. Writing in "Appropriating Postmodernism" (1996), the American Merold Westphal, Professor of Philosophy at Fordham University (1841), critically engages this contemporary mindset, found in the postmodern claim "the truth is that there is no Truth,"[4] published in a volume of essays entitled *Overcoming Onto-Theology: Toward a Postmodern Christian Faith* (2001). For this Christian philosopher, the significance of this statement lies in the last word "Truth" with a capital T, namely, the undermining of modernity's supposed faith in the use of reason, found in the recognition of the human capacity to achieve access to such Truth in the first place, the foundation of modern thought whether expressed as Cartesian rationalism or Lockean empiricism. Nevertheless, considerable caution should be exercised when engaging this sceptical form of philosophical and literary analysis, commonly criticized as an instance of unbridled relativism, wherein we find a denial of any objectivity or certainty for our ideas, only "better or worse interpretations."

A way of thinking driven by one of its major proponents, the Algerian born French philosopher Jacques Derrida's (1930–2004) radical denial of traditional Western philosophy characterized as "logo-centrism" along with its "metaphysics of presence," detailed in his seminal *Of Grammatology* (1967), wherein he questions the possibility of any coherent meaning found in reading a written text, circumstances which informed the contemporary "crisis of truth" in the estimation of Pope John Paul II in his encyclical *Veritatis Splendor* (1993). Approached from this postmodern perspective, characterized by a "gnawing pessimism," there is no privileged position concerning interpretation, such as that given to an author's intention or contact with reality, which confers significance to what is read, thinking in these literary circumstances meaning is to be found in Derrida's understanding of *différence*. An awkward expression which formulates an equally ambiguous movement known as "deconstruction," understood as a "philosophy of alterity" defined as "the very experience of the (impossible) possibility of the impossible, of the most impossible."[5] Employing such apparent unintelligible language we find the application of Derrida's novel term, which designates the constant interplay within our patterns of thought, one which overcomes the traditional binary opposition generated by an "either/or" way of thinking, such as between "body and soul," in favour of a radical "otherness." A radical movement towards the "other," interrupted by Derrida's novel use of parody which prompts unsolicited

---

4. Westphal, *Overcoming Onto-Theology*, 81.
5. Derrida, *On the Name*, 43.

laughter, a characteristically human phenomenon, used as a means to counter Hegel's uncompromising dialectic.

This wanton way of postmodern thinking exercised a direct impact on how we think about ourselves as being human, a theme taken up by K. J. Ozborne, creator of "The Scariest Movie Ever Made" (2016) online channel, who engaged the consequences of "living in the age of anything goes" in response to "a personal awakening to the true nature of our shared rigged reality." An uninhibited way of scientific thinking, which came to characterize contemporary thought and exercised a direct impact on how we think about ourselves as human beings, discussed by scholars meeting in Leuven, which initiated a movement of thinking "beyond humanism," in the assessment of Ihab Hassan, "humanism may be coming to an end as humanism transforms itself into something one must helplessly call posthumanism."[6] This movement of current thought beyond humanism is best approached by its contemporary progeny, "transhumanism," a way of thinking taken up during the first years of the twenty-first century.

While the term "pansexuality" was originally attributed to Sigmund Freud, the Austrian father of psychoanalysis, who reminded his readers, in his preface to the fourth edition of the *Three Essays on the Theory of Sexuality* (1905), that it was Arthur Schopenhauer (1788–1860), the German philosopher "rebel and outsider," who "confronted mankind some time ago with the extent to which their aims and actions are determined by sexual impulses."[7] Towards the end of the twentieth century, this expression came to represent a new category of sexual identity which was gender blind. One which moved beyond familiar binary terms, such as heterosexual, homosexual, or bisexual, toward an idea of pansexuality which represents the blurring of traditional lines of gender differentiation, whereby sexual, physical, or romantic attraction to others is indifferent to their physical gender identity or biological sex, found in the evolving acronym LGBTIQA+. These inclusive though ambiguous circumstances prompted Ozborne to speak of "a new world order," which he claimed promoted whatever is "more disgusting, more profane and more debauched." Operating within this excessive ethos of "a new normal" which has emerged, this is especially found in the

---

6. Hassan, "Prometheus as Performer," 830.
7. Gay, *Freud*, 149.

entertainment industry where "practically anything you see anymore is controlled and dictated by spiritual wickedness."

As such, I return to the thought of Leslie Williams, "the world we live in is changing. Rapidly. For the worse."[8] Understood as the practical consequence of living in our contemporary world following "the death of God" where *anything goes*, namely, understood a post Christian world in the absence of religion. Originally used as the title of Cole Porter's 1934 smash-hit musical comedy, the confined setting on board the ocean liner USS *America* was significantly expanded when later used as the title for a portrayal of American society during the 1920s, the "roaring twenties," characterized as an era of uninhibited excess, characterized by drinking, shameless flappers, jazz and gangland war. Recently, this expression was used to identify the contemporary philosophical, cultural and social orientation of twenty-first-century postmodern thought, found in Leslie Williams' *When Anything Goes: Being Christian in a Post-Christian World* (2016). Living today in an age which has yet to come up with a new label for itself, Williams argues, western culture now defines itself in terms of what it has lost, namely the influence of Christianity. To counter this claim, she offers a bold affirmation of the meaning and purpose living in a world that loudly proclaims that all is meaningless, wherein individual belief still stands. Recalling her thought that as human beings we are "beggars for love, with our hands outstretched," we are now understood as "a soul-hungry creature that's made for more (and made of more) than immediately meets the eye."

While Aldous Huxley's (1894–1963) *Brave New World* (1932) narrated a futuristic dystopian society whose citizens are environmentally, scientifically and socially engineered within an intelligence based social hierarchy, his older brother Sir Julian Huxley (1887–1975), the renowned evolutionary biologist and secular humanist, coined the expression "transhumanism": "I believe in transhumanism: once there are enough people who can truly say that, the human species will be on the threshold of a new kind of existence," taken from his article "Transhumanism" in a publication entitled *New Bottles for New Wine* (1957). A remarkable way of thinking endorsed by the Australian Elise Bohan, author of *Future Superhuman: Our Transhuman Lives in a Make-or-Break Century* (2022), wherein we are challenged to think about humanity in the same way we view other species, not only to survive but to thrive!

---

8. Jasper and Sardine, "About," para. 1.

Under these circumstances, "humanity stands to be profoundly affected by science and technology in the future," so begins "The Transhumanist Declaration" of March 2009. A way of thinking which envisages the expansion of human potential in a state of continual movement, "overcoming aging, cognitive shortcomings, involuntary suffering, and our confinement to planet Earth." Living with "the accelerating pace of technological development and scientific understanding," we are entering "a whole new stage in the history of the human species," a salient claim made in *The Transhumanist FAQ* (2003), published by the *World Transhumanist Association*. A recognizable intellectual and social phenomenon of the twenty-first century, which promotes being human into the future. A way of thinking captured in the single edition of the *National Geographic Society* magazine for April 2017 entitled "The Next Human." While humanists believe that "humanity matters," that our individual lives can be improved by promoting rational thought, the use of freedom, and concern for our fellow human beings, through the traditional means of education, cultural development, and ethical activity; transhumanists are prepared to take a step further in their choice to live longer, the optimal word being "choice."

Moving into the twenty-first century, this way of thinking has been directed by proponents of a distinctive way of thinking designated during the 1990s as "transhumanism," used in the modern sense by the American philosopher and futurist Max More,[9] who claimed current scientific developments and biotechnological improvements had led to an enhanced form of humanity, the creation of a new species of "trans-humans," or "beyond" human following Nietzsche's thought. While there appears no definitive position shared among the proponents of this secular way of thinking, all agree that being human is fundamentally a material and biological condition, understood as being malleable or susceptible to change. Approached as the defining characteristic of being human, the capacity to transform humanity into a new species, whereby the traditional understanding of the 'capacity for transcendence' is misappropriated to designate the initiation of a new era, namely, that of transhumanism.

Interestingly, along with his equally famous brother, the writer philosopher Aldous Huxley (1894–1963), author of *Brave New World* (1932) and *The Perennial Philosophy* (1945), these English men joined

---

9. Bostrom, "History of Transhumanist Thought," 1–25.

the ranks of prominent intellectuals and thinkers who were invited to participate in an international colloquium held in Mexico 1947 to discuss the origins and philosophical foundations of human rights in preparation for the Universal Declaration on Human Rights adopted by the United Nations on December 10, 1948. Another equally influential thinker during these deliberations, though approaching "what is human" from an entirely different perspective was the French Catholic philosopher, Jacques Maritain. Commemorating the seventieth anniversary of the Declaration of Human Rights, the editors of the UNESCO *Courier* (2018–24) chose to "take a detour into the past to enable us to better orient ourselves in the future," an approach encapsulated using the title "Back to the Future," namely, to revisit the significance of this preparatory symposium organized prior to the acceptance of the Universal Declaration on Human Rights (1948), a similar approach undertaken in this book, which informs my discussion of the human and philosophical background which informs conciliar humanism.

While twentieth-century secular humanism reflected a Godless rational and scientific way of thinking about the human condition as a species with definite ethical overtones, understood as a meaningful form of existence which emphasized human welfare and the dignity of being human as one biological species among many, certainly not essentially different from other forms of animate life, now transhumanists, equally atheistic, build on this thoughtful legacy to further explore the potential found in this scientific approach. While similarly anti-religious, their understanding of the human reliance on the use of reason, scientific technology, and the use of human creativity to surmount human limitation, has generated a new form of humanity, beyond humanity, characterized by "an open-ended lifespan" in the words of the transhumanist Max More. A radical way of thinking which follows "the removal of political, cultural, biological, and psychological limits to continuing development" found in being human, writing in his essay "The Philosophy of Transhumanism."[10] Moving 'beyond' humanism, the proponents of this twenty-first-century way of thinking, who similarly denigrate any form of religious faith, build on the use of reason and scientific technology to unexpectedly transform the human condition as a material being. Whereby progress is not viewed as inevitable nor free from danger, but rather expressed through the principle of "self-transformation."

10. More and Vita-More, *Transhumanist Reader*, 5.

Namely, in the provocative words of More, the continual process of "ethical, intellectual, and physical self-improvement through critical and creative thinking, perpetual learning, personal responsibility, proactivity and experimentation." Whereby being human represents one stage along the continual process of evolution towards a new species of human "beyond human"; however, this reductive way of thinking fails to address the conundrum whether this new form of being human is any different from other forms of animate life?

Confronting the numerous existential crises which challenge humanity in the twenty-first century, from the ongoing nuclear annihilation, global warming and living amid "bioengineered pathogens and unaligned AI" in the words of Elise Bohan, the Oxford based researcher from Australia, she offers an ingenious ethical account of how human beings possess the capacity to "own our evolution," by transforming ourselves into new, artificially enhanced beings. Advocating a sustainable posthuman future by means of integrating ourselves with advanced robots and the use of artificial intelligence, she concludes her "love letter to humanity, though an unconventional one" by recalling the thought of the English philosopher John Stuart Mill (1806–73): "better to be a Socrates dissatisfied than a fool satisfied" from *Utilitarianism* (1861) quoted n *Fraser's Magazine*. Whereby she claims: "Superhumans can pave the way for more radiant beings to enjoy the wonders of existence for millions of years to come." Currently Senior Research Scholar at the University of Oxford's Future of Humanity Institute (2005), with a doctorate in evolutionary microhistory, she is well placed within this multidisciplinary research organization which "asks the big-picture questions about humanity and its prospects." However, we might ask where do we find ingredients for this picture? To which I respond, in the tenets of conciliar humanism.

Given the characteristic denial of God during the last century in preference for a form of scientific, biological materialism which continues to this day, one lacking the necessary thoughtful foundations, the denial of any human nature emerged as the inevitable conclusion in the opinion of the atheist Jean-Paul Sartre writing in *Existentialism and Humanism* (1945). Summarily approached as one biological organism among many, in the thought of Nancy Pearcey, the American evangelical author of *Finding Truth* (2015), the human species is constantly changing and evolving, whereby individuals must find themselves "in the ceaseless flux of life, constantly creating and re-creating themselves,"[11] perhaps recalling the pre-Socratic thought of Heraclitus "the Obscure" (c. 535–c. 475 BC). The shadowy figure from Ephesus who, notwithstanding his original notion of *logos* or principle which governs and unifies all things, he is primarily remembered for the "doctrine of flux," encapsulated in the claim "no one ever steps in the same river twice." This way of thinking re-emerged in the postmodern thought of the French philosopher historian Michel Foucault (1926–84), who envisaged the "dissociation of the self" as a fictional entity "fluid and fragmented," the consequence of various forces pulling in many directions within continual movement.

Moving beyond traditional humanism, transhumanists similarly denigrated any form of religious faith, in favour of the use of reason and scientific technology to transform the human condition as a material being, wherein progress is not viewed as inevitable nor free from danger, but rather expressed through the principle of "self-transformation." Understood as a continual process of "ethical, intellectual, and physical self-improvement through critical and creative thinking, perpetual learning, personal responsibility, proactivity and experimentation," whereby the human condition represents one phase along the continual process of evolution towards a new species of human. Nevertheless, how can we account for being human compared to other forms of animate life?

Notwithstanding our human shape or our current biological genetic makeup, transhumanists claim human beings are defined by our aspirations, our experiences, and the kinds of lives we lead, which determine our value, found in the choices we make; in the words of *The Transhumanist* "progress occurs when more people become more able to shape themselves, their lives, and the ways they relate to others, in accordance with their own deepest values." Approached from within this ethical orientation, human life is valuable no matter what the cost! Furthermore, as a living human organism, we have the potential to choose to use contemporary science and biotechnology to prolong our biological life, to move beyond the parameters and limitations which might be considered "human." Edited by Max More and Natasha Vita-More, internationally acclaimed founders of the philosophy and social movement of transhumanism, the appearance of *The Transhumanist Reader* (2013) marks the consolidation of this remarkable way of contemporary ethical thinking about humanity

---

11. Pearcy, *Finding Truth*, 208.

which seeks to expand the frontiers of being human through the use of science moving into an uncertain future.

Set against the rapid growth of emergent forms in scientific and biotechnological thought, transhumanists seek to overcome our fundamental human limitations, thereby expanding our natural biological life expectancy and enhancement, and in so doing, the associated ethical implications and concerns with such an approach are relatively ignored by its proponents; however, while this way of thinking attracts many supporters, this is critically discussed by many detractors, especially from contemporary Catholic intellectuals, such as the American Catholic philosopher Steven J. Jensen in his article "the roots of transhumanism." Published in a remarkable compilation of critical essays in *Thomas Aquinas: Teacher of Humanity* (2015), wherein "transhumanism" is approached from Wojtyła's understanding of "alienation." Namely, as a denial of our God given capacity as human beings "to choose," that is, to act ethically and religiously in a movement of transcendence towards another, either another human person or towards God, a way of thinking inspired by Maritain's *Integral Humanism* (1936) and Scheler's ethical personalism.

33

Definitely Something More

WHILE TRANSHUMANISTS RECOGNIZE HUMAN beings have sought to expand the boundaries of our being human. Approached as a biological *Homo sapiens*, human beings search for a way around every obstacle which might jeopardise human life and strive to surpass every limitation which might thwart our personal happiness. However, this way of thinking is not unlimited as being in a continual state of flux; there are definite boundaries and limitations of which we are aware being human. A way of thinking recently taken up by the Australian biologist and non-religious writer Jeremy Griffith in *A Species in Denial* (2003). Introducing this most expansive exploration of his original thought he claims, "humanity's historic denial of the issue of the human condition began when consciousness first emerged from the instinct-dominated state some 2 million years ago."[1] Building on his earlier work, *Free: The End of the Human Condition* (1988) and *Beyond the Human Condition* (1991), he clarifies his original use of this expression.

While he claims, "human nature" appears in dictionaries, little attention has been given to a contemporary understanding of the "human condition," to which he draws attention. Rather than referring to its physical and medical orientation, "the state of poverty or disease that afflicts much of humanity" is found he thinks in dealing "with human's psychological predicament." Wherein we find the real problem living on planet Earth, namely, the "humans' predicament or condition of being insecure, unable to confront, make sense of and deal with the dark side

---

1. Griffith, *Species in Denial*, 34.

of human nature,"[2] that is, confronting the fundamental enigma of being human. A realization which provides the only instance when Griffith actually employs the word 'predicament' to elaborate his original understanding of 'condition.' Namely, as the ethical predicament confronting humanity, previously expressed by Pope Paul VI as "being *Janus* like" or found in the thought of the French Catholic philosopher Blasé Pascal in *Pensées* (1670) paras. 127–132,[3] wherein he claims, "man's condition is dual" (para. 131). Thought which defines the paradox of human nature as being corrupt, drawn to evil action, but also equally capable of transcendence, found in doing good, variously approached from either the perspective of instinct or experience.

The emergence of a new form of hybrid humanity, found within the Godless world of postmodern thought, is characterized by the moral value we attribute to other human beings shown in our care for humankind, expressed in acts of compassion and kindness directed towards others, regardless of species nor religious affiliation. A vague way of thinking which sets the scene for the ethical orientation of the World Transformation Movement (1983), as a form of ethical secularism. Introducing *Beyond The Human Condition* (1991), it's founder the Australian biologist Jeremy Griffith claims, while the traditional understanding of "human nature," a philosophically oriented expression which speaks of something essential or "immutable" about being human, wherein we find something more has been prioritized in the past, he asserts that this is rather "the symptom of a condition—the human condition" which will inevitably disappear once "the condition is relieved."[4]

An ambiguous though commonly used expression within contemporary discourse, the use of "human condition" by Griffith incorporates "all of the characteristics and key events that compose the essentials of human existence," as such, it remains a very broad and ongoing topic approached from many perspectives, including anthropology, art, biology, history, literature, philosophy, psychology, and religion. One recently incorporated within an artistic event, "The Human Condition: A Poets & Artists Exhibition" opened on November 1, 2018 at the AnArte Gallery & Studio (2001) in Alamo Heights, San Antonio Texas; supporting contemporary art, this gallery recently sponsored an

2. Griffith, *Species in Denial*, 27.
3. Pascal, *Pensées*, 61–66.
4. Griffith, *Beyond the Human Condition*, 22.

exhibition "Painting the figure now." Curated by the prolific American artist, Steven DaLuz, who is highly regarded for his "sublimely luminous landscapes and sensitively figurative painting," wherein he sought to explore the various manifestations of humanity, with each selected artist given "very wide latitude in creating their expressions of the human condition" as critically reviewed by Richard Pursey, the Australian cofounder of *Beautiful Bizarre Magazine*.[5]

This exhibition is indicative of the ongoing interest in the enigma of being human, found in the juxtaposition between "human" and "condition," which implies, according to Pursey, the connotation shared by Griffith, that to be human is not only a taxonomical categorization as a biological species of primate, a mammal classified as *Homo sapiens* or "thinking ape" but also as a pathological state, namely, as a harmful deviation from the normal structural or functional state of an organism, usually observed by certain signs and symptoms. Commonly understood within this medical diagnostic context, during the late nineteenth and twentieth centuries this was significantly broadened, found in the definition of "the human condition" in the *Oxford Living Dictionary* as "the state or condition of being human, especially regarded as being inherently problematic or flawed" which informs the human enigma. Reflecting the earlier thought of John Alday, the sixteenth-century English translator of semi-philosophical works, the Australian specialist in Information & Communications Technology management suggested these artists were more than observers of the figural form, in the opinion of Pursey, they are witnesses to humanity itself.

Writing in *Irrational Man: A Study in Existentialist Philosophy* (1958), the twentieth-century American philosopher William Barrett (1913–92) claims "no age has been so self-conscious as ours."[6] As such, he draws attention to the mindset which informed twentieth-century European intellectuals and artists who sought to creatively engage in the ongoing conversation about the meaning of the "human condition," especially conducted between philosophy and science in the search for something more? Writing in the "Profiles" section of *The New Yorker* published November 6, 1954, there is an entry concerning the French novelist Andre Malraux (1901–76), author of *La Condition Humaine* (1933), whereby it is claimed this expression entered

---

5. Pursey, "Human Condition," 37.
6. Barrett, *Irrational Man*, 23.

the French language, subsequently translated into English as *Man's Fate* (1934) or predicament? Inspiration for this expression "condition" can be found in the earlier thought of French thinkers, proponents of the study of human existence, building on the notable assertion that "every man has within himself the entire human condition" from Michel de Montaigne's (1533–92) *Essays* (1595) and the reflective thought found in Blaise Pascal's (1623–62) *Pensées* (1670) para. 117, wherein he attributes the source of a soldier's bravery or the cleverness of a workman as "inclinations and choice of conditions."

Whether found in the religious thought of the creation accounts in the Book of Genesis wherein humanity first appears in sacred scripture or in the religious writings of the seven *sapiential* books in the Hebrew Old Testament, the Septuagint, in the philosophical thought of Socrates and his student Plato, in Shakespeare's literary account from his pastoral comedy *As You Like It* (1599) of the seven phases of human life in Jacques' famous monologue "All the world's a stage and all the men and women merely players," or in the scientific literature of Darwin's biological theory of natural evolution documented in *On the Origin of Species* (1859), or in the theory of hierarchy of human needs proposed by the American founder of humanist psychology Abraham Maslow (1908–70) in his 1943 paper "A Theory of Human Motivation" in the journal *Psychological Review*, or finally in the eye witness account of suffering humanity chronicled by the Holocaust survivor, the Austrian Victor Frankl (1905–97) in *Man's Search for Meaning* (1946) which inspired *logotherapy* as a psychotherapeutic method, understanding the human "condition" remains a particular subject of ongoing interest.

Approached from different perspectives, these seek to capture the breadth found in the human condition, especially in the aftermath of the dehumanising effects occasioned by the Great War (1914–18). As documented by the French novelist André Malraux's *La Condition Humaine* (1933) or used as a title by the Belgian artist René Magritte (1898–1967). Currently found in Washington's National Gallery of Art (1937), "The Human Condition" (1933) was used as the title for two works of art produced by this Belgian surrealist. Driven by his belief that reality is a matter of perception, this art was produced to surprise with an unexpected juxtaposition of unrelated imagery seemingly illogical and unnerving. Whereby Magritte employed the technique of "a painting within a painting" by depicting an easel mounted with a canvas of an artist's just completed portrayal of a scene. Characteristically personal insofar as it is believed Magritte's exterior demeanor concealed a very different interior disposition, "The Human Condition" (1933) was produced to surprise, something seemingly illogical and unnerving. Approached as an instance of surrealist art, this sought to capture the enigma of humanity as part of a broader intellectual and cultural movement in response to the phenomenon of human disenchantment and disillusionment which followed the Great War.

Recognized as containing "striking originality bursting with unexpected insights," the Jewish born Austrian Holocaust survivor and political philosopher Hannah Arendt's (1906-76) *The Human Condition* is in many respects more relevant now than when it was first published in 1958, one which introduced "condition" as subject matter for twentieth-century philosophical discourse. To avoid confusion with the 1933 novel by the French writer André Malaux, Arendt's book was originally published in French as *Condition de l'homme modern*, and only later retitled as *L'Humaine Condition*. Writing her original account of modern humanity, Arendt approaches her subject from the perspective of human agency, set against its current demise along with the exercise of political freedom she personally experienced as a political refugee, namely, the enigma that as human powers increase through the use of scientific technology and humanist inquiry, we are less equipped to control the consequences of our actions.

As such, she joined the ranks of other twentieth-century European philosophers, who along with intellectuals and artists, sought to capture the breadth found in human existence under this rather ambiguous expression, "human condition." Whereby existential philosophers like Hannah Arendt, artists such as Magritte, or writers such as Malraux, all sought to capture the enigma of being human by portraying ordinary objects in extraordinary ways, whereby "we are only allowed to see what we are allowed to see" in the words of Magritte.

Her insightful philosophical and sociopolitical account of humankind documented in her book, which foreshadows the dilemma of transhumanism found in the consequential use of science to enhance being human, was based on a study of the actions we can perform and their consequences. As such this was a continuation of her earlier thought published in *The Origins of Totalitarianism* (1951) wherein she critically compares the consequences arising from the dehumanizing political ideologies of Nazism and Stalinism. A Jewish political philosopher who lived in European countries under the Nazi regime before emigrating to the United States in 1941, her philosophical career began in 1924 when she studied at the University of Marburg (1527) under Martin Heidegger, a major proponent of existential phenomenology who at that time was a practicing Catholic. Four years later she relocated to the University of Heidelberg (1386) to write her doctorate in philosophy *Love and Saint Augustine* (1929) under the supervision of Karl Jaspers (1883–1969), another Christian existentialist.

However, given the prevalent atheism and ethical ambivalence concerning extreme forms of competitive cruel or violent behavior perpetrated by humans from diverse ethnic backgrounds towards each other, especially over the twentieth century, a further meaning of humanity has emerged, as being "a global identity." An original idea of the American historian Bruce Mazlish (1923–2016) in *The Idea of Humanity in a Global Era* (2009), which is accompanied by ethical considerations. Namely, given that our shared human behavior, found in the phenomenon of racism was not only directed towards other human beings, as tragically experienced during the twentieth century. But now it also appears, living in the twenty-first century, during an era characterized by climate crisis, environmental degradation, and multiple species extinction, the ethical issue concerning human behavior was significantly broadened to include how human beings interact with non-human forms of life, not only towards animal and vegetative life, but also towards what might be characterized as non-human machines, such as hybrid forms of non-human life such as robots and those who utilize Artificial Intelligence, which exhibit levels of what might be considered consciousness. All of which raise the ongoing question concerning the criteria used in the determination of what it means to be human moving in the future, and especially its questionable ethical status found in transhumanism, namely, "what sense does it make to aspire to a single global identity as billions of human beings?" Is more necessarily better?

Questions which inspired the World Transformation Movement, established by Jeremy Griffith in Sydney Australia in 1983 as the Centre for Humanity's Adulthood to promote and develop an understanding of the human condition in response to the human problems we share in common, intense, and interdependent existential issues which challenge the survival of humanity as a species during the twenty-first century and which can only be "solved internationally not just nationally." While as a biological species humans are continuing to evolve, now moving into the twenty-first century, this evolution is driven as much by our culture and as by our genetic makeup, by the emergent forms of bio and nano technology we've invented. Characterized as "transhuman" or "beyond human," a way of thinking inspired by Nietzsche's ethical vision of *Übermensch*. Portrayed in *Thus Spoke Zarathustra* (1883) as a vison for humanity, an idea of a powerful human being, an 'overman' who transcends the boundaries of classes, creeds, and nationalities, thereby overcoming human nature itself. Moving into the twenty-first century, it seems the thoughtful spectre of Nietzsche's *Übermensch* invades contemporary thought, namely, as a model of a "superior humanity" found in transhumanism.

This one-dimensional scientific way of thinking about humanity, with its accompanying atheistic denial of our human spiritual resourcefulness found in our "capacity for transcendence," was adopted by the German metahumanist philosopher Stefan Lorenz Sorgner in his seminal article "Nietzsche, the Overhuman, and Transhumanism," a discussion of Nietzsche and European post humanist philosophies published in the January 2010 issue of the *Journal of Evolution and Technology*. As a contemporary form of philosophical and intellectual thought about being human, "transhumanism" promotes the enrichment of humanity as an ethical issue, especially found in the enhancement of our natural span of life and our capacity for knowledge, using emergent forms of biotechnology. An evolutionary inspired scientific way of thinking about humanity, whereby human beings as biological organisms may transform themselves into a "new concept of human," using advanced forms of scientific and biotechnology, complemented by the promotion of "transitional" lifestyles and futurist worldviews.

Approached from this Nietzschean perspective these "posthuman beings" are somehow "super" or "above" what is normally attributed to being human, with an enriched form of being human, whatever that may be, with greatly extended and enhanced capacities and abilities. This contemporary scientific way of thinking was based on the evolutionary thought of Sir Julian Huxley (1887–1975), whereby he announced a new era of technologically enhanced human beings with superior intelligence, strength, and perception such that they "transcend" the limitations of human nature, outlined in his 1957 essay wherein he coined the expression "transhumanism." Originally titled "New Bottles for New Wines," set against the increasing accumulation of new scientific knowledge which has generated a "new understanding of the universe" Huxley promotes "the fullest realization of man's possibilities, whether by the individual, by the community, or by the species in its processional adventure along the corridors of time."

A way of thinking taken up by the *National Geographic Society* (1888), a global non-profit organization committed to "exploring, illuminating and protecting the wonder of our world," in the publication of a series of discussion pieces on the "theory of evolution," a shortened form of the expression "theory of evolution by natural selection," culminating in the publication *The Next Human: Taking Evolution into Our Own Hands* (2017). Based on their observations of how different biological forms of animate life adapt to their natural environment, a theoretical mechanism for genetic change was co-proposed by the leading evolutionary thinkers of the nineteenth century, Charles Darwin (1809–82) and Alfred Russel Wallace (1823–1913), the former having read Wallace's essay "On the Tendency of Varieties to Depart Independently from the Original Type" (1858).

Addressing the use of ideas to explain how organisms change emerged during the 1880s, the *National Geographic Society* directs attention to the pioneering thought of Anaximander of Miletus (c. 610–547 BC), who speculated about the beginnings and origin of animal life. Currently, few would disagree on the growing power of technology to modify humanity, with its increasingly powerful ability to transform humanity by enhancing our physical and mental capacities, a claim used as a convenient approach to understanding contemporary society, a way of thinking accepted by the Christian Transhumanist Association. Set against this contemporary background, we can appreciate the contribution offered by conciliar humanism in response to the perennial question, "what is human," approached through the human person's "journey of conscience," found in the recognition of our God given capacity as human beings to exercise free will through personal "choice."

While the human species has been approached as "the culmination of a grand experiment of nature that we call life," in the opinion of the Australian biologist Jeremy Griffith, wherein we find nature's most astonishing creation, "the human mind," currently environmental issues dominate twenty-first-century discourse, such as whether the possibility of nuclear war, overpopulation, starving millions, species extinction, family breakdown or despair, even sickness. However, he considers these symptoms of a deeper problem, namely, to better understand the human condition: "While 'human nature' appears in dictionaries, 'human condition' doesn't," a remarkable claim made by

Griffith in his introduction to *Beyond The Human Condition* (1991). Wherein he rejects the traditional claim that human nature is somehow immutable and being human is rather a symptom of a condition, what he calls "the human condition," furthermore, that this condition will disappear once it is relieved. Namely, quoting his words, "through a journey that explores the biology of the human condition" and by an examination of the source of our current distress, understanding ourselves, "our upset state or nature or condition."[7]

Original thought which supports the opinion of the American biologist and naturalist, Edward O. Wilson (1929–2021): "the human condition is the most important frontier of the natural sciences." Taken from *Consilience: The Unity of Knowledge* (1998), which together with *The Meaning of Human Existence* (2014) are Wilson's most philosophical works, wherein we find a multidisciplinary conversation about being human, to better understand the aesthetic and ethical implications found in the underlying assertion: "the person who appreciates Michelangelo's art is still capable of murder."[8] Written by Tim Macartney-Snape, the Australian professor of sustainable design from the University of Wollongong (1951) as a Foreword to *Beyond The Human Condition* (1991), written by Jeremy Griffith as a sequel to his seminal *Free: The End of the Human Condition* (1988). The questionable ethical orientation and essential ambiguity found in this way of thinking is indicated by the first word used in the title. Namely the word "free" and the accompanying freedom found in the performance of supposedly good and evil actions, or lack of it, as these contemporary scientists strive to understand the meaning of "human transformation" through the use of biology, the science of life, expressed by Griffith in the words, "the human species must surely be the culmination of this grand experiment of nature that we call life."

An original way of thinking characterized as "the breakthrough biological explanation of the human condition, expressed in *Transform Your Life and Save the World—Through the Dreamed Of Arrival of the Rehabilitated Biological Explanation of the Human Condition* (2016): a very lengthy title for a very short book, written in response to a "world in crisis" by Jeremy Griffith, founder of the World Transformation Movement (1983), taken from his address to the June 2016 launch of FREEDOM at the Royal Geographical Society in London. Claimed as a

---

7. Griffith, *Beyond the Human Condition*, 22–23.
8. Griffith, *Beyond the Human Condition*, 11.

"sensational world-shaking and spectacular world-saving" account about human behavior, *Transform Your Life* is a condensation of the thought of this remarkable scientist who has devoted his career to understanding and documenting the primal paradox which informs "humanity," understanding the ethical tension occasioned by the exercise of freedom, the choice embedded between our "good and evil afflicted human condition," expressed succinctly in the words of Tim Macartney-Snape. However, notwithstanding the originality of this overt scientific orientation, little critical thought is directed to a consideration of how to achieve "the psychological rehabilitation and transformation of our species" which is necessarily affected through the biological explanation of the human condition. While Griffith certainly rehabilitated the ethically nuanced expression "transformation" within contemporary discourse as a means to better understand our humanity, others have adopted a broader multidisciplinary approach, which includes the spiritual and personal life of being human, found in the tenets of conciliar humanism.

34

Together in Christ

As ALWAYS, THERE IS another side to thinking in the postmodern era. Wherein our received notions of what and who we are as being human are critically scrutinized, and in doing so we find further opportunities to rethink our humanity, "to open our eyes to new ways of being human" in the words of Ms. Julie Clague, a lecturer from the Department of Theology and Religious Studies at the University of Glasgow (1451). And I would add, being human together with God in the Person of Christ. While obviously a theological way of thinking, this was approached from a philosophical perspective during the Council.

A process of rethinking taken up by a group of international scholars, philosophers, theologians, and social scientists, who were tasked with "re-imagining human," the theme of the 17 Biennial Conference of the "International Society for Religion, Literature and Culture," held in the medieval university city of Leuven, during September 2014 under the auspices of the *Katholieke Universiteit Leuven* (1425). This world-famous institution of higher learning and scientific research retains an illustrious reputation for its continued multidisciplinary promotion of the study of humanity, found in the international journal *Humanistica Lovaniensia* (1928). A series of monographs on the history of humanism at Leuven, especially pursued in the *Collegium Trillingue* (1517), established under the patronage of the fifteenth-century humanist Hieronymus van Busleyden (c. 1470–1517) where the classical languages of Latin and Greek, as well as Biblical Hebrew were used for instruction. Thinking within this ethos of Christian higher education, known for its capacity to reflect on the mysterious yet revelatory nature of being human, this Biennial conference took up the challenge of retrieving a sense of humanity living in our postmodern world. As it recalled the initial experience of disenchantment following the Great War (1914–18), characterized as "emblematic of the catastrophes that shattered every humanist illusion in the twentieth century."

Guided by *Anthropos*, this interdisciplinary Research Group of fundamental theologians and theological ethicists attached to Leuven's Faculty of Theology and Religious Studies, assumed a postmodern approach wherein no definition was taken for granted, with the deliberate omission of the definite article, and invited those attending to rethink their ideas of being human. An approach similarly adopted by members of the faculty in a series of essays published under the title *Questioning the Human: Towards a Theological Anthropology for the Twenty-First Century* (2014). A subject later taken up during the 2019 December Conference of the International Red Cross and Red Crescent meeting in Geneva, "on being human now and in the future," to promote the "power of humanity," whereby once again we return to the fundamental question "what is humanity and what is the power behind this slogan?" Critical questions asked and answered by Hugo Slim, a British academic, trained theologian, and author of *Humanitarian Ethics: The Morality of Aid in War and Disaster* (2015), who worked as a research fellow at the Centre for Humanitarian Dialogue in Geneva. Writing in his 2019 blog post "Humanitarian Action/Humanitarian Principles/Identity" Slim identifies three different meanings of humanity, which reflect different dimensions of a contemporary understanding of humanity discussed by the American historian Bruce Mazlish (1923–2016) in *The Idea of Humanity in a Global Era* (2009), namely, "humanity as a species," "humanity as ethical behavior," and "humanity as global identity." Wherein we find the anthropological, sociological, and what I understand as a "theological" orientation found in preference to a global or universal orientation found in twenty-first-century thought. A way of thinking wherein we can access the legacy of conciliar humanism.

Approached as a remarkable network of thoughtful connections thinking about our shared humanity, conciliar humanism emerged as the consequence of an extraordinary moment of *sapiential* consciousness which drew attention to three basic ideas. Namely a discussion of "conscience" as informed by the anthropological orientation found in the Council's understanding of "human person," the related sociological orientation found in the idea of "participation" as it informs the Council's idea of a "community of persons," interrelated ideas which are ingeniously brought together within the Council's idea of "human solidarity," as being expressive of our shared human access to God, should we choose through the Person of Christ, wherein we find the theological orientation of conciliar humanism. Original thought found in this "symphony of ideas" which speaks to the distinctive character, that "something more" found within a Christ centred integral philosophical understanding of our shared humanity found in the 'human person.' Wherein we find the legacy of conciliar humanism in conversation with certain trends associated with twenty-first-century thought.

Living together in this so-called "post Christian" world where everything is permitted, the gauntlet is certainly thrown to those who share religious faith to rethink our identity as being a human person as a first step, an essentially philosophical task towards this conversation. Whereby, in light of this faith filled thinking about our shared humanity, to recover our philosophical awareness of being drawn together with God as human beings expressed in the idea of "human solidarity," approached theologically as an instance of Incarnational soteriology. Namely, the Council's promotion of a renewed sense of our personal Christ centred and Incarnational understanding of our shared humanity in dialogue with contemporary thought. As Pope Francis observes, "in our times, divine Providence is leading us to a new order of human relations which, by human effort and even beyond all expectations, are directed to the fulfillment of God's superior and inscrutable designs," writing in his Apostolic Exhortation *Evangelii Gaudium* (2013), whereby "the joy of the gospel fills the hearts and lives of all who encounter Jesus" (para. 84).

Understood as "being together with God" as human persons, these highly original ideas found in conciliar humanism direct our attention to a renewed awareness of our "being" human, namely, what makes us truly and genuinely human. A way of thinking which directs attention to the Council's original understanding of the human person's "journey of conscience" as a shared moral and religious interaction between human persons socially oriented within a "community of persons," one which provides thoughtful access to God through the recognition of what Scheler describes as the "sphere of the Absolute," an integral component of being human. Understood as a constitutive feature of the human person, both individual and communal, defined by the capacity for transcendence, wherein we find our human "openness to God through the Person of Christ" who is lovingly encountered living together in human solidarity.

This Christ centred integral philosophical understanding of our shared humanity was recently reflected in the thought of Pope Francis. Once again quoting from *Evangelii Gaudium* (2013) wherein he claims those who encounter Jesus "accept his offer of salvation are set free from sin, sorrow, inner emptiness and loneliness," para. 1, as expressed in the religious art, *Descent from the Cross* (1435) and *In His Image* (1967)

While in the opinion of Christian Smith "we humans are perhaps the most mysterious of all to ourselves," conciliar humanism affords the theoretical, especially philosophical means to better understand the distinctive and characteristic awareness of "something more" which informs the human enigma. Approached as "an orchestra that performs well" conciliar humanism represents a thoughtful legacy, one recognized by Pope Francis on April 4, 2017 when he used these words in his address to participants attending a Conference to celebrate the fiftieth anniversary of Pope Paul VI's encyclical *Populorum Progressio* (1967), organized by the Dicastery for Promoting Integral Human Development (2016). A department of the Roman curia which combined the work of four Pontifical Councils established following the Second Vatican Council, especially that of Pontifical Commission *Justitia et Pax* institute by Paul VI on January 6, 1967 which "in a certain way applies to the teaching of the Council" found in the tenets of conciliar humanism.

Approached by Pope Francis as an instance of "transcendent humanism," one which is ordered to the Creator, "united with the life-giving Christ," conciliar humanism speaks of the "harmonious integration of our human nature." A vision of humanity based on "the deep thought and reflection of wise men" in search of a new humanism, one which will, in the opinion of Pope Paul VI, enable our contemporaries to enjoy the higher values of love and friendship, of prayer and contemplation, a means to self-understanding which marks the "transition from less human conditions to truly human ones." While recording the attention the Council gave to understanding the nature of the Church, "with herself and with her relationship of union with God, but with man—man as he really is today" in his summation on December 7, 1965, in the opinion of Pope Paul VI, the Council addressed "the religion of the God who became man," rather than "the religion (for such it is) of man who makes himself God." Found in conciliar humanism, the former represents a "new type of humanism," found in an original Christ centred integral philosophical vision of our shared humanity, which was focused on, in the words of the pope, "humanity's ever twofold facet, namely, man's wretchedness and his greatness, his profound weakness—which is undeniable and cannot be cured by himself," an enigma resolved in the freedom we possess to recognize in "the human face of Christ, especially when tears and sorrows make it plain to see, the countenance of our heavenly Father," as the pope recalls the words of the Gospel: "he who sees me, sees also the Father" (John 14:9).

Now on the cusp of a new millennium, humanity's love story remains a concern shared by all, when once again like our forebears we search for an answer to "the mystery of humanity," to unravel the primal paradox of being human together. While the twentieth century was characterized by the "crisis of humanity," the twenty-first century is characterized by what Pope John Paul II in *Veritatis Splendor* (1993) described as "*the crisis of truth*" (para. 34). Whereby he addressed living in a postmodern world, one characterized by unprecedented levels of uncertainty and by unbridled secular relativism, the consequence of the absence of the Christian God. Wherein "there are not truths, only interpretations" in the opinion of Daniel Dennett, the prominent American atheist and philosopher, named in 2004 "Humanist of the Year" by the American Humanist Association, one of the "Four Horsemen of New Atheism." An expression taken from sacred scripture, referring to figures in the Book of Revelation known as "Four Horsemen of the Apocalypse," the harbingers of the Last Judgement which we still await.

Little seems to have changed from the time of the Council when gauging the intellectual and cultural climate of our day as observed in the recent publication of a series of essays entitled *Philosophers and God* (2009). Written at "the frontiers of faith and reason" by a group of philosophers and theologians in response to what they call the continued "popular polemic against theism" living in a world wherein "aggressive secularism" and "secular humanism" remain our critical opponents as found in *The God Argument: The Case against Religion and for Humanism* (2013). Written by the prominent British philosopher A. C. Grayling, the founder of New College of the Humanities (2011) in London and someone commonly associated with a new form of Godless thinking, a contemporary movement known as the "Fifth Horseman of New Atheism." An expression used to describe the current way of thinking found among some twenty-first-century atheists, coined by the British journalist Gary Wolf in 2006, a journalist for the *New Statesman* (1913), a leading British political and cultural magazine "of the Left and 'sceptical' politics." Namely, the British evolutionary biologist Richard

Dawkins, the American philosopher and neuroscientist Sam Harris, the Anglo-American Christopher Hitchens (1949–2011), and Dennett, who collectively use rational arguments to criticize and reject all forms of superstition, religion, and irrationalism. Current forms of thinking which Jacques Maritain characterized as "an active struggle against everything that reminds us of God" writing in *The Range of Reason* (1953).[1]

Defined as "the belief that God does not exist," approached historically 'atheism' emerged as a "modern phenomenon," as a way of thinking that denies the existence of a personal God"[2] in the words of Cornelio Fabro (1911–95), the Italian Catholic priest and scholastic Thomist philosopher. One which the Council specifically addressed in *Gaudium et Spes* in response to the claim concerning "the human incapacity to say anything about God" (para. 19), an incapacity initially discussed in terms of our human capacity for natural theology during the First Vatican Council. Now during the Second Vatican Council, following its distinctive human agenda, the many shades of meaning associated with this phenomenon were discussed, demonstrating the challenge to generalize about atheists. Broadly characterized, these either make a deliberate choice to deny any belief in the existence of God or gods or choose to reject the content of religious teachings, especially pertaining to the Christian idea of God as being inherently unreasonable, untenable, and irrelevant, wherein the Council finds significance in the word "choice" in its human context. A mindset which informs thinking in an era of unbridled secular relativism characterized by the absence of the Christian God, wherein 'there are no truths, only interpretations' in the words of Daniel Dennett, the prominent American atheist and philosopher.

Years later this expression was used by Greg Epstein, the Humanist Chaplain at Harvard University (1636) for his book *Good without God: What a Billion Nonreligious People Do Believe* (2010) in response to these "New Atheists." Approached as a more benign way of thinking found within secular humanism, rather than the former hostility and intolerance directed toward organized religion which characterized previous forms of aggressive atheistic humanism during the twentieth century which "defied" the Council, and which set the parameters for a constructive response understanding our shared humanity which generated the idea of 'human solidarity' in conciliar humanism. These

---

1. Maritain, *Range of Reason*, 104.
2. Fabro, "Atheism," 25.

contemporary forms of atheism reflect a positive approach to human life as a socio-secular phenomenon, informed by humanistic values and morality, found in the practice of tolerance, and an awareness of life shared as members of a society of equals, an ethical stance living without God following the thought of Nietzsche.

Set against this twenty-first-century intellectual background wherein "western societies today are coming unmoored in the face of an earth-shaking ethical and cultural paradigm shift, summarily expressed as 'what it means to be human and how are we meant to live.'" So begins the promotional blur for *Healing Humanity: Confronting Our Moral Crisis* (2020). The publication of a series of essays by a group of Orthodox Christian scholars who gathered in the spring of 2019 in response to the ethical crisis which speaks to "the world of today." A critical situation generated by an adherence to a way of thinking expressed by the words "good without God," the motto used for the Humanist society. Words which emerged through a survey held in 1965 by the British Humanist Association, formerly known as the Union of Ethical Societies (1896), to design a logo for the humanist movement, as a universal symbol which signifies a commitment "to non-religious people who seek to live ethical lives on the basis of reason and humanity."

Established to counter the current "war on God," the religiously inspired web site, "Jasper and Sardine" took up the phenomenon of "transhumanism" which it characterized as "corrupting the image of God." Although described on this site as "the world's most dangerous idea," this biological approach to understanding humanity, which seeks to utilize all available scientific and technological resources to eliminate the natural aging process and to optimize our human intellectual, physical and psychological resourcefulness to achieve a "posthuman future," probably "provokes more ridicule than fear." However, this resolutely atheistic ideology contains certain religious aspirations, as observed by Michael Cook, when he cites the vision of Zoltan Istvan, the American futurist, transhumanist philosopher and author of *The Transhumanist Wager* (2013). Inspired by Pascal's original use of the idea of a wager, he defines this approach to humanity as "the radical field of science that aims to turn humans into, for lack of a better word, gods." That is, by assuming the creative role of God through our use of science to enhance humanity. This marks a curious development for Cook when he observes: "While many prominent scientific thinkers want to abolish

God and treat man as one beast amongst many, transhumanists want to abolish evolution and create God (or gods)."

The appearance of *Healing Humanity* (2020) raised a few contemporary eyebrows. Written as a counter-cultural critical response to living in a postmodern situation, wherein Western thought is portrayed by the authors as being increasingly "unhinged and unmoored." Especially as humanity continues to be disenfranchised from its religious inspired philosophical foundations in the face of earth-shaking scientific, ethical, and cultural paradigm shifts, such as the separation of gender from biological sex, or the promotion of "a smorgasbord of lifestyles." All of which calls into question the traditional answers concerning our identity as human beings being *imago Dei*. Unpredictable circumstances which still demand clarity of thought, not only concerning moral issues we encounter, but also the articulation of the philosophical foundations within which these are to be approached. A way of thinking found in conciliar humanism and its network of three basic ideas "human person," "community of persons," and "human solidarity." Wherein we find its legacy based on the theological premise that it is only though our participation in the life of the Incarnate Person of Christ, Son of God who became human, that we can find the necessary healing of our shared humanity, portrayed in the religious art of the twentieth century, *In His Image* (1967) by Wllliam Zdinak (1925–93), the Slovakian born American commercial illustrator.

The well-informed awareness of these Orthodox Christians in response to the challenges arising from the current state of confusion and chaos living in a postmodern world is shared by many contemporaries, such as the author of this book, characterized as a "solidarity of purpose." A critical awareness found in the thought of Julene Siddique, a Fellow of the World Academy of Art & Science (1960), driven by her recognition of "interacting forces both systemic as well as social" in the opinion of someone "at the cutting edge of research and innovations taking place in the music—health—and culture interface" writing in her 2018 article "The Emerging New Paradigm of Education: Critical Knowledge for Critical Times." Confronting these circumstances requires more than knowledge, namely, we need "critical thinking coupled with constructive creativity" by people with "personal strength and integrity based on values and belief in a higher purpose." Aspirational words which might well have come from the thought of someone infused with *sapiential* consciousness.

Inspiration for her way of thinking was drawn from an address given on June 3, 2013 by Kassym-Jomart Tokayev, the former Kazakh diplomat, and United Nations Under-Secretary General, during a conference held at the UN headquarters in Geneva, "Opportunities and Challenges for the Twenty-First Century—Need for a New Paradigm," organized in conjunction with the World Academy of Art and Science. Amid changing political, economic, and social balances, wherein new dynamics have come into play, as the Under Secretary observed in his words "moving centres of gravity, from east to west, and from north to south." However, at the same time, amid this relocation there was also the experience of "increasing division and distrust among communities—both ethnic, religious and national" wherein the human family seems "more distant from one another," found in the growth of extremist rhetoric and activity based on religious and ethnic hatred. All of which generates the question, "can humanity realize the apparently conflicting goals of prosperity, security, sustainability, and social justice?"

Attentive to this critical situation wherein the world confronts multiple crises, each of which appears intractable and resistant to resolution, the World Academy of Art and Science (1960), under the honorary presidency of the Croatian nuclear and particle physicist Ivo Šlaus, sought an effective solution to meet all of these challenges facing humanity today through a series of sponsored conferences and workshops between 2013 until 2017 which examined the "root causes of these multiple challenges" in order to formulate "an integrated perspective from which to develop a comprehensive strategic policy framework," one found in the network of ideas which constitute conciliar humanism. Drawing inspiration from the French Catholic philosopher Étienne Gilson, a colleague of Jacques Maritain who worked together to promote lived Thomism, the World Academy of Art and Science was founded on December 24, 1960, as an international non-governmental scientific organization, a global network of scientists, artists, and scholars drawn from more than ninety countries, numbering distinguished fellows of the Academy such as Arthur C. Clarke (1917–2008), the English science-fiction writer, author of *2001: A Space Odyssey* (1968), Sir John Eccles (1903–97), the Australian neurophysiologist, Abraham Maslow (1908–70), the American psychologist, Yehudi Menuhin (1916–99), the American Lithuanian born violinist, and Margaret Mead (1901–78), the American cultural anthropologist.

Established under the auspices of the UN Economic and Social Council in the immediate aftermath of World War II by concerned scientists and academics who had witnessed the potential for the ongoing destruction of humanity by its own hand. An early concept for the foundation of the academy was proposed in an article in *Time* magazine on published on October 1, 1938 by Étienne Gilson, which was taken up during the 1940s. Written shortly before the German invasion of Poland on September 2, 1939, when the so-called "last French humanist" wrote an article *"Erasme: citoyen du monde"* whereby Gilson sought to understand the circumstances for the forthcoming war in order to avoid these by means of a peaceful resolution. In so doing he drew inspiration from Desiderius Erasmus of Rotterdam (1466–1536), the Dutch Catholic humanist, philosopher and former teacher at Leuven's *Collegium Trillingue*, by quoting his words: "[who] wanted to end all wars and to liberate men to work out their salvation in the context of personal freedom," this goal was achieved by a form of education which fostered the acquisition of moral virtue through the integration of thought from the writings of the Roman writers Cicero (106–43 BC,) the Stoic philosopher Seneca the Younger (4 BC—AD 65) and the teachings of Christ.

This integral way of thinking was developed by Gilson between 1932 and 1946, when he gave a series of courses at the *Collège de France* (1530), located in Paris near the *Sorbonne*, the University of Paris (1150), including "the foundations of medieval realism" and "origins of medieval humanism" (1936), in preparation for a series of lectures at Harvard University (1636) in Cambridge, Massachusetts, between August 29 and September 2, 1936 on "'Medieval Universalism' and Its Present Value." Whereby he adopted a similar philosophical approach found in his colleague's *integral humanism*, the other foremost French interpreter of the writings of Aquinas. Approached differently, from a historical existential, rather than a sociopolitical perspective, but with same God centred orientation, Gilson was convinced that "medieval universalism," as a form of human thought with foundations in rationalism, realism, personalism and the philosophical quest for "truth universal in its own right," contained the thoughtful ingredients which promoted "the ultimate health of the human condition" and "the best antidote to the venom of war," foundations for the attainment of personal freedom. Following its outbreak on September 2, 1939, he continued his usual practice of lecturing between continents, when he returned to North America which afforded him further opportunity to explore this original way of thinking about humanity in a series of public lectures, "Roman Classical Culture from Cicero to Erasmus" at Harvard and at Toronto's Pontifical

Institute of Medieval Studies, which he had founded in 1929, based on the Christian premise that philosophical analysis was best approached within the context of the lives of those who lived it. Thinking by those infused with the same *sapiential* consciousness.

Over the remarkable course of human history, we continually evolve as human animals that naturally think and live together, but we still remain animals, a salutary observation thinking in the twenty-first century. Nevertheless, understanding the natural evolution of being human, clouded with mystery as being comprised of both "body and soul," Francis Fukuyama writing in *Our Posthuman Future: Consequences of the Biotechnology Revolution* (2002)[3] recognized "the intimate connection that exists between human nature, values, and politics" which defines *human nature* as "the sum of the behavior and characteristics that are typical of the human species, arising from genetic rather than environmental factors,"[4] later characterized as "Factor X," whereby he strips away a person's contingent and accidental features to reveal "the essential human quality underneath," which the Council finds in the human person. Understanding this revelatory process Fukuyama refers to original source of this idea, namely Pope John Paul II's recognition of an existential "ontological leap," wherein the natural evolutionary process which informs being human as essentially material and biological was radically transformed through the acquisition of a living spiritual soul by a deliberate intervention from outside. Namely, through a personal act of creative love by God, revealed as an all creating and loving Being. This definitive Divine intervention makes a world of difference, as recognized in conciliar humanism.

Critical of the traditional mechanistic explanations of humanity, based on an 'either or' way of thinking, the English theoretical physicist and Anglican priest, John Polkinghorne (1930–2021) recognized this transition to the personal within an integral understanding of the human being, directed towards what he characterized as "a realm of experience in which testing has to give way to trusting,"[5] namely, approached from the "whole realm of human experience," which recognizes the spiritual dimension of being human, found in living together within the religious community wherein we find, in his words, "the chance of a personal experience, an encounter with the sacred reality of God." Found in the

---

3. Fukuyama, *Our Posthuman Future*, 149–50.
4. Fukuyama, *Our Posthuman Future*, 129–30.
5. Polkinghorne, "Belief in God in an Age of Science," 10.

recognition that the "search for truth" informs "both" science and religion, during his talk given on October 29, 2003 as part of the series "Conversations from Socrates in the City." Wherein this Cambridge priest scientist acknowledged a different level when asking questions of meaning and purpose, which are based on the use of trust rather than testing, what he calls "*meta-questions*—questions that take us beyond," namely, about understanding religion and our human nature. As he claims concerning the latter, personal relationships are built on trust and are seriously undermined when these are submitted to critical scrutiny by one of the parties involved, whether human or Divine.

Thinking within the legacy of conciliar humanism, while the realm of the spiritual is "not something that can be observed in the same way," the pope considers this realm equally accessible through philosophical analysis and critical reflection on what he calls "a series of very valuable signs of what is specifically human life," found in what might be approached as traditional characteristics of the person, "the experience of metaphysical knowledge, of self-consciousness and self-awareness, of moral conscience, of liberty, or of aesthetic and religious experience" (para. 6). Wherein 'experience' is the critical word for this professional phenomenologist and prelate from Kraków infused with *sapiential* consciousness.

35

Loving in God

LIVING IN A POSTMODERN world hurtling towards a superhuman future, whether we like it or not—this is the opening premise which informs *Future Superhuman: Our Transhuman Lives in a Make-or-Break Century* (2022). Having negotiated the existential crises of the twentieth-century, humanity is not indifferent to the forthcoming challenges for human beings living in the twenty-first century "with global warming, novel and bioengineered pathogens and unaligned AI," as we take on a life filled with "promise and peril." Remarkable words coming from "a love letter to humanity, though an unconventional one" written by Elise Bohan, a Senior Research Scholar at the University of Oxford's Future of Humanity Institute, who wrote the first book-length history of "transhumanism." Characterized as "corrupting the image of God," this twenty-first-century way of thinking has been described as "the world's most dangerous idea," whereby the denial of God found in twentieth-century atheistic humanism set the scene for the re-emergence of this biological approach to humanity found in secular transhumanism. Previously characterized as a wager, a radical way of thinking whereby humanity replaces the creative will of God through the unprecedented use available scientific and technological resources to eliminate the natural aging process and to optimize our human potential, our intellectual, physical, and psychological resourcefulness. To achieve this "posthuman future," recalling the thought of Comte, humanity assumes the creative role in place of God. A way of thinking which probably provokes more ridicule than fear, characteristically dismissed as "uploading one's brain onto the internet [which] seems to defy common sense."

By way of a generalized response, it appears the traditional understanding as a thinking animal, *Homo sapiens* which emerged from within a religious philosophical mindset, under current circumstances seems on unsteady ground, remarkably insufficient living in an entertainment driven world inhabited by humanoids, alien beings with a body structure generally like that of a human being, like a real person or like biological mutants who exhibit superhuman abilities or qualities. In the media driven world of the twenty-first century more influenced by science fiction rather than science, how can we assess these beings who are "suspiciously human?" A world view critically challenged by Donovan Riley, the American Lutheran pastor and conference speaker, in his essay "21st Century Digital God," wherein he claims "our smartphones, tablets, and laptops tempt us to enter into a virtual world without flesh and blood," rather than turning to God in the act of personal prayer to ask for all we need, we turn to the various forms of social media, as he claims: "A new god for a new, digital age."

However, engaging these critical circumstances Riley envisages an opportunity, perhaps understood as a moment of trust, when he asserts that "it's time for Christians to close our laptops and shut off our smartphones" at least for a moment and ask "what good is social media really doing for me, my relationships, and my overall well-being?" While access to social media can be of great benefit, spiritually speaking it is no substitute for an authentic encounter with a concrete, real Saviour, perhaps it's time to "return to our first love, our God and Savior, the man Jesus Christ, who comes to us through concrete words, water, bread and wine in a real place he calls, 'The Church.'" Evocative thought from the author of *Crucifying Religion: How Jesus Is the End of Religion* (2020).

Taking up the postmodern gauntlet, conciliar humanism offers a thoughtful response in thinking "what and who we are" as an essentially philosophical task infused with *sapiential* consciousness, as a first step in faith filled thinking, following a logic of trust which leads to the awareness of God, through the incarnate Person of Christ, namely, through a logic of discovery. Wherein following the thought of St. Augustine, we discover the presence of God Who is already within us, articulated in his *Confessions*, though of course Being God, essentially different. Namely, by means of critical thinking within the tradition of lived Catholic Christianity infused with *sapiential* consciousness, wherein Truth represents itself in manifold ways, especially found in the human face of the crucified Christ, the combined philosophical and pastoral orientation found conciliar humanism as a network of original ideas represents a "good news story" for everyone, approached as "a beacon of hope" in the words of the Council. Furthermore, it represents an opportunity for dialogue with those living in "the world of today," marked by an openness of mind towards other human minds who might think differently, and to that of God approached using Sacred Scripture and Tradition. Whereby together as a community of human beings living in "human solidarity" we continue to "grapple with the age-old questions," living in constantly changing environments wherein we find new opportunities "to speak the truth in the mode of that which the receiver can receive it," to paraphrase the insightful thought of Aquinas "teacher of humanity." Namely, found in "the truth about the human person" which reflects a radical and innovative way of thinking about our shared humanity speaking to humanity, expressed in the concluding words of *Gaudium et Spes* "Christians can have nothing more at heart than to be of ever more generous and effective *service to humanity* [emphasis added] in the modern world" (para. 94).

Approached within the context of conciliar humanism, Fukuyama's "Factor X" is encapsulated in the expression "whole human person" taken from the *Catechism of the Catholic Church*, para. 36. The result of the Council's original Christ centred integral philosophical understanding of our shared humanity, its belief in humanity, as an integrative way of thinking about our common humanity which brings together the modern understanding of the self-aware and self-sufficient modern "person," now used to describe an individual human being "who" is a biological sentient being, a "what" with an immortal spiritual soul, understood as a multi-dimensional being equally capable of conscious rational thought, self-awareness, with an emotional life directed towards others in ethical and religious activity.

However, "you can't have it both ways, there are irreconcilable differences," was the remarkable claim made by Richard Dawkins, author of *The God Delusion* (2006), in his article for the *Skeptical Inquirer* (August 1999). Thought which marks the continuation of the ideological battle between the use of science and the claims found in Catholic thought as the twentieth century began. Now writing in its final years, the noted atheist responds to Pope John Paul II's message to the Pontifical Academy of Sciences on October 22, 1996, the anniversary of the opening of the Council. Directing attention to the pope's helpful recognition of the presence within human life of "a different ontological order," the consequence of a so-called "ontological leap," which informs the transition between physical and spiritual realms of being human, found in the human person. The moment in the evolution of humans when according to Dawkins, "God intervened and injected a human soul into a previously animal lineage," whereby humanity assumed the status of a thinking species of animal or *Homo sapiens*.[1]

The presence of "a different ontological order," one of a philosophical rather than scientific orientation, informs the Council's recognition of an integral understanding of the human person, one approached as being "nutritional," which speaks to the state of the person's well-being as a value oriented consumption of a variety of activities directed towards the enhancement of our humanity, which contribute to our personal openness, especially our capacity to think about God and our capacity for transcendence. Thereby the pope seeks to disengage "the great ontological discontinuity" found in the traditional dualistic separation between "body and soul" in Platonic and later Cartesian philosophical thought with its emphasis on the significance of the latter over the former, the spiritual aspect of human nature. Set against the apparent "irreconcilable differences," the tension between contemporary atheistic and Christian ways of thinking about humanity assumes significance as the former characterized as "good without God" promotes a material biological being approached through a scientific methodology, whereas the latter, an integral understanding of a human being with a God given immortal soul can be approached through philosophical analysis.

Namely, the awareness of the human being as essentially multidimensional, who as a human person operates on another level, that "something more" which incorporates the spiritual and personal dimensions in being human. An understanding which informs the human predicament in having the capacity to choose, to exercise freedom, and to choose to think about God, or not to do so. Thinking philosophically on the ontological level the human person is essentially irreducible and unapproachable outside the confines of personal love; however, thinking within an "integral" understanding, the human person as a material and bodily being remains accessible to study from the perspective of science.

Approached as a "beacon of hope," conciliar humanism is offered by the Catholic Church under the guidance of the Holy Spirit, as an original form of thinking about "the noble calling of humanity" in the

---

1. Dawkins, "You Can't Have It Both Ways," 62.

words of the Council, it remains the forgotten legacy of the Council. Defined as "being a unity of body and soul," wherein our physical dimension engages the impersonal elements of the material world through our bodily life; this unity also includes the intellectual and spiritual nature of the human person, through the exercise of the human mind, the consequence of an extended moment of *sapiential* consciousness "which gently draws the human mind to seek and love what is true and good," reflecting the influence of Augustine, whereby the mind is lead "through visible realities to those which are invisible." Namely, living in a world characterized by progressive improvements in scientific technology, through the necessary exercise of wisdom "to humanize its new discoveries" as detailed in *Gaudium et Spes*, para. 15

"God created man in his own image, in the image of God he created him, male and female he created them" (Gen 1:27). The opening lines in the Bible, whereby humans are recognized as being created "in the image of God," as the concluding part of an account of creation that God continually calls "very good," wherein we find the inherent dignity of human nature. A way of thinking taken up in the *Catechism of the Catholic Church* (1992), which was officially promulgated on October 11, 1992 by Pope John Paul II in his Apostolic Constitution *Fidei depositum*, published to mark the thirtieth anniversary of the opening of the Second Vatican Council. Prepared to incorporate Conciliar thought, which begins with "the life of Man—to know and love God," following what I call a "logic of discovery," whereby we find, expressed in the words of the Prologue, "God, infinitely perfect and blessed in himself, in a plan of sheer goodness, freely created man to make him share in his own blessed life," in so doing, "God draws close to man" (para. 1). However, the means to accomplish this salvific task is the belief in a "soul" received from God, defined in the *Catechism* as "the immaterial dimension or essence of a human being." To accomplish this task, "when the fullness of time had come," God sent his Son as Redeemer and Saviour, who then chose apostles which he sent forth, commissioned to proclaim the Gospel: "Go therefore and make disciples of all nations" (Matt 28:18–20).

As such, "God draws close to man. He calls man to seek him, know him, to love him with all his strength. He calls together all men, scattered and divided by sin, into the unity of his family, the Church," aspirational words taken from the Prologue to the *Catechism of the Catholic Church* (1994) which speak of the mutual reciprocity found in personal love between the Divine initiative and our human response lived within a community of faith, a mutuality shared in an unsolicited act of reciprocal love. Documented in the canonical structure of the Genesis creation narratives in chapters 1 and 2; notwithstanding the obvious textual differences found within them, they communicate a coherent theological vision about the wisdom of God the Creator, the goodness of creation and God's purposeful design for humanity, expressed within the activity of mutual love. Being created "in the image and likeness of God; male and female he created them" (Gen 1:26–27), these words determined the theological concept of *imago Dei* as the source of the dignity of human life, the basis of Catholic social teaching as it emerged towards the end of the nineteenth century. A way of thinking especially championed by the popes of the twentieth century.

Unlike the origins of other ancient religions, those of Christianity came to be understood as distinctively personal. The former found in some form of heavenly or spiritual intervention, an intellectual process of enlightenment or infusion of learning as the means of salvation, found in Gnosticism, a second-century quasi-religious movement and way of interpreting reality which persists to this day. Whereas Christian faith was initiated in response to God's unconditional creative love, embedded within a decisive and revelatory event, understood as a personal encounter with the Incarnate Word, the Person of Jesus Christ, wherein the earthly Jesus invited his disciples to follow him: "I am the way and the truth and the life. No one comes to the Father except through Me" (John 14:6), an approach made through mutual love. Approached as a philosophical way of thinking about our shared humanity, conciliar humanism represents an innovative Christ centred approach, a reasonable way of thinking accessible to both "believers and unbelievers alike." Based on understanding the distinctive human activity of personal love, originally discussed by Max Scheler, wherein we find the meaning of human existence as the foundation of conciliar humanism, captured in the words of Pope Benedict XVI: "Jesus' entire earthly existence, from conception to death on the Cross, was a single act of love." Words he used to introduce his understanding of *Jesus Caritas*, "Jesus Love," the subject of his Angelus address on September 25, 2005.

Ever the consummate theologian, the recently elected pope explores this thought through the lens of these words which I have already quoted: "God's love can become concrete and can almost be experienced in history with all its painful and glorious vicissitudes," circumstances which characterize the enigma of being human. These words were later quoted by his successor Pope Francis in his Closing World Youth Day homily on January 27, 2019 during the final open-air mass in Panama City's Metro Park. Reflecting on the thought which begins Jesus' public ministry, found in the Gospel of Luke (4:20–21): "today it has been fulfilled," Pope Francis speaks to the "now of God" revealed in the humanity of the person of Jesus, through his face and flesh, "a face that is fraternal and friendly, concrete and familiar," a way of thinking generated by mutual love which encapsulates conciliar humanism. However, philosophically speaking, it is difficult to understand Christ's "new commandment" to love which moves simultaneously in several directions towards God, our neighbor, and one's enemies, and by implication oneself, not to mention commanding love in the first place.

Building on the biblical inspired understanding of love as directional, the more theologically nuanced Johannine metaphysical claim "God *is* love" only exacerbates this situation wherein the identity of God is found within the activity of mutual love, with its distinctive emphasis on action rather than being an entity, whereby the nature of God is understood as a verb rather than a noun, expressed as *actus essendi* in the original words of Aquinas. Thinking within this religious philosophical context, our finite human being was lovingly and purposefully created *ex nihilo* by a loving God who takes the initiative, loving us first and from within this relationship, the one who loves knows God. A spiritual journey of self-disclosure narrated by the "greatest Christian thinker" in his famous *Confessions*, written between 397–400. The syncretism which informs early Christian thought as it absorbed pagan ideas only compounds this spiritual distinctiveness with the emergence of two competing notions of love, the Platonic *eros* and the Johannine *agape*.

A subject discussed by the Oxford lay theologian C. S. Lewis (1898–1963) in his publications *The Allegory of Love: A Study in Medieval Tradition* (1936) and *The Four Loves* (1960), based on a 1958 series of radio talks on the BBC. Beginning with the Johannine claim "God is love," wherein Lewis speaks of "gift-love," epitomized by God's love for humanity, he then approached the nature of love from Greek philosophical and Christian perspectives, moving from passionate love (*eros*), human affection or friendship, to "brotherly love" (*philia*), to the unique form of Christian love found in charity (*agape*). Commenting on this particular relationship based on love, the Munich Catholic philosopher Romano Guardini (1885–1968) observed in *Freedom, Grace, and Destiny* (1948), "from the moment I know my personal existence to be "God's handiwork, I experience the encounter of another person 'in God.'" Set against this Augustinian background, we can understand the existential significance of Scheler's original expression *amare in Deo* as it informs the legacy of conciliar humanism, found in the mutual love shared between the individual human person, the community of persons and our human solidarity lived together "in" God.

"More than a feeling, that's the power of love," words which express the wonder and resourcefulness of humanity found in the enigmatic yet wonderous character of personal love, a distinctly authentic phenomenon associated with being human and being together; defined by a set of instructions, humanoids are incapable of taking the risk of authentic love or a breakdown of trust. However, as a human phenomenon personal love can be "messy" and prone to misunderstanding. Originally entitled "do you believe in love" (1982) for the first top-ten hit for the American rock band Huey Lewis and the News, the title "The Power of Love" was later used as the soundtrack for the 1985 blockbuster film *Back to the Future*.

Prototypically ambiguous, love informs the very fabric of our human lives as individuals and as social beings, and following Christ's original commandment to love God and neighbor, love lies at the heart of Christian life.[2] Within these circumstances, love has been characterized by the American psychologist Bernard Murstein (1929–2020) as "an Austro-Hungarian Empire uniting all sorts of feelings, behaviors and attitudes, sometimes having little in common."[3] Narrated in sacred scripture as the principle of God's saving action and the believer's response lived in the religious community, understood as a love story wherein humanity is saved, a narrative encapsulated within the network of ideas found in conciliar humanism.

Thinking as a Christian theist and realist inspired by the thought of Augustine, Scheler claims in his essay "*Ordo Amoris*" (1914–15) "prior to our being an *ens cognitans* or an *ens volens*, the human is a loving being, an *ens amans*."[4] Considered the *leitmotiv* of his philosophical thought, Scheler indicates the direction of his nascent philosophy of love, the driving force behind his critical exchange with Nietzsche with his claim: "*Our heart is primarily destined to love*, not to hate," wherein Scheler reveals the influence of Augustine's "philosophy of the heart." In the opinion of

2. Carroll, "Deceptive Ambiguity," 156–208.
3. Murstein, "Taxonomy of Love," 33.
4. Scheler, "*Ordo Amoris*," 110–11.

Margaret R. Miles, Harvard professor of Historical Theology, "Augustine was the first Christian author to begin his thinking and writing with an analysis of human experience," namely, approached from a consideration of human "restlessness" which informs his *Confessions*. A way of thinking later taken up by the French philosopher Blaisé Pascal with his original claim of the existence of an *ordre du coeur*, an "order of the heart" whereby he contrasts this intuitive knowledge found in personal love as being inherently reasonable which operates according to its own reasons, with traditional deductive thought which operates according to the rational principles used in logic and mathematics. All of which informs the philosophical background to Scheler's critical engagement with Friedrich Nietzsche's subversive assertion in *Assorted Opinions and Maxims* (1879): "'*Love*'—the subtlest artifice which Christianity has over the other religions is a word; it spoke of *love*."[5] As Scheler claimed in his essay "Love and Knowledge" (1915): "Augustine expressly made love the *original* power of movement of the divine as well as the human spirit."[6]

Given these current circumstances, living in the twenty-first century, the question persists as to the possibility of participating in the perennial search for the *why* of human life, namely thinking in an intellectual milieu generated by atheistic nihilism and cultural relativism wherein *anything goes;* if God is dead, everything is permitted? A situation further aggravated by an aggressive "Beyond Christ" mentality,[7] which has infiltrated every aspect of contemporary culture, with the dismissal of traditional systems of Christian thought and practice as intellectually irrelevant, misguided, or simply not interesting; perhaps the postmodern world is characterized by lack of interest and indifference!

---

5. Nietzsche, *Assorted Opinions and Maxims*, in *A Nietzsche Reader*, 172.
6. Scheler, "Love and Knowledge," 149.
7. Williams, *When Anything Goes*, xiv.

36

A Thoughtful Legacy

Moving into a new millennium, recognized as "indispensable for living," the distinctive human phenomenon identified by the capacity to choose, remains a critical issue for ongoing discussion, which speaks to the "something more" about being human, found in the activity of the human person characterized as ethical and religious. Wherein we find the legacy of conciliar humanism as a celebration of our God-given human capacity to exercise freedom, the foundation of compassionate ethics and religious life. Understood as an observance of humanity in action, whereby we encounter the person of Christ through this activity as we literally look into the human faces of those looking back, living around us as our sisters and our brothers; in the words of Pope Francis: "God invites us to evaluate and choose. He created us free and wants us to exercise our freedom" during his weekly general audience in Paul VI Hall on September 1, 2022.

Taking ownership of this thoughtful legacy, the pope found inspiration in Jesus' response to Phillip's request "to show us the Father" recorded in the Gospel of John, which the pope extended to understanding humanity as such: "to remember how in everyone we can and must recognize the countenance of Christ" (14:9). In so doing the Council offered an invitation to humanity to rediscover God in the narrative of mutual and reciprocal love between persons, to lovingly "follow a score shared by all" in the pursuit of wisdom, "which gently draws the human mind to seek and love what is true and good" in the words of *Gaudium et Spes*, para. 15.

A way of thinking which characterized the subsequent thought of Pope John Paul II during the twenty-six years he occupied the Chair of St. Peter as a faithful shepherd and teacher: "Help the Pope and all those who wish to serve Christ and with Christ's power to serve the human person and the whole of mankind." Expressive words prayed during his inauguration as pope on October 22, 1978, which marked the anniversary of the opening of the Second Vatican Council and which directed the subject of his inaugural encyclical written "at the close of the second millennium," *Redemptor Hominis* "the Redeemer of Man, Jesus Christ," published on March 4, 1979. Recalling the theme of ecclesial consciousness "as a loving mother of all men," previously outlined by Pope Paul VI in his encyclical *Ecclesiam Suam* published on August 6, 1964, wherein he showed a mindset which seeks renewal through the employment of "dialogue," the new pope used this encyclical to outline the ingredients of conciliar humanism which would inform his pontificate, namely its Christ centred integral philosophical understanding of our shared humanity, fallen and redeemed through the salvific action of Christ suffering and death, wherein "the human person is *from* and *for* God in Jesus Christ" (para. 9), expressed in the religious art, *Descent from the Cross* and *In His Image*.

More than seventy years on from one of the most seminal moments in Catholic history, the concluding words of Pope Paul VI at the end of the Council continue to challenge the inattention of contemporary Catholic scholarship "to recognize our own type of humanism," especially as a means of thoughtful dialogue with the "world of today." While conciliar humanism emerged in response to the twentieth-century "crisis of humanity," its legacy is best approached from within a renewed understanding of *being human*, living through the twenty-first-century *crisis of truth* and its impact on understanding our humanity within the postmodern malaise of relativism, scepticism, and excessive individualism, a consequence of the ongoing denial of our human capacity to know the truth.

Originally used within a pre-modern theological context, the idea of 'person' received philosophical significance within modern thought pertaining to a human being's self-awareness in possession of a particular identity, which was integrated within conciliar humanism as the "human person," wherein "human" is employed within the scientific biological term used to describe a sentient being who is also a "person," namely, a spiritual being in possession of a soul. Whereby the Council employs a complex form of philosophical reflection to describe a human being who is conscious of an identity in the modern sense, capable of rational thought and emotional activity, but also someone in possession of a spiritual soul, someone capable of personal love and religious belief, ingeniously subsumed within the original expression "human person," as an integral understanding of being human.

While this expression remains the emblematic product of Conciliar thought, this is embedded within a comprehensive philosophical understanding of our shared humanity found in conciliar humanism, one which not only recognizes our personal life lived with other human persons, understood as a "community of persons," but also our personal openness to God shared with other human persons, found in the idea of "human solidarity." While incorporating the insightfulness of Maritain's social philosophy, this way of thinking reflects the particular philosophical influence of Scheler's original understanding of the "communal person" discussed by Wojtyła in *Person and Act*, wherein he claims, "a person is both an individual subject and the subject of a community," later published as "The Person: Subject and Community" (1976).

Set against this background, Pope John Paul II seeks the recovery of universal truth about the good, accessible through human reason, as he introduces his encyclical *Veritatis Splendor* (1993): "Truth enlightens man's intelligence and shapes his freedom, leading him to know and love the Lord. Hence the Psalmist prays: 'Let the light of your face shine on us, O Lord' (*Ps* 4:6)." A companion piece to *Evangelium Vitae* (1995), written by the former professor of Christian ethics at the Catholic University of Lublin (1918) between 1956 till his election as pope in 1978, devoted to the analysis of moral praxis, this complements his foundational philosophical book, *Person and Act* (1969). Written during the Council, wherein we find his understanding of "conscience," later defined as "a judgement of reason by which the human person recognizes the moral quality of a concrete act" in the *Catechism of the Catholic Church*, para. 1796.

As a remarkable human phenomenon, the exercise of conscience remains an enigma for many; in the face of confusion as to its meaning, whether understood as an "inner voice" or some form of Freudian "superego" which makes us aware of conventional social standards, the pope sought conceptual clarity about the nature of conscience, one consistent with the philosophy of Aquinas wherein we find the legacy of conciliar humanism, "taking hints from the past," understood as an "act" of the human person. Namely, conscience represents the exercise of the human person's act of practical intelligence, found in the judgement of reason based on moral truth and value, "to do good and avoid evil." Wherein we find the manifestation of the person's capacity for transcendence as the revelation of our inherent human spirituality directed towards another person, whether finite or Divine. Addressing what Wojtyła calls the "journey of conscience" as a moment of transcendence, within the context of moral theology, the pope identifies the extreme consequences of its denial, namely, once the idea of a universal truth about the good, accessible using human reason is denied, "this individualism leads to a denial of the very idea of human nature," whereby we find ourselves confronted by a series of unrelated "better or worse interpretations" found in postmodern thought. In response, Wojtyła offers a way of thinking which informs how we think and act as a human person, wherein "each individual is faced with his own truth, different from the truth of others" in the words of *Veritatis Splendor*, para. 32. Written in response to the "radical opposition between moral law and conscience, between nature and freedom" which captures the spirit of postmodern thought and its individualistic ethic, the pope once again reveals his indebtedness to the seminal thought found in *Gaudium et Spes* and *Dignitatis Humanae*, wherein we find the Church's understanding of the dignity of human nature, envisaged as the "human person," an integral unity of "body and soul," one which affords an opportunity for thoughtful engagement with the "world of today," wherein we find the legacy of conciliar humanism.

The consequence of taking "hints from the past," this original way of thinking about our shared humanity represents an original appropriation of three ideas, "conscience," "participation," and "solidarity," initially discussed by Wojtyła in *Person and Act*. Whereby the pope recalled his original understanding of the "journey of conscience" and its anthropological orientation as an "act of the human person" and its human connection embedded within the Council's understanding of a "community of persons."

While the idea of "human person" was found within emerging papal thought on social justice, the idea of a "community of persons" was unprecedented, an instance of original thought generated during the Council, especially though the influence of Wojtyla's familiarity with Scheler's innovative use of a thoughtful distinction devised by the German sociologist Ferdinand Tönnies' (1855–1936) influential *Gemeinschaft und Gesellschaft* (1887), wherein he distinguishes between "community" and "society." A way of thinking recently found in *Living Together: Combining Diversity and Freedom in 21st-Century Europe* (2011), a report of a group of "eminent persons of the Council of Europe" based on the premise that "relationships" are essential in understanding our human identity, that our human connections with other people are fundamental to our physical, mental health and wellbeing.

While much has changed since the time when Tönnies' classical form of social analysis was used by Scheler, this fundamental distinction remains relevant; expressed colloquially, "there is something artificial about being a member of a 'society' I choose to join," such as a trade union or political party comprised of other skilled or likeminded persons, whereas there is something organic and personal about the bonds which unite a "community" into which I am received and for which I am prepared to offer my life, such as within a family, a nation or a church. Expressed philosophically, these human communities express a relational ontology, one which connects the human being living together with other beings, as synthesis of anthropological, sociological, and theological concerns found in twenty-first-century discourse. Expressed by the formative idea of living within a "community of persons," being human, being together with other human beings, and being together with God. Exemplified by means of the Council's original understanding of "conscience" as an activity within the moral life of the individual human person, based on the Council's innovative use of the idea of "participation."

While Wojtyła's 1977 lecture "Participation or Alienation" drew attention to the Platonic origin of the former, found in *Parmenides* (132d, 151e) and *Symposium* (510, 511a), he was indebted to the original research of Cornelio Fabro (1911–95), the Italian scholastic Thomist philosopher, author of *The Metaphysical Notion of Participation according to St. Thomas Aquinas* (1939), which initiated a revival of twentieth-century Thomistic thought. Whereby he drew attention to the significance of "participation" in Aquinas' metaphysics of goodness, found in his doctrine of God's goodness discussed in the *Summa Theologica* (1,q.6), which relates to Aquinas' original doctrine of creation, wherein he claims that "all things are good by participation in the divine Goodness" including humanity, whereby Fabro affirms "God as the foundation and goal of human existence itself."[1] While drawing attention to the reawakened interest in the use of 'participation' among

---

1. Dodds, "Introduction," ix.

Thomists, its broader significance lies in Fabro's lifelong interest in the "question of God," which haunts "every human life and every age of human history" as he claims in *God: Introduction to the Theological Problem* (1953) and his confrontation with the problem of modern atheism, found in *Introduction to Modern Atheism* (1964).

Publications well known to Wojtyła, these form the broad background to this lecture, wherein he detailed his emergent philosophy of the human person found in his original use of what he calls the "attitude of participation" compared with the recent idea of "alienation" or "estrangement" employed within both Hegelian Absolute idealism and atheistic Marxism. Employed in the latter to understand human nature as being self-alienated, an insufficient material being awaiting transformation through the productive process found in the working class or proletariat. Another instance of "taking hints from the past," Wojtyła recalls Aquinas' understanding of the connection between the Aristotelian act-potency with the Platonic idea of participation, which informs his original idea of *actus essendi* to better understand the Being of God. In so doing, recalling Conciliar thought found in *Gaudium et Spes* which he presumably worked on, Wojtyła now employs the idea of "participation" in support of his claim that "human acts are performed 'together with others.'"[2] As such, the sociological orientation found within a "community of persons" naturally leads to the Council's original idea of "human solidarity," and its implied theological orientation, whereby we gain access to the Triune God as human persons.

Was COVID-19 just the beginning? The last few years of this pandemic have reminded us that humanity is far from invincible. While we may be the most powerful sentient beings living on Earth, incredibly intelligent and resourceful as *Homo sapiens*, however, just like the great civilizations in the past, we have also succumbed to the natural limitations and weaknesses we share as human beings. Confronting this global health crisis, understood as "a human crisis that calls for 'solidarity'" in the opinion of the Portuguese diplomat Antônio Guterres, the ninth secretary-general of the United Nations, speaking on March 19, 2020 who sought to explore the shared awareness of the social implications arising from this existential crisis, one which unites human beings, wherein "our human family is stressed, and the social fabric is being torn. People are suffering, sick and scared" in the words of Guterres.

---

2. Wojtyła, *Person and Act*, 377–78.

While the idea of "solidarity" is commonly associated with a sociopolitical movement of passive resistance founded by Lech Wałęsa, the Polish electrician and trade union activist from the Lenin Shipyard in Gdańsk, when he used this in the title of Poland's first "Independent Self-Governing Trade Union 'Solidarity'" in 1980, for a broad anti-authoritarian social movement to promote the issues of worker's rights and social change living under the Communist inspired Polish United Workers Party; however, this word was embedded within the broader human ethical context of Catholic social teaching, especially found in German thinkers.

Originally applied within nineteenth-century European sociopolitical thought as "solidarism," used to identify the "principle of social solidarity" promoted by the German Jesuit ethicist Heinrich Pesch (1854–1926), author of *Liberalism, Socialism, and Christian Order* (1900), the founder of the Solidarist school as a "bilateral type of social order," colloquially expressed as "one for all and all for one," a way of thinking which informed Pope Pius XI's social encyclical *Quadragesimo Anno* (1931). Later described as "the socio-philosophical corollary of the anthropology of Realism" by Franz H. Müller (1900–1994), the German sociologist and author of *The Church and the Social Question* (1984), an understanding originally employed by Scheler in his essay "The Reconstruction of European Culture," (1917) wherein he claims the states of Europe "must learn to act in *solidarity*, i.e., in conformity with the principle of mutual responsibility,"[3] thought first expressed in an address given in the Urania, a public educational institute and observatory built in 1909 in Vienna. Thought later employed by Scheler within his phenomenological understanding of the triadic structure found in religious experience, one which incarnates the individual person and community alike, directed towards the Absolute or Divine Person, a way of thinking developed in the Council's appropriation of the idea of "human solidarity."

Set against the natural disposition that "man exists and acts together with others," Wojtyła defines "solidarity" as an attitude, "a constant readiness to accept and realize the share that falls to each due to the fact that he is a member of a given community," furthermore, an attitude in "conformity with the principle of participation."[4] When this original thought is brought together, the idea of "human solidarity," taking ideas found in Scheler's phenomenological ethical personalism, offers as a way

---

3. Scheler, *On the Eternal in Man*, 410.
4. Wojtyła, *Person and Act*, 401.

of thinking about our personal access to God, found through sphere of the Absolute, a constitutive part of being human, which in faith we call the Triune God, namely, the theological orientation found in conciliar humanism. Namely, as finite individual human persons living together in a "community of persons," wherein together we are also directed in human solidarity towards God as Infinite Person through the activity of personal love. Characterized by Scheler as *amare in Deo*, an appropriation of ideas from Augustine's original Christian anthropology which formed the foundation of Scheler's original sociological demonstration of God's existence through a "logic of discovery," whereby he distanced himself from contemporary forms of Thomistic proofs.

Living in a postmodern world characterized by progressive improvements in scientific technology, conciliar humanism, the consequence of a necessary exercise of wisdom, offers an opportunity "to humanise its new discoveries." Embedded within this integral understanding of humanity, the Council concludes *Gaudium et Spes* with a discussion of "conscience," understood as "the most intimate centre and sanctuary of a person," approached through the exercise of "genuine freedom" which informs the practical judgement of conscience made by the human person, one which offers the means of personal access filtered through the sphere of the Absolute with God as Divine Person, a manifestation of the Divine image in humans living as a "community of persons." Concluding this thought, the Council draws attention to the ultimate enigma of being human, namely death and the fear of "perpetual extinction," which is overcome through the restorative action of "an all-powerful and merciful saviour," "being in communion in Christ" (para. 18). A remarkable way of thinking about the idea of our shared human nature gifted by the Church as "the universal sacrament of salvation." Thinking in this context, conciliar humanism is best approached through "living in the eyes of others," looking into the "face of the other" within a community of persons who not only embrace Christ, portrayed in the religious art of van der Weyden, but also reflect His human image as portrayed by William Zdinak.

As such, conciliar humanism represents an original network of ideas, found in the Council's understanding of "conscience" which speaks to our identity as an individual human person, through "participation" which speaks to the our human identity lived with other human beings within a "community of persons," and our "human solidarity" which informs this shared awareness that as human beings we not only exist as individual persons with a particular consciousness and identity, but also as inherently social personal beings accessible to other persons through the mutual act of revelatory love. A remarkable way of thinking whereby we chose to reveal our identity to others including God through the bond of personal relationships, based on trust, wherein "truth lies in the eye of the beholder." Reflecting the orientation of conciliar humanism, truth is found in the face of a person "Jesus Christ, the true light that enlightens everyone."

37

A Vision of Humanity

GIFTED BY THE CHURCH as "the universal sacrament of salvation," conciliar humanism is best approached as something wondrous, characterized as "living together in the eyes of others" through the connected ideas of the human person's act of conscience, through our loving participation as members of a community, bound together through the recognition of our human solidarity, our shared awareness as being in God's presence. Drawing these ideas together, as human beings we are formed and informed by our social interactions and personal relationships with others including those with God. Wherein we find a truthful vision of humanity which is accessible to all people, found in the human person who we are, generated by the Church's mandate "to contemplate the 'mystery of the Word Incarnate' in whom 'light is shed on the mystery of man,'" in the much-quoted thought of *Gaudium et Spes*, para. 22. Recalling the introductory words of *Veritatis Splendor* (1993): "Truth enlightens man's intelligence and shapes his freedom, leading him to know and love the Lord. Hence the Psalmist prays: 'Let the light of your face shine on us, O Lord'" (Ps. 4:6).

Not for the first time the pope used a public address to promote the legacy of conciliar humanism, found in these seminal ideas taken from the Pastoral Constitution, which he helped to draft as a Council father, acknowledged during a general audience the previous year on November 8, 1995. Approaching the thirtieth anniversary of *Gaudium et Spes* he used this occasion to explore the "legacy of this conciliar Constitution," namely, the confirmation that the destiny of humanity is definitively revealed "in the light of the crucified and risen Christ" (para. 2), an instance of Incarnational soteriology. Understood as the "means to embrace the world" while "looking at men in the light of Christ" the pope envisaged the significance of this document, which somehow reflected the "apex of the Council's journey" as "a sort of 'Magna Carta' of human dignity to be safeguarded and promoted" (para. 9). Ideas the pope explored the following year during his address to the assembled Academy of scientists on the limitations of the explanatory value of evolution. As such, accessing the legacy of conciliar humanism is best approached through the thought of one of its major proponents, Pope John Paul II.

"Man is the only creature on earth that God wanted for its own sake," whereby "the human person" has an irreducible value of one's own. These words express the orientation of Christian thought which informs conciliar humanism and its constitutive network of three ideas which Pope John Paul II recalled in his "Message on Evolution" (para. 5) to the plenary session of the Pontifical Academy of Sciences on October 22, 1996, on the anniversary of the opening of the Council. Defined as "intelligent and capable of free will," the human person is understood as someone "capable of entering into relationship, of communion, of solidarity" with others like himself, who are called into a "loving relationship with God himself." Now recalling the scriptural wisdom, as he concludes his Message, which informs a better understanding of the "highest forms of existence" found in humanity, the pope drew attention to his previous encyclical *Evangelium vitae* on "the value and inviolability of human life," published on March 25, 1995, the traditional Feast of the Annunciation.

Narrated in Luke's Gospel (1:26–28), this documents the liberating encounter between the angel Gabriel and Mary, a virgin living in Nazareth, Galilee, betrothed to a man named Joseph, wherein we find the liberation of humanity initiated through the Incarnation and birth of Christ, wherein God reveals to us the dignity of human life. Approached from the perspective of the conciliar humanism's recognition of "a community of persons," the Annunciation represents a twofold encounter, one which celebrates God's entrance into the human world through Jesus, the Incarnate Word, and Mary's willingness on behalf of humanity to accept God's saving plan, all of which sets the climactic scene portrayed in van der Weyden's *Descent from the Cross*, wherein the community of faith embraces and supports the crucified lifeless body of Christ. Namely, the consequence of Jesus' death, his sharing the lowliest and most vulnerable conditions of human life our mortality embraced by those around him, whereby he makes human life the instrument of our salvation. As the Son of God Christ reveals the priceless value of human life, the foundations for building a *culture of life* which penetrates every part of human society, as an answer of ongoing significance.

Initially established in 1603, the Pontifical Academy of Sciences was re-founded in 1936 by Pope Pius XI (1922–39) to promote progress in the mathematical, physical, and natural sciences, and the study of related epistemological issues. Now celebrating the sixtieth anniversary of the Academy, Pope John Paul II takes up Pope Pius XII's (1876–1958) engagement with the doctrine of "evolutionism" in his encyclical *Humani Generis* (1950), which sought to counter "some false opinions" which threatened Catholic doctrine, as an opportunity to move beyond the various "theories" concerning human evolution, the "diversity of explanations of the mechanism of evolution" and "the diversity of philosophies involved," and to address the underlying truth concerning "the conception of man" (para. 5). While approached within the domain of observable nature, the "spiritual realm" found in human life, which is inaccessible through scientific observation but approachable through philosophical reflection on "a series of very valuable signs," wherein we find the Council's original understanding of the human person. Defined as "being a unity of body and soul," the integral understanding of humanity envisages the biological and physical dimension of being human, the impersonal elements of the material world shared with other forms of animate life through our bodily existence, which also incorporate the rational and spiritual nature of the human being, found in the exercise of the mind, brought together within the "whole human person."

A product of an extended moment of *sapiential* consciousness, conciliar humanism represents a distinctive form of shared philosophical awareness, with its God centred, synthetic and unitive orientation, generated through the original thought of millennial thinkers in Catholic tradition, namely, Augustine's Christian anthropology, Aquinas' metaphysics of participation found in *actus essendi*, and Woytła's original understanding of the human person, which informed the fundamental ideas of this original way of thinking about our shared humanity, "human person," "community of persons," and "human solidarity," which constitute the thoughtful legacy of conciliar humanism as a "beacon of hope," offered by the Catholic Church under the guidance of the Holy Spirit, about "the noble calling of humanity," one hitherto unrecognized. This way of thinking found in conciliar humanism informs the irreducible and integral character of the human person, as a rational being through the use of reason, as an emotional being through the exercise of free will, and as a social being, someone capable of "entering into relationship, of communion, of solidarity of the gift of himself to others like himself," and ultimately, to "enter into a loving relationship with God himself." Thought taken up in this Address which invokes the Council's renewed interest in the theme of the image of God, found in *Gaudium et Spes*, and man's fundamental orientation to God, recognized as the "basis of human dignity and the inalienable rights of the human person" (para. 21).

Personally awakened to the true nature of our shared humanity through the influence of sociopolitical forms of humanism, the Egyptian born American literary theorist Ihab Hassan (1925–2015) extended this thought by the observation: "humanism may be coming to an end as humanism transforms itself into something one must helplessly call posthumanism." Another philosophical and intellectual way of thinking which promotes the improvement of the human condition, especially our longevity and cognition, through ever sophisticated forms of emergent technology, as discussed in the *Journal of Posthuman Studies* (2017). Original thought which once again ask the question, "will robots make good friends" typically asked by human beings living in the twenty-first century, let alone trusting in a Personal God? A response found in the legacy of conciliar humanism. An understanding which offers a vision of our shared humanity within a threefold personal connection hitherto undiscussed. Based on the truthful recognition of what it means to be a human person, the dignity of human life and the meaning of and desire for love shared with other human beings and with God, "burning for love," these Conciliar ideas have consequences. Namely, the recovery of thoughtful connections found between biblical anthropology and Christology, particularly enriched by Karol Wojtyła's philosophical appropriation of ideas taken from both the medieval synthesis of the "teacher of humanity," and original ideas from Scheler's ethical personalism, whereby we still have much to learn from conciliar humanism. Understood as an emergent way of thinking about the integrity of being human in our personal exercise of "conscience," the recognition of our "responsible stewardship" as physical beings sharing a common world with other physical beings, and of our communal identity shared with other human beings as human persons, which reflects our radical likeness to the triune God, wherein we find the legacy of conciliar humanism.

Humanism remains reliably persistent. Notwithstanding the provocative claim *Humanism in Ruins* (2019) made by Asli Igsiz, the American professor of Middle Eastern and Islamic studies at New York University, used for her book subtitled *Entangled Legacies of the Greek-Turkish Population Exchange*, approached as a way of thinking about being human. While her sociopolitical account of the demise of liberal humanism delivers "an urgent message about the politics of difference" living in a postmodern world marked by "the reincarnation of fascism," there is merit in an alternative approach. One found in the legacy of conciliar humanism which offers a valuable contribution, found in a Christ centred integral philosophical understanding of our shared humanity. One based on the call of the Gospel for the promotion of peaceful coexistence found in mutual respect that we give to each other as human beings.

While the popular expression "we are all in this together" spoke to our collective sense of connection as vulnerable human beings during the COVID-19 pandemic, conciliar humanism builds on this shared awareness with an emphatic, "we are not alone," living together with each other in human solidarity, and if we choose, together with God. Original thought graphically captured by William Zdinak (1925–93) in his religious art *In His Image* (1967), a remarkable depiction of the crucified head and shoulders of Jesus crowned with thorns. While this book began with van der Weyden's graphic *Descent from the Cross*, the religious art of this American artist, somewhat less familiar, concludes this book as a celebration of our shared humanity in Christ. Namely, as individual human persons living within a community of persons in human solidarity, perhaps the sense of Christian personalism originally intended by Wojtyła for the Council. Received as a "message of salvation for everyone" living in a world which at times seems radicalized and unequal, conciliar humanism and its remarkable network of three interrelated ideas has much to offer.

While the depiction of Jesus in pictorial form was controversial in the early Church, due to the "flow on" effect of the Jewish prohibition of "graven images" in the Decalogue, the earliest surviving Christian art is found on the walls of Rome's ancient catacombs from between the second and fourth centuries, such as the third-century fresco of the 'Good Shepherd' in the Catacomb of Saint Pope Callistus (218–222/3) in the cemetery of Calepodius on the Aurelian Way, a favorite image of mine which I saw during a visit to Rome. However, notwithstanding emergent differences within the practice of Christianity, over the centuries a standardized physical appearance was generated, one recognizable by all, as portrayed by van der Weyden. Interestingly, these images of Jesus generally show the ethnic characteristics which match the culture in which the image has been created, such as a bearded Caucasian male portrayed in *Descent from the Cross*.

However, given the general assumption that Christians have always "contextualized" Jesus in their own image, what are we to make of the religious art of the Slovakian born American commercial illustrator Zdinak? An original study which I understand to express the Christ centred integral philosophical understanding of our shared humanity found in the tenets of conciliar humanism. As a remarkable synthesis of three original ideas within a network of thoughtful and lived personal connections found in those around us. As we look into their faces and they look in return, through the eyes of faith we look together at "the human face of Incarnate truth" lived in human solidarity.

As a portrayal of our human solidarity, *In His Image* remains an artistic expression of extraordinary originality incorporating the faces of others, known and unknown. With only a blank canvas in front of him, in a moment of frustration following numerous failed sketches, a vision of faces came to the artist which constitute the image of the Divine Person found in the numerous faces of these human beings he has recalled. In the words of his son Matthew Zdinak "what followed was a 15-hour marathon session to complete the painting that he titled *In His Image*,"[1] a piece of religious art to be auctioned the next day to raise funds for the local Catholic church charity drive. While operating within a Christian setting it may be assumed this is the bearded head and broad shoulders of the crucified Jesus crowned with thorns, however, upon closer scrutiny, this image is simply formed by multiple human faces. Whereby this art receives universal significance as a celebration of our shared humanity expressed as human solidarity at its most diverse embraced by the crucified Christ, and in so doing, captures the spirit of conciliar humanism, the consequence of the Council's pastoral outreach to a broken and wounded humanity living in the "world of today."

While there is no direct evidence to support this connection with the Council, as a practicing Catholic from the local parish of Our Lady of Fatima in the town of Wilton in Connecticut, William would certainly have heard about the Council in the local news, perhaps through his wife Mary or their seven children who went to the local parish primary school, and he would have experienced its practical effects during the

---

1. Zdinak, "In His Image," 17.

celebration of the Sunday mass in his local parish church. Indications which inform a remarkable, perhaps mysterious symmetry between his religious art and the original ideas which constitute conciliar humanism, a celebration of our shared humanity, the philosophical consequence of a pastoral Council following its human agenda.

An agenda recalled by his inclusion of numerous human faces which constitute when placed together the face and shoulders of the suffering Christ, such as the two popes who had convened the Council, saints John XXIII and Paul VI, along with other prominent contemporary Catholic figures, notably John F. Kennedy (1917–63), America's first Catholic President who was sadly assassinated during the Council on November 22, 1963, also the popular media personality, commonly recognized as "one of the first televangelists," the Venerable Bishop Fulton J. Sheen (1895–1979), a postgraduate from Leuven's Higher Institute of Philosophy whose doctorate earned him "the Cardinal Mercier Prize for International Philosophy" in 1923, and finally, the Venerable Pope Pius XII (1939–58), an outspoken critic of all forms of racism as a "champion of humanity," these men of faith constitute a "community of persons" living and thinking in the tradition of Catholic Christianity.

Furthermore, as recognizable human beings they share a human solidarity with the much revered Indian lawyer and political ethicist Mahatma Gandhi (1869–1948) or American Baptist minister and leading figure in the civil rights movement, Dr. Martin Luther King Jr. (1929–68), all of whom in their own particular manner personify the Council's pastoral concern with social justice issues, or the innovative use of science by Dr. Jonas Salk (1914–95), the American Jewish medical researcher who developed one of the first successful polio vaccines. Incorporated within this religious art are also images of a personal nature, family images of his wife Mary, his three sons and a daughter and extended members of his family, all of whom constitute an indiscriminate assemblage of photos used by William to portray the human face and shoulders of the crucified Christ. As observed by the artist, "while there are recognizable faces, it really doesn't matter which persons are depicted. We are 'all one in Christ' as St. Paul has told us. Hurting one, we hurt all; helping one, we help all. That is the idea behind—'In His Image.'"

A depiction of the crucified head and shoulders of Jesus crowned with thorns, which recalls the evocative thought of *Gaudium et Spes*: "Since the human nature which was assumed in him was not thereby destroyed, it was by that fact raised to a surpassing dignity in us also. For by his incarnation the Son of God united himself in some sense with every human being" (para. 22). Expressed succinctly as "Christians [are] conformed to the image of the Son." Original thought of the Council, found in the network of three ideas which constitute conciliar humanism portrayed *In His Image*. Namely, the portrayal of Christ through the life of the individual human person, lived in a community with other persons in human solidarity, expressive of a structured purposefulness based on Gospel values.

Original thought, initially recognized by Scheler and appropriated by Wojtyla, which provided the foundation of conciliar humanism, and its network of ideas, human person, community of persons and human solidarity. Approached philosophically, from Aristotle onwards humans have been recognized as wilful, intelligent and social beings; however, during the seventeenth-century philosophers, like the Englishman Thomas Hobbes (1588–1679) directed particular attention to the study of how the human use of will influenced their social and political interaction, their forms of behavior, relationships, and institutions, as discussed in *The Matter, Forme, and Power of a Commonwealth Ecclesiasticall and Civil*, commonly known as *Leviathan* (1651), which concerns the structure of society and legitimate government, based on the self-interested consent of citizens. A way of thinking later adapted by Ferdinand Tönnies in his classic *Gemeinschaft und Gesellschaft* (1887), wherein he distinguished between two social groupings, based on the natural will *Wesenwille* and rational will *Kürwille*.

Whereby the former involved a judgement of the will concerning the intrinsic value or final end of an act rather than its practicality, whereas the latter involved a conscious choice of the means directed toward a specific end, pragmatic and purposeful. On the basis of this distinction, the natural will was found in the human 'community,' characterized by a universal sense of solidarity, which Scheler identified as either family, nation or Church or a combination of these, social groupings for which a person might be willing to sacrifice one's life, whereas human 'society' was based on a theory of social union through mutual agreement, through the exercise of choice, found in a 'social contract.' Set against these generalized observations, and the characterisation between something integral and organic, and something arbitrary and artificial, the religious art portrayed *In His Image* represents another remarkable synthesis, found in the use of family pictures, as well as pictures of recognizable Church and political figures, wherein we find the Council's recognition of our human solidarity, understood as a moment of structured purposefulness, found in the recognition of our shared humanity, "we are not alone."

Conclusion

"THE SECOND VATICAN COUNCIL enabled the light of faith to illumine our human experience from within, accompanying the men and women of our time on their journey of faith." Aspirational words taken from Pope Francis' inaugural papal encyclical *Lumen Fidei: On the Light of Faith* (2013; para. 6). An unprecedented papal document having been co-authored by his predecessor Pope Benedict XVI, it seemed somewhat fitting as I finish this unprecedented book which narrates the story of conciliar humanism. A celebration of our shared humanity, approached philosophically and pastorally, centred on the Person of Christ.

Conclusions always seem such an anti-climax, and often made in haste. Nowhere is this more apparent than attempting to bring to some form of closure a conversation which is deliberately intended to "open up" a subject hitherto undiscussed. Namely, to identify the complex philosophical and human connections which inform the original thought generated during the twenty first ecumenical Council of the Catholic Church. To explore the broad circumstances and personalities which serve as the background necessary to understand a remarkable "symphony of ideas." Composed during the Council, approached as an extraordinary moment of *sapiential* consciousness during the twentieth century. Whereby we can appreciate the genesis of this remarkable though hitherto neglected way of thinking about our shared humanity generated during the Council. Or in words taken from UNESCO *Courier* (2018–4) "[to] take a detour into the past to enable us to better orient ourselves in the future."

Now on the cusp of the Church's third millennium, there is still much to be learnt from the collective thought of this extraordinary moment of *sapiential* consciousness, encapsulated in the words from *Gaudium et Spes*: "to create a synthesis, or to preserve among men and women capacities for contemplation and wonder which lead to wisdom" (para. 55). A way of thinking certainly found in conciliar humanism as a means to better understand our shared humanity and to marvel at God's loving creation, approached through an original network of three interrelated ideas, human person, community of persons, and human solidarity. Wherein we find the Council's belief in humanity, one which leads to wisdom through understanding our shared humanity as God given and received.

"My dear people, let us love one another since love comes from God and everyone who loves is begotten by God and knows God" (1 John 4:7). Addressed to humanity, these Johannine words best express the spiritual orientation which inspired conciliar humanism as a "love story." Namely, that each human person is created in the image and likeness of God, and is loved by God, wherein we find that "something more" about being human which enables access to ourselves as a "human person," to each other within a "community of persons," and to God, the Divine Person through our "human solidarity." Namely, through a Christ centred integral philosophical vision of our shared humanity, approached as a "service to humanity" which emerged during the Second Vatican Council. One which affords the universal Church, approached as a communion of salvation, with the theoretical means for dialogue with the contemporary world, found within an integral vision of our shared humanity looking towards the future, into the human faces of our sisters and brothers with love, wherein we discover that we are not alone.

Built on the Council's recognition of our inherent capacity for transcendence, the something more about human beings directed towards others through the exercise of choice and in the activity of personal love, conciliar humanism represents "a good news story" constructed around the great insight of St. Thomas Aquinas, paraphrased in words worth repeating "to speak the truth in the mode of that which the receiver can receive it." Namely, a remarkable way of thinking about our shared humanity accessible to all, which represents a truthful and loving exchange undertaken in the language of our shared humanity. An evocative way of thinking inspired by the words of someone who became the great philosopher pope of the twentieth century: "Defend your humanity. This is the great heritage of Christianity, the great heritage of our faith: that we maintain high regard for mankind," heartfelt and aspirational words of Cardinal Karol Wojtyła during his pastoral visit to the village of Wiśniowa in southern Poland, on September 25,

1970 when he exhorted the young people to a truthful promotion of what we share in common, our humanity. An assertion whereby this leading Council father not only took up the challenge of Pope Paul VI, namely, to take seriously the original form of humanism which emerged during the Council, namely conciliar humanism, but more importantly, invites future generations to recognize its thoughtful legacy wherein we recover the profound awareness that living in the presence of God through Christ "we are not alone." A vision of humanity which continues to inspire, looking back into the future.

Bibliography

Ackerman, Diane. *The Human Age: The World Shaped by Us*. London: Headline, 2014.
Acosta, Miguel, and Adrian J. Reimers. *Karol Wojtyła's Personalist Philosophy: Understanding Person & Act*. Washington, DC: The Catholic University of America Press, 2016.
Adamson, Peter. *Classical Philosophy: A History of Philosophy without Gaps*. Oxford: Oxford University Press, 2014.
Aeschliman, Michael D. *The Restoration of Man: C. S. Lewis and the Continuing Case Against Scientism*. Seattle: Discovery Institute, 2019.
Allen, E. L. *Christian Humanism: A Guide to the Thought of Jacques Maritain*. New York: Herder & Stoughton, 1951.
Anselm of Canterbury. "Letter to Archbishop Lanfranc." In *Anselm of Canterbury: The Major Works*, edited by Brian Davies and G. R. Evans, 3–5. Oxford: Oxford University Press, 2008.
Appelby, David F., and Teresa Olsen Pierre, eds. *On the Shoulders of Giants*. Toronto: Pontifical Institute of Medieval Studies, 2015.
Aquinas, Thomas. *Summa Theologica*. Translated by the English Dominican Province. 5 vols. Notre Dame: Christian Classics, 1948.
Archer, Margaret S. *Being Human: The Problem of Agency*. Cambridge: Cambridge University Press, 2000.
Arendt, Hannah. *The Human Condition*. Chicago: University of Chicago Press, 2018.
———. *Love and Saint Augustine*. Chicago: University of Chicago Press, 1996.
Astley, Neil, ed. *Being Human*. Tarset: Bloodaxe, 2011.
Augustine. *The Confessions*. Translated by John K. Ryan. New York: Image, 1960.
———. *On Genesis*. Translated by Roland J. Teske. Washington, DC: The Catholic University of America Press, 1991.
———. *The Soliloquies*. Translated by Rose Elizabeth Cleveland. Boston: Little, Brown, and Company, 1910.
———. *Teaching Christianity*. Translated by Edmund Hill. Hyde Park, NY: New City, 1996.
———. *The Trinity*. Translated by Edmund Hill. Hyde Park, NY: New City, 1991.
Ball, Philip. *Universe of Stone: Chartres Cathedral and the Invention of the Gothic*. New York: Harper, 2008.
Balthasar, Hans Urs von. "On the Concept of Person." *Communio* 13 (1986) 18–23.

BIBLIOGRAPHY

Báñez, Dominic. *The Primacy of Existence in Thomas Aquinas: A Commentary on Thomistic Metaphysics*. Translated by Benjamin S. Llamzon. Proctorville, OH: Wythe-North, 2012.

Banning, Tim. *The Triumph of Music: The Rise of Composers, Musicians, and Their Art*. Cambridge: Belknap, 2010.

Barnhart, Bruno. *The Future of Wisdom: Toward a Rebirth of Sapiential Christianity*. New York: Continuum, 2007.

Barré, Jean-Luc. *Jacques and Raïssa Maritain: Beggars for Heaven*. Translated by Bernard E. Doering. Notre Dame: University of Notre Dame Press, 2005.

Barrett, William. *Irrational Man: A Study in Existential Philosophy*. New York: Anchor, 1990.

Barron, Robert. *Catholicism: A Journey of the Heart of the Faith*. New York: Image, 2011.

Belcher, David. "When Comedy Gets Better with Age." *The Glasgow Herald*, February 9, 2009.

Berlin, Isaiah. *Concepts and Categories*. Princeton: Princeton University Press, 2013.

———. *The Proper Study of Mankind: An Anthology of Essays*. New York: Farrar, Straus, and Giroux, 2000.

Berger, Lee, and John Hawks. *Almost Human: The Astonishing Tale of Homo naledi and the Discovery That Changed Our Human Story*. Washington, DC: National Geographic, 2017.

Billias, Nancy Mardas, et al., eds. *Karol Wojtyla's Philosophical Legacy*. Washington, DC: Council for Research in Values and Philosophy, 2008.

Blackburn, Simon. *The Oxford Dictionary of Philosophy*. Oxford: Oxford University Press, 1994.

Blondel, Maurice. *Action*. Translated by Olivia Blanchette. Notre Dame: University of Notre Dame Press, 1984.

Blondel, Maurice, et al. *A Monument to Saint Augustine: Essays on Some Aspects of His Thought Written in Commemoration of His 15th Centenary*. London: Sheed and Ward, 1930.

Boeve, Lieven, et al., eds. *Questioning the Human: Toward a Theological Anthropology for the Twenty-First Century*. New York: Fordham University Press, 2014.

Bochenski, Joseph F. *Contemporary European Philosophy*. London: Bloomsbury, 1982.

Boniecki, Adam. *The Making of the Pope of the Millennium: Kalendarium of the Life of Karol Wojtyła*. Stockbridge, MA: Marian, 2000.

Borghesi, Massimo. *The Mind of Pope Francis: Jorge Mario Bergoglio's Intellectual Journey*. Collegeville, MN: Liturgical Press Academic, 2017.

Bostrom, Nick. "A History of Transhumanist Thought." *Journal of Evolution and Technology* 14 (2005) 1–25.

Boyd, Malcolm, ed. *J. S. Bach: Oxford Composer Companions*. Oxford: Oxford University Press, 1999.

Boyle, Nicholas. *Who Are We Now? Christian Humanism and the Global Market from Hegel to Heaney*. Notre Dame: University of Notre Dame Press, 1997.

Brague, Rémi. *The Legend of the Middle Ages: Philosophical Explorations of Medieval Christianity, Judaism, and Islam*. Translated by Lydia G. Cochrane. Chicago: University of Chicago Press, 2009.

Bregman, Rutger. *Humankind: A Hopeful History*. Translated by Elizabeth Manton and Erica Moore. London: Bloomsbury, 2021.

Brezik, Victor B., ed. *One Hundred Years of Thomism: Aeterni Patris and Afterwards: A Symposium*. Houston: University of St. Thomas Press, 1981.

Brown, Peter. *Augustine of Hippo: A Biography*. London: Faber and Faber, 1967.

Buckley, Michael J. *At the Origins of Modern Atheism*. New Haven: Yale University Press, 1987.

Burgos, Juan Manuel. *An Introduction to Personalism*. Translated by R. T. Allen. Washington, DC: The Catholic University of America Press, 2018.

Butler, Cuthbert, Dom. *The Vatican Council, 1869–1870*. London: Collins and Harvill Press, 1962.

Cahoone, Lawrence E. *From Modernism to Postmodernism: An Anthology*. Oxford: Blackwell, 1993.

Camille, Michael. "The Dissenting Image: Postcard from Matthew Paris." In *Criticism and Dissent in the Middle Ages*, edited by Rita Copeland, 115–50. Cambridge: Cambridge University Press, 1996.

Campbell, Lorne. *Van der Weyden*. London: Chaucer, 2004.

Cantore, Enrico. "Science and Humanism: The Sapiential Role of Philosophy." *Dialectica: International Review of Philosophy and Knowledge* 24 (1970) 215–23.

Carmody, John. "Muldoon, Thomas William (1917–1986)." In *Australian Dictionary of Biography*. Vol. 18, *1981–1990: L–Z*. Melbourne: Melbourne University Press, 2013.

Carroll, Thomas D. "*Amare in Deo*: Max Scheler's Understanding of Religious Experience: A Retrieval and Appropriation of Certain Augustinian Insights." PhD diss., Katholieke Universiteit Leuven, 1997.

———. "A Deceptive Ambiguity: Revisiting Scheler's Philosophy of Love and Religious Activity." In *Confessions of Love: The Ambiguities of Greek Eros and Latin Caritas*, edited by Craig J. N. de Paulo et al., 156–208. New York: Lang, 2011.

———. "A Human Activity." In *An Introduction to Catholic Theology*, edited by Richard Lennan, 36–55. New York: Paulist, 1998.

Chadwick, Henry. *Augustine*. Oxford: Oxford University Press, 1986.

Chesterton, G. K. *Saint Thomas Aquinas/Saint Francis of Assisi*. San Francisco: Ignatius, 1986.

Clarke, Norris W. *The Creative Retrieval of Saint Thomas Aquinas*. New York: Fordham University Press, 2009.

———. *Explorations in Metaphysics: Being, God, Person*. Notre Dame: University of Notre Dame Press, 1994.

Cohen, Paul Michael. "Reason and Faith: The Bergsonian Catholic Youth of Pre-War France." *Historical Reflections/Réflexions Historiques* 13 (1986) 473–97.

Colberg, Kristin. "Vatican I and Vatican II as Coherent Christian Discourse: A Relationship of Complementary, Continuity, and Difference." PhD diss., University of Notre Dame, 2008.

Collins, James. "Leo XIII and the Philosophical Approach to Modernity." In *Leo XIII and the Modern World*, edited by Edward T. Gargan, 179–209. New York: Sheed & Ward, 1961.

Congar, Yves. *The Meaning of Tradition*. Translated by A. N. Woodrow. San Francisco: Ignatius, 2004.

Congregationes Generales. *Acta et Documenta Synodalia Sacrosancti Concilii Oecumenici Vaticano II*. 62 vols. Rome: Liberia Editrice Vaticana, 1970–97.

Conkin, Paul K. "The Religious Pilgrimage of Thomas Jefferson." In *Jefferson Legacies*, edited by Peter S. Onuf, 19–49. Charlottesville: University Press of Virginia, 1993.

Connelly, Paul. "Modernity in the Sequence of Historical Eras." http://www.darc.org/connelly/religion5.html.

Copeland, Rita, ed. *Criticism and Dissent in the Middle Ages*. Cambridge: Cambridge University Press, 1996.

Cornwell, John, and Michael McGhee, eds. *Philosophers and God: At the Frontiers of Faith and Reason*. London: Continuum, 2009.

Cottier, Cardinal George M. M. "Faith and Reason in the Blessed John Paul II's Teaching." Doctor Communis, The Proceedings of the XII Plenary Session. The Thomistic legacy of Blessed John Paul II and his Refounding of the Pontifical Academy of St. Thomas Aquinas. June 29–July 1, 2012.

Cowburn, John. *Personalism & Scholasticism*. Milwaukee: Marquette University Press, 2005.

Cox, Brian, and Andrew Cohen. *The Human Universe*. London: Collins, 2015.

Creve, Felix M. *The Giants of Pre-Sophistic Greek Philosophy: An Attempt to Reconstruct Their Thoughts*. 2 vols. The Hague: Nijhoff, 1973.

Crosby, John F. *The Personalism of John Paul II*. Steubenville, OH: Hildebrand, 2019.

Cross, Richard. *The Medieval Christian Philosophers: An Introduction*. London: Taurus, 2014.

Crossan, John Dominic. *The Birth of Christianity*. London: HarperCollins, 1998.

D'Ambrosio, Marcellino. "*Ressourcement* Theology, *Aggiornamento*, and the Hermeneutics of Tradition." *Communio* 18 (1991) 52–61.

D'Arcy, M. C., et al. *A Monument to Saint Augustine: Essays on Some Aspects of His Thought*. London: Sheed & Ward, 1930.

D'Ercole, Giovanni. "The Church, an Instrument of Peace in the Contemporary World: 50 Years On. Encyclical *Pacem in Terris*." Talk given at the 2013 Telos Conference, Religion and Politics in a Post-Secular world." February 17–25, 2013.

Dauphinais, Michael, Matthew Levering, eds. *John Paul II & St. Thomas Aquinas*. Ann Arbor, MI: Sapientia, 2006.

Davies, Brian, and Eleonore Stump, eds. *The Oxford Handbook of Aquinas*. Oxford: Oxford University Press, 2012.

Dawkins, Richard. "You Can't Have It Both Ways: Irreconcilable Differences." *Skeptical Inquirer* (1999) 62–64.

Dennett, Daniel C. *Consciousness Explained*. New York: Back Bay, 1991.

Derrida, Jacques. *On the Name*. Edited by Thomas Dutoit. Stanford: Stanford University Press, 1995.

———. *The Post Card: From Socrates to Freud and Beyond*. Translated by Alan Bass. Chicago: University of Chicago Press, 1987.

———. "Psyche: Inventions of the Other" in *A Derrida Reader: Between the Blinds*, edited by Peggy Kamuf, 200–220. New York: Harvester Wheatsheaf, 1991.

Descartes, Rene. *The Philosophical Works of Descartes*. 2 vols. Translated by John Cottingham et al. Cambridge: Cambridge University Press, 1967.

Dodds, Michael J. "Introduction." In *Selected Works of Cornelio Fabro*. Vol. 9, *God*, translated by Joseph T. Papa, ix–xvi. Westmont, IL: IVE, 2017.

Dougherty, Jude P. *Jacques Maritain: An Intellectual Profile*. Washington, DC: The Catholic University of America Press, 2003.

Dreher, Rod, et al., eds. *Healing Humanity: Confronting our Moral Crisis*. Jordanville, NY: Holy Trinity Seminary Press, 2020.

Dreyer, Nathaniel, ed. *Selected Works of Cornelio Fabro*. Translated by Joseph T. Papa. Westmont IL: IVE, 2017.

Düwell, Marcus, et al. *The Cambridge Handbook of Human Dignity*. Cambridge: Cambridge University Press, 2014.

Eadmer. *The Life of St. Anselm, Archbishop of Canterbury*. Edited by R. W. Southern. Oxford: Clarendon, 1972.

Eco, Umberto. *On the Shoulders of Giants*. Translated by Alastair McEwen. London: Secker, 2019.

Eucken, Rudolf. *The Meaning and Value of Life*. Translated by Lucy Judge Gibson and W. R. Boyce Gibson. London: Adam and Charles Black, 1913.

———. *The Problem of Human Life: As Viewed by the Great Thinkers from Plato to the Present Time*. Translated by William S. Hough and W. R. Boyce Gibson. London: Unwin, 1914.

Evans, G. R., ed. *The First Christian Theologians: An Introduction to Theology in the Early Church*. Oxford: Blackwell, 2004.

———, ed. *The Medieval Theologians: An Introduction to Theology in the Medieval Period*. Oxford: Blackwell, 2001.

Fabro, Cornelius. "Atheism." In *Selected Works of Cornelio Fabro*, translated by Joseph T. Papa, 25–48. Westmont, IL: IVE, 2017.

Faggioli, Massimo. *John XXIII: The Medicine of Mercy*. Collegeville, MN: Liturgical, 2014.

Faggioli, Massimo, and Andrea Vicini, eds. *The Legacy of Vatican II*. New York: Paulist, 2015.

Fanu, James Le. "Between *Sapientia* and *Scientia*—Michael Aeschliman's Profound Interpretation." *Evolution News*, September 9, 2019. https://evolutionnews.org/2019/09/between-sapientia-and-scientia-michael-aeschlimans-profound-interpretation/.

Feuerbach, Ludwig. *The Essence of Christianity*. Translated by George Eliot. New York: Harper, 1957.

Fitzgerald, Allan D., ed. *Augustine through the Ages: An Encyclopedia*. Grand Rapids: Eerdmans, 1999.

Flynn, Gabriel, and Paul D. Murray, eds. *Ressourcement: A Movement for Renewal in Twentieth-Century Catholic Theology*. Oxford: Oxford University Press, 2012.

Foster, David Ruel, and Joseph W. Koteriski, eds. *The Two Wings of Catholic Thought: Essays on Fides et Ratio*. Washington, DC: The Catholic University of America Press, 2003.

Francis. *Laudato Si'*. https://www.vatican.va/content/francesco/en/encyclicals/documents/papa-francesco_20150524_enciclica-laudato-si.html.

Francis, Gavin. *Adventures in Human Being: A Grand Tour from the Cranium to the Calcaneum*. New York: Basic, 2015.

Frankl, Viktor E. *Man's Search For Meaning: The Classic Tribute to Hope from the Holocaust*. Translated by Ilse Lasch. London: Rider, 2004.

Frossard, André, and Pope John Paul II. *"Be Not Afraid!" Pope John Paul Speaks Out on His Life, Beliefs, and His Inspiring Vision for Humanity*. New York: Image, 1985.

Fukuyama, Francis. "The End of History?" *The National Interest* 16 (1989) 3–18.

———. *Our Posthuman Future: Consequences of the Biotechnology Revolution.* New York: Farrar, Straus, and Giroux, 2002.
Gaillardetz, Richard R., ed. *The Cambridge Companion to Vatican II.* Cambridge: Cambridge University Press, 2020.
———. "The Ecclesiological Foundations of Modern Catholic Social Teaching." In *Modern Catholic Social Teaching: Commentaries & Interpretations,* edited by Kenneth R. Himes, 75–102. Georgetown University Press, 2017.
———. *An Unfinished Council: Vatican II, Pope Francis, and the Renewal of Catholicism.* Collegeville, MN: Liturgical, 2015.
Gardner, John Eliot. *Bach: Music in the Castle of Heaven.* New York: Knopf, 2013.
Gargan, Edward T., ed. *Leo XIII and the Modern World.* London: Sheed and Ward, 1961.
Garrigou-Lagrange, Reginald. *Reality: A Synthesis of Thomistic Thought.* Translated by Patrick Cummins. St. Louis: Herder, 1950.
Gay, Peter. *Freud: A Life for Our Time.* London: Dent & Sons, 1988.
———. *Weimar Culture: The Outsider as Insider.* London: Penguin, 1974.
González, Orestes J. *Actus Essendi and the Habit of the First Principle in Thomas Aquinas.* New York: Einsiedler, 2019.
Grayling, A. C. *Descartes: The Life of Rene Descartes and Its Place in His Times.* New York: Free, 2005.
Griffith, Jeremy. *Beyond the Human Condition.* Sydney: WTM, 1991.
———. *A Species in Denial.* Sydney: WTM, 2003.
Guardini, Romano. *The World and the Person.* Translated by Stella Lange. Chicago: Regnery, 1965.
Guiton, Jean. *The Pope Speaks: Dialogues of Paul VI with Jean Guiton.* New York: Meredith, 1968.
Gwozdz, Thomas L. "Young and Restless: Jacques Maritain and Henri Bergson." *American Catholic Philosophical Quarterly* 84 (2010) 549–64.
Hamilton, Marc A. "On the Tenth Anniversary of the 2005 Philadelphia Grand Jury Report on Child Sex Abuse in the Archdiocese." *Justia,* October 29, 2015.
Hannam, James. *The Genesis of Science: How the Christian Middle Ages Launched the Scientific Revolution.* Washington, DC: Regnery, 2011.
———. *God's Philosophers: How the Medieval World Laid the Foundations of Modern Science.* London: Icon, 2009.
Hanvey, James. "Dignity, Person, and *Imago Trinitatis.*" In *Understanding Human Dignity,* edited by Christopher McCrudden, 209–28. Oxford: Oxford University Press, 2013.
Harari, Yuval Noah. *21 Lessons for the 21st Century.* London: Vintage, 2019.
———. *Homo Deus: A Brief History of Tomorrow.* London: Secker, 2015.
———. *Sapiens: A Brief History of Humankind.* London: Vintage, 2011.
Harcourt, Alexander H. *Humankind: How Biology and Geography Shape Human Diversity.* New York: Pegasus, 2015.
Haskins, Charles Homer. *The Rise of Universities.* London: Cornell University Press, 1965.
Hassan, Ihab. "Prometheus as Performer: Toward a Postmodern Culture?" *Georgia Review* 31 (1977) 830–50.
Hawking, Stephen, ed. *On the Shoulders of Giants: The Great Works of Physics and Astronomy.* Philadelphia: Running, 2002.

Heaney, John. *The Modernist Crisis: von Hügel*. London: Chapman, 1969.
Heidegger, Martin. *Basic Writings*. Edited by David Farrell. London: Routledge, 1978.
———. *Being and Time*. Translated by John Macquarie and Edward Robinson. New York: Harper & Row, 1962.
———. *The Metaphysical Foundations of Logic*. Translated by Michael Helm. Bloomington, IN: Indiana University Press, 1984.
Henold, Mary J. *The Laywoman Project: Remarking Catholic Womanhood in the Vatican II Era*. Chapel Hill, NC: University of North Carolina Press, 2020.
Hildebrand, Dietrich von. *The Sacred Heart: An Analysis of Human and Divine Affectivity*. Baltimore: Helicon, 1965.
Himes, Kenneth R., ed. *Modern Catholic Social Teaching: Commentaries & Interpretations*. Washington, DC: Georgetown University Press, 2011.
Hinckley, Gordon B. *Teachings of Gordon B. Hinckley*. Salt Lake City: Deseret, 1997.
Hittinger, John P., ed. *The Vocation of the Catholic Philosopher: From Maritain to John Paul II*. Washington, DC: The Catholic University of America Press, 2010.
Hittinger, John P., and Daniel C. Wagner, eds. *Thomas Aquinas: Teacher of Humanity*. Newcastle: Cambridge Scholars, 2015.
Huebsch, Bill. *Vatican II in Plain English: The Council*. Notre Dame: Ave Maria, 1997.
Leclercq, Jean. *The Love of Learning and the Desire for God: A Study of Monastic Culture*. Translated by Catherine Misrahi. New York: Fordham University Press, 1961.
Lewis, Suzanne. *The Art of Matthew Paris in the Chronica Majora*. Berkeley: University of California Press, 1987.
Ivereigh, Austen. *The Great Reformer: Francis and the Making of a Radical Pope*. London: Allen & Unwin, 2008.
Jasper and Sardine. "About." https://jasperandsardine.wordpress.com/about/.
John, Helen James. *The Thomist Spectrum*. New York: Fordham University Press, 1966.
John of Salisbury. *The Metalogicon: A Twelfth-Century Defense of the Verbal and Logical Arts of the Trivium*. Translated by Daniel McGarry. New York: Dry, 2009.
John Paul II. *Augustine of Hippo*. Sydney: St. Paul, 1986.
———. *Centesimus Annus*. https://www.vatican.va/content/john-paul-ii/en/encyclicals/documents/hf_jp-ii_enc_01051991_centesimus-annus.html.
———. "The Cross Illumines All Human Life." *L'Osservatore Romano*, June 16, 1999.
———. *Fides et Ratio*. https://www.vatican.va/content/john-paul-ii/en/encyclicals/documents/hf_jp-ii_enc_14091998_fides-et-ratio.html.
———. *Memory and Identity: Personal Reflections*. London: Weidenfeld & Nicolson, 2005.
———. *Sapientia Christiana*. https://www.vatican.va/content/john-paul-ii/en/apost_constitutions/documents/hf_jp-ii_apc_15041979_sapientia-christiana.html.
———. *Sollicitudo Rei Socialis*. https://www.vatican.va/content/john-paul-ii/en/encyclicals/documents/hf_jp-ii_enc_30121987_sollicitudo-rei-socialis.html.
———. *The Whole Truth about Man: John Paul II to the University Faculties and Students*. Edited by James V. Schall. Boston: St. Paul, 1981.
John Paul II, and André Frossard. *"Be Not Afraid": Pope John Paul II Speaks out on His Life, His Beliefs, and His Inspiring Vision for Humanity*. Translated by J. R. Foster. New York: Image, 1985.
Johnson, Paul. *Socrates: A Man for Our Times*. New York: Penguin, 2011.
Kamuf, Peggy, ed. *A Derrida Reader: Between the Blinds*. New York: Columbia University Pres, 1991.

Kant, Immanuel. "An Answer to the Question: 'What Is Enlightenment?'" In *Kant's Political Writings*, edited by Hans Reiss, translated by H. B. Nisbet, 54–60. Cambridge: Cambridge University Press, 1971.

Kasper, Walter. "The Theological Anthropology of *Gaudium et Spes*." *Communio* 23 (1996) 129-38.

Kelly, Joseph F. *The Ecumenical Councils of the Catholic Church: A History*. Collegeville, MN: Liturgical, 2009.

Kemperdick, Stephan. *Rogier van der Weyden: Masters of Netherlandish Art*. Potsdam: Ullmann, 2013.

Kerr, Fergus. *Twentieth-Century Catholic Theologians: From Neoscholasticism to Nuptial Mysticism*. Oxford: Blackwell, 2007.

———. "Yves Congar and Thomism." In *Yves Congar: Theologian of the Church*, edited by Gabriel Flynn, 67–97. Leuven: Peeters, 2005.

Kelly, James J. *Baron Friedrich von Hügel's Philosophy of Religion*. Leuven: Leuven University Press, 1983.

Kelly, J. N. D. *Early Christian Creeds*. London: Longmans, Green, & Co., 1950.

Kiesel, Theodore. *The Genesis of Heidegger's Being and Time*. Oakland: University of California Press, 1995.

King, Martin Luther, Jr. *The Measure of a Man*. Minneapolis: Fortress, 2001.

Knowles, David. *The Evolution of Medieval Thought*. London: Longmans, Green, and Co, 1963.

Kobler, John F. *Vatican II, Theophany, and the Phenomenon of Man: The Council's Pastoral Servant Leader Theology for the Third Millennium*. New York: Lang, 1991.

———. *Vatican II and Phenomenology: Reflections on the Life-World of the Church*. Dordrecht: Nijhoff, 1985.

Komonchak, Joseph, ed. *History of Vatican II*. 5 vols. Leuven: Peeters, 1996–2006.

Koterski, Joseph W. *An Introduction to Medieval Philosophy: Basic Concepts*. Oxford: Wiley-Blackwell, 2009.

Krápiec, Miczysław, and Andrzej Maryniarczyk. "The Lublin Philosophical School: Founders, Motives, Characteristics." *Studie Gilsoniana* 4 (2015) 405–22.

Kuehn, Heniz R., ed. *The Essential Guardini: An Anthology of the Writings of Roman Guardini*. Chicago: Liturgy Training, 1997.

Küng, Hans, et al., eds. *Council Speeches of Vatican II*. New York: Paulist, 1964.

Kupczak, Jaroslaw. *Destined for Liberty: The Human Person in the Philosophy of Karol Wojtyła/John Paul II*. Washington, DC: The Catholic University of America Press, 2000.

Lacroix, Jean. *Maurice Blondel: An Introduction to the Man and His Philosophy*. Translated by John C. Guinness. New York: Sheed and Ward, 1968.

Lafont, Ghislain. *God, Time, and Being*. Translated by Leonard Maluf. Petersham, MA: Saint Bede's, 1992.

———. *Imagining the Catholic Church: Structured Communion in the Spirit*. Translated by John J. Burkhard. Collegeville, MN: Liturgical, 2000.

Lamberts, Emiel, and Jan Rogiers. *Leuven University, 1425–1985*. Leuven: Leuven University Press, 1990.

Lennan, Richard, ed. *An Introduction to Catholic Theology*. New York: Paulist, 1997.

Leo XIII. *Aeterni Patris*. https://www.vatican.va/content/leo-xiii/en/encyclicals/documents/hf_l-xiii_enc_04081879_aeterni-patris.html.

———. *Rerum Novarum*. https://www.vatican.va/content/leo-xiii/en/encyclicals/documents/hf_l-xiii_enc_15051891_rerum-novarum.html.

Levering, Matthew. *An Introduction to Vatican II as an Ongoing Theological Event*. Washington, DC: The Catholic University of America Press, 2017.

Levinas, Emmanuel. *Humanism of the Other*. Translated by Nidra Poller. Chicago: University of Illinois Press, 2006.

———. *Totality and Infinity: An Essay on Exteriority*. Translated by Alphonso Lingis. Pittsburgh: Duquesne University Press, 1969.

Lewis, Suzanne. *The Art of Matthew Paris in the Chronica Majora*. Berkeley: University of California Press, 1987.

Lombo, José Angel, and Francesco Russo. *Philosophical Anthropology: An Introduction*. Woodridge, IL: Midwest Theological Forum, 2014.

Lubac, Henri de. *At the Service of the Church: Henri de Lubac Reflects on the Circumstances That Occasioned His Writings*. Translated by Anne Elizabeth Englund. San Francisco: Communio, 1993.

———. *Augustinianism and Modern Theology*. Translated by Lancelot Sheppard. New York: Herder & Herder, 2000.

———. *The Drama of Atheist Humanism*. San Francisco: Ignatius, 1983.

Lyotard, Jean-Francois. *The Postmodern Condition: A Report on Knowledge*. Translated by Geoff Bennington and Brian Massumi. Manchester: Manchester University Press, 1984.

Mace, Emily. "Williams, George Hunston (1914–2000)." *Harvard Square Library* July 28, 2012. https://www.harvardsquarelibrary.org/biographies/george-huntston-williams/.

MacIntrye, Alasdair. *God, Philosophy, Universities: A Selective History of the Catholic Philosophical Tradition*. Plymouth: Rowman & Littlefield, 2009.

Mader, Wilhelm. *Max Scheler*. Hamburg: Rowohlt, 1980.

Malikow, Max. *The Human Predicament: Towards an Understanding of the Human Condition*. Chipley, FL: Theocentric, 2013.

Malinski, Mieczyslaw. *Pope John Paul II: The Life of Karol Wojtyła*. Translated by P. S. Falla. New York: Image, 1982.

Mantel, Hilary. *Wolf Hall*. London: Henry & Colt, 2009.

Maritain, Jacques. *An Introduction to Philosophy*. Translated by E. I. Watkin. New York: Sheed & Ward, 2005.

———. *The Degrees of Knowledge or Distinguish to Unite*. Translated by Gerald B. Phelan. Notre Dame: University of Notre Dame Press, 1998.

———. *Existence and the Existent: An Essay on Christian Existentialism*. New York: Image, 1956.

———. Foreword to *Walls Are Crumbling: Seven Jewish Philosophers Discover Christ*, by John M. Oesterreicher, vii–ix. London: Hollis and Carter. 1953.

———. *Integral Humanism, Freedom in the Modern World, and a Letter on Independence*. Translated by Otto Bird et al. Notre Dame: University of Notre Dame Press, 1996.

———. Introduction to *Human Rights: Comments and Interpretations: A Symposium*, edited by UNESCO, vi–ix. New York: Wingate, 1949.

——— *The Peasant of the Garonne: An Old Layman Questions Himself about the Present Time*. Translated by Michael Cuddihy and Elizabeth Hughes. Eugene OR: Wipf & Stock, 2011.

———. *The Person and the Common Good*. Translated by John J. Fitzgerald. Notre Dame: University of Notre Dame Press, 1966.

———. *A Preface to Metaphysics: Seven Lectures on Being*. New York: Mentor Omega, 1962.

———. *The Range of Reason*. London: Bles, 1953.

———. "St. Augustine and St. Thomas." In *A Monument to Augustine*, 197–294 London: Sheed and Ward, 1930.

Mattei, Roberto. *The Second Vatican Council (An Unwritten Story)*. Translated by Patrick T. Branna et al. Fitzwilliam, NH: Loreto, 2012.

McBrien, Richard. *Catholicism*. Rev. ed. San Francisco: HarperSanFrancisco, 1994.

McCool, Gerald. *The Neo-Thomists*. Milwaukee: Marquette University Press, 1994.

———. *Nineteenth-Century Scholasticism: The Search for a Unitary Method*. New York: Fordham University Press, 1977.

———. "Thomism (1), Modern." In *The Oxford Companion to Christian Though*, edited by Adrian Hastings et al., 703. Oxford University Press, 2000.

McCrudden, Christopher, ed. *Understanding Human Dignity*. Oxford: Oxford University Press, 2013.

McGrade, A. S., ed. *The Cambridge Companion to Medieval Philosophy*. Cambridge: Cambridge University Press, 2003.

McGrath, Alister. *The Twilight of Atheism: The Rise and Fall of Disbelief in the Modern World*. New York: Doubleday, 2004.

McGuckin, Terence. "A Century of 'Pontifical Thomism.'" *New Blackfriars* 72 (1991) 377–84.

McInerny, Ralph, ed. *Thomas Aquinas: Selected Writings*. London: Penguin, 1998.

———. *The Very Rich Hours of Jacques Maritain: A Spiritual Life*. Notre Dame: University of Notre Dame Press, 2003.

Meagher, Robert Emmet. *Albert Camus and the Human Crisis*. New York: Pegasus, 2021.

Melloni, Alberto. *Vatican II: The Complete History*. New York: Paulist, 2015.

Mercier, Cardinal. *The Origins of Contemporary Psychology*. Translated by W. H. Mitchell. London: Kennedy & Sons, 1918.

Mettepenningen, Jürgen. *Nouvelle Théologie—New Theology: Inheritor of Modernism, Precusor of Vatican II*. London: T. & T. Clark International, 2010.

Miles, Margaret R. "The Body and Human Values in Augustine of Hippo." In *Grace, Politics, and Desire: Essays on Augustine*, edited by H. A. Meynell, 55–70. Alberta: University of Calgary Press, 1990.

Moeller, Charles. "History of the Constitution, Preface and Introductory Statement." In *Commentary on the Documents of Vatican II*, edited by Herbert Vorgrimler, 5:1–115. London: Herder and Herder, 1969.

Moore, Lucy. *Anything Goes: A Biography of the Roaring Twenties*. New York: Overlook, 2010.

Moran, Dermot, and Timothy Mooney, eds. *The Phenomenology Reader*. London: Routledge, 2002.

More, Max, and Natasha Vita-More, eds. *The Transhumanist Reader: Classical and Contemporary Essays on Science, Technology, and Philosophy of the Human Future*. Hoboken, NJ: Wiley-Blackwell, 2013.

Morrisey, Paul. "An Examination of Servais-Théodore Pinckaers, O.P., as a Sapiential Theologian in the Tradition of St. Thomas Aquinas." PhD diss., Sydney College of Divinity/Catholic Institute of Sydney, 2014.

Mounier, Emmanuel. *Personalism*. Translated by Phillip Mairet. Notre Dame: University of Notre Dame Press, 1952.

Murstein, Bernard I. "A Taxonomy of Love." In *The Psychology of Love*, edited by Robert J. Sternberg and Michael L. Barnes. London: Burns & Oates, 1988.

Nichols. Aidan. *Reason with Piety: Garrigou-Lagrange in the Service of Catholic Thought*. Naples, FL: Sapientia, 2008.

Nietzsche, Fredrich. *A Nietzsche Reader*. Translated by R. J. Hollingdale. London: Penguin, 1977.

Norris, Christopher. *Deconstruction: Theory and Practice*. London: Methuen, 1986.

Nota, John H. "The Development of Max Scheler's Philosophy of Religion." In *The Papin Festschrift: Wisdom and Knowledge*, edited by Joseph Armendi, 257–65. Philadelphia: Villanova University Press. 1976.

———. *Max Scheler: The Man and His Work*. Translated by Theodore Plantinga and John H. Nota. Chicago: Franciscan Herald, 1983.

Novak, Michael. "The Achievement of Jacques Maritain." *First Things*, December 1990. https://www.firstthings.com/article/1990/12/the-achievement-of-jacques-maritain.

———. *A New Generation: American and Catholic*. New York: Herder & Herder, 1964.

Nussbaum, Martha. "Inheriting Socrates." *The Point*, January 3, 2010. https://thepointmag.com/criticism/inheriting-socrates/.

O'Collins, Gerald. *Living Vatican II: The 21st Council for the 21st Century*. New York: Paulist, 2006.

O'Collins, Gerald, and Mario Farrugia. *Catholicism: The Story of Catholic Christianity*. Oxford: Oxford University Press, 2003.

O'Donnell, James J. *Augustine's Confessions*. 3 vols. Oxford: Oxford University Press, 2012.

———. *Augustine, Sinner & Saint: A New Biography*. London: Profile, 2005.

Oddie, William, ed. *John Paul the Great: Maker of the Post-conciliar Church*. San Francisco: Ignatius, 2005.

Oesterreicher, John M. *Walls Are Crumbling: Seven Jewish Philosophers Discover Christ*. London: Hollis and Carter, 1953.

O'Malley, John W. *What Happened at Vatican II*. Cambridge: Belknap, 2008.

———. *When Bishops Meet: An Essay Comparing Trent, Vatican I, and Vatican II*. Cambridge: Belknap, 2019.

Orsy, Ladislas. "The Divine Dignity of Human Persons in *Dignitatis Humanae*." In *50 Years On: Probing the Riches of Vatican II*, edited by David G. Schultenover, 347–64. Collegeville, MN: Liturgical, 2015.

Packman, Carl. Review of *Our Posthuman Future: Consequences of the Biotechnological Revolution*, by Francis Fukuyama. *Rethinking Marxism: A Journal of Economics, Culture & Society* 21 (2009) 141–47.

Pascal, Blasé. *Pensées*. Translated by A. J. Krailsheimer. London: Penguin, 1966.

Passelecq, Georges, and Bernard Suchecky. *The Hidden Encyclical of Pius XI*. Translated by Steven Rendall. New York: Harcourt Brace & Company, 1997.

Paul VI. *Dignitatis Humanae*. https://www.vatican.va/archive/hist_councils/ii_vatican_council/documents/vat-ii_decl_19651207_dignitatis-humanae_en.html.

———. *Gaudium et Spes*. https://www.vatican.va/archive/hist_councils/ii_vatican_council/documents/vat-ii_const_19651207_gaudium-et-spes_en.html.

———. *Populorum Progressio*. https://www.vatican.va/content/paul-vi/en/encyclicals/documents/hf_p-vi_enc_26031967_populorum.html.

Paulo, Craig J. N. de, et al., eds. *Confessions of Love: The Ambiguities of Greek Eros and Latin Caritas*. New York: Lang, 2011.

Pearcey, Nancy. *Finding Truth: 5 Principles for Unmasking Atheism, Secularism, and Other God Substitutes*. Colorado Springs: Cook, 2015.

Pearson, Keith Ansell, and Large Duncan, eds. *The Nietzsche Reader*. Oxford: Blackwell, 2006.

Pecknold, C. C., and Tarmo Toom, eds. *T. & T. Clark Companion to Augustine and Modern Theology*. London: Bloomsbury, 2013.

Peddicord, Richard. *The Sacred Monster of Thomism: An Introduction to the Life and Legacy of Reginald Garrigou-Lagrange, O.P.* South Bend, IN: St. Augustine's Press, 2005.

Pedersen, Olaf. *The First Universities: Studium Generale and the Origins of University Education in Europe*. Translated by Richard North. Cambridge: Cambridge University Press, 1997.

Phillips, Francis. "William Oddie: Dynamic, Passionate, and Provocative." *Catholic Herald*, November 14, 2019. https://catholicherald.co.uk/william-oddie-dynamic-passionate-and-provocative/.

Pieper, Josef. *In Defense of Philosophy*. Translated by Lothar Krauth. San Francisco: Ignatius, 1992.

———. *Scholasticism: Personalities and Problems of Medieval Philosophy*. South Bend, IN: St. Augustine's Press, 2001.

———. *The Silence of Thomas: Three Essays*. Translated by John Murray and Daniel O'Connor. South Bend, IN: St. Augustine's Press, 1999.

Pippin, Robert B. *Modernism as a Philosophical Problem*. Oxford: Blackwell, 1991.

Pius XI. *Quadragesimo Anno*. https://www.vatican.va/content/pius-xi/en/encyclicals/documents/hf_p-xi_enc_19310515_quadragesimo-anno.html.

———. *Studorium Ducem*. https://www.papalencyclicals.net/pius11/p11studi.htm.

———. *Ubi Arcano Dei Consilio*. https://www.vatican.va/content/pius-xi/en/encyclicals/documents/hf_p-xi_enc_19221223_ubi-arcano-dei-consilio.html.

Polkinghorne, John. "Belief in God in an Age of Science." In *Life, God, and Other Small Topics: Conversations from Socrates in the City*, edited by Eric Metaxas, 1–36. London: Penguin, 2011.

Przywara, Erich. "St. Augustine and the Modern World." In *A Monument to St. Augustine*, translated by E. I. Watkin, 249–87. London: Sheed & Ward, 1930.

Pursey, Richard. "The Human Condition: A Poets & Artists Exhibition @ AnArte Gallery." *Beautiful Bizarre*, September 11, 2018. https://beautifulbizarre.net/2018/09/11/the-human-condition-a-poets-artists-exhibition-anarte-gallery/.

Ratzinger, Joseph. *Called to Communion: Understanding the Church Today*. Translated by Adrian Walker. San Francisco: Ignatius, 1996.

———. "Catholicism after the Council." *The Furrow* 18 (1967) 3-9.

———. "The Dignity of the Human Person." In *Commentary on the Documents of Vatican II*, edited by Herbert Vorgrimler, 5:115–63. London: Herder & Herder, 1969.

———. *Introduction to Christianity*. Rev ed. San Francisco: Ignatius, 2004.

———. *Milestones, Memoirs, 1927–1977*. Translated by Erasmo Leiva-Merikakis. San Francisco: Ignatius, 1998.

———. "What Is Man?" *Humanitas*. http://www.humanitasreview.com/16-anthropology-culture/15-what-is-man.

Reardon, Bernard M. G. *Roman Catholic Modernism*. Stanford: Stanford University Press, 1970.

Ricoeur, Paul. *Freud & Philosophy: An Essay on Interpretation*. Translated by Denis Savage. New Haven: Yale University Press, 1970.

Rigali, Justin. "*Gaudium et Spes* and Catholic Higher Education." *Journal of Catholic Social Thought* 3 (2006) 273–81.

———. *Reliving Vatican II: It's All about Jesus Christ*. Chicago: Liturgy Training, 2006.

Riley, Donovan. "21st Century Digital God." *1517*, November 14, 2019. https://www.1517.org/articles/21st-century-digital-god.

Rist, John M. *Augustine: Ancient Thought Baptised*. Cambridge: Cambridge University Press, 1994.

Robinson, James M., and Helmut Koester, eds. *Trajectories through Early Christianity*. New York: Fortress, 1971.

Routhier, Gilles. "Finishing the Work Begun: The Trying Experience of the Fourth Period." *History of Vatican II*, edited by Giuseppe Albergio, 5:49–184. Leuven: Peeters, 2006.

Rowland, Tracey. "Saint John Paul II: Doctor of Incarnate Love." *ABC Religion & Ethics*, April 26, 2014. https://www.abc.net.au/religion/saint-john-paul-ii-doctor-of-incarnate-love/10099278.

Rush, Ormond. *Still Interpreting Vatican II: Some Hermeneutical Principles*. New York: Paulist, 2004.

———. *The Vision of Vatican II: Its Fundamental Principles*. Collegeville, MN: Liturgical Press Academic, 2019.

Sadler, Gregory B., ed. *Reason Fulfilled by Revelation: The 1930s Christian Philosophy Debates in France*. Washington, DC: The Catholic University of America Press, 2011.

Sartre, Jean-Paul. *Existentialism Is a Humanism*. Translated by Carol Macomber. New Haven: Yale University Press, 2007.

Saunders, Clare, et al. *Doing Philosophy: A Practical Guide for Students*. 2nd ed. London: Bloomsbury, 2013.

Scanlon, Helen. "Bishop Thomas William Muldoon (1917–1986) April Lecture." *Australian Catholic Historical Society Inc. Newsletter* 21 (2010) 17.

Scanlon, Michael J. "Modern Theology." In *Augustine through the Ages: An Encyclopedia*, edited by Allan D. Fitzgerald, 825–27. Grand Rapids: Eerdmans, 1999.

Schall, James V. *The Mind That Is Catholic: Philosophical & Political Essays*. Washington, DC: The Catholic University of America Press, 2008.

Scheler, Max. *Formalism in Ethics and Non-Formal Ethics of Values*. Translated by Manfred S. Frings and Robert L. Funk. Evanston, IL: Northwestern University Press, 1973.

———. "Love and Knowledge." In *Max Scheler: On Feeling, Knowing, and Valuing: Selected Writings*, edited by Harold J. Bershady, 147–65. Chicago: University of Chicago Press, 1992.

———. *Man's Place in Nature*. Translated by Hans Meyerhoff. New York: Noonday, 1961.

———. *Max Scheler Centennial Essays, 1874–1928*. Translated by Daniel Liderbach. The Hague: Nijhoff, 1974.

———. "The Meaning of Suffering." In *Max Scheler Centennial Essays, 1874–1928*, translated by Daniel Liderbach, 121–64. The Hague: Nijhoff, 1974.

———. *The Nature of Sympathy*. Translated by Peter Heath. London: Routledge, 1970.

———. *On the Eternal in Man*. Translated by Bernard Noble. London: SCM, 1960.

———. *On Feeling, Knowing, and Valuing: Selected Writings*. Edited by Harold J. Bershady. Chicago: University of Chicago Press, 1992.

———. "On the Idea of Man." Translated by Clyde Nabe. *Journal of the British Society for Phenomenology* 9 (1978) 184–98.

———. "On the Positivistic Philosophy of the History of Knowledge and Its Laws of Three Stages." In *The Sociology of Knowledge: A Reader*, translated by Rainer Koehne, 161–69. New York: Praeger, 1970.

———. "Ordo Amoris." In *Selected Philosophical Essays*, translated by David R. Lachterman, 98–135. Evanston, IL: Northwestern University Press, 1973.

———. *Problems of a Sociology of Knowledge*. Translated by Manfred Frings. London: Routledge, 1980.

———. *Ressentiment*. Translated by William W. Holdheim. New York: Schocken, 1972.

———. *Selected Philosophical Essays*. Translated by David R. Lachterman. Evanston, IL: Northwestern University Press, 1973.

Schultenover, David G., ed. *50 Years On: Probing the Riches of Vatican II*. Collegeville, MN: Liturgical, 2015.

Schwarz, Hans. *The Human Being: A Theological Anthropology*. Grand Rapids: Eerdmans, 2013.

Schweitzer, Albert. *J. S. Bach*. Translated by Ernest Newman. 2 vols. London: Dover, 1966.

Shaw, Russell. *Eight Popes and the Crisis of Modernity*. New York: Ignatius, 2020.

Smith, Christian. *What Is a Person? Rethinking Humanity, Social Life, and the Moral Good from the Person Up*. Chicago: University of Chicago Press, 2010.

Smith, James K. A. *Who's Afraid of Postmodernism? Taking Derrida, Lyotard, and Foucault to Church*. Grand Rapids: Baker Academic, 2006.

Southern, R. W. *The Making of the Middle Ages*. New York: Folio Society, 1998.

———. *Medieval Humanism and Other Studies*. New York: Harper & Row, 1970.

———. *Scholastic Humanism and the Unification of Europe*. 2 vols. Oxford: Blackwell, 1995–2001.

Spencer, Mark. *The Irreducibility of the Human Person: A Catholic Synthesis*. Washington, DC: The Catholic University of America Press, 2022.

Spiegelberg, Herbert. *The Phenomenological Movement: A Historical Introduction*. The Hague: Nijhoff, 1982.

Spinello, Richard A., ed. *The Encyclicals of John Paul II: An Introduction and Commentary*. New York: Sheed and Ward, 2012.

Staude, John Raphael. *Max Scheler, 1874–1828: An Intellectual Portrait*. New York: Free, 1967.

Stein, Edith. *Finite and Eternal Being*. Translated by Kurt F. Reinhardt. Washington, DC: ICS, 2002.

———. *Life in a Jewish Family, 1891–1916: Her Unfinished Autobiographical Account*. Translated by Josephine Koeppel. Washington, DC: ICS, 1986.

———. *On the Problem of Empathy*. Translated by Waltraud Stein. Washington, DC: ICS, 1989.
Sternberg, Robert J., and Michael L. Barnes, eds. *The Psychology of Love*. London: Burns & Oates, 1988.
Stengel, Richard. "The Power of Ideas." *Time*, May 13, 2008.
Sullivan, Maureen. *The Road to Vatican II: Key Changes in Theology*. New York: Paulist, 2007.
Swieżawski, Stefan. *St. Thomas Revisited*. Translated by Theresa Sandok. New York: Lang, 1995.
Tanner, Norman P. *The Councils of the Church: A Short History*. New York: Herder & Herder, 2016.
———, ed. *Decrees of the Ecumenical Councils*. 2 vols. London: Sheed and Ward, 1990.
Taylor, Joan E. *What Did Jesus Look Like?* London: Bloomsbury T. & T. Clark, 2018.
Torrell, Jean-Pierre. *Saint Thomas Aquinas*. Vol. 1. Translated by Robert Royal. Washington, DC: The Catholic University of America Press, 1996.
Tranzillo, Jeffrey. *John Paul II on the Vulnerable*. Washington, DC: The Catholic University of America Press, 2013.
Tucci, Roberto. "The Proper Development of Culture." In *Commentary on the Documents of Vatican II*, edited by Herbert Vorgimler, 5:246–87. London: Herder & Herder, 1969.
Tuchman, Barbara W. *Bulletin of the American Academy of Arts and Science* 34 (1980) 16–32.
———. *A Distant Mirror: The Calamitous 14th Century*. New York: Ballantine, 1978.
Vanhoozer, Kevin J., ed. *The Cambridge Companion to Postmodern Theology*. Cambridge: Cambridge University Press, 2003.
Vaughan, Roger Bede. *The Life and Labours of Saint Thomas of Aquin*. London: Burns and Oates, 1890.
Velmans, Max, and Susan Schneider, eds. *The Blackwell Companion to Consciousness*. Oxford: Blackwell, 2007.
Vincelette, Alan. *A Reader in Recent Catholic Philosophy*. St. Louis: En Route, 2020.
———. *Recent Catholic Philosophy: The Nineteenth Century*. Milwaukee: Marquette University Press, 2009.
———. *Recent Catholic Philosophy: The Twentieth Century*. Milwaukee: Marquette University Press, 2011.
Walsh, Kevin J. *Yesterday's Seminary: A History of St. Patrick's Manly*. London: Allen & Unwin, 1998.
Warren, Nicolas de, and Thomas Vongehr, eds. *Philosophers at the Front: Phenomenology and the First World War*. Leuven: Leuven University Press, 2017.
Weigel, George. *To Sanctify the World: The Vital Legacy of Vatican II*. New York: Basic, 2022.
———. *Witness to Hope: The Biography of Pope John Paul II*. New York: HarperCollins, 1999.
West, David. *An Introduction to Continental Philosophy*. New York: Polity, 1996.
Westphal, Merold. *Overcoming Onto-Theology: Toward a Postmodern Christian Faith*. New York: Fordham University Press, 2001.
"When Father Joseph Ratzinger Predicted the Future of the Church." *Aleteia*, June 13, 2016. https://aleteia.org/2016/06/13/when-cardinal-joseph-ratzinger-predicted-the-future-of-the-church/.

Whitehead, Kenneth D., ed. *John Paul II—Witness to Truth*. South Bend, IN: St. Augustine's Press, 2001.

Williams, George Huntston. *The Mind of John Paul II: Origins of His Thought and Action*. New York: Seabury, 1981.

Williams, Leslie. *Night Wrestling: Struggling for Answers and Finding God*. Nashville: Nelson, 1997.

———. *When Anything Goes: Being Christian in a Post-Christian World*. Nashville: Abingdon, 2016.

Wojtyła, Karol. *The Acting Person: A Contribution to Phenomenological Anthropology*. New York: Springer, 1979.

———. *Considerations on the Essence of Man*. Translated by John Grondelski. Lublin: Polski Towarzystwo Tomasza z Akwinu, 2016.

———. *Faith according to St. John of the Cross*. Translated by Jordan Aumann. New York: Ignatius, 1981.

———. *Fruitful and Responsible Love*. Stanmore: Chapman Australia, 1978.

———. "The Intentional Act and the Human Act That Is Act and Experience." *Analecta Husserliana* 10 (1976) 269–80.

———. *Love and Responsibility*. Translated by H. T. Willetts. San Francisco: Ignatius, 1981.

———. *Person and Act and Related Essays*. Translated by Grzegorz Ignatik. The English Critical Edition of the Works of Karol Wojtyła/John Paul II 1. Washington, DC: The Catholic University of America Press, 2021.

———. *Person and Community: Selected Essays*. Translated by Theresa Sandok. New York: Lang, 1993.

———. *Sign of Contradiction*. Stanmore: Chapman Australia, 1978.

———. *Sources of Renewal: The Implementation of the Second Vatican Council*. San Francisco: Harper & Row, 1980.

Wright, N. T. "Reading Paul, Thinking Scripture." In *Scripture's Doctrine and Theology's Bible: How the New Testament Shapes Christian Dogmatics*, edited by Markus Bockmuehl and Alan J. Torrance, 59–71. Grand Rapids: Baker, 2008.

Wuerl, Donald. "Fellowship of Catholic Scholars." *L'Osservatore Romano*, February 2, 1978. https://www.ewtn.com/catholicism/library/fellowship-of-catholic-scholars-9996.

Wulf, Maurice de. *An Introduction to Scholastic Philosophy*. New York: Dover, 1956.

Vorgrimler, Herbert, ed. *Commentary on the Documents of Vatican II*. 5 vols. London: Herder & Herder, 1966–69.

Zdinak, Ashley. "Painting: 'In His Image.'" *Falcone's Crossroads*, January 24, 2016. https://grandefalcone.wordpress.com/2012/08/18/painting-in-his-image/.

Zdinak, Matthew Liam. "In His Image." *Manresa Matters* (Fall/Winter 2019) 17.

Zimmerman, Jens, ed. *Humanism and Religion: A Call for the Renewal of Western Culture*. Oxford: Oxford University Press, 2012.

———. *Incarnational Humanism: A Philosophy of Culture for the Church of the World*. Downers Grove, IL: IVP Academic, 2012.

———. *Re-envisioning Christian Humanism: Education and the Restoration of Humanity*. Oxford: Oxford University Press, 2017.

www.ingramcontent.com/pod-product-compliance
Lightning Source LLC
Chambersburg PA
CBHW071229290426
44108CB00013B/1341